Harvard Historical Studies · 126

Published under the auspices
of the Department of History
from the income of the
Paul Revere Frothingham Bequest
Robert Louis Stroock Fund
Henry Warren Torrey Fund

THE
Greatest Nation
of the Earth

REPUBLICAN ECONOMIC POLICIES
DURING THE CIVIL WAR

Heather Cox Richardson

HARVARD UNIVERSITY PRESS
Cambridge, Massachusetts • London, England

For Catherine Cox Richardson

and

Irving Richardson, Sr.

Library of Congress Cataloging-in-Publication Data

Richardson, Heather Cox.
  The greatest nation of the earth : Republican economic policies
during the Civil War / Heather Cox Richardson.
    p. cm.—(Harvard historical studies ; v. 126)
    Includes bibliographical references and index.
    ISBN 0-674-36213-6 (cloth : alk. paper)
    1. United States—Economic policy—To 1933. 2. United States—
Economic conditions—To 1865. 3. United States—History—Civil
War, 1861–1865. 4. Republican Party (U.S. : 1854–)—History.
I. Title. II. Series.
HC105.6.R53   1997
338.973—dc21   96-46707

Contents

Preface

This book began as an attempt to understand the ideology of the late-nineteenth-century Americans who built industrial America. Many, I knew, had been enthusiastic supporters of the Republican party during the Civil War. How could people who had worked to save the nation and end slavery later seem to put their fortunes ahead of their country and humanity? Their memoirs and letters were not much help in answering that question. It was not until close to the turn of the century that these rich and powerful men either argued confidently that the stratification of wealth served the public good or recognized any impropriety in their government dealings. In the immediate postwar decades, they seemed to be bewildered by attacks and defended themselves in an almost pathetic way as good Americans doing what they were supposed to do. Gradually I found myself pulled back in time: to understand the Gilded Age, I came to realize, required understanding wartime Republicanism. And in the pages of the *Congressional Globe* for the years 1861–1865 I saw the construction of both a world view and a newly active national government designed to promote that view. The ambitious vision of wartime Republicans and the extraordinary institutional development that followed from it would determine the course of the United States for at least half a century.

This is the story of how those men who controlled the North during the Civil War tried to shape the postwar world as they struggled to defeat the South. It tells that story largely from their perspective while calling attention to the weaknesses of their vision. In the course of my research I found the inevitable opportunists and corrupt dealers in the wartime Union, but I gained enormous respect for men such as William Pitt Fessenden, who gave his sons as well as his own health and peace of mind to the cause in which he so passionately believed. Those like Fessenden, I am convinced, outnumbered and outweighed others in the wartime Union who acted solely for profit rather than for what they believed to be the public good. The story of those dedicated Republicans is a classical tragedy, since their vision for the American future contained the seeds of its own destruction.

＊   ＊   ＊

In the years that this book took shape I incurred many debts. Whatever errors and omissions remain are certainly my responsibility, since the generous help of so many good people should have removed them all. David Herbert Donald and William E. Gienapp advised the dissertation on which this book is based. I am grateful not only for their substantive contributions, but also for their unflagging patience and good humor.

For their careful reading of the manuscript and comments and suggestions for its improvement, I thank Tyler Anbinder, Donna Bouvier, Thomas Brown, Douglas Forsyth, Richard R. John, Pauline Maier, Peter Temin, Merritt Roe Smith, Michael Vorenberg, and Grace Won. The bibliographical essay benefited from the aid of Stephen Chen. Many other friends and colleagues offered insights on this project, including Kim Lamp Acworth, Richard Bennett, Caroline Castiglione, Rebecca D. Larson, Robert Martinez, David M. Osher, and Mary Foster Peabody. For their hospitality when manuscript sources took me to their cities, I am grateful to Felicia Eckstein Lipson, John Loiselle, Christine Reuther, and Nancy White.

I would like to thank Peter T. Harstad and the Indiana Historical Society for awarding me a research fellowship in 1988. Peter Parish, the Institute of United States Studies, and the Institute for Historical Research, all at University College, London, welcomed me in 1990–1991 when I was finishing my dissertation, and I thank them for their kindness.

Of the many excellent librarians and archivists who helped me find my way through manuscripts and libraries, Fred Bauman at the Library of Congress manuscript reading room, Radames Suarez at the New York Public Library, and Linda Stanley at the Historical Society of Pennsylvania were especially helpful. I owe an enormous debt to all of the people at the Government Documents Division of the Harvard University Library system, particularly David Paul, Stephen W. Tanner, and John Collins.

I would like to offer special thanks to Karin Daley, who has kept my home fires burning with such devotion that I have been able—sometimes, anyway—to turn my attention elsewhere.

My greatest debt is to my husband, Michael R. Pontrelli, for always asking one more question and never accepting an easy answer.

If the Republican party of this nation shall ever have the national house entrusted to its keeping, it will be the duty of that party to attend to all the affairs of national house-keeping. Whatever matters of importance may come up, whatever difficulties may arise in the way of its administration of the govern-ment, that party will then have to attend to. It will then be compelled to attend to other questions, besides this question which now assumes an overwhelming importance—the question of Slavery.

—*Abraham Lincoln, March 6, 1860*

A Note on Quotations

Throughout this work I have corrected spellings
and have replaced the ubiquitous ampersand with "and."
Nowhere have I added emphases; all italics are in the
original documents.

Introduction

With all its faults and errors, this has been a great and self-sacrificing Congress. If the rebellion should be crushed, Congress will
have crushed it. We have assumed terrible responsibilities, placed
powers in the hands of the government possessed by none other
on earth short of a despotism, borne contumely and reproach,
taken the sins of others upon ourselves and forborne deserved punishment of flagrant offenses for the public good, and suffered
abuse for our forbearance. Well, future times will comprehend our
motives and all we have done and suffered.

—William Pitt Fessenden, 1863

During the Civil War, Republicans transformed the United States. In
1860, Northerners lived east of Kansas Territory or tried their fortunes on the remote Pacific Coast; small businessmen provided goods
and services for their local areas; low tariffs illustrated America's
commitment to agriculture. Hopes and loyalties, as well as local
investments and state currency, tied individuals to their respective
states rather than to the nation. The national government did little
to merit the interest that citizens devoted to their local concerns.
When Lincoln took office, the nation's army had fewer than 16,000
men, and the new president's first report from the Treasury listed only
four sources of income. The national government did little more
than deliver the mail, collect tariffs, and oversee foreign affairs. By
the time of Appomattox, the world had changed. Northerners were
poised to spread across the continent on a transcontinental railroad;
businesses had begun to operate on a national scale; and high tariffs
bolstered Northern manufacturing. Individuals gave their allegiance
to a nation that not only held their investments, provided their currency, and promoted their economic welfare, but also claimed their
hopes and pride with its promise to become "the greatest nation of
the earth."[1] A strong central government dominated the postwar
nation. It boasted a military of over a million men; it carried a national
debt of over $2.5 billion; and it collected an array of new internal
taxes, provided a national currency, distributed public lands, char-

tered corporations, and enforced the freedom of former slaves within state borders.

Although forced by the war, these changes were not haphazard. The members of the Republican party who controlled the Union during the Civil War worked consciously to create a new nation, both on the battlefields, where they insured the survival of their new country, and in the halls of Congress, where they constructed the framework for the postwar era. The Republicans acted on a belief that the United States could become the wealthiest, strongest, and most egalitarian nation on earth. Surprised when they found themselves in such a bloody war, they quickly understood that the war years would both compel and enable them to pass sweeping novel legislation to bring their optimistic vision of the nation's future to life. Ultimately, however, these revolutionary efforts crushed their dream under the tumultuous new world of the Gilded Age. How the Republicans tried and failed to usher in a millennium for America is the subject of this book.

Civil War Republicans were members of a new political party that had coalesced around the issue of the spread of slavery into the national territories after the passage of the Kansas-Nebraska Act in 1854. The fear that an aggressive Slave Power would dominate the developing western lands and eventually the whole North, undermining the North's distinctive political economy of free labor, brought together old Whigs, nativists, many Northern Democrats, and abolitionists. With regional emphases on different prospective policies, Republicans at the time of the election of 1860 had articulated as a national policy little but an opposition to the extension of slavery.

While they had not agreed on a legislative plan for the nation, Republicans did share a world view that they had inherited from the rural antebellum world of farming and small towns from which most of them had come. Having seen their communities develop from agricultural beginnings, party members believed that God had given man the ability to create value with the labor of his hands. Every individual could thus build capital, which would accumulate faster than it was consumed. The resulting national prosperity would guarantee that the American standard of living would always increase, making the United States the envy of the world.[2] In their optimistic conception of economic development, all elements in society would work together to increase individual and national wealth, so long as no one monopolized money or power. The belief that workers would create an ever-increasing spiral of prosperity inclined many (though not all) Republicans to favor governmental intervention in the economy to accelerate labor's development of the nation.

Their lack of a national policy platform and general belief in free labor did not mean that Republicans were indistinguishable from Northern Democrats, many of whom also disliked slavery. Despite their shared belief in free labor, Northern Democrats tended to follow their ideas to quite different conclusions than their opponents. Many Democrats, especially those with immigrant constituencies, recognized the limitations on upward mobility. They disagreed with the Republican belief in a harmony of all interests, arguing that individual self-interest led to conflicts in society that pitted labor against capital. Democrats tended to adhere to a strict construction of the Constitution and to oppose government intervention in the economy out of a conviction that any increase in government activity would create monopolies of power and wealth that would further entrench a wealthy aristocracy and destroy individual liberties.[3]

Rather loose antebellum Republican and Democratic leanings probably would not have made much difference in the course of the nation's development had it not been for the outbreak of war between the North and the South in April 1861. When Southern Democrats gave their determined farewell speeches and left their congressional seats and administrative posts, they surrendered control of America's government to their opponents. Left behind with poor leadership and in the unenviable position of having to choose between supporting an opposition government or opposing the war, Northern Democrats undermined their influence by clinging to a belief in state sovereignty and a strict understanding of the powers of the national government under the Constitution, which, if accepted, would have meant the dismemberment of the nation. As Democrats condemned increasingly far-reaching Republican legislation as revolutionary and abhorrent, they retreated into harsh racism and strident states' rights rhetoric, attacking the Republicans as rich capitalists bent on destroying labor while exploiting the tyrannical government they had built. Alienating moderates with their inflammatory language and tactics of obstruction, Democrats were never able to challenge national Republican policies effectively.

As the dominant party in the North, the Republicans had a unique opportunity to direct the nation for four years with virtually no opposition. Congressmen listened to the opinions of their constituents and translated their needs and desires into law.[4] They did so with impunity, convinced that Democratic criticisms of their measures were tainted by a desire for Southern victory, and that occasional protests from agricultural districts were incited by traitorous Democrats. So the Republicans, largely alone, changed the nation during the war. They did so by enacting laws shaping each segment of society to their own plan, and, ultimately, by establishing the pattern and scope of the federal government's involvement in society for the rest of the century.

Historians who have examined the political and economic developments of the war years disagree about both the causes and the consequences of the changes wrought by the Republican wartime Congresses. Scholars in the Progressive Era argued that the wartime government was dominated by capitalist interests, which worked in tandem with Radical Republicans to guarantee a laissez-faire postwar government that would permit business and industry to crush labor and farming interests. A revision of this interpretation began in the 1950s. Quantitative studies indicated no deliberate wartime combination of radicals and industrialists; analyses of congressional voting showed little correlation between economic and social issues. Subsequent studies of postwar legislation revealed no unity among Republicans on postwar economic issues. While they effectively countered the old interpretation of the aims of the wartime legislators, these studies, which tended to concentrate on discrete postwar issues rather than wartime domestic policies generally, suggested that wartime laws represented a haphazard reaction to wartime conditions, and offered no new interpretation of the war years as a whole. In 1968, Leonard P. Curry addressed this gap when he examined the domestic legislative activity of the Thirty-seventh Congress (1861–1863) in his *Blueprint for Modern America;* but, with this exception, the economic policies of the war years have received no comprehensive treatment since the early twentieth century.[5]

Instead of concentrating on the war years, historians since the 1970s have offered explanations of mid-nineteenth-century Republican behavior by examining the ideological roots of the party. In 1970, Eric Foner's pathbreaking book *Free Soil, Free Labor, Free Men* launched a new debate by arguing that Republican party unity sprang from a commitment to the economic and social world engendered in the concept of free labor. Responses to this work emphasized the power of different elements and ideas in the Republican coalition, explored the importance of the breakdown of the party system in the

1850s, and outlined the chronological formation of the antebellum Republican organization. With the exception of Gabor S. Boritt's portrait of the president in *Lincoln and the Economics of the American Dream* (1978), however, those examining the importance of the free labor ideology did not venture into the war years.[6]

Yet it was during the war that the Republican party changed the nation, and it did so according to a set of ideas revealed by party members' extensive economic legislation. In order to wage a war requiring millions of dollars a day and hundreds of thousands of men on the battlefields, Republicans were forced to create a sweeping new system of domestic legislation. Beginning in July 1861, when party members passed novel revenue and confiscation laws, through the passage of the Thirteenth Amendment in 1865, the Republicans tailored fundamentally important national legislation in accordance with their economic beliefs. As they did so, they articulated a new national policy that altered the course of the nation.

Wartime Republicans began their congressional activities convinced that all Northerners would support what party leaders defined as the national good, especially in the face of the South's frightening challenge to the integrity of the Union. Their initial belief in a harmony of interest between capitalists and government quickly broke down, however, when bankers refused to provide money on the terms the government wished. Revising their belief in a harmony of economic interests, Republicans deliberately turned away from bankers and placed the financial security of the Union in the hands of individual Americans by selling bonds to the public, revamping the national banking system, and instituting broad-based domestic taxes. Fitting nicely with the idea that individual wealth would benefit all, this change then required that national legislation promote individual prosperity so that the public could meet its new obligations. Republicans ultimately designed agricultural policies, transcontinental railroad legislation, and eventually even the Thirteenth Amendment, to foster a wealthy populace and a strong nation.

The Civil War forced Republicans to test their ideas about the way the economy and society worked, and changed their traditional understanding of the role government should play in economic growth. As they struggled to pay for an extraordinarily expensive war, the Republicans began to extend the government's reach throughout the economy. Increasingly confident of the government's authority to promote growth, party members speaking for different factions and interests promoted measures designed to benefit their constituents. Ultimately, they channelled wartime and regional pressures into a set of domestic policies that reflected initial Republican economic beliefs and increasingly strengthened some aspects of the national government while leaving others untouched. Wartime domestic legislation established a firm precedent that the American government could promote development in all sectors of the economy, but the Republicans created no corresponding government role in the regulation of large interest groups or the protection of economically disadvantaged segments of the population.[7]

Republican politicians had neither a static world view nor simple political aims; they shaped legislation according to their evolving ideas, a need to accommodate constituents, and inevitable compromises with other party members. Republican beliefs were not monolithic; divisions within the party were dynamic factors in the construction of both policies and ideas. Although Republicans shared a general economic belief based on the idea that labor created value, they rarely enjoyed unanimous support for party measures. They clashed constantly over personal, regional, and factional differences; and Democratic opposition, despite its inability to thwart Republican measures completely, often altered legislation. In short, there was seldom a direct line from theory to legislation; rather, a variety of factors usually affected the final version of Republican policy. At the same time that various Republican tendencies shaped policies, laws themselves changed the way party members thought. Each new law seemed to provide more latitude for later initiatives even as it created unanticipated problems which demanded that party members revise their theories.

Although circumstances made Republicans refine their economic ideas and drastically changed the way they approached the world, their basic premises remained intact. Forced by the war to legislate on a wide range of economic issues, the Republicans nonetheless always passed legislation that reflected a general vision of universal harmony and a determination to foster economic progress. They refused to recognize that their vision might be wrong or incomplete; as a result, their increasingly sweeping legislation often had unexpected results. The Republicans' self-righteous determination that they were correct helped to cause the breakdown of their vision in the postwar years.

Civil War Republicans were neither great capitalists bent on advancing the interests of northeastern business nor befuddled combatants reacting haphazardly to the events of the war. Rather, Republicans tried to create an activist government that encouraged the prosperity of all sectors of the economy; that balanced the needs of each region of the country; that consolidated the government without destroying the states; that freed the slaves without infantilizing them; that was innovative without undermining the Constitution. Using the government to develop the country by placing land in the hands of free individuals and educating farmers, by building railroads to transport emigrants and crops, and by increasing tariffs to nurture industry seemed to party members a way to make America a prosperous nation of small producers while they fought a desperate civil war to guarantee that their plan would be unchallenged. But the Republicans' actions undermined their goals and obscured their vision. In their single-minded dedication to their world view, unable to recognize the implications of their own legislation, wartime Republicans paved the way for the transformation of their party from one dedicated to labor and reform to one unabashedly advancing big business. Trying to recreate a more extensive and prosperous version of the antebellum world of independent individuals from which they came, the Republicans instead set the stage for an entirely new, industrial America.

1   "The Cares of Your Country Are a Paramount Duty": The Republicans in 1861

The attention of the world is naturally turned to the exciting
scenes which are being enacted, and are expected to be enacted by
the hosts of armed men now confronting each other. But war is in
its nature temporary . . . The civil transactions . . . at Washington
will make their impression upon ages to come, when the battles
on the Potomac and Tennessee will be regarded as mere accidents
in history.

—Montreal *Herald,* 1862

Responding to Lincoln's call for a special session of Congress, the men
who were to create the nation's economic legislation during the Civil
War convened in the hot, humid city of Washington on July 4, 1861.
They were not the first arrivals who would be important for wartime
economic policy. The President himself had been in the White House
for four months, and although his attention would be focused almost
exclusively on military matters during the war, his influence often
added momentum to his party's economic measures. Lincoln's new
Secretary of the Treasury, Salmon P. Chase, had also been in Washington since March, arranging bank loans to fill the Union's empty
war chest.

The city to which Republican congressmen came in the summer of
1861 was, a visitor from Maine recalled, "a squalid, unattractive, in-
sanitary country town infested by malaria, mosquitoes, cockroaches,
bed bugs, lice and outdoor backhouses . . . surface drainage, muddy
or dusty streets, . . . and no end of houses of ill-fame." Congressmen
who would soon legislate over the nation's finances and economic
development crowded into the area northeast of Pennsylvania Avenue,
within sight of the construction on the unfinished Capitol. Here the
rooming houses stood clustered on the dirty streets, and entertainment
spots offered diversions for weary legislators. While still "ragged,"

Washington had lost its habitual sleepiness in the summer of 1861.[1] Republicans arriving in Washington entered a city already immersed in war. "It is much like living in a military camp here," wrote Vice-President Hannibal Hamlin to his wife. "Troops are quartered everywhere in and around the city and more daily arriving . . . The roll of the drum and the tramp of armed men, are in our ears all the time."[2]

When the House and Senate convened, Republican congressmen divided into several committees that directed economic legislation. In the House, the Committee on Ways and Means controlled all financial bills. Its chairman in the Thirty-Seventh Congress (1861–1863) was Pennsylvania's scowling, clubfooted Thaddeus Stevens. The House's undisputed leader, as one man called him, Stevens "ruled in grim and relentless mastery."[3] Authoritative on all economic affairs, he controlled tax debates, railroad laws, and currency issues. Stevens spoke well and easily with a keen wit, which he often turned mercilessly on his opponents. Ruthless in political debates, he was often kind, charitable, and lavish to a fault when approached by the needy or oppressed. In Congress, he often defended the interests of the poor.[4]

Stevens's second on the committee was his friend Justin Smith Morrill of Vermont. A blacksmith's son who had made a small fortune in business, Morrill was the acknowledged expert on tariff matters throughout the war and a pivotal figure in the development of tax legislation. A Whig before he became a Republican, Morrill believed strongly that a system of protective tariffs would enrich the nation. The intimacy of the friendship between Morrill and Stevens was legendary. The bachelor Stevens would often play with Morrill's young son during House sessions, raising the boy's hand during roll call votes. In the Thirty-Eighth Congress (1863–1865), Morrill replaced Stevens as the chairman of the committee.[5]

Two other Republican members of the Ways and Means Committee concerned themselves primarily with banking legislation. The first was wealthy Boston financier Samuel Hooper. Hooper and his friends, who were among the first large purchasers of government war bonds, invested almost $1.5 million in government securities in April 1861. The second Republican banking authority on the committee was New York's Elbridge G. Spaulding. As a young lawyer, Spaulding had married a banker's daughter and shortly thereafter began a banking career in Buffalo. In the Thirty-Seventh Congress, he would help to develop key currency legislation.[6]

Another Republican on the committee who contributed materially to economic legislation was Ohio's Vermont-born Valentine B. Horton. A Western representative with Eastern ties, Horton brought to the committee a broad perspective on economic issues. Speaking as a Westerner in congressional debates, his justification of financial measures carried weight with other Westerners who had qualms about bills in question.

The Senate Committee on Finance paralleled the House Ways and Means Committee. Its powerful chairman was Maine's William Pitt Fessenden. A man "of majesty in . . . figure and brow" with "integrity perfect," as a colleague remembered him, the acerbic Fessenden dominated Senate debate with strong, well-reasoned speeches. Despite his short temper and obvious exasperation with those who challenged his measures, he commanded great respect in both Congress and the White House. Frequent personnel changes in the committee gave Fessenden extraordinary influence as its driving force.[7]

The only man who rivaled Fessenden's power in the Finance Committee was Ohio's John Sherman, who was to replace Fessenden as committee chairman in 1864. With a broad forehead, high cheekbones, and piercing eyes, Sherman looked much like his older brother, William Tecumseh Sherman. Although placed on the committee as a junior member, Senator Sherman quickly became instrumental in the development of Union financial policy. He enjoyed the friendship of both the Secretary of the Treasury and Jay Cooke, a financier who would be critical to the Union finances.

The Senate initially placed Rhode Island's James F. Simmons on the Senate Finance Committee as its second most experienced member. A Providence cotton trader who had, in years past, chaired the Senate Committee on Manufacturing, Simmons's tenure on the wartime Finance Committee was short. He resigned from the Senate in 1862 under a cloud of disapprobation for his involvement in a corrupt deal regarding wartime supplies to the government, but not before he had helped to commit the Republican party to a novel system of income taxes.

When Simmons resigned, Fessenden secured the vacated seat on the Finance Committee for his friend Jacob Collamer of Vermont. A colleague described the former judge simply as "a wise man." He was also "conservative in his nature, [and] he was sure to advise against rashness," a tendency that led him to oppose important banking and currency measures. Collamer's conservatism came from his unwillingness to let expediency bend principles: years before, as a judge, he had defended the right of freedom of speech "even if the disruption of the Union was being plotted." The Vermont man served on the Finance Committee only during the third session of the Thirty-Seventh Congress, for in 1863, congressmen angry at his continual opposition to proposed measures ousted him from it.[8]

Timothy Otis Howe of Wisconsin stayed on the Finance Committee throughout the war. Although a native of Maine, Howe joined Sherman in providing a crucially important Western voice on the committee.

While members of the House Ways and Means Committee and of the Senate Finance Committee developed financial legislation, members of other committees controlled agricultural and railroad bills. In the Thirty-Seventh Congress, Owen Lovejoy of Illinois chaired the House Committee on Agriculture and sat on the Committee on Territories. Famous as the brother of an abolitionist editor murdered at the hands of a proslavery mob, the minister Lovejoy's fortunes grew with his fame as an abolitionist. A native of Maine's poor agricultural region, Lovejoy was also a dedicated farmer and the prime advocate of key agricultural legislation.

The House Committee on Agriculture worked closely with the House Committee on Public Lands, which Wisconsin's John Fox Potter chaired. Like Lovejoy, Potter had emigrated to the West from a town in Maine's agricultural region. Their hometowns were near each other, and it is entirely possible that the two men had heard of each other, or even met, before they struck out for the West.[9]

Lovejoy and Potter found their work easier because the Speaker of the Thirty-Seventh Congress, Galusha A. Grow, strongly supported agricultural legislation. Grow's father had died when the boy was four, leaving six children and little to support them. After living with her father for seven years, Grow's mother took her family West, where it prospered on a farm. Convinced that cheap Western land would help others as it had him, Grow became, as his biographers called him, "the father of the Homestead Law."[10]

Congress passed its most important agricultural measures in 1862, but until 1863, when the Senate created the Committee on Agriculture with John Sherman at its head, no one Senate committee had jurisdiction over agricultural bills. At least one bill benefited from the support of the chairman of the Committee on Territories, Ohio's fierce abolitionist Benjamin Franklin Wade. Like Grow, Wade knew the benefits of Western migration. A rough, brash man, he came from a poor Massachusetts family that had moved West. Wade had worked as a cattle drover and as a laborer on the Erie Canal before he managed to study law and to enter politics.[11]

No one of either party in either house ignored transcontinental railroad legislation. In the Thirty-Seventh Congress, Pennsylvania's James H. Campbell led debate from his position as the head of the House Committee on the Pacific Railroad. His Senate counterpart was the hard-drinking California War Democrat James A. McDougall, whose disastrous overland trip West from Illinois made him a staunch advocate of a transcontinental railroad by almost killing him. Samuel C. Pomeroy, representing the new state of Kansas, took the Republican lead on the Senate Committee on the Pacific Railroad. A Massachusetts native, Pomeroy had moved to Kansas, as he wrote, "to be early upon the ground to occupy some of the best points upon the 'Pacific R. Road'—which is destined to cross the Territory Some where." As a member of the Committee on Territories, Pomeroy's Kansas colleague, James H. Lane, also did all he could to help promote a railroad.[12]

During the war, the Senate created a Select Committee on Slavery and Freedmen and the House created a Select Committee on Emancipation, but the radical antislavery men who chaired the committees, Massachusetts senator Charles Sumner and Massachusetts representative Thomas D. Eliot, often found themselves unable to press their measures through Congress. Much of the Republicans' wartime legislation regarding slaves or freedmen, therefore, came from the chairman of the Senate Judiciary Committee, Illinois senator Lyman Trumbull. Trumbull's previous position as a judge and his formative experiences successfully challenging his conservative state's toleration of slavery helped him to develop moderate but effective antislavery measures.[13]

Wartime economic debates among these men and their colleagues tended to reveal three splits among Northern Republicans. The first was the traditional tension between the old Northeastern states and the less developed, Western ones. This schism manifested itself primarily during currency and banking debates, although it also appeared in debates of agricultural and railroad legislation. Easterners tended to speak for the banking and industrial interests of their developed regions, while congressmen from Ohio, Illinois, Indiana, and Iowa often spoke for farming interests.

The split between the East and the West arose not only from

different economic interests, but also from political jealousies and cultural differences. Westerners complained that the East was indifferent to the West, and they bitterly resented what they perceived as slights. In Washington, Easterners formed a visible and powerful clique against which Westerners fought. A jealous Western newspaper correspondent complained that New England monopolized "every thing worth having—eleven chairmanships of committees in the Senate, a Vice-Presidency, a Cabinet office, the highest foreign mission, and two others of the first class, and a myriad of lesser appointments." Indeed, in a time when the mean length of service of a Northern representative was only two and a half years, many of the Easterners in Washington had served in previous Congresses long enough to hold important positions by seniority. So complete did New England domination appear in the Senate that in 1863 Western congressmen protested strongly enough to force a Republican caucus to call for committee reorganization, but a New England man killed the accord in the Senate.[14]

Equally galling to any Westerner trying to break a New England phalanx must have been the close ties among Eastern delegations. Vermont's entire congressional delegation, for instance, had been friends for years, while Maine's delegation made Vermont's look like a group of strangers. As Westerners noted, by the end of 1862, five out of the eight Maine representatives to Congress were from two families, one led by Senator Lot Myrick Morrill and the other by Senator William Pitt Fessenden. Westerners correctly assumed that such close ties made these delegations work together. Even when not related by blood, Easterners shared ties of education, business, and friendship, and they often boarded together in Washington.[15]

Related to this East-West tension was a less obvious one between city and country. It showed up primarily in bond policy, as country dwellers showed increasing prejudice against New York City, which, a member of Lincoln's Cabinet complained to his diary, "is . . . leprous and rotten." A city is a place, agreed a Republican from Iowa, "where the masses climb in despair to garrets or go down to the death-damps of cellars, struggling like a pitcher of tamed Egyptian vipers each to get the head above the others." Drawing on a long heritage of American dislike of urban life, many Republicans, especially Westerners, did not trust cities, for they seemed to threaten the existence of free, independent labor. "The tendency of city growth is invariably to produce classes, and to widen the differences between those already existing," explained the editor of the Chicago *Tribune*. "In the country the equality of man is generally successfully maintained through a course of many years."[16]

The third split was one between the New England–influenced upper Northwest and the Southern-influenced lower Northwest. This schism affected tax, tariff, and railroad legislation. The division corresponded to different settlement histories. The region known as the upper Northwest—Wisconsin, Michigan, Minnesota and the upper portions of Illinois and Indiana—had been settled primarily by emigrants from the Northeast, who had arrived after the opening of the Erie Canal in 1825. When Democratic members of the Indiana legislature suggested breaking the Northwest away from New England during the war, a Republican newspaper editor called it "a terrible mistake—a fatal mistake," and explained: "scattered all through our Western country—are thousands of New England families that look fondly back on their old homes." Several congressmen from the upper Northwest had emigrated from the East and kept ties there from their youths. In Washington, these emigrants often formed friendships with Easterners.[17]

Easterners and Northwesterners formed a group against which lower Northwesterners defined themselves. The portions of lower Ohio, Indiana, Illinois, and Iowa that lay in the Ohio or Missouri River valleys had been settled much earlier than the upper halves of the states, primarily by Southerners. Together with those parts of Missouri, Tennessee, and Kentucky that also lay in the valleys, these areas formed a cohesive section that grew different crops, used different political structures, and had a different culture than its Northern neighbors. An Illinois representative maintained that men from this region could be identified on sight. They had their own "tall, large-boned . . . stature, figure, dress, manner, voice, and accent." Men from this area distinguished themselves from the hated Northerners, who often poked fun at their backwoods lower Northwestern neighbors. "I have an aversion to Yankees," wrote a young lower Northwesterner, and his sentiments were not uncommon.[18] Indiana novelist Edward Eggleston later recalled how jealous he and his young friends had been "that the manners, customs, thoughts, and feelings of New England country people filled so large a place in books, while our life [did not]." Partly in self-defense, the region had begun to develop its own distinct literature, the "Cincinnati School." During the war, Democrats fueled this region's antagonism to the East, and the lower

Northwest's frequent threats to secede from the Union and join the Southern confederacy caused many Republicans great anxiety.[19]

Despite the stresses within the party, experience, religion, and economic theory joined to give most Republicans a general world view that celebrated individual labor. In 1861, when congressmen from all across the North traveled the hard roads to Washington, America was still the land of the self-made man. In the 1840s and 1850s the economy had expanded and flourished. Immigrants had poured in, providing an extra labor force for the nation, and railroads had steamed across the eastern half of the continent. The country had grown, and new states entered the Union: Texas in 1845, Iowa in 1846, Wisconsin in 1848, California in 1850, Minnesota in 1858, and Oregon in 1859. The opening of Western lands brought new opportunities for Easterners. On the frontier, "work and wit give quick returns," one man proclaimed. "I can say boldly and freely," another man wrote home on the back of one of his newly printed business announcements, "I like the West . . .—I like the people—I like the go ahead, enterprising spirit, and I . . . can do better, make more money . . . here than in any New England town."[20]

Many of the Republicans who developed the economic legislation of the Civil War years embodied the story of self-made success. During the war, commentators made much of Lincoln's rural boyhood and eulogized him as a representative laboring man of the country, but Lincoln was hardly unique. Treasury Secretary Chase could also claim to have earned his own success. His father had died when the boy was nine, leaving Chase's mother with ten children. An uncle adopted him, and Chase was supporting himself by the time he was sixteen. He taught school until he passed the bar, then went West to seek his fortune. He chose Cincinnati "chiefly because he believed that it offered the largest opportunity for brains and ambition."[21]

Congress's financial leaders claimed similar backgrounds. Thaddeus Stevens's father had been a shiftless shoemaker who abandoned his wife and four sons. Thaddeus, crippled and sickly, managed to get a college education before emigrating from Vermont to Pennsylvania. He supported himself by teaching school until admitted to the bar. Stevens quickly became a prosperous lawyer. Later in life he advised, "Learn to rely through life upon your own unaided efforts." William Pitt Fessenden would have felt that he had worked hard for his success even if his difficult early days as a lawyer on the Maine frontier had been easier. Fessenden's father was a prominent lawyer, but he had not married Fessenden's mother. The senator carried the cross of illegitimacy all his life.[22]

John Sherman had also made his own prosperity. His father died when the boy was six, leaving eleven children. An uncle took John for four years, until the pressures of the man's own new family made him unwelcome. He returned to his mother's home at age twelve. Three years later, he had become a superintending engineer at a river improvement company and worried that "it depends upon my conduct whether I sink or swim live or die survive or perish." In 1855, when he was thirty-two, Sherman was sitting in the U.S. House of Representatives and had presided over the first Republican convention in Ohio.[23]

Many of the Republican congressmen had histories similar to those of their financial leaders. Republicans in general, and perhaps congressmen in particular, believed that individuals could make their own successes. "A determined, persistent industry will secure your success anywhere," wrote Senator James W. Grimes, who had settled in a frontier section of Iowa only three years after the Indians had left. "Without it," he added, "no one can succeed."[24]

Most of the Republican congressmen arriving in Washington in 1861 had made their own fortunes by their own efforts. They had also watched their nation grow and, ignoring the contributions that British capital had made to development, Republicans attributed this growth solely to individual effort. "Labor has made this country what it is," Chase wrote. It was no surprise, then, that Republicans believed labor generated economic development, and that it was the sole creator of value. Capital, Republicans believed, was simply the value of accumulated unconsumed labor, or, in Lincoln's words: "Capital is only the fruit of labor, and could never have existed if labor had not first existed." In 1865, Republicans still stated axiomatically, "Labor is the great source of national wealth."[25] From the theory that the amount of labor expended on a product creates its exchangeable value came the ideas of economic individualism, free labor, and the progressivism that marked Republican thought.

The belief in labor's fundamental role in economic life, and therefore in society, arose from what seemed to be the inherent sense of the proposition. In a nation with great resources that needed only work to make them profitable, the idea that labor creates value seemed obvious. Most Americans survived by basic manual labor, which brought products forth from nature; agriculture dominated Northern society, and even most manufacturing simply processed agricultural products. An individual's efforts transformed untamed nature into a salable product, seeming to illustrate that labor alone added value to natural resources.[26]

One contemporary economist pointed out that the principles of political economy and moral philosophy were "so closely analogous, that almost every question in the one may be argued on grounds belonging to the other"; indeed, Republican beliefs about labor also had a religious basis. God had decreed that "in the sweat of thy face shalt thou eat bread," recalled one Republican newspaper editor, and he wondered: "Does any body suppose he can circumvent an eternal decree . . . ?" To work, he concluded, was the fate of mankind, and "the great majority of the human race" would always "have to get their living by bodily labor." Despite the invention of labor-saving devices and the increase of knowledge, the writer asserted that he could not "conceive of a condition in which the greater portion would not have to labor." In his memoirs, one man recalled how this theory was put into practice. In the days before the Civil War, he wrote, "the strenuous and inexorable mandates of 'Poor Richard's Almanac' were virtuously and vigorously enforced and obeyed as if they were holy Scripture, and when even young children learned by heart, with the purpose of making them rules of conduct, such prudential maxims as 'God helps them who helps themselves'; and 'The sleeping fox catches no poultry.'"[27]

Republicans believed that God must have established humane laws to govern human intercourse. God had given man the inherent ability to survive by endowing him with the ability to work. The Creator had also insured that the labor of each individual harmonized with the efforts of everyone else, so that the struggle for survival would become progressively easier. The editor of the Chicago *Tribune* mused that the economist who discovered the primacy of labor "believed in God, and the immutable laws of His creation, and he saw the senseless folly of attempting to interfere with, or change them by human exactments." As the light of this economic theory dawned on Henry Carey Baird, later a political economist in his own right, he wrote in the style of a religious convert to an economist who expounded the labor theory, describing with fervent ecstasy the gradual unfolding of his thought. He now understood, he wrote, "that the Almighty in placing man upon the Earth had established laws for his movements as fixed and unalterable as the laws which govern the movements of the planets." When mankind completely conformed to God's laws, "a perfect harmony will exist in all the movements of man." Just as Baird finished writing, the arrival of the most violent thunderstorm he had ever witnessed cemented his conviction that his ideas about labor illuminated God's plan.[28]

America's thriving economy strengthened Republicans' simple faith that a good God would not have created a world inadequate to supply everyone's needs. Democratic labor leaders turned to the theories of Ricardo and Malthus, and to the history of England, to show that the condition of workers steadily, if gradually, declines. Republicans rejected this miserable conclusion, perceiving that the propositions of Ricardo and Malthus could only lead to a polarization of wealth and inevitable economic class conflict. Labor must become either wealthier or poorer, Republicans argued, and they pointed to high American wages as proof that it was becoming richer.[29]

Economic writers bolstered the beliefs that Republicans brought from their experience and religion. Political economy in the mid-nineteenth century was a much more accessible science than it became just decades later, and most men were conversant with the leading economic theories of the day. Newspaper editors frequently ran editorials discussing how the economic world worked. Asking an economist to explain his ideas, one writer revealed why he, and many other nineteenth-century Americans, studied political economy so closely. "Painting is well," he wrote, "sculpture and poetry are well . . .—but Political Economy is *bread;* and people must, first of all, be kept alive."[30] Essentially optimists, Republicans followed economic theorists who emphasized the potential of society to create wealth and prosper without creating a poor or downtrodden class. Because their beliefs were founded primarily on their experience, the Republicans had little problem with contradictions in economic texts. They simply followed the specific aspects of economists' work with which they agreed.

The foundations of Republican political economic theory lay in the work of Adam Smith. In *The Wealth of Nations,* party members noted, Smith attacked the view "that wealth consisted solely of money," arguing instead that "the universal agent in the creation of wealth is labor." Smith's concentration on the creation of new national wealth instead of the confiscation of existing foreign wealth described a world of potentially unlimited plenty. Like him, the Republicans were optimistic about their world. Smith's work had "contributed more towards the happiness of man" than any legislators had ever accomplished, the editor of the Chicago *Tribune* insisted.[31]

Smith had introduced the idea of the primacy of labor; American economic thinkers repeated and embellished it. First in the pantheon of Republican economic heroes was Alexander Hamilton, who, in his *Report on Manufactures,* wrote that "every fabric is worth intrinsically the price of the raw material and the expense of fabrication." Hamilton was "the greatest of all American statesmen," one party member insisted, and, wrote another, "the ablest practical financier and economist that ever lived, certainly without a rival in this country." The genius Hamilton "delved deep in the mines of perpetual prosperity," proclaimed one Republican congressman, and "he haunts us yet with the maxims he has left."[32]

Although the labor theory of value underlay much of American economic theory in the mid-nineteenth century, the Republicans primarily followed two political economists, Francis Wayland and Henry Charles Carey. Wayland's easily read 1837 work, *The Elements of Political Economy,* which was one of America's most popular texts in the 1840's, stated that exchangeable value "is derived . . . from human labor." What cost two days of labor to produce would be exchangeable only for something of similar value, Wayland argued. He went on to define capital as "pre-exerted labor."[33] Wayland had been Republican leader William Henry Seward's tutor and was so renowned among congressmen that allusions to "that great and good man" crept into congressional debates. As the President's December 1861 Message showed, Lincoln "ate up, digested, and assimilated . . . Wayland's little book."[34]

Published in the same year as Wayland's *Elements* was Carey's tremendously influential *Principles of Political Economy.* "Labor is . . . the sole cause of value," he wrote, and capital was "the accumulated results of past labor." Carey, one historian recounts, was the "most broadly influential American economist before the Civil War," and Ralph Waldo Emerson called him America's greatest political economist. Republicans certainly respected him: one Democratic paper charged that Carey was the Republican New York *Daily Tribune's* "great idol." "We follow . . . the principal of political economy of which you are so distinguished an advocate," wrote the congressman owner of the Providence, Rhode Island, *Daily Journal* to the economist; and congressmen consulted him on tax and tariff issues. Secretary of the Treasury Salmon P. Chase wrote to Carey for advice, and some people assumed that "the most intimate relations exist[ed] between" the two men.[35]

From the idea of the primacy of labor Republicans derived several economic principles. First, party members believed that a healthy political economy rested on individual self-sufficiency. Convinced that labor created value, the Republicans saw a man's ability to work as his ticket to success. The labor in a man's arms was his "pecuniary resource," stated a Rhode Island representative; and as long as a man could work, Republicans argued, he could better himself. Horace Greeley, the powerful editor of the New York *Daily Tribune,* assured his readers that the first thing to do to ameliorate poverty was to make sure individuals were "at perfect liberty to help themselves." "Charity is sweet," agreed a columnist in the Chicago *Tribune,* "but the joy of honest and busy labor is sweeter still." Believing that the ability to work was, in a sense, money in the bank, Republicans were unsympathetic to the unemployed. In New York City, Greeley, for instance, warned against "a very numerous class . . . who too readily resort to the Poor-House rather than earn their bread by honest industry."[36]

In an 1864 New York *Daily Tribune* editorial, Greeley justified Republican ideas by illustrating the legitimacy of a society based on the labor of self-sufficient individuals. Hearing agitators encourage poor workers to strike for better wages, Greeley, who was himself a reformer whose "zeal for 'strange Gods'" (as one party member wrote to another) led him to embrace causes from abolition to Fourierism, protested against what he perceived as the basis of Communism. Better conditions could not come from any theory except that based on the worth of labor, he said. Making the need of the laborer instead of the value of his work the basis of demands for higher wages made the worker "a solicitor of charity rather than of justice." Greeley contended that "the *worth of the work* is the true and only sure measure of the worker's compensation." As an illustration of his point, he compared the wages of two men, one a bachelor and the other a married man with a sick wife and six children. Even if the bachelor was by far the better worker, when need dictated compensation the married man would have the higher wages. The injustice of this principle seemed so patently obvious that Greeley felt unobliged to spell it out. Rather he asked "those who aspire to instruct and guide the laboring class . . . [to] be careful first of all to think."[37]

Belief in the primacy of labor also strengthened the Republicans' commitment to free labor, for if work created value, slavery was clearly unjust. Wayland, whose hatred of slavery and stand against the Kansas-Nebraska Act had earned his books expulsion from the South, asserted, "Moral Philosophy teaches us, that if a man expend labor in the creation of a value, this labor gives him a right to the exclusive possession of that value; that is, supposing the original elements belonged to no one else." The free laborer, agreed a Republican correspondent, has vested rights "in the produce of his hands, in the fabrics he manufactures, and in the values he may create, whether by the direct or indirect application of his labor." In 1861, few Republicans extended this logic to support emancipation, but their fear that the Southern system would usurp their own labor if it spread fed their advocacy of slavery's containment in the South.[38]

Republicans saw the Northern political economy as one based on the value of labor and consisting almost entirely of free, self-sufficient workers—a category from which they excluded only a handful of unproductive capitalists. From this perception came their general beliefs about the way the American economy operated. Northern society in 1861 still consisted primarily of farmers, small manufacturers, and employees of the first two; and every employee planned one day to become a farmer or a manufacturer himself. Having themselves often begun as poor laborers, Republicans perceived not fixed economic classes, but a fluid society in which a man could move readily from being an employee to being an employer. Emphatically denying that "the free hired laborer [was] fixed to that condition for life," Lincoln affirmed in his December 1861 Message to Congress that "the prudent, penniless beginner in the world labors for wages awhile, saves a surplus with which to buy tools or land for himself; then labors on his own account another while, and at length hires another new beginner to help him."[39]

This belief in economic fluidity permitted party members to make a key assumption, which would underlie their wartime economic legislation: Republicans believed that a harmony of interests existed between labor and capital. Carey and Wayland supported this perception. There was a "harmony of all real interests" of the country, from laborers to capitalists, wrote Carey. "Nothing can . . . be more unreasonable than the prejudices which sometimes exist between . . .

different classes of laborers," agreed Wayland, "and nothing can be more beautiful, than their harmonious co-operation in every effort to increase production, and thus add to the conveniences and happiness of man." The popular poet Alexander Pope provided the epigram of Carey's *Principles:* "All discord harmony not understood."[40]

The Republicans' simplistic understanding of the laws of production explained their belief in economic harmony. Each man's labor created more capital than he could consume, Carey wrote, so "capital has a tendency to increase more rapidly than population." This surplus capital provided money for more industry, which in turn employed more labor. A laborer "adds his mite to the prosperity of all branches of industry, and this, so far as his mite goes, increases the demand for labor," explained a Western newspaper. These were "natural laws of production and distribution," agreed the editor of the Chicago *Tribune,* with which it was useless to interfere. "Nothing is gained by the community except by labor and the increase of capital . . . It is capital only that employs labor." As men moved up the economic scale, they would progress from employee to employer, thus perpetuating a growth spiral.[41]

Republicans believed that capital promoted the interests of labor not only by providing employment but also by making labor more productive. "The *quantity* of capital in use in a community and the *quality* of its labor are necessarily in uniform relation to each other," wrote a newspaper columnist. Using Smith's famous comparison of a nail-making machine to a hammer and anvil, the writer went on to explain: "Labor gains increased productiveness in the proportion that capital contributes to its efficiency . . . Every improvement in the efficiency of labor, so gained by the aid of capital, is so much increased faculty of accumulation." Republicans believed that men should plow only as much surplus capital into consumption as was imperative, for most consumption destroyed value. They encouraged investment in increased production, which would employ more laborers and augment their productivity, thus helping more workers to rise.[42]

The Republican belief in economic harmony depended on party members' conviction that increase of individual wealth meant the spread of national prosperity. That conviction in turn made the sanctity of private property and the right of every man to accumulate wealth basic Republican values. Carey maintained that it was a universal law that "whatever has a tendency to prevent the growth of capital, is injurious, while every thing that promotes its growth is advantageous." From Wayland came assurance that God had ruled that a man should "be allowed to gain all that he can . . . and that . . . he be allowed to use it as he will." Wealth was deserved, for God had ordained that "the hand of the diligent maketh rich." Private property was the basis of this system, for it created a motive for "regular and voluntary labor," which in turn created more property, and so on. Private property, Wayland concluded, "lays at the foundation of all accumulation of wealth, and of all progress in civilization." The necessity for the protection of property was clear: if the enjoyment of accumulation were uncertain, men would lose the desire to labor and would cease to rise. Without immunity from unjust legislation attacking property, "capital emigrates, production ceases, and a nation . . . sinks down in hopeless despondence." If individuals did not enjoy protection of their assets, Wayland warned, "the progress of a nation in wealth will be slow."[43]

Belief in the protection of property did not mean a desire for polarization of wealth. Republicans feared monopolization of money or resources because they believed that such monopolies would force individuals to work permanently for others or, at best, to pay exorbitant prices for land and other materials they needed to become independent. Party members abhorred the aristocratic Slave Power, and some also worried that the Northern drive for accumulation of wealth would cause "the money-power" to become "too much centralized—that the lands and property of the country, in the course of time may come to be held or controlled by a comparatively small number of people." Republicans believed that European society illustrated the evils of money and land monopolies, and they shuddered when they looked to the starving poor and rich aristocracy of the Old World. Shunning the creation of rich or poor classes, Republicans hoped to perpetuate a society of similarly prosperous, independent families. "Small farms, small towns, manufacturing communities and villages, rather than cities or large estates, are among the conditions of true national greatness," one Republican declared.[44]

Opposing a polarization of wealth, party members took comfort from the idea that an economically well-adjusted society would not develop economic classes. Proponents of the labor theory of value maintained that capital constantly depreciated while labor, because of its increasing productivity, constantly became more valuable. This murky doctrine "has come to be considered correct, by all thinkers upon the relation of capital to labor," claimed the editor of the

Chicago *Tribune.* "It therefore follows that labor is steadily growing in power to command capital, and that the power of capital over labor is constantly diminishing . . . that labor and capital combined are producing a larger return for the same outlay, of which a larger share should go to the laborer."[45]

To reject the natural laws of political economy that dictated economic harmony, and instead to "resort to appropriation, and to monopoly," maintained economic theorists, would create discord and conflict, disrupting the natural harmony of the universe. Slaveowners who stole their slaves' labor and oppressed poor white people, Europeans who monopolized land, and Northern industrialists who stockpiled money and cheated their employees during the war were flying in the face of the divine economic plan. Unfortunately, public condemnation was the only available punishment for such misdeeds, at least for those occurring in the North. During the war, Republicans attributed poverty to a dislocation of the true economic system by either war or greedy men. Seeing the poor working at low wages, the editor of the Chicago *Tribune* blamed evil employers whose lack of humanity enabled them to justify fattening themselves on wartime economic confusion.[46]

The Republicans' belief in a harmony of all economic interests gained strength in the battle with the South's peculiar political economy, which, party members maintained, fostered aristocracy and peonage. Although Northern Democrats clearly perceived laborers and capitalists as different classes, Republicans identified the belief in a permanent laboring class with "the extreme Southern theory . . . that the condition of labor is servitude." They recognized that this idea would create "castes—making master and capitalist, slave and laborer, convertible terms, and change the Republic into an oligarchy." In the face of a Democratic newspaper's assertion that in the North, "where the capitalist is one person and the laborer another," labor was "servile or involuntary," a Republican editor exploded that such "slavery" was not "the natural condition of the working man." The editor specifically called this debate to the attention "of the free white laboring men of the North." Indeed, wrote another Western editor, the only kind of capital that attacked labor was capital in slaves, for slavery degraded white labor and kept wages low. Ironically, the contrast that Southern slave labor provided to Northern free labor enabled Republicans to ignore any shortcomings of their theories. They could dismiss the poor in American cities as aberrations when they looked at the larger and much more visible Southern slave population.[47]

Republican newspapers trumpeted the idea of economic harmony. "We are very certain," ran an editorial in the staunchly Republican Philadelphia *Inquirer* during the war, "that . . . there is no enmity between capital and labor, but an actual unity of interests, and concert of movement in the functions and affairs of all the classes concerned in . . . production." A Western editor agreed: "In the usual conditions of life," he wrote, "the interests of capital and labor are believed to be generally the same. Capital is dependent upon labor, and labor derives employment from the enterprises and investments of capital." An editorial in the Chicago *Tribune* assured readers, "There is a complete identity of interest between agriculture, manufactures and commerce"; and, in the New York *Daily Tribune,* Greeley proclaimed: "We hold that the true interests of Capital and Labor are identical." To make this harmony work in the everyday struggle over wages, Greeley called for cooperative unions of workers and employers to adjust wages so that laborers would receive an appropriate share of the profits from their production.[48]

Republicans could wholeheartedly embrace the idea of economic harmony because, during the war, their theories suffered no telling attacks. Although Democrats took exception to the Republican vision of a harmony of economic interests, repeatedly accusing Republicans of "denying the general nature of man," their opposition fell flat. Democrats denied that the accumulations of selfish individuals could be used to promote the general good, insisting instead that "enterprise, industry and grasping avarice will always command more of earth's possessions than their opposites; the general inequality of wealth cannot therefore be avoided." Recognizing that there would always be poor, the Democrats insisted that "natural justice" demanded that "general comfort, the absence of pinching want and the possession of substantial necessities of life . . . should be fixed facts in all true social conditions." Democratic wartime association with Southern sympathy, however, undermined Democratic protests by tainting them with disloyalty to the government. On occasions when trouble arose between laborers and employers, the Republicans attributed it to "conniving demagogues and mischief-makers" who were trying to "excite a feeling against the 'merchants' and the 'wealthy classes,' the better to 'divide the North,' and strengthen Secession."[49]

The lack of a strong labor movement during the war also prevented effective challenges to the idea of economic harmony. As men poured into the army and navy, leaving those at home to provide for them, the North clamored for workers. The Union enjoyed high employment rates, which meant low union membership. During the war years, as Carey said, "every man who had labor to sell could sell it if he would." Even had employment been low, intense nationalism tended to silence the voices of a labor interest. "It having been resolved to enlist with Uncle Sam for the war," one organization declared, "this union stands adjourned until either the Union is safe, or we are whipped." This lack of significant labor unrest enabled Republicans to admit on the one hand that it was a "fundamental truth," as Horace Greeley said, that "every free laborer . . . has a right to fix his own price on his labor, and insist on it; he has a right to combine with all who choose to so establish and uphold that price"; while at the same time criticizing strikes, and quelling them with the military, if necessary, on the grounds that cessation of production would hurt the war effort.[50]

The Republican belief in an economic system grounded on the value of labor, with its consequent faith in self-sufficiency, free labor, and economic harmony, fostered in the party a tremendous optimism about the future of the nation. Republicans fervently believed in American progress. As men worked, they created value, so "every laborer in the community adds to the aggregate wealth." Part of the wealth a laborer created enabled him to create another product. Another part of the wealth went for his support; that is, he consumed it. Many of the articles he bought were the products of others, so he enriched these individuals as he consumed. "Every new production forms the capital for another, and the means of buying something for sale," explained the editor of the Chicago *Tribune*. "Commodity pays for commodity . . . Until every beggar is provided with a coach and six, there will be no such thing as overproduction . . . one want will create another, and one supply will become the means of another supply, to the end of time. We shall never get out of business in this world."[51]

The condition of all would improve as the population worked, Republicans believed, giving America unlimited potential to grow and prosper. According to Carey, natural law guaranteed that "with the increase of population and of capital, and with the extension of cultivation, there is a steady improvement in the condition of both labourer and capitalist." In a passage that could easily have been a booster tract for the sparsely settled American West, Carey wrote:

> As capital increases . . . habits of kindness and good feeling take the place of the savage and predatory habits of the early period. Poverty and misery gradually disappear, and are replaced by ease and comfort. Labour becomes gradually less severe, and the quantity required to secure the means of subsistence is diminished, by which [one] is enabled to devote more time to the cultivation of his mind. His moral improvement keeps pace with that which takes place in his physical condition, and thus the virtues of civilization replace the vices of savage life.

Increasing production was "hope for the future," agreed Congressman Israel Washburn, Jr. "The greatest power of production is indispensable to the greatest good."[52]

The Republican party, true to its initial commitment to keep the territories open for the expansion of free labor, dedicated itself to growth and progress. Party members looked forward to a time when "a score of mighty and prosperous States, the pride of the Republic and the admiration of the world, will leap forth from the great valleys, prairies, and forests of the West, like youthful giants rejoicing in their strength." At a Republican rally before the 1860 election, wagons representing various types of industry followed a cart draped with a favorite Republican adage: "Westward the star of empire takes it[s] way." Republicans considered themselves, as one said, "a rising party, with the glittering hopes of the future."[53]

Before the Civil War, the American national government's economic activities were as limited as one would expect from a country capital mired in a swamp. When circumstances required it, the government issued bonds; it collected customs from a tariff; and it sold public land. The nation had no system of national taxation, no national banking system, no national currency. It almost never aided economic expansion other than to grant public lands to states to use as they wished, often on internal improvements.

Believing that God's orderly system directed America's economic affairs, Republicans saw little need for the national government to manage the economy. "If God have given to all men faculties for labor;

if he have made labor necessary to our happiness; if he have attached the severest penalties to idleness, and have preferred the richest rewards to industry," as Wayland wrote, "it would seem reasonable to conclude, that all that was required of us, was, so to construct the arrangements of society, as to give free scope to the laws of Divine Providence."[54]

Some Republicans, however, wanted to use the national government to facilitate labor's development of the country. "The Government was not established . . . simply to take care of itself, to collect revenues, and pay officeholders," Israel Washburn, Jr., told the House shortly before he helped to organize the Republican party. It was created, he said, "for higher purposes and objects, having regard to the protection and promotion of the vast and varied interests of a great people. And its legislative power clearly extends to the passage of laws affecting the trade, commerce, and labor of the country."[55]

However, even Republicans who hoped that the national government could help labor to expand the economy did not wish to involve the government in directing or regulating specific developmental projects. They wanted only national legislation freeing lands, easing restrictions on business growth, and releasing national monies to fund large internal improvements. Party members profoundly distrusted government enterprise, for they believed that unsupervised power and access to public funds would corrupt managers of government projects and encourage them to build what Republicans most feared: a vast government monopoly of money and power that would destroy the free labor economy. Only individuals with personal financial stakes in projects should operate them, Republicans maintained, for they would be frugal and efficient and would check each other's power. Similarly, party members conceived of no role for government regulation of large businesses, for they believed that individual stockholders, who had invested their hard-earned money, would scrutinize company operations.

Before the Civil War, even these limited Republican attempts to make the government more economically active always met strong arguments from those who interpreted the Constitution strictly, primarily Democrats, who contended that such activity was unconstitutional. The coming of the war, however, eased constitutional scruples about the government's role in economic activity. The Republicans developed a concept of "war powers," which maintained that the Constitution authorized any Congressionally approved measures designed to maintain the government in times of insurrection. During such a crisis, the government could act in ways that might be considered unconstitutional in peacetime. While this theory gave the government great latitude in military matters, it also opened the way for economic legislation. Troops needed supplies, and the government needed railroads to move those supplies. The Treasury required a new system of taxation to pay for both the troops and their maintenance. Taxes and tariffs, railroads, banking and currency laws, aid to immigration and agriculture, and the confiscation of Southern slaves could all be justified as ways to strengthen the Union.[56]

The new government activity in turn changed the way legislators thought of the Constitution and of precedent, thereby enabling them to promote economic legislation that was not strictly necessary for the war effort. Representative James H. Campbell of Pennsylvania justified the new legislation he advocated by proclaiming, "The Constitution was made for the people—to secure to them and their posterity the blessings of free government." Another congressman put his vision of the Constitution even more clearly: "I . . . construe it in the light of the rule authoritatively announced for our action: 'The Sabbath was made for man, and not man for the Sabbath.'" Once over the constitutional hurdle, Republicans argued that the government should promote the natural economic development of the nation, for it must manage public affairs "in accordance with the wishes of the people." Areas other than politics, "of equal importance to the people at large, . . . should receive the profoundest attention of our legislators," Senator Joseph A. Wright of Indiana concluded. Republicans thought that since the government represented the people it shared in the harmony of American society, and thus it could safely encourage economic growth without destroying the premises of the Constitution.[57]

Radically altering the traditional concept of precedent, Republicans argued that in order truly to emulate the Revolutionary fathers, they must not merely follow the dicta their venerable ancestors had provided, but must act decisively in new ways, exactly as the founding fathers themselves had approached a new situation. Their actions were not always expressly sanctioned by the Constitution, Republicans argued, but were in accord with the spirit of it. Charged by Democrats with violating the Constitution, one Senator retorted that men should not blindly "follow in the footsteps of their ancestors . . . we should do better to practice their virtues and try to avoid their errors."[58] With this adventuresome attitude, the Republicans came to use a growing national government not only to shore up the wartime economy, but also to promote economic growth and progress.

The Republicans who gathered in Washington in 1861 would work together over the next four years to solve a series of financial crises. They would also create domestic legislation designed to develop America's economy. There was rarely complete consensus within the party about contemplated measures, but despite their regional and personal differences, the Republicans agreed on a series of major innovative laws. Their shared general economic beliefs, which stemmed from the proposition that labor created value, ran much deeper than their differences. During the war, circumstances made Republicans refine their economic ideas, but their basic premises remained. Forced by the war to legislate on a wide range of economic issues, the Republicans' work reflected their general vision of universal harmony and their determination to foster economic progress.

"Now Is the Time for Making Money, by Honest Contracts, Out of the Government": War Bonds

How much misrepresentation there is about my financial policy!
And yet how plain it must be to any one willing to understand it.

—Salmon P. Chase, 1864

"I see Chase is in the Treasury," wrote Jay Cooke, a young Philadelphia banker, to his brother in March of 1861, "and now what is to be done[?]"[1] Cooke was not the only person curious about the nation's financial future. Less than a month before, Southern states had declared themselves the Confederate States of America, adopted a constitution, and elected Jefferson Davis their provisional president. Northern businessmen had panicked. Inauspiciously, the man who would have to hold Union finances together, the new Secretary of the Treasury, had virtually no experience in financial management.[2]

In the four months between Lincoln's inauguration and the first session of the Thirty-Seventh Congress, events set some important parameters for Republican wartime economic policy. In these months, desperate for funds to fill the Union's empty war chest, the new Secretary of the Treasury maneuvered to raise revenue. Fleshy, balding, Salmon P. Chase, a political appointee more ambitious and self-confident than knowledgeable about finances, entered office not with a preconceived policy, but only with a desire to raise money to fill the empty Treasury. His first tentative financial forays enabled party members to test their ideas about a national harmony of economic interests.

Chase took office on March 7, 1861, and Lincoln promptly requested a statement of the Union's financial situation. The President's concern was well founded. The Treasury was running a deficit of $65 million and had little cash on hand. Coming due were short-term

Treasury notes, issued during the recession of 1857 by James Buchanan's Secretary of the Treasury. A new tariff went into effect in March 1861, and the South, which abhorred the new law, refused to permit the Union government to collect duties from it or, in fact, to collect any customs duties in Southern ports. Worse still, the Confederate government talked of setting a low tariff, or none at all, which would pull foreign trade South. Since the Union government depended almost entirely on customs duties for revenue, the situation threatened to cripple Union finances. Indeed, it was not long before the Charleston *Mercury* gleefully proclaimed that trade was going South and the North would starve. "At this moment there are fifty thousand human beings in New York who know not where they will be able to get their breakfast tomorrow morning," its editor crowed.[3]

Chase's report to Lincoln contained little good news. The Secretary cited four sources of money. The first was the customs, which had received almost $1.5 million from New York, Boston, Philadelphia, and Baltimore for the two weeks ending March 13, 1861. Chase projected that the cities' receipts from March 14 to July 1 would be around $11 million, of which only $1.5 million could be realized by April 1. There were also three loans, totaling around $41 million, that Congress had authorized since 1860 but that had not yet been placed on the market. These would take time to negotiate. On the debit side, Chase projected over $3 million in government expenses before April 1. The Treasury needed money fast.[4]

The simple accounting that the Secretary gave to Lincoln revealed the crudeness of the government's financial supports. The Union had no system of national taxation to which Chase could turn for revenue. He would also have to raise money without the help of a national currency, for the country did not have one. A national bank could not help either, for there had been no such institution since the Jacksonians destroyed the Second Bank of the United States. Instead, state-chartered local institutions assumed the functions of banking in America, including the issue of paper currency based on a limited reserve of capital. The national government had no infrastructure for raising or transferring large amounts of money.

Chase's search for revenue was further complicated by a general distrust of national debt. Americans worried that national indebtedness would destroy workers' ability to accumulate capital and would rise while it created a permanent wealthy class because, they believed, indebtedness would require grinding taxation of the poor to pay interest to rich bondholders. Distrustfully eyeing Britain's example, Americans saw a national debt as "an encumbrance upon the national estate" that was "anti-republican" in its unequal burdens and benefits. Knowing that debt would undoubtedly require taxation, and aware of his critical role in determining the terms of any debt, Chase sought to keep bond interest rates as low as possible. While protecting the public from unnecessary tax burdens, this would also help to prevent a popular image of bondholders as profiteers gouging the taxpayers. Low interest rates, however, would make fund-raising difficult.[5]

Under these formidable constraints, yet obliged to raise money quickly, Chase embraced traditional government fund-raising practices. In the past, when it needed money, the Treasury had turned to two types of financial instruments. It either sold long-term, interest-bearing bonds to bankers and financiers, who usually bought them as investments; or it issued short-term Treasury notes, which could circulate as currency. Though investors could often buy Treasury notes directly from the Treasury, two kinds of notes could be issued exclusively to government creditors. These were "demand notes"—that is, notes, usually without interest, payable by the government upon presentation by the holder—and "certificates of indebtedness," which bore interest and were payable one year from the date of issue.

In March 1861, Chase decided to sell government bonds to banks and financiers. This was not an ideological decision so much as a reflection of deep and immediate need. Although existing banks were not organized into any one group with which Chase could negotiate, their concentration in large cities would enable him to sell large blocks of bonds to them at one time. The banks would then distribute the bonds throughout their regions by reselling them at a profit to smaller investors. In 1861, the nation's financial centers were New York City, Boston, and to a lesser degree Philadelphia and Providence. New York was Chase's first priority, for it had the most capital and its banks were loosely organized. A trip to New York convinced the Secretary that the financial mood there was good. Since business had stagnated after the secession crisis, banks had a surplus of gold to invest. At the end of March, New York banks held an unprecedented almost $40 million worth of gold. At that time, Chase offered to the banks and to financiers an $8 million loan at 6 percent interest, a rate established by a previous Congress.[6]

Although Chase turned without hesitation to bankers and investors to help the nation out of its crisis, much of the Republican party could not share his easy dependence on financiers. Within the party were two warring perceptions of wealthy people and bankers, which reflected the party's heritage from both the traditionally pro-bank Whigs and the bank-hating Democrats. Their feelings toward bankers also separated the party's wealthier members, living primarily in large Eastern cities or developed regions, from its cash-poor Western farmers. Very few Republicans held anything against the wealthy in general, for most rich men, Republicans believed, had worked hard for their money. Bankers and financiers seemed to some to be a special case, however, for many Republicans believed that their wealth came not from their own productive efforts, but from the manipulation of the fruits of other people's labor. They were thus not producers, but parasites.

Most Republicans, especially those from the East, thought Chase's resort to bankers a wise and beneficial plan, as well as the only choice he had. If, as economic theorists insisted, there was a "perfect harmony of interest" between all groups in society, capital could not have interests different from those of a good government. Eastern Republicans, who knew banks and bankers as part of the social fabric of their own communities and did not find them threatening, found it easy to believe, as Alexander Hamilton had suggested, that honorable businessmen shared the interests of the public and its government. Remembering well that financiers had saved the nation during the Revolutionary War, Eastern Republicans believed that bankers and investors would again come gladly to the aid of the Union government for, even should patriotism fail, capitalists knew that their own security depended on the survival of the Union. Eastern Republicans strongly advocated Hamilton's vision of uniting the nation's capital with its government to secure financial and political stability. They welcomed Chase's bond offer because they believed it would begin that process.[7]

Other Republicans, especially those from Western areas, distrusted Chase's reliance on banks. States like Illinois and Indiana had suffered from the undercapitalized "wildcat" banking of the last several decades. Blaming Easterners for the financial disasters, people from these areas tended to associate banking with ill-gotten gains. One Western Republican referred to bankers as "this army of little leeches that are sucking the life blood, in small quantities, out of the laboring people of this country." Across the Union, the image of bankers also suffered

from association with New York City. New York often drew fury as
it ran afoul of the interests of other regions. The war aggravated
Republican prejudice against bankers and New York City interests,
for Democratic New York was a lukewarm convert to the Union
cause. While many wealthy Democrats from the city voiced their
opposition to the war, Union newspapers noted that key financiers
were talking with Jefferson Davis and offering to float Confederate
bonds. During the war, radical newspaper editor Horace Greeley
lamented that Cornelius Vanderbilt's son "is about the only rich man's
son among us who is a Republican."[8]

Chase's bond offer, his first negotiation with the banks, was a test
of whether or not bankers shared the same interests as the nation.
While the bankers explored the sense and sentiments of the Secretary,
the government could examine the willingness of financiers to loan
funds, and the public could test its ideas about bankers. While some
expressed confidence that the financiers' loyalty would open their
purses, others rumbled warnings that bankers were "looking entirely
to their own interests" and planned to make low bids, guaranteeing
a half-million dollar profit on the bonds.[9]

With their response to the Treasury's first bond offer, bankers
indicated that their plans did, in fact, coincide with the public interest.
They turned out magnificently. On April 2, 1861, Chase opened
almost $30 million worth of bids at rates from ninety to par for $8
million worth of bonds. Jubilation from all quarters greeted the large
subscription. Chase wrote immediately to the pleased President, declaring a "decided improvement in finances." The Philadelphia *Inquirer* reported that the bids were "the subject of much congratula-
tion, not only among the money Kings of Wall street, but by people
elsewhere, who are gratified to see the Government credit thus handsomely sustained."[10]

The grand cooperation of the bankers convinced the Secretary that
financiers would support the government in all events; and since he
spoke for the government on financial issues, Chase mistakenly believed that bankers would support any measure he declared good for
the nation. In a move correctly calculated to please the public, the
Secretary accepted only about $3 million worth of bids for the loan,
rejecting all bids that offered less than 94 cents on the dollar. Claiming
sole responsibility for the rejection of low bids, Chase wrote to a
friendly financier, "I have no doubt the people will approve what I
did." Indeed, the editor of the New York *Times* rejoiced that the

Secretary had advanced the public credit, promoted public confidence, and rebuked capitalists who were so greedy as to make low bids for the loan. The editor of the Philadelphia *Inquirer* asserted that Chase's action proved his honesty and good intentions.[11]

In his easy confidence, Chase had miscalculated the extent to which financiers would support the government. Chase assumed, as did many of his Republican colleagues, that citizens and the government could never have opposed interests; what was good for the nation was good for financiers, and vice versa. Bankers, however, would cooperate with the government only when they believed that it was acting in the best interests of the nation's citizens, including, of course, themselves and their stockholders. Far from approving the Secretary's bid rejection, then, bankers were furious at his assault on their interests. They felt that they had leapt patriotically to the aid of the government, only to be ill-treated. Chase had not listed any restrictions when he had advertised the loan, and since all bids were close to 94, bankers perceived the cutoff for bids as arbitrary. A single bank got over half of the issue, and some suggested that Chase had tipped it to bid 94. A rumor ran through Wall Street that one man intended to sue the Treasury Secretary to force him to issue the remainder of the bonds. A good relationship between financiers and the Treasury was imperative to keep bankers behind government credit, but Chase's bid rejection won him the permanent distrust of much of the financial community. Some men darkly hinted that the Secretary could wait a long time before they would be so helpful again.[12]

Chase tried to mollify the financial community by selling almost $5 million worth of the Treasury notes for which it clamored. These notes ran for a short period of time, bore interest, and were payable in gold. Unlike long-term bonds, they could circulate as money, which would help to fill the void left by a dearth of negotiable paper on the market. Unfortunately, the Secretary so irritated bankers by rejecting private bids for the notes that they virtually refused to bid for the Treasury notes at all. The escalating conflict at Fort Sumter cemented the bankers' aloofness by destroying the market for Union securities. New York bankers, who had been wild for Treasury notes only days earlier, now had no interest in them.[13]

The belief that a harmony of interest would make all bankers automatically do the government's bidding was incorrect, and both

Chase and some members of the public began to realize it. The Secretary privately asked a close New York friend if there had been "a concerted effort of Wall St. men to prevent the taking of the Treasury notes." Like the Treasury Secretary, those who thought that "honorable" businessmen would support the government wondered if the New York troublemakers were loyal to the Union. Well might they wonder. New York's Democratic mayor publicly insisted on the city's neutrality in the conflict, and rumors flew that New York hovered on the brink of insurrection. Newspapers reported that New York bankers supported the Confederacy or at least favored making New York a "free city." Republicans who assumed that all financiers would closely cooperate with the government watched uneasily.[14]

In sharp contrast to those financiers who refused to buy Treasury notes stood young Philadelphia banker Jay Cooke. Cooke appeared in many ways to epitomize the ideal Republican financier. He was an energetic and shrewd businessman who was also well known for his religious scruples, honesty, and patriotism. By undertaking government business, he hoped to benefit both himself and the nation. He planned to turn a healthy profit not by bilking the government—as only evil bankers would do—but by providing good service. If the government allowed a percentage on its business, whether it be selling bonds, transferring funds, or any other financial transaction, then Cooke believed that he could collect more profit than any competitor simply by working hard enough to do more of that business. "Now is the time for making money, by honest contracts, out of the Gov[ern-men]t," Cooke's father counseled him.[15]

Cooke had ties to the government that, to a friendly Republican eye, reflected the ideal joining of finance and government. Like Chase, the young man hailed from Ohio, where his father had shared political speaking platforms with the new Secretary. Cooke's brother, H. D. Cooke, a sometime newspaper editor now working with Jay on financial deals, had become good friends with Chase and had supported his political career. H. D. Cooke had similarly befriended John Sherman, who was now in the Senate as Chase's replacement and who sat on the powerful Finance Committee. Believing that his good and the government's coincided, Jay Cooke could un-self-consciously ask the Secretary of the Treasury for "those natural advantages that would legitimately and honestly flow towards us from your personal friendship." Cooke was a calculating financier, but at the heart of his willingness to use personal influence to win favors for himself and others was the conviction that he was acting in the best interest of the nation.[16]

Cooke had previously found little opportunity to work with Chase, but once he discovered that New York bankers had not taken all of the Treasury notes, he organized Philadelphia bankers to bid for them. When Chase opened the offers on April 11, he found a $200,000 bid at a slight premium from Cooke and his associates. Cooke had struggled to get even this subscription, but it was enough to get the Secretary to look favorably on the young man.[17]

The negotiations and ultimate sale of almost $5 million worth of Treasury notes had several results. Bankers' early reluctance to buy undermined the idea that financiers would support the government at all costs. This made Chase solicitous of the few bank supporters he had and anxious to draw other capitalists to his side. He assured one banker that the help of "public spirited capitalists" in marketing the notes gave him great satisfaction and that it would be his "constant endeavor so to administer the Department as not to forfeit their confidence." The bankers' reluctance also made Chase look elsewhere for support. This opened a path for Jay Cooke to make himself indispensable to the government. Finally, despite, or perhaps because of, the rift the Treasury note negotiations revealed in bankers' loyalties, the sale encouraged public confidence in the strength of the Treasury. These results would determine Republican bond policy throughout the war.[18]

On April 12, 1861, the day after the Treasury note loan was taken, the war began. While Northern ships sped vital supplies to Fort Sumter, Confederate forces opened fire. On the same day, the Indianapolis *Daily Journal* reported that a package addressed to President Lincoln had broken open in the Washington post office and two angry copperhead snakes had slithered out. With the coming of a devastating war to both the South and the North, the Union was going to need more money.[19]

The outbreak of war introduced new financial anxieties for the Republicans. Going into the war, they worried that a ruined and beggared country would limp out of it. Republican economic theorists argued that war withdrew men from productive activities at the same time that marauding armies destroyed previous production. Francis

Wayland maintained that war was thus destructive of value, and one of the worst possible calamities for a nation. "All this immense Army add nothing by their labor to the wealth of the country," a Republican lamented during the war. "What a mighty drain this war is upon the productive energies and resources of the country. It is, indeed, an exhausting as well as a bloody war." Such gloomy fears made Republicans cling fervently to their faith that "it is the grand purpose of Providence to build up, on these Western shores, a great world-power." They also began nervously to reassure themselves that the Union's financial resources would enable the government to meet its obligations.[20]

Despite the Republicans' worries about debt, the Union needed money and Chase set out to find it. Under the spell of popular enthusiasm for the war, he fell back again on the idea that bankers would support the endangered government at all hazards. He ill-advisedly decided to invite bids for $14 million worth of bonds which, by law, could only be issued at par. He told New York bankers that patriotism should make up the difference between par and market price. The members of the New York Chamber of Commerce unanimously agreed the loan could not be negotiated under these terms, but Chase pressed on. For the next three weeks, he ordered, coaxed, begged, and badgered bankers in Boston, New York, Providence, and Philadelphia to subscribe for the par bonds. Bankers, who believed that Chase was exploiting the patriotic feeling in the country to force better terms from them, steadfastly refused to deal.[21]

In the second week of May, Chase finally conceded. After conferring with New York bankers, Chase invited bids for $9 million worth of bonds that had no par restriction. Newspapers correctly surmised that he would not reject bids below par. He promised that he might also issue Treasury notes, then consulted financial men to see "whether my views meet their convenience or not." Apparently appeased, bankers bought over $7 million worth of bonds and over $1.5 million worth of Treasury notes. Newspaper editors, who were glad to see the government and bankers getting along, cheerfully noted "the open-handed alacrity of Northern capitalists."[22]

While the Secretary and the New York bankers warily jockeyed, Chase and Cooke became increasingly cordial. Still eyeing government contracts, Cooke volunteered with two other Philadelphia bankers to help sell the May loan. Chase accepted, and the Cooke brothers scrambled to get $300,000 in subscriptions from Philadelphia bankers. Further illustrating his financial skills, in June Cooke sold Pennsylvania's $3 million state loan at par in a matter of days. Excited and justly proud, he telegraphed word of the success to Chase. In mid-June, Chase told the Assistant Treasurer in Philadelphia to confer with Cooke about Department business, and the Treasury Secretary himself consulted Cooke about his upcoming Report to Congress.[23]

If Chase was ever going to have a coterie of financiers like Cooke, which would jump to meet the government's needs, he would have to improve his relationship with New York bankers. A confidential adviser suggested that the Secretary meet with the New York capitalists and bankers "and have some understanding with them about the loans of the Government . . . [A] personal acquaintance with you by our leading business or monied men would secure more sympathy and cooperation and perfect confidence on their part." Recognizing the merit of this idea, the Secretary invited the New York Chamber of Commerce to Washington to confer. Another of Chase's friends, an important banker, heartily approved. Clearly harboring a vision of bankers and the government in perfect harmony, he encouraged Chase to build a circle of active financiers in every city to help the Secretary stimulate financial support for the government.[24]

Chase could not, however, build a supportive bank network in time to avert trouble. The Treasury had not realized the revenues he had hoped from bond or Treasury note sales, and the government would probably run a deficit of almost $11 million by August 1. Worse, in two days at the end of June, war expenditures reached over $2 million. Panicked, Chase wrote to Lincoln and insisted that the departments use "vigilance and economy," but thrift alone could not fund a war. It was time to overhaul traditional methods of government funding. Chase and Lincoln called the leading members of the House and Senate finance committees together two weeks before a special session of Congress began in July to discuss strategy and prepare financial bills. When the Secretary reported to the special session of the Thirty-Seventh Congress on July 4, 1861, he called for two new measures to solve the Treasury's woes: a foreign loan and a popular loan.[25]

The idea of a foreign loan was an extension of the idea that the government should borrow from capitalists. It merely changed their nationality. New York financiers, who worried that New York could not or would not produce the money the Union needed, encouraged this plan. It was not new; Chase had begun exploring the feasibility of a European loan when it seemed that the banks would not subscribe to the May loan.[26]

The idea of a popular loan, however, was an experiment in America. New York merchants had suggested in April that Chase try such an approach instead of depending on the banks, probably to prevent the government from draining the banks' specie. Cooke felt strongly that Chase should ask the public to provide money and had privately urged the Secretary to do so instead of pursuing a foreign loan. The newspaper that expressed Cooke's views, the Philadelphia *Inquirer,* called repeatedly for Chase to tap the wealth of the "great mass of the people of the country," which could furnish huge sums.[27]

In addition to hoping that a popular loan would raise money, Chase and his congressional advisers wanted to encourage national enthusiasm for the war, and they believed, as Hamilton had, that a financial interest in the government would draw men to its unconditional support. A popular loan was "probably the happiest and shrewdest mode of strengthening and consolidating a government that ever was adopted," one newspaper editor later commented. Fittingly, Chase placed Hamilton's portrait on some of the first bond issues. "You see who I would fain emulate if I might," he wrote, "[the man] whose spirit animates . . . our Constitution, our institutions, and our history."[28]

Along with many other Republicans, the Treasury Secretary hoped to reduce the nation's dependence on uncooperative bankers, who were certainly not acting as if their interests were the same as those of the government. Chase and his congressional allies modeled their popular loan plan on Napoleon III's successful 1859 loan in France. One of Chase's correspondents recalled that Napoleon had simply bypassed self-dealing middlemen and thieving bankers and gone straight to the people. Reducing ties to the belligerent bankers would also defuse Democratic accusations that bond sales to "favorite bankers" robbed the war effort.[29]

Shortly after the July session of Congress began, House Ways and Means Committee chairman Thaddeus Stevens called up a loan bill (H.R. 14). Although Chase had requested only $100 million, the bill authorized him to borrow up to $250 million in long-term bonds, Treasury notes, or demand notes in the year following the passage of the act. Up to $100 million of the loan could be sold in any foreign country. As Chase had requested, the interest rate for the loan could be as high as 7.3 percent, a rate that daily gave one cent interest on fifty dollars and that was perceived as high enough to encourage sales. Creating a popular loan, Congress specified that Treasury notes were to be sold by subscription and gave the Secretary of the Treasury discretion to appoint agents to do so. The House had originally pledged duties on tea, sugar, coffee, spices, wines, and liquors and other revenue to pay back the loan but, in an amendment indicative of the trouble the Union would have funding the debt, the Senate changed this to read that the "faith" of the nation was pledged to pay back the loan. The bill passed the House by a vote of 150 to 5, with only Democrats in the minority. The Senate, too, easily passed the bill.[30]

Now needing about $1 million per day for expenses, Chase had little faith in the popular loan, which promised to be cumbersome and slow even if it could eventually produce money. He turned first to the foreign loan for which the law provided, privately asking financier August Belmont, who was embarking on a trip to Europe, to explore the possibility of a European loan at a reasonable rate. The prospects were not good. Having suffered repeatedly when states defaulted on their bonds, English financiers so despised American loans that Charles Dickens had Scrooge dream in terror that his solid investments were changed into "a mere United States' security." Even before sailing, Belmont warned Chase that he was not optimistic about a European loan, for foreign governments hoped to force an American peace by withholding aid. Even more disheartening, the London *Times* and the London *Economist,* among other English papers, had disparaged Union securities. Foreign capitalists showed no disposition to bid for the loan.[31]

Most Republicans did not share Chase's preference for a foreign loan. In response to English scorn, Northerners were developing a hearty dislike of England and had no desire to turn to it for money to settle an internal dispute. The war "will rebuild the decayed dislike of the British name in this country with ten times its former strength," wrote one newspaper editor. This animosity called out American pride. "We are, if we may believe the London *Times* and its American echoes," fumed the editor of the Boston *Daily Evening Transcript,* "too poor to assert our nationality." The chairman of the Senate Finance Committee mused that American credit fortunately seemed so strong within the nation that "we need not go abroad for a dollar."[32]

Thwarted by foreign investors and pressured by much of Congress and the public, Chase had to move forward with the popular loan. Because he needed money long before funds could be realized from public subscriptions, however, he first negotiated an advance on the loan from New York, Boston, and Philadelphia bankers. Fortunately, the Secretary had found some influential bankers with whom he could work. George S. Coe, the president of New York's American Exchange Bank, and John A. Stevens, president of the New York Bank of Commerce, among others, helped to induce the financial community to advance funds covering $50 million worth of the loan at par. The banks received a second option to take another $50 million on October 15 and a third on December 15. As bonds sold to the public, Chase would reimburse the banks the money they had initially advanced, so that they would have funds to cover the next installment. If bonds sold slowly, the Secretary would reimburse the banks with the bonds themselves. While Chase was effusive in his thanks to the financiers, the public and a senator were less laudatory. The Philadelphia *Inquirer* called the banks patriotic but pointed out they must support the government or they would go under when it did. Senate Finance Committee chairman William Pitt Fessenden agreed but reflected that, in any case, the banks' example "has given confidence to all who have money to invest."[33]

Once he had secured an advance from the banks, Chase turned to the public. On September 1, 1861, he issued an "Appeal from the Secretary of the Treasury" explaining that Congress had wisely provided "that the advantages, as well as the patriotic satisfaction of a participation in this loan" should be offered to individuals as well as banks. The loan consisted of three-year bonds at 7.3 percent interest, which were quickly nicknamed the "seven-thirties." Chase promised to open public subscription books soon.[34]

In September, requiting Cooke's lobbying for a contract to handle the government's popular loan and his brother's attachment of Sherman's "invaluable aid" for a "plan of agencies, commissions [etc.]," Chase appointed Cooke one of the Treasury Department's General Subscription Agents for the loan. Acting on commission, agents were required to open subscription books in their cities and to take money from and issue bonds to investors. Given to an enthusiastic and well-proved salesman, Cooke's appointment was as good for the Treasury as it was for him. He threw himself into his new job. After Cooke's first day of work, Chase congratulated him on his sales and thanked him for aiding the government "in this hour of trial." By the end of a week, while others told Chase they could not help the Treasury, Cooke was selling over $100,000 of bonds per day. He ultimately sold over $5 million worth of the loan. The other 147 agents together sold slightly less than $25 million worth.[35]

Republicans hoped that the bonds would tie individuals to the government, and indeed the loan attracted a new class of Americans to government securities. Cooke catered to small investors, advertising heavily, keeping night hours, and carefully explaining to each person the benefits and terms of the loan. Newspapers encouraged people to take their savings from "broken crockery or old stockings" and invest them, thus helping the Union, making a profit, and keeping their money safe from thieves. A letter to the editor of the Boston *Daily Evening Transcript* reassured anxious investors that the treasurer's office "is as accessible *to ladies* as gentlemen, and no one need hesitate to visit it, as they will find every facility in the way of blanks for application, and not the least 'red tape' or hindrance of any kind." The loan was popular; the Republicans of Erie County, Pennsylvania, adopted resolutions praising it, while Chase's law partner from Ohio wrote that the Secretary would "have all you want from the pockets and stockings of the poor."[36]

The bonds touched the lives of many Northerners who had previously had little contact with the national government. The new instruments were popular as circulating currency, especially in the West, where bank paper had disappeared after successive bank failures. Anxious to move their mature crops, farmers willingly adopted the new money for their agricultural transactions. When the first bills arrived in a small Ohio town, one man reported, "many persons called to see them, and with glad hearts rejoiced at the event." "I never doubted but you fellows out West would *take* anything you could lay your hands on," one Republican senator teased a Western colleague who had boasted of the seven-thirties' popularity in Iowa.[37]

In late September and October, as bond sales drew support to the Union, the popular financial mood lifted. In the face of European disdain, the success of the loan stirred American pride. One newspaper reporter watched the distribution of the loan and proclaimed that "not a dollar of it will be offered abroad; so that we shall have the honor as well as the profit of conducting our own war for our own nationality." Another claimed that the war would emancipate America financially from England. As the notes sold, Chase felt less need for European money. He found himself able to begin reimbursing bankers for their advances on the loan, and this lightened their spirits, too. The bankers' willingness to take the second $50 million install-ment seemed to prove the strength of the Union's credit.[38]

While the public gained confidence in the Union's financial power, Chase and the bankers, who were privy to knowledge of unpaid government expenses and actual bank deposits, gradually stumbled into despair. By October, it was clear that bond sales were not equal-ing, or even approaching, daily expenditures. The empty Treasury forced Chase to pay creditors with Treasury notes. Much of the army went unpaid, and desperate generals demanded funds. Chase began to reconsider seeking foreign capital, but Belmont advised that there was no chance of a large European loan. Banks were anxious, for Chase had demanded specie for loan payments and Westerners were exchanging Treasury notes for gold. Specie was not returning to the banks as quickly as they needed it, and their gold was draining away.[39]

On top of this uneasy financial situation, Chase's tenuous relation-ship with the New York banking community disintegrated. The trouble sprang from Chase's interpretation of the ideal relationship between capital and government. Although aware of the need for a tractable banking group, Chase insisted that he alone spoke for the financial good of the nation. In an argument about the bankers' motives when they purchased the Treasury's loans, the Secretary main-tained that financiers bought for the hearty investment profits the loans offered. Furious, many New York and Boston bankers, who had risked bankruptcy if government stocks proved unsalable, insisted that they had "from a spirit of patriotism undertaken a burthensome responsibility, not from a desire to make money out of it, nor from any other interested motive." When this spat had just calmed, Chase again stirred up wrath when he angrily implied that bankers were trying to cheat the government in a wrangle over a mathematical error. It was not long before the Secretary and his men suspected disloyalty whenever bankers challenged policies that threatened to ruin them.[40]

For their part, many bankers increasingly distrusted the austere, distant Treasury Secretary. They could not believe he conceived of a mutually beneficial program, for he ignored their most basic prob-lems. He refused to moderate his calculations of the nation's financial needs in his annual report, even though his large estimates, by de-stroying the market for Union securities, might ruin the bankers who had loyally absorbed government bonds. Even Chase's efforts to create a body of sympathetic banks caused trouble. After unsuccessfully asking individual banks to join cooperative organizations to facilitate the loan distribution, he floated the idea of joining existing state banks into a national bank plan. Because this would cut his dependence on the difficult New York Banking Association, rumors of Chase's plan were enough to "scatter our Bank gentlemen in alarm," one observer commented.[41]

By December, the situation was critical. The financial community credited rumors that the Secretary would enact a policy crippling to the banks, and a small but important group of New York bankers threatened to break all relations with the Treasury.[42] Although these men backed down, most bankers' unrest continued through December. Tales of corruption in the War Department hurt public morale and slowed bond sales. Then rumors began of war with England over the *Trent* affair, in which Union officers boarded a British vessel and removed Confederate commissioners traveling to England, and stocks plummeted. Despite bankers' opposition to the plan, Congress began to develop legislation that would create a national currency, while at the same time specie continued to drain from the banks.[43] Chase tried to calm financiers by visiting New York and prophesying military triumphs, but his attempt failed. After a month of threatening to suspend specie payments, the New York banks finally did so at the end of December. While most bankers blamed the suspension on the Treasury Secretary's rigidity, or on Congress for hesitating to back bonds with adequate taxation, Chase felt the suspension was unnecessary and "deplore[d] [it] exceedingly." His men whispered to him that "there are strong indications of an attempt to make direct war upon the Treasury."[44]

The public had only limited information about negotiations between the Treasury and the financiers. As people saw little of the positive efforts of bankers and instead read in the press primarily about quarrels, popular Republican sympathies from the start were with the Secretary and the government. The nation seemed prosperous and bond sales indicated that there was plenty of money in the country—at least in the East—so many concluded that the financiers' problems with the Treasury must be caused by their greed. As bankers fought with Chase, many Republicans, especially Westerners, grew angry at the bankers. The editor of the Cincinnati *Daily Commercial* warned that the banks were threatening specie suspension because Chase had proposed a national bank, and declared that such a suspension "would not be warranted in any event."[45]

Specie suspension further tarnished the banks' image. It, too, looked like an Eastern plot, for major banks in Indiana and Ohio did not suspend until forced to do so by runs on their gold after the Eastern banks proceeded with suspension. Republican newspaper editors, even those whose conviction of the unity of interests between capital and government had made them see banks as the supports of the government, questioned whether suspension was necessary. Bankers seemed disloyal.[46]

Bankers continued to undermine their reputation after suspension. While trying to protect their own vulnerable position, they challenged the Treasury in ways that infuriated both the public and the Treasury Secretary. They refused to take the final $50 million loan installment for which they had an option, leaving the Treasury without funds. They then prodded Chase and Congress to help them out of their own plight. While the government had no money, and the printing of bonds was running hundreds of thousands of dollars behind sales, New York bankers demanded that Chase send them the bonds he owed them from their advances to the government. Bankers then destroyed the value of government demand notes by refusing to accept them, thus preventing the Secretary from relieving the Treasury of some of its most pressing debts by issuing notes to creditors. Bankers instead advised Chase to raise money by selling bonds to them at whatever discount the market commanded. Ignoring the very real crises that many banks had reached by helping Chase, newspapers across the country attacked the "presumptuous and insolent banks."[47]

Facing the emergency at the beginning of 1862, Congress created a paper currency, the "greenbacks," to fund the war, but it still looked to raise much of the Treasury's revenue from bond sales. In February 1862, Congress authorized the issue of $500 million worth of bonds bearing 6 percent interest, redeemable in five years at the pleasure of the government, and payable in twenty years. These were quickly dubbed "five-twenties." To reinforce the value of the new currency, Congress made the greenbacks convertible into five-twenties. Convertibility meant that the relationship between the notes and bonds was stable; $100 in notes would always buy $100 worth of bonds, regardless of market conditions.

Beginning to move away from bankers, Congress designed these bonds to benefit taxpayers, not financiers. Many Easterners and New Yorkers in Congress still spoke well of financiers, but some Western congressmen were fed up with "city bankers." Any man who "hawks the credit of the Government in the markets . . . to make the best bargains for himself that he can" was simply "dust . . . compared to the rights and interests of the people of this country," according to an Ohioan. More anxious to keep debt down than to please bankers, Congress dropped the interest rate on the bonds to 6 percent. Further, although financiers preferred long-term bonds, Chase himself, with his desire to keep the national debt low, opposed giving the new bonds a twenty-year maturation date. He refused to make the public responsible for paying high interest for so long a time and demanded a five-year maturation date so that the government could pay the bonds early.[48]

More conservative than the House, the Senate refused to move quite so quickly away from bankers for it knew it could not afford to sacrifice the support of the financiers. It added to the bill a significant concession to financial interests. To encourage investors, some Republicans favored making interest on the new bonds payable in gold rather than in the new paper money. This clause was not won without a fight, however, for many congressmen, as well as the public, resented the pretensions of uncooperative capitalists. The Senate agreed to the provision reluctantly, and three of the House's strongest financial specialists vigorously opposed it. Elbridge G. Spaulding, Samuel Hooper, and Thaddeus Stevens, all wealthy men who strongly supported the government, were examples of the Republican ideal of unity of capital and government and their opposition to the plan reinforced the idea that uncooperative bankers were attacking the interests of the government. Stevens, a staunch defender of the poor, insisted that the gold clause would distinguish between the two kinds of government creditors: the rich investor, who lent money, and the poor soldier, who offered his life. The soldiers had to accept paper money as pay, while bondholders received gold. Stevens complained that he was tired of permitting bankers to dictate to the government.[49]

Despite the Republicans' efforts to formulate bond policy in the public interest, newspapers soon attacked the Treasury Secretary for catering to bankers. While waiting for sales of five-twenties to begin bringing money from the public to the Treasury, Chase quietly sold seven-thirties to banks. In June 1862, when these bonds sold at a 6 percent premium on the market, he sold $2.25 million worth of them to two New York banks at a 3 percent premium paid in demand notes. The Secretary's supporters argued that he made this deal to reduce the supply of demand notes in circulation, for they were being used to pay customs duties instead of gold, which the Treasury desperately needed. Newspapers and some bankers cried foul, however, for the men making the deal were friendly to Chase and had bid above the 94 cutoff of the first bond sale. Angry men charged the Secretary with favoritism if not corruption for letting bankers walk off with a $40,000 profit by simply unloading at a 6 percent premium the bonds they had bought at 3 percent.[50]

The press's attack on Chase's work with bankers reflected the public's confidence in its financial strength. "The monetary affairs of the country were never in a position which bespoke a greater degree of activity and buoyancy," wrote one newspaper correspondent. The press rejoiced that the nation had no need of foreign aid. "We are . . . every day becoming less and less dependent upon others," proclaimed one editor. Another maintained that soon England and France would be begging for American friendship, but, he warned, "we should pursue our path of glory and greatness without any dependence upon other nations." One correspondent saw the hand of God in the finances: "Providence has singularly blessed this country with everything necessary to render it independent of the world," he stated.[51]

Despite public confidence bond sales were sluggish, and the Secretary tried two things to speed them up. His first measure, an additional issue of $150 million worth of greenbacks, passed Congress in June 1862 fairly easily. A new issue would guarantee that a shortage of circulating currency would not prevent bond sales. It would also please the public, especially in the West, where currency was tightest.[52]

Chase's second measure for speeding up bond sales inflamed Congress's previously ambivalent feelings about the bankers. He asked Congress to repeal the provision for convertibility of greenbacks to five-twenties, for he was convinced that this provision destroyed the viability of the bonds. The nation's financial market dropped precipitously with each rumor of failure on the battlefields and rose sharply with each victory. Playing the market with all government securities except the five-twenties, financiers cleared huge profits if they timed their movements well. Investors could not speculate with five-twenties, however, because the convertibility clause kept the bonds always at par. When one could play the market with other bonds, the 6 percent interest of the five-twenties was unalluring, and large investors refused to buy them.[53]

Congressmen correctly interpreted the repeal of convertibility as a sop to banking interests. While some Republicans, mainly Easterners, defended the patriotism and goodwill of the bankers, others, mainly Westerners, were fed up with financiers and accused the Secretary of favoring them. Speculation in bonds was one of the activities that had made bankers popularly distrusted, for profits so made were not the result of a man's labor, but of his manipulation of money. In the case of war bond speculation, such transactions seemed doubly evil, for by injuring the Union's credit they hurt the war effort. Congress refused to repeal the convertibility clause.[54]

Furious at Congress's intractability, by September 1862 Chase was also frantic about the state of the nation's finances, especially after the second battle of Bull Run completely destroyed the market for five-twenties. Running a deficit of nearly $36 million, the Treasury was almost without resources. By September 30, 1862, only slightly over $2.5 million worth of five-twenties had sold. In October, financiers confirmed the Secretary's belief that he had been right about convertibility. He explored selling five-twenties directly to banks but was quickly rebuffed when bankers demanded a price well below par to insure a large profit on the bonds.[55]

Congress's refusal to repeal the convertibility clause encouraged Chase to turn again to the public for funds. Realizing that selling the five-twenties to banks at a discount would cost the nation at least $1 million extra, he determined to induce the public to take the bonds at par. The popular financial mood was good, despite Chase's worries. The first heavy wartime tax went into effect in October, and people were both pleased that the debt was being funded and convinced that the feared taxation bore as lightly as it did because the Union was strong and prosperous. A good harvest, which promised to bring gold from Europe in its exchange, further buoyed popular financial morale. Chase decided to take advantage of the public's confidence by making the sale of five-twenties "the second great national or popular loan."[56]

Although he intended to let people buy bonds from Assistant Treasurers in major cities, the Secretary knew that the government had no adequate facilities to market the loan itself. Recalling Cooke's signal success with the seven-thirties, Chase believed that the Philadelphian could market the five-twenties better than anyone else. In an ironic maneuver, Chase turned to Cooke—the man who would later come to symbolize the Republicans' unsavory ties to financiers—in an attempt to free the Treasury from the aggressive demands of bankers.

Chase wanted Cooke to bring popular support to the nation's finances so that the Treasury could operate without worrying about the plans and actions of a few rich men, who had so far proved unmanageable.[57]

The Secretary trusted Cooke for he knew him well. The respected Philadelphia financier had been courting Chase while the New York men had been irritating him. Cooke had deluged the Secretary with patriotic advice on financial matters, entertained his daughters, presented the Secretary with a carriage (which Chase eventually refused), and invested borrowed money for the older man's personal account. With Cooke's flattery and sound advice contrasting sharply with New York's demands, Chase and Cooke became friends. Certain of the young man's honesty and rectitude, the Secretary hired Cooke, confident that an arrangement could be negotiated that would satisfy everyone in the nation, even "carpers and cavilers."[58]

In October 1862, Chase appointed Cooke the General Subscription Agent for the whole country. Hoping that Cooke could sell $1 million worth of bonds per day, the Secretary authorized him to hire his own agents and buy liberal advertising. He offered Cooke a commission of one-half of one percent on the first $10 million of sales, and one quarter of one percent on the rest. From this Cooke was to pay his agents at least one-eighth of one percent on the first $10 million and one-tenth on the rest, and to pay all advertising expenses. The Secretary calculated that this method of bond sales would be much cheaper for the Treasury than allowing banks to buy discounted bonds.[59]

Enthusiastic and energetic, Cooke acknowledged the Secretary's desire to make the public a mainstay of the Treasury. He assured Chase that he would not only sell the five-twenties but also "enlighten the whole community fully and constantly on the subject of the nation's resources and finances." He would hire editors, advertise widely, and give to his subagents at least the commission Chase had suggested. Cooke was so enthusiastic that Chase had to remind him to retain his own one-eighth of one percent commission, "which all agree is a very moderate compensation for the services you render, and the responsibilities you assume."[60]

Cooke mounted an aggressive sales campaign to bring the public to the support of the Treasury. "Every newspaper in the country [was] made his assistant," commented one newspaper editor. In addition to advertising the loan and reporting each day's sales in the press, Cooke and his associates pressed different cities to take more bonds than a local or regional rival. They also wrote editorials on the wisdom of investing in the five-twenties. In 1863, Cooke published a series of articles entitled "The Best Way to Put Money Out at Interest," which, of course, recommended the government bonds. The young financier employed subagents throughout the country to tap every town. "His agents are among the gold fields of California, and the delvers for silver in the mountains of Nevada, Idaho and Colorado," recorded one editorial. "They reach every military post and city," it added, and follow the Union armies to reach loyal men in the South.[61]

In mid-November 1862, the Secretary complimented Cooke on his marketing success, but the Treasury was still running a deficit. Treasury note sales to banks and a temporary bank loan helped only slightly, but they confirmed public faith in the finances. Since most bankers had made it clear that they invested only in secure stocks, their willingness to support the Treasury showed "the[ir] unwavering confidence . . . in the Government," asserted one reporter. The news of the bank loan went "through the country like the news of a victory."[62]

Well aware of growing popular discontent with the banks—even New York newspapers were shifting away from their support of financiers—Republican congressmen continued to move bond policy away from the bankers. As head of the House Committee on Ways and Means, Thaddeus Stevens had opposed the gold clause in the 1862 currency act as a gross concession to financiers. Then, after months of complaining bitterly that Treasury measures favored banks at the expense of the public, he launched an attack on Chase's policies. In December 1862, he introduced a novel bill to reorder drastically the Union's financial system by severely weakening state banks and subjecting them to strong national government control. "It is known to this House," Stevens commented in a masterpiece of understatement, "that I do not approve of the present financial system of the Government."[63]

Although willing to wean the Treasury from bankers, Chase was aghast at Stevens's wholesale attack on them, for they were still vital for the solvency of the government. The Secretary sent Congress a monumental financial package by which he acknowledged popular pressure to decrease dependence on bankers at the same time that he tried to retain financiers' support. His financial proposal reintroduced an earlier banking plan he had advocated that, instead of destroying state banks, offered them the opportunity to join a national banking system. National banks could issue a newly created national currency, which would rest on a capital fund of government securities. This new banking system would provide a new, certain market for government loans, and it would give the Secretary a supportive group of banks on which to rely. It would solidify the "community of interest" between the banks and the government for which Chase had striven.[64]

Chase's plan was popular with the public. Some financiers, too, notably Cooke, backed the Secretary and became more closely allied with the government. Most bankers, however, furiously opposed the plan. Representatives of the two sides battled it out in Congress; the bill passed in February 1863. The Secretary had at first been obliged to kneel to the bankers, wrote the editor of the Chicago *Tribune,* but then, "after weeks of dangerous anxiety and vacillation, Mr. Chase succeeded in turning the financial tide toward, instead of away from, the Federal Treasury." Despite the Secretary's high hopes for the new banking law, however, it did little, and Congress completely rewrote it in 1864.[65]

Another part of the Secretary's plan was an unprecedented $900 million loan package, which would cover the needs of the wartime government through June 1865. Republicans, who had sustained losses in the congressional elections just past, were anxious to forestall antiwar Democrats by voting military appropriations before the newly elected congressmen arrived. They passed the sweeping loan bill, and Lincoln signed it on March 3, 1863. The new law offered Chase great flexibility. It authorized the Secretary of the Treasury to issue $300 million worth of securities for the current fiscal year, which would end on June 30, and $600 million for the next fiscal year. Encouraging the Secretary's efforts to keep the national debt as low as possible, it allowed him to issue bonds bearing not more than 6 percent interest, which would mature in no less than ten nor more than forty years. In addition, Congress allowed the Treasury Secretary to issue $300 million worth of interest-bearing Treasury notes. Finally, trying to encourage Chase to turn still further away from bankers and toward the public for funds, Congress officially permitted—and privately urged—the Secretary to issue another $150 million worth of greenbacks.[66]

This new loan package indicated the Republicans' growing confidence in the public's ability to support the government financially. The Union had found money in its own pockets to fund the war, and Republicans had become increasingly sure of the nation's financial strength. This confidence combined with ill-feeling toward Europe over its neutral role in the war to make Republicans proud of the nation's self-sufficiency. "It is an indisputable fact," said one congressman, "that the material interests of the North were never more prosperous than at present." That the country could prosper in the midst of a war so destructive of value indicated the true wealth and potential of the nation, Republicans believed. After three years of war, noted the Indianapolis *Daily Journal,* "instead of showing any signs of exhaustion, the loyal States are just beginning to develop their real power and exhaustless abundance." The Union, reported the press, seemed finally to be waking to its "stupendous . . . [financial] strength." The columns of the New York *Times,* among others, regularly touted the country's prosperity and insisted that the Union could fund its own war effort, thus preventing the debilitating drain of capital to Europe, which had contributed to the Republicans' fear of national debt at the start of the war. Keep the debt at home, demanded a newspaper correspondent. *"What is owed to our own people is no loss,"* he wrote; "the nation is no poorer for it."[67]

The new Western gold mines reinforced public confidence about the nation's finances. Newspapers across the country picked up the first rumors of gold in the territories and embellished them throughout the war. Chase, too, pursued Western gold. Since early 1862, he had received letters describing the incredible wealth of the Colorado and Nevada gold mines and suggesting that the government find a way to take some of it, either by taxation, fees, licensing, land sales, or government ownership. In 1863, Chase asked the Secretary of the Interior for a report on gold production in the Western states and territories. In May 1863, the administration attempted unsuccessfully to assert the government's ownership of Western mining lands—a right specifically reserved in state constitutions and Western regulations. While the attempt failed in the face of Western outrage, neither the administration nor the public abandoned the hope of exploiting the rich Western mines for the benefit of the Treasury.[68]

Even Chase's quiet exploration of a foreign loan in March 1863 revealed the Union's growing financial self-confidence. The Secretary asked two bankers on their way to Europe to pursue unobtrusively the negotiation of foreign loans. He authorized another financier to "remove erroneous and create true impressions" in Europe about the North and its national credit. "It has not been thought advisable hitherto [to] take any steps whatever towards any Foreign Loan," the Treasury Secretary reflected. "It was thought important to demonstrate to the world the ability of the country to provide for the large demands on the Treasury created by the existing rebellion from its own resources. This is now plainly seen; and the question of a Foreign Loan has become one not of necessity but of expediency and economy." Europe still had little interest, however, in lending money to the Union except at exorbitant rates.[69]

In the summer and fall of 1863 the financial situation seemed to be steadily improving. In April 1863, sales of five-twenties had increased dramatically. Cooke's efforts to reach investors in every city and town had paid off: he was selling over a million dollars' worth of bonds a day. From the Finance Committee, William Pitt Fessenden reflected that "our financial system must be regarded as a success." In May, despite the disastrous Union defeat at Chancellorsville, Chase was ebullient about the nation's finances. Accounts at the Treasury were paid in full, and he had almost ceased to issue Treasury notes because revenue from bond sales, customs, and taxes amply covered expenditures. And the Treasury's affairs only got better. In July, the battle of Gettysburg and the fall of Vicksburg sent Union morale skyrocketing. Five-twenties sold in flurries, and newspapers hailed the power of the Union's pocket. When the loan closed at the end of January 1864, Chase discovered that the tremendous run on five-twenties had gone too far. Sales had exceeded the authorized $500 million issue.[70]

Backed by the public, Union finances were strong enough to permit Chase to ease away from both bankers and Cooke. In April, the Secretary felt able to decline the invitation of a group of sixty New York bankers to dine at Delmonico's in honor of his "public services and private character." He also felt secure enough in the summer of 1863 to cool his professional relationship with Cooke. Cooke's honest declaration that he was "doing about 20 times as much to help . . . as [most others] put together" could no longer soothe Chase's irritation at the financier's lack of punctual accountings. In June, the Secretary reduced Cooke's commission on bond sales; then, skittish about accusations of financial impropriety, he haughtily declined to accept a check for money Cooke had made for him in what he suspected were government stocks. Their professional relationship remained distant from this time on, but their personal relationship quickly warmed again.[71]

On the strength of such a positive financial situation, Chase launched a bid for the 1864 Republican presidential nomination. In October 1863, he went to Ohio to vote in the fall elections. The West, especially, liked his popular loans, greenbacks, and national bank plan, and Chase made the most of the region's approval in speeches there. At the Indianapolis State House, catering to the shifts in Republican financial attitudes, Chase delivered to a crowd of Western farmers and laborers a popularized overview of his financial measures. To great applause, he explained that he had spurned England and turned to America for money. Ignoring the still close ties of his department to cooperative banks, he accused bankers of trying to overcharge the Treasury. He refused to pay extortionate rates, he claimed, so he did just what "Mr. Smith, a farmer, and . . . Mr. Jones, a mechanic, and . . . Mr. Robinson, a merchant" would have had him do: he turned to the public. "My business," said Chase, "was only to interpret your will." This was just what people wanted to hear. His speeches attracted "wide and profound attention," and his friends intended to publish them as campaign documents.[72]

In 1864, the apparent security of the nation's finances permitted an examination of Republican bond policy. The Thirty-Eighth Congress, seated in late 1863, had many more Democrats than the previous Congress. In January 1864, vigorously opposed to the Secretary's presidential candidacy, congressional Democrats turned on him. The popular reputation of bankers was now so tarnished that Democrats found an easy target in Chase's relationship to Cooke, who, ironically, had been hired to cut Republican ties to banks. Since Cooke was footing many of the Secretary's political bills, an attack on the young banker could seriously damage the Secretary's campaign.

In their assault, Democratic congressmen glossed over the emerging Republican distinction between cooperative and uncooperative financiers and accused the Republicans of fostering financial monopoly and corruption. Ignoring the fact that Chase had hired Cooke as an individual, Democrats emphasized Cooke's presidency of a banking concern. In January 1864, they introduced a House resolution demanding that Chase explain the services and fees of Cooke's company to the government. Attributing bond sales to favorable battle news instead of Cooke's efforts, Democrats suggested that Chase had venally enriched an unneeded financier. One senator referred to Jay Cooke and Company as "this rich banking firm that has been made rich by the drippings from the Treasury." It had pocketed "perhaps a million dollars . . . by being made the special and exclusive agent of the Treasury Department in disposing of the bonds of the Government, which might have been disposed of by the ordinary machinery of that Department." Democratic newspapers joined the chorus, impugning Cooke's character and patriotism and calling for Congress to make his government office a salaried public one.[73]

Chase's supporters defended him fiercely, but the final word on his relationship with Cooke came from the Secretary himself. In early April 1864, he answered the House resolution. Recognizing that the Democrats were using Cooke's Treasury work to try to brand the Republicans as friends of corruption and the discredited banks, Chase emphasized that he had hired Cooke individually, not his banking house. The Secretary insisted that the Treasury, with its lack of both nationwide branches and infrastructure, could never have distributed bonds with anywhere near the success Cooke enjoyed. He reminded the House of Cooke's great salesmanship; as one of 148 agents for the seven-thirty loan of 1861, Cooke alone had marketed over one-fifth of the total bonds sold. The Treasury was deeply indebted to the Philadelphian, Chase insisted.[74]

Refuting the accusation that Cooke had profited unduly and to the detriment of the Treasury from his commission, the Secretary highlighted the positive aspects of a close relationship between the government and helpful financiers. For his work with the seven-thirty loan Cooke had been paid a fixed rate of under $7,000, Chase explained. Although Cooke had advanced over $3,000 for expenses incurred marketing the bonds, he was reimbursed only $150. According to the Secretary, Cooke's five-twenty agency had been even more of a boon for the Treasury. Negotiating the five-twenties through bankers would have cost the country $2 to $3 million on every $100 million of bonds, a total of over $12 million. Cooke's total payment was $1,350,000, of which less than $500,000 went to Cooke himself. The total cost of selling the loan was eighteen days' interest on the whole amount, "less than the cost of any other great loan either American or English hereto-fore negotiated," according to Chase.[75]

With satisfaction, Chase proclaimed that his report was regarded in Congress as "unanswerable," and many Republican newspaper editors throughout the country agreed. The editor of the New York *Times* praised Cooke; the Cincinnati *Daily Gazette* reported that the Secretary's answer would "silence the shameless clamors" against the Department.[76]

Despite strong Republican support for Chase's position, the Democratic challenge to the Secretary's arrangement with Cooke revealed weaknesses in the Republican ideal of cooperation between the government and friendly financiers. The idea that a private entrepreneur on commission would serve the Treasury better than uninspired public servants forced to deal with unscrupulous bankers seemed proved by Cooke's example, but the new, extraordinary amounts of Treasury activity meant that commissions could reach unreasonable levels. Further, critics understood that the personal ties of financiers to politicians, which Cooke exemplified at the beginning of the war, could easily allow dishonest men to win lucrative government contracts from corrupt politician friends. Chase's close personal acquaintance with Cooke correctly convinced the Secretary that the financier was honest, but many men—notably those Chase appointed to handle captured Southern cotton—called on their friendships with the credulous Chase to hide dishonesty. "By communicating a word, a single word to a friend, the Secretary of the Treasury can make him a rich man," a Democratic senator accurately insisted. Recognizing the dangers of government ties to financiers, some Republican newspaper editors suggested that Chase should never again work with Cooke.[77]

Noting the increasing Republican desire to minimize government ties to bankers and to rest the Treasury on the financial strength of the public, Chase made a grievous mistake in bond policy. When the five-twenty loan closed triumphantly in January 1864, he declined to issue more of the popular five-twenties, for which the Northern public clamored. Trying to keep the national debt as low as possible, Chase decided to issue 5 percent bonds redeemable in ten years and payable in forty. Warnings from financiers that investors both small and large would spurn a 5 percent loan after the 6 percent five-twenties only hardened Chase's resolve. Also following popular inclinations for the marketing of the new bonds, the Secretary bypassed Cooke and marketed the bonds through Assistant Treasurers and the new national banks.[78]

After an initial surge when the ten-forties entered the market in late March 1864, sales slowed drastically, doing little to relieve the Treasury. Bankers, congressmen, and eventually even the President, who generally let Chase make his own decisions, asked the Secretary to raise the bonds' interest rate. Ignoring advice, Chase pressured Congress to raise revenue by higher taxation and issued Treasury notes and certificates of indebtedness to meet government expenses. He quickly glutted the already fat money market, into which, on top of local currencies, he had pumped $750 million worth of greenbacks, legal tender Treasury notes, and certificates of indebtedness since taking office.[79] In June, Congress pointedly invited Chase to turn back to the five-twenties by passing a new loan act that authorized the Secretary of the Treasury to issue $400 million worth of bonds at interest not more than 6 percent, to mature in five to forty years. Finally acquiescing, the Secretary advertised for bids on a new $32 million issue of five-twenties at the end of June, but the sodden money market had so killed interest in the loan that he withdrew the offer.[80]

The public, continuing to believe in the nation's financial strength, blamed the collapse of Union securities on traitors. After a tour of the North, a New York *Times* correspondent reported that "the war, so far, has produced no injurious effect whatever, on the wealth, strength, and stability of this country." Troubles with securities were clearly caused by Confederate sympathizers, Republicans decided. "The deepest stab which any traitor could give, at this time, to the national life," read another article in the New York *Times,* "would be a blow at the public credit." The editor of the New York *Daily Tribune* claimed in his columns that Northern Democratic papers that attacked the Union's finances were "animated by a joyful hope of producing a hopeless collapse and paralysis of the national credit" to secure a rebel triumph.[81]

Chase's ten-forty bond fiasco was his last effort as Secretary of the Treasury. At the end of June 1864, after months of petulantly pressuring Congress to follow his orders, he abruptly tendered his resignation when Lincoln declined to appoint his nominee for Assistant Treasurer in New York. Lincoln, now safely renominated, astonished the Secretary by accepting his resignation. Though angry and chagrined, Chase felt that he had done a good job. He assured his successor that "all the great work of the Department was now fairly blocked out and in progress."[82]

Indeed, Chase's wartime bond activities had established a trend in Republican financial policy at the same time that they had critically shaped Republican financial attitudes. Watching the Secretary fence with uncooperative bankers made many Republicans gradually adopt the negative Western Republican view of bankers. They began to advocate the reduction of government ties to all but a few helpful financiers; and gradually, as public pressure combined with fiscal needs, Republican policy had turned toward resting the government's finances on popular support. Chase's successful issue of over $1.5

billion worth of debt without causing national ruin eased the initial Republican horror of national debt and confirmed the belief of party members that America was financially powerful. Republicans continued to worry about the deficit, and few were ever convinced it was a good thing, but they no longer expected debt to cause instant disaster because they were firmly convinced of the Union's ability to generate increasing amounts of capital. While the new Treasury Secretary would inherit a cash crisis of larger proportions than any that Chase had confronted during his tenure, he would have the advantage of working with a nation that believed in its financial strength.[83]

After the President's first choice to succeed Chase declined the nomination, Lincoln nominated Senator William Pitt Fessenden. Desperately unhappy with the appointment, the chairman of the Finance Committee nonetheless perceived that the "feverish condition" of the money market and military reverses were so undermining public confidence that his refusal to accept the position would precipitate a crash. Such an event could very well result in Lincoln's defeat in the upcoming election, and might shatter the whole war effort. A shower of telegrams, letters, and newspaper editorials encouraged him to accept the post, and Fessenden took office on July 5.[84]

The Treasury needed money badly. Daily expenses ran about $2.5 million, while the outstanding drafts on the Treasury—mostly army paychecks—were around $50 million. Army pay requisitions on September 1 would be another $50 million. Also outstanding were over $160 million worth of certificates of indebtedness. Chase's large issue of circulating financial instruments had so terribly weakened the money market that a House financial leader begged Fessenden not to inflate the currency further.[85]

Fessenden had no grand financial plan when he took office; he merely wanted to find money for the Union. Pushed by circumstances, he coincidentally retraced much of Chase's path and, in so doing, confirmed that, until his most recent loan, the previous Secretary had responded appropriately to the nation's financial circumstances.

Fessenden was determined not to risk his reputation on a relationship with Jay Cooke, and so, as Chase had done back in 1861, the new Secretary turned first to bankers for funds. In order to raise the money the Treasury needed, he tried to negotiate a $50 million loan from New York, Boston, and Philadelphia financiers. Despite some hopeful reports that "the entire money and business interests of the nation are indissolubly intertwined with the interests of the government," bankers told Fessenden, as they had his predecessor, that they could not accommodate him unless the Treasury made significant policy changes in their favor. The banks, an observer recalled with disgust, viewed the Treasury crisis only "in the light of their own interests." Underneath the mutual expressions of esteem as negotiations broke off, one Republican read the Secretary's "bold . . . reject[ion of] the pretensions of the New York banks."[86]

Despite the soft money market, Fessenden turned to the public, as Chase had done before him. He began to sell $200 million worth of seven-thirties. Fessenden followed Chase's lead in turning from Cooke's agency to the new national banks and Assistant Treasurers, for these were supposed to be the agents of the people. The Secretary appealed to the public to buy the bonds, assuring them that the Union was strong and prosperous. "It is your war," he wrote. "Much effort has been made to shake public faith in our national credit, both at home and abroad," Fessenden reflected. "As yet we have asked no foreign aid. Calm and self-reliant, our own means thus far have proved adequate to our wants. They are yet ample to meet those of the present and the future." Newspapers echoed the Secretary's sentiments and called for loyal men and women to subscribe.[87]

Fessenden's appeal had some effect; sales were around $1 million per day for a few days. This initial enthusiasm soon waned. The upcoming presidential election made investors worry about the security of government bonds, especially since Republicans were again assuring them, as they had in 1862, that Democratic victory would mean repudiation. News from the battlefields was dull, and Jubal Early's spectacular raid on Washington hurt Northern morale. Bond sales fell off. In August, Fessenden ruefully wrote to his assistant: "We are not meeting with the hoped for success with regard to the loan . . . and I am afraid we shall find ourselves in trouble unless General Grant can help us." After two months, less than one-fifth of the $200 million loan had sold.[88]

Claims on the Treasury mounted throughout the summer of 1864 while the Treasury's receipts fell. In the fall, Chase's first popular loan came due, and the $150 million worth of seven-thirties issued in the fall of 1861 compounded the problems caused by each day's large expenditures. Fessenden issued certificates of indebtedness to meet bills, and by September there was an unbelievable $247 million worth of them on the market. In this swollen money market, government securities fell until even the solid five-twenties sold below par. By

November, neither the new seven-thirties nor Chase's ten-forties were selling, and the financial situation was dire.[89]

As disaster approached, Fessenden began to see why his predecessor had relied so heavily on Cooke. Despite the public's confidence in the nation's financial strength and its increasing desire to run all financial operations directly through a strong national system, the Treasury's national infrastructure was still completely inadequate to market huge bond issues effectively. In the New York *Daily Tribune,* Horace Greeley complained that the new national banks could not accomplish the task, for there were too few of them to reach into every hamlet as Cooke's agents had done. Somehow, Greeley wrote, Fessenden must find a way to reach everyone. Desperately, the Secretary gave the national banks one more chance to market his seven-thirty loan, but they failed.[90]

With the start of the new year and his own reelection to the Senate, Fessenden committed himself at last to Cooke. Lincoln's reelection had calmed financial fears, while Sherman's March to the Sea and the Battle of Nashville bolstered morale. Fessenden hoped that, with Cooke's help, he could market new seven-thirties. He got permission to issue up to $400 million worth of them, and on January 28, 1865, Fessenden named Cooke the "general agent of the Treasury Department for disposing of Government loans." Beginning work on February 1, Cooke's operations were immediately successful. Fessenden claimed on February 4 that "we begin to feel the new agency already." In one day alone, Cooke sold over $3 million worth of bonds. In the last week of the month, his agents sold over $35 million worth of bonds—almost as much as the national banks had managed to market in five months. Once again, Cooke's sales teams and advertising accomplished what others could not.[91]

By the spring of 1865, it was clear that the Union was winning the war and that the Treasury was out of the woods. Bonds sold rapidly as Cooke flooded newspapers with advertisements and as Grant's long, bloody war of attrition began to yield results. Even Europeans began to invest in Union bonds. This development, years too late to soothe Northern anger at Europe, elicited both Republican glee that Union credit was so strong and chagrin that foreigners were assuming some American debt. Proved financially secure, the North was determined to hold its own bonds.[92]

Fessenden sent a new loan bill to Congress in order to maintain the momentum of the bond sales. Approved by Lincoln on March 3, the act authorized the issue of another $600 million worth of bonds. Like the previous one, this act gave the Secretary great discretion. It called for bonds of from five to forty years at interest rates of no more than 6 percent in coin or 7.3 percent in currency. In the House, Republicans from the East as well as the West showed increasing dislike of the provision for paying interest in gold, which they identified as favoring financiers. Nonetheless, the House passed the bill by a party vote of 78 to 35, for the Treasury needed money. The Senate passed the bill without a roll-call vote.[93]

A new Secretary carried the Treasury to the end of the war. In order to take his seat in the Senate, Fessenden surrendered his office on March 3, 1865, to Hugh McCulloch, an Indiana banker who had worked closely with the Treasury during the war. Although forced to ride the swells and ebbs of the stock market as the war's end unsettled prices, McCulloch ultimately did little but finish Fessenden's final loan. The public knew that the war's victorious conclusion would halt bond issues, and the popular demand for the now-secure bonds enabled Cooke to market quickly the final $300 million worth of seven-thirties.[94]

The day the North heard of Richmond's fall, Cooke hung from his office a sign that embodied the Treasury's wartime activity. Between two large inscriptions, "5–20" and "7–30," an even larger banner read:

> The Bravery of our Army
> The Valor of our Navy
> Sustained by our Treasury
> upon the Faith and
> Substance of
> A Patriotic People.

The Union's patriotic people had in four years absorbed a national debt of over $2.5 billion.[95]

That the Treasury's soundness was perceived in 1865 as the people's triumph indicated the important effects of bond policy, despite the early demise of the image of popular assumption of the national debt. Although Democrats continued to develop the theme of Republican ties to favored bankers, most Republicans believed both that they had financed the war without the help of uncooperative financiers and that the cooperative bankers who had helped in the war effort were representative of the people. Successful domestic bond sales also

made Republicans stress the nation's newfound financial independence from the moneyed men of Europe. "If there is one conviction
resting on the popular mind," read an 1864 New York *Post* article
reprinted in the West, "it is that the nation is able to bear its own
[financial] burdens."[96]

The perceived public strength behind the national debt cemented
individuals' ties to an increasingly strong Union government. Chase
had tried, as he reported, to distribute the debt "into the hands of the
greatest possible number of holders," and at the end of the war a
Western newspaper reflected that "there has never been a national
debt so generously distributed among and held by the masses of the
people as all the obligations of the United States. This shows at once
the strength of popular institutions, and the confidence the people
have in their perpetuity."[97]

Popular bond sales helped the Republicans to emerge from the war
with a strong belief in the triumphant destiny of America and its
people. The public's steady purchase of bonds allayed the Republicans' initial fear that the war's destruction of wealth would bankrupt
the Union. "We began without capital and if we should lose the
greater part of it before this [war] is over," Chase wrote in 1863,
"labor will bring it back again and with a power hitherto unfelt
among us." It seemed that America must be fabulously rich and
Americans favored of God to thrive in such adverse circumstances.
America is "to-day the most powerful nation on the face of the globe,"
a Western congressmen told an Indiana crowd in 1864. "This war has
been the means of developing resources and capabilities such as you
never before dreamed that you possessed."[98] Pride in the nation's
financial power and fiscal independence from Europe convinced Republicans of America's future as one of the greatest nations in the
world.

The popular belief in national financial strength, the identification
of the public with the government, and the conviction of America's
great destiny long outlived the country's immediate postwar financial
euphoria. Despite Jay Cooke's repeated and increasingly shrill insistence that "out of three million subscribers to our various public
loans, over nine-tenths are of the class called *the people*," by 1867 a
significant group of Northerners observed the frenzied postwar Wall
Street traffic in United States bonds, including their increasing sales
overseas and, echoing Democrats' wartime accusations, argued that
rich bondholders were soaking poor laborers. This group found a

voice in the 1868 Democratic "ragbaby" presidential campaign. Re-calling Democratic wartime class rhetoric, tapping Western distrust of Eastern wealth, and feeding Western fondness for greenbacks, the Democrats in 1868 proposed the redemption of war bonds not in gold, but in depreciated paper money.[99]

Grant's triumph in 1868 reaffirmed a Republican commitment to honoring the wartime bonds in gold, but some Republicans defected to the idea of redeeming bonds in greenbacks, although they were probably driven by enthusiasm for greenbacks rather than by class resentments. The fracture in Republican support for bondholders indicated not only the fragility of the idea of the popular assumption of the national debt and the consequent emphasis on a popular com-munity, but also the tensions over national policy that could emerge from the identification of the American government with the Ameri-can people when the image of a popular community splintered.[100]

3 | "A Centralization of Power,
Such as Hamilton Might Have
Eulogised as Magnificent":
Monetary Legislation

> In a nation's wealth, business, and resources consists the greatest
> strength; and these almost entirely depend upon the wise, uni-
> form, and safe conduct of the finances. Success in business, the de-
> velopment of resources, the comparatively even accumulations of
> wealth, and the national success and prosperity, call for a system
> of finance which will preserve uniformity of values, stability of
> credit, and the highest attainable confidence.
>
> —Reuben E. Fenton, 1863

Their conflicts with bankers over bond negotiations and their increasing faith in the public's ability to support the Union's finances helped
to convince Republicans that the nation's banking and currency system needed an overhaul. Party members were forced initially to consider emergency legislation when the banks suspended specie payments and destroyed the nation's money. Then, in order to give the
public more control over the nation's capital and to weaken the power
of bankers, Republicans asserted the power of the national government to control the nation's finances and acted to institutionalize their
idea of a harmony of interest between financiers and the government.
As they created a national currency and centralized the country's
banks, Republicans were building a new economic role for an increasingly powerful national government, permanently involving it in the
country's monetary affairs.

Before the Civil War, America had neither a national currency nor,
after the dissolution of the Second Bank of the United States, a
national banking system. State-chartered local institutions were the
nation's sole banks, and they issued their own currencies based on a
limited reserve of capital. The issue of notes proved very profitable
for these banks, for they expanded an institution's ability to lend.

Notes, which could nominally be exchanged on demand for specie at the bank of issue, entered circulation when banks made loans. An institution that could not honor its notes closed its doors, and its notes became worthless. Accepting such an unstable currency was always risky, and for that reason banks or businesses would "discount" the notes of other banks before taking them. Thus, a $10 bill from a Maine bank might be worth only $8 in Boston, or $5 in New York. One historian estimated that there were seven thousand different kinds of bank notes in circulation before the war, not including ever-present counterfeits.[1]

When the war began, Republicans had different attitudes about the state bank system depending on the region from which they came. In general, they dreaded the consolidation of the "money power" into a monopoly that usurped the products of labor, but they were divided over whether or not state banks exercised such evil control. In the East, where strong state banks issued secure notes, Republicans believed that banks were a healthy element of society, that capitalists had the same interests as a good government, and that bankers would cooperate heartily with government measures to fill the Treasury.

In the West, whose many stable banks were obscured in the popular mind by "wildcat" banks that issued worthless currency, Republicans distrusted bankers. Having watched state bank notes depreciate in their pockets, they tended to associate banking with ill-gotten gains and believed that bankers manipulated the value created by the labor of others rather than producing anything themselves. Western Republicans thought that, far from contributing to society, bankers were parasites who sucked up the profits of Western agriculture. For decades, Westerners had searched unsuccessfully for ways to stabilize their currency. Before the formation of the Republican party, some Western Whigs, notably Abraham Lincoln, had called for a new national bank to provide a secure currency, while other Westerners, especially Democrats who had loathed the old Bank of the United States, worried that such a powerful bank would simply hold an even greater monopoly than the state banks already had. Although Western Whigs and Democrats brought into the Republican party different ideas about the solution to the bank problem, they shared a dislike of the current arrangement.[2]

Western Republican dislike of the state bank note system grew even stronger when the outbreak of hostilities made Western currencies crumble. A reserve of Southern state bonds backed much of the West's currency; when secession made the bonds worthless, the currency instantly collapsed. The West fell desperately short of money and business stagnated.[3] As early as April 1861, the Philadelphia *Inquirer* reported on "the deranged state of Western currency," and in June, the collapse of Wisconsin currency incited mobs that stormed Milwaukee's banks, forcing the governor to declare martial law. By September, a Republican congressman reported that "the Northwest [was] almost destitute of paper currency of their own," and by the end of 1861, most Western money was so heavily discounted it was almost entirely out of circulation except in the localities from which it came.[4]

When the Union's lack of a national financial infrastructure and a national system of taxation forced Treasury Secretary Chase to raise revenue by selling Union bonds to state banks, Republicans across the North saw that bond sales did not bring in enough money to fund the war, and grew angry at bankers' apparent reluctance to help the Union. At the same time that it became imperative to find new sources of revenue, Chase, and many of the Republicans who watched him tussle with the banks, began to think of weakening state banks and reducing the government's dependency on them.

On December 9, 1861, with the Union's financial situation becoming critical, and expecting little help from bankers without some pressure, Chase delivered his annual Report to Congress. In it, he discussed novel monetary reforms that would both raise revenue and reduce the power of state banks.

The Union had two options to solve its financial woes, Chase told Congress. Its first alternative, he said, was to force state banks to retire their bank notes and replace them with national government demand notes. These government notes would become the nation's only currency, entering circulation when the government paid them to creditors. This plan would destroy state bank note issue altogether and would base the nation's currency solely on government credit. Reflecting his roots as a hard-money Democrat, Chase specified that such a government currency must be convertible to specie.[5]

The Secretary's explication of this first alternative noted the growing Republican dislike of bankers, but warned that such a drastic revision of the nation's financial system might be imprudent. He acknowledged that a currency of government notes "would be equivalent to a loan to the Government without interest . . . and without expense . . . ; while the people would gain the additional advantage of a uniform currency, and relief from a considerable burden in the form of interest on debt"; but a government currency was hazardous as well as beneficial, the Secretary continued. There was an ever-present danger of overissue, panic, depreciated currency, and "the immeasurable evils of dishonored public faith and national bankruptcy." Chase also implied that this plan would raise Republican fears of creating a powerful government money monopoly.[6]

The Union's second option, Chase said, was to create a new national currency that existing state banks would circulate in place of their own notes. Unlike government demand notes, this currency would be secured by private capital as well as by government credit. Adapting to a national scale a plan successfully operating in New York, the Secretary suggested that banks could invest their capital in government bonds, which they would deposit with the Treasury. In return, the Treasury would provide them with national notes to circulate. This plan would bring money to the Treasury by increasing demand for bonds at the same time that it would cement the cooperation of state banks with Republican financial policies by tying them to the national government.[7] Leaving state banks the privilege of issuing currency—only now it would be national currency rather than their own notes—this plan would avoid great interruption in the financial community. It would leave the nation's currency secured first by private capital and second by the government or, as Republicans conceived of it, by the American people and their ability to fund their bonds through their productive labor. This second option, Chase said, offered a uniform, secure currency, safeguarded as much as possible from depreciation, "without rising the perils of a great money monopoly."

Chase's presentation of these two plans was a thinly veiled threat to the bankers who had refused to do his bidding during bond negotiations. He remarked that the policy of issuing government Treasury notes—which would take from existing banks their very profitable business of circulation—had already commenced, for Congress had authorized the issue of $50 million worth of demand notes in July 1861. Although he claimed to dislike this option, he warned bankers that a plan to continue such issues would "hardly fail of legislative sanction" if sufficient safeguards against overissue could be devised. The second plan, however, which the Treasury Secretary preferred, would allow banks that cooperated with the government to continue to circulate currency. "Through the voluntary action of the existing institutions, aided by wise legislation," Chase rhapsodized, "the great transition from a currency heterogeneous, unequal, and unsafe, to one uniform, equal, and safe, may be speedily and almost imperceptibly accomplished."

While most New York bankers were furious at the suggestion of a national currency, Republicans outside of banking circles, primarily in the West, liked the scheme. Some welcomed the promise of a permanent, stable currency; some made much of the idea that a national currency would promote a sentiment of nationality; and some hoped to break the power of the state banks. The editor of the Cincinnati *Daily Commercial* reported that the currency plan was popular, and, worrying that pressure from the bank lobby would keep Congress from passing it, he encouraged his readers to challenge the power of the banks. "If a class interest is likely to control the action of Congress prejudicially, and to embarrass the administration of the Treasury Department in its present extremity," he wrote, "it were high time that the people were looking more jealously upon the exercise of such power."[8]

A subcommittee of the House Ways and Means Committee, consisting of Elbridge G. Spaulding of New York as chairman, Republican Samuel Hooper, a retired Boston merchant and financier whose business ventures had netted him a tidy fortune, and Democrat Erastus Corning, an Albany millionaire, went right to work on a national currency bill, but before the subcommittee could mature Chase's plan the bottom fell out of the Union's financial system. The bankers' anger, threats of a war with England over the *Trent* affair, low Northern morale, and rumors that Chase planned to issue several millions of dollars of paper currency fueled financial fears and gold hoarding.[9] Chase rushed to New York to reassure bankers of both his own goodwill and the safety of the country's finances, but despite his efforts, Northeastern banks suspended specie payments on December 30. The government followed suit, for it honored in coin its demand notes and bank suspension caused a run on what little gold remained in the Treasury. Within three weeks, almost all Northern banks were unable to redeem their notes. Lacking even a nominal right of redemption in coin, the value of state bank currency now had no foundation at all. People refused to use such volatile currency and searched wildly for a secure medium of exchange. "We must not only have money," declared a New York assemblyman, "but we must have it *at once*."[10]

Meanwhile, the government desperately needed funds to finance the war. Feeding, clothing, and equipping an army of half a million men and a growing navy was costing up to $2 million each day, and the Treasury was empty. Selling more bonds would be ruinous, for government securities commanded only a fraction of their face value. Taxation could not solve the immediate crisis either, for implementing a sweeping revenue system would take much too long. Treasury notes were useless because many New York bankers refused to accept them until Congress provided for their repayment.[11]

As soon as it heard that New York bankers had voted on December 28 to suspend specie payments, the subcommittee realized that its sixty-section bank bill embodying Chase's suggestions for a rather complicated national currency system could not be enacted quickly enough to provide emergency funds. Now convinced that the government could not rely on state bankers for help, the subcommittee wrote a bill that would create the government paper money that Chase had mentioned unenthusiastically in his report. Spaulding introduced the bill to the House on December 30—the day New York banks suspended specie payments—and Horace Greeley printed it in the New York *Daily Tribune* on December 31, 1861. Bypassing bankers, the plan dropped the idea of placing bank capital behind a new national currency and called instead for the government to issue Treasury notes that would enter circulation when Chase used them to pay the government's outstanding bills. Unlike the government currency Chase had mentioned in his report, these proposed government notes were not redeemable in specie. They were based instead on the good faith of the government.[12]

In the three weeks before Congress began debating the unprecedented and momentous plan, public emotions about government currency ran high. There were two related issues: the idea of irredeemable paper money, and the idea that the government was to issue that money. Most Republicans had a long-standing horror of irredeemable paper currency. Because gold and silver were uniquely stable, distinctive, and internationally accepted media of exchange, most Republicans retained a belief that specie was the only true standard of value. They thought that, unlike specie, paper notes were a debt—"a mere memorandum of an unfulfilled contract"—payable in specie in the future.[13]

Republicans refused to consider paper as money because unlike specie, whose even production kept its value stable, paper money's worth fluctuated, threatening the bedrock Republican principle that value was a product of labor. Unstable paper money detached value from the labor employed in production and attached it instead to conditions in the money market. Volatile currency destroyed people's desire to engage in steady and productive work. All commerce and business slowed while "knavery and swindling" flourished, claimed Greeley in the New York *Daily Tribune*.[14]

The fact that the government would issue the proposed paper money compounded Republican dislike of it. Taking their cue from the rural world of small enterprise from which they had come and from their favorite economists, most Republicans conceived of national finance as simply a larger version of individual finance. A penniless person could not buy goods with a mere promise to pay sometime in the future; nor could a nation, they thought. "Business may be carried on with cash or on credit," wrote a Boston newspaper editor. "Governments must adopt the same principle . . . Who ever heard of a merchant or manufacturer carrying on a successful business by means of loans payable . . . when convenient to himself?"[15]

Some Republicans also worried, as Chase had suggested in his report, that government control over all currency issues would create a great money monopoly. The theorist who had provided the blueprint for Chase's bank plan admitted that government currency would indeed create an "unqualified government monopoly," although he defended it as a legitimate and beneficial constitutional power of the government and claimed that all Americans would share in the advantages of the monopoly. The editor of the Cincinnati *Daily Commercial* nonetheless reflected that a currency of Treasury notes might plant "the seed of a power in the government that may be easily debased to the worst uses and become a fearful oppressor of the political rights of the people."[16]

Republicans feared that government paper currency would always be susceptible to overissue. The South had turned quickly to paper money, and it well illustrated the potential disasters of such a policy. As early as June 1861 a Philadelphia *Inquirer* correspondent had laughed at the instant depreciation of Southern bills. By May 1862, Greeley reported in the New York *Daily Tribune* that the South was wallowing in the "fetid trash" of overissue; its currency had turned into "greasy mementoes of typographical barbarism." "Southern zanies," he declared, ""were rioting in a "great carnival of rags."[17]

Spaulding's plan for a government paper currency added one more objectionable element to the idea of government paper money by declaring the government's paper to be legal tender for all debts; that is, by law the new notes would have to be accepted in payment for obligations. This would prevent New York bankers from snubbing the government paper. Some argued that Congress had constitutional power only to "coin" money, not to declare paper a currency. They further pointed out that the Constitution forbade states to make anything but gold or silver legal tender, and that, by implication, the national government could not either. Finally, and most powerfully, some Republicans held that the creation of a paper legal tender would unconstitutionally impair contracts made in specie.[18]

Reactions to the currency plan reflected the two different Republican attitudes about the role of bankers in the economy. Many Republicans, primarily in the East, clung firmly to their dislike of paper money and hoped that capitalists and the government would cooperate to solve the crisis in some other fashion. A Philadelphia paper admonished that "symptoms of disagreement" between the government and the banks were not "looked upon with approbation" and were already producing "mischief." Horace Greeley agreed. "In a time like this," he wrote, "a difference between the Government and the moneyed capitalists would be suicidal." Bankers blamed the crisis on Chase's refusal to listen to them. They opposed the currency plan because they predicted the Union would collapse in worthless paper money and, less openly, feared measures that would weaken the country banks whose profits depended on bank note issues, for the deposits of rural organizations in New York City banks were the major source of profits for the New York bankers. They called for more of the measures that they and the Secretary had adopted together: loans, taxes, and interest-bearing demand notes. One went so far as to call for a board of loan commissioners, comprised of businessmen, to negotiate government bonds on whatever terms they saw fit. The government, he wrote, needed the help of the experienced financial men whose loyalty in buying bonds was solely responsible for the maintenance of the Treasury so far.[19]

Other Republicans, primarily Westerners, were so angry at banks that they backed the currency plan, answering their old dislike of paper money with a new conviction that the government represented the people and must be upheld against the banking interests. Calling for exclusive government control of finances, they asserted that irresponsible—and probably disloyal—banks were attempting to set themselves above the government by dictating terms to the country. Fulminating against New York "stock gamblers," the editor of the Chicago *Tribune* claimed that Westerners wanted government legal tender to replace state bank notes. Noting that the creation of government notes would bring the people's capital to the government instead of to banks, he insisted that the government must make and control its own currency, even if that would destroy state banks. A Republican from Ohio agreed, writing to his congressman, "We are all in favor of the citizens of the Republic becoming its *creditors*, rather than the *debtors* of the bankers and capitalists." The editor of the New York *Times* declared that the vast loyal majority of people would applaud the issue of national currency stamped as legal tender, for they desired "to see the sovereign power of this Government asserted." Newspapers picturesquely reported that the cry in the streets was "Down with the banks, and give us a national currency."[20]

Spaulding's subcommittee continued the Republican attack on banking interests when it released its long bank bill in the midst of the currency controversy. This unworkable bill, which died quickly in the Ways and Means Committee, called for the establishment of national banks to operate alongside state banks. Like the currency plan, the call for national banks was popular, especially among Western Republicans, while it confirmed many Eastern bankers' dislike of Republican financial policies.[21]

Anxious to reestablish good relations with the Eastern bank lobby, whose opposition to even his less radical currency ideas had been much more strident than he had expected and whose support he still needed to raise revenue, Chase privately threw his weight against the subcommittee's legal tender plan and invited bankers from New York, Philadelphia, and Boston to help him solve the crisis. They gathered at Chase's home on January 13, 1862. After the Secretary rejected the bankers' proposal that he sell bonds at whatever price they could command, Chase and the bankers drafted a plan that they believed would solve the money problem. They returned to the idea of funding the war with bonds, calling for the Treasury to pay to its creditors seven-thirty bonds and interest-bearing notes, which were convertible to the bonds. The agreement squelched the idea of currency based on government credit, rejecting further issues of demand notes and limiting the government to the $50 million worth authorized the previous July. This limit would guarantee the banks' monopoly on bank notes. In exchange, the banks promised to receive and pay out both government demand notes and the proposed interest-bearing notes.[22]

While even many bankers disliked this solution to the problem, the public was outraged. Republicans who had previously hoped the banks and the government would cooperate began to call for government control of the nation's finances. The New York *Times* dismissed the plan as a bankers' scheme, and the New York *Daily Tribune* claimed that the suggestions of "so-called financiers" had not impressed the Ways and Means Committee, which had determined to push the Treasury note bill. The New York *Post* trumpeted that Ways and Means Committee members opposed the plan two to one. In Philadelphia, the moderate *Daily Evening Bulletin* accused arrogant financiers of conspiring to dictate a selfish policy to the Government and called for Congress to make Treasury notes legal tender.[23]

With most of the public angry about the solution that Chase and the bankers had proposed, Congress returned to a plan of paper currency issued by the national government. On January 22, 1862, from the Committee on Ways and Means, Spaulding introduced a bill (H.R. 240) that would become the Legal Tender Act. This bill authorized the issue of $100 million of non–interest-bearing Treasury notes for use as legal tender in payment of all public and private debts. The newly created paper money would enter circulation when it was paid to such government creditors as army contractors and soldiers. Revealing that Republicans were still reluctant to believe that paper could be stable enough to serve the same purpose as specie, the bill provided that the proposed notes would not technically be irredeemable but would be redeemed at the pleasure of the government. At the option of the holder, they could also be converted into interest-bearing government bonds, of which the bill authorized the issue of $500 million worth. When Spaulding consulted Chase about the bill, the Secretary, who was still trying to soothe angry bankers, neatly avoided responsibility for the legal tender plan and, in so doing, placed Congress at the head of the movement for a popular government paper currency. He said that he regretted that "it [was] found necessary to resort" to such a measure, but that he was "heartily desirous" of cooperating with the Ways and Means Committee.[24]

The next day, the New York *Times* reported that "the unanimity with which [the bill] is received in this commercial City is scarcely qualified by a show of respectable or loyal opposition." That was hardly true, for the staunchly Republican New York *Daily Tribune*, for one, was set against the legal tender clause. Although inaccurate, the assertion illustrated that the battle over the plan was becoming associated with loyalty to the government. Bankers who disliked the bill were already suspect for their refusal to cooperate with Chase's requests over bonds, and Democrats both in and out of Congress were beginning to oppose the plan out of their increasingly fervent dislike of any expansion of the national government's power. From the co-operation of Democrats and financiers would come two results: Re-publicans—eventually including Greeley—would rally behind the pro-posal; and the bank lobby, which had originally opposed the plan, would acquire the taint of disloyalty.[25]

Congressional discussion of the bill began a week after Spaulding introduced the measure. Citing the nationalist Alexander Hamilton as its authority for constitutional interpretation, Spaulding's opening speech revealed that the Republican party was beginning to advocate centralization of the Union's monetary system in order to place it in the hands of the people, rather than at the mercy of unpopular bankers. Spaulding assured the House that the plan would remedy the perilous state of the nation's finances and, addressing constitutional objections to government paper money, he insisted that "the war power must be exercised to its full extent" to maintain the army and to coin and to regulate the value of money. Catering to popular aversion to the banks, Spaulding claimed that the bill would keep the government from going "into Wall street, State street, Chestnut street, or any other street begging for money" and would instead "assert the power and dignity of the Government."

Spaulding's advocacy of the bill revealed that Republicans anxious to increase government control over the nation's finances had begun to distinguish between two groups of bankers: those cheerfully coop-erating with the Treasury, whom Republicans believed to be the na-tion's true statesmanlike capitalists acting in concert with the people; and those opposing the Treasury's policies, whom party members saw as unpatriotic, greedy speculators. As one Western Republican ex-plained: "The true capitalists of the country are patriotic; they have furnished their means liberally; but there is a class of bankers . . . who would make merchandise of the hopes and fears of the Republic." In early February, Spaulding introduced a letter from Chase, which deftly illustrated that even the Treasury Secretary had begun to make this distinction. In his letter, Chase abandoned his hard-money principles, urging the bill's passage despite his regret that a simple issue of Treasury notes would not suffice in the crisis. The people and many banking institutions would have accepted such a remedy, he wrote, but unfortunately, the refusal of some uncooperative bankers to trade in Treasury notes made it necessary to declare Treasury notes legal tender.

Republican opponents of the bill, however, still adhered to the traditional Eastern belief that capital and government shared a harmony of interest. Resisting central control of the finances, they portrayed state banks as loyal partners of the government. Justin Smith Morrill of Vermont, a longtime shareholder in a state bank, launched an all-out assault on the bill's legal tender clause, contending that it was unconstitutional and immoral, would destroy the national credit, and would cause inflation. From the minority of the Ways and Means Committee he introduced a substitute to the bill, which generally followed the terms of the bankers' January agreement with Chase. New York Republican Roscoe Conkling, who spoke for the New York banking interest, followed Morrill. Emphasizing the loyalty and self-sacrifice of banks during the early days of the war, he accused advocates of both the currency bill and the banking scheme of being prompted by hostility to state banks.[26]

Proponents of the bill acknowledged that it would strengthen the national government's influence in financial matters, but representatives from different regions placed different emphasis on what that increased involvement meant. A few Easterners in favor of the measure tried to reassure bankers that the bill would not replace state banks with a government system, claiming that the plan simply combined government and business. A Massachusetts representative, for instance, emphasized Hamilton's friendship with leading merchants and financiers, and recalled that the cooperation of government and bankers had created the means to fund the American Revolution. But Westerners militantly argued that the government must take control over the nation's finances from uncooperative financiers. Although acknowledging that "many bankers . . . have been patriotic and self-sacrificing in the cause of the country," Republican John A. Bingham of Ohio protested efforts "to lay the power of the American people to control their currency . . . at the feet of brokers and of city bankers." Need also helped to drive Western support for the government money. Insisting that they desperately needed currency, Westerners maintained that their region would welcome the proposed government notes, for they would be more secure than those with which the region had suffered.

On February 6, Committee on Ways and Means chairman Thaddeus Stevens closed the House debate only two weeks after the bill had been introduced. He supported a strong central government, and, with the characteristic self-assurance that marked this dictatorial man, he contended that a uniform national currency would be better than any other. He declared the proposed measure constitutional and expedient and denied that supplementary issues of currency would be necessary after the proposed bills entered circulation. Dubbing Morrill's substitute for the bill—one advocated by the minority of his own committee—a ridiculous "curiosity," the powerful Pennsylvanian hailed Spaulding's bill as "the most auspicious measure of this Congress."[27]

Revealing that most Republicans no longer trusted banks to be the cooperative partners of the government, the House rejected Morrill's substitute plan by a vote of 95 to 55. Then, in order to free the government from bank demands and to promote national control over the finances, Republicans overcame their dislike of paper currency and their constitutional scruples about the creation of government paper money. The Treasury note bill, adjusted upward to authorize $150 million worth of notes, passed by a vote of 93 to 59. The votes for the bill came almost entirely from Republicans; Democrats, who strongly opposed the centralization inherent in the bill, led the opposition. Most of the twenty-two Republicans who voted against the bill came from New England, New York, and New Jersey, areas with strong banking interests.[28]

While the House debated the bill, two members of the Senate Finance Committee, William Pitt Fessenden and John Sherman, were deluged with letters, most of which supported the currency bill. Opposed to the legal tender clause, moderate committee chairman Fessenden left sponsorship of the bill to Sherman. Still two years short of forty, Sherman had climbed rapidly up Ohio's political ladder and had enjoyed a prewar camaraderie with Chase. He had also made friends with a politically sympathetic newspaper editor, H. D. Cooke, whose brother, Jay, bankrolled Sherman's campaign finances. Young, hardworking, earnest, interested in finance, and anxious to prove as useful to the Union as his fighting brother promised to be, Sherman would become the driving force behind the Republicans' wartime monetary legislation.[29]

The Treasury note bill went to the Senate on February 7, and three days later, with the Treasury on the brink of insolvency, Fessenden reported the bill from the Finance Committee with amendments. Making concessions to bankers, the amendments revealed the hand of Fessenden, who, according to the caustic Thaddeus Stevens, had "too much of the vile ingredient, called conservatism." One amendment called for the establishment of a fund to pay interest on bonds and to create a sinking fund for the whole debt, and another allowed large investors in Treasury notes to earn interest on them. In an attempt to reassure the country that Treasury note issues would not replace bond sales in revenue policy, the committee inserted an amendment permitting the Secretary of the Treasury to sell bonds at market rates so that par restrictions would not hamper bond sales in the future. The most important and controversial of the committee's amendments, however, was its stipulation that, in order to keep government credit strong and exhibit good faith to the nation's creditors, interest on the proposed bonds should be paid in coin rather than in the proposed notes.[30]

After introducing the committee's amendments, Fessenden illustrated his dislike of the groundbreaking ideas embodied in the bill by launching into a passionate harangue against the legal tender clause. He claimed that such a measure was tantamount to a declaration of bankruptcy because it impugned government credit. In a speech probably intended for a wider audience than those in the Senate chamber, Fessenden defined the basis of government currency in order to challenge Chase's declaration that the clause was "a vital necessity." Fessenden powerfully defended the Union's credit by reminding his listeners that the nation's ability to labor supported the proposed government currency. Everyone knew, he said, that the government would one day be able to redeem the notes in specie, for regardless of the outcome of the war, the North would always retain everything necessary to make "a great, a prosperous, and a glorious people." It would still have "the capital which those who framed the Constitution considered the best capital that a nation could have": that is, "labor; the power and the will to work; and the disposition, the desire, the anxiety, the policy to make that labor more productive by educating it; under which policy of educating labor and thus increasing the power of production, the country has grown up with such unexampled, unparalleled rapidity." Notes based on such ample security needed no legislative fiat to guarantee their worth, Fessenden concluded.[31]

It was left to Fessenden's conservative friend Judge Jacob Collamer of Vermont to test the strength of the basic Republican idea of a harmony of all interests. Collamer, who believed the legal tender clause unconstitutional because it would impair contracts, followed Fessenden's attack with an effort to strike out the clause making the notes legal tender for private debts. This would be a test vote preliminary to killing the entire provision. Congressmen who voted for Collamer's amendment must believe that everyone would honor treasury notes because they would recognize the nation's power to fund them with the proceeds of labor.

Henry Wilson of Massachusetts, who styled himself the voice of the common man, revealed that Republican understanding of finance had evolved beyond Fessenden's basic ideas. Opposed to striking the legal tender clause, Wilson explained that the sheer power of the public credit, which ideally should secure the notes as Fessenden argued, could not do so because of the machinations of newly recognized uncooperative bankers. Without the legal tender provision, Wilson said, evil men would destroy the value of the notes by refusing to take them. As the notes depreciated, the government would be forced to go to the market for money, where it would get fleeced. "I look upon this contest as a contest between the . . . brokers, the . . . money-changers, and the men who speculate in stocks, and the productive, toiling men of the country," Wilson said.

Westerners agreed wholeheartedly with Wilson. Accusing opponents of the legal tender clause of selfishness and a lack of patriotism while hoping to favor state banks, one Western man declared that "in the great and loyal West I do not believe there can be found one man in a hundred who does not wish [the notes] to be issued with that promise [of legality]."[32]

Like the House, the Senate overcame constitutional scruples about the legal tender clause to protect the government's finances. Those nervous about affronting bankers could take comfort from Sherman's assurance that financiers wanted the legal tender clause if any Treasury note bill passed, for bankers doubted that they, in their turn, could pay out government notes unless they were legal tender. The Senate rejected Collamer's amendment by a vote of 22 to 17. Western Republicans generally supported the legal tender clause; those opposed to it tended to hail from New England.

Reluctant to move away from bankers as quickly as the House advocated, however, the Senate adopted all of the committee's amendments before it passed the bill by an overwhelming vote of 30 to 7. Although only three Republicans ultimately clung to their dislike of the new monetary centralization and opposed the bill, few voted aye cheerfully. As Fessenden had written home earlier: "This thing has tormented me day and night for weeks . . . the thing is wrong in itself but to leave the government without resources at such a crisis is not to be thought of." The Senate passed the bill on February 13, 1862, the day after news of General Ambrose E. Burnside's victory at Roanoke Island "electrified" Wall Street. Businessmen gathered outside the Stock Exchange congratulating each other "that the beginning of the end of the rebellion was in view." Three days later, General Ulysses S. Grant took Tennessee's strategic Fort Donelson, and the North rejoiced. Opponents of the bill declared the creation of paper currency unnecessary, for it appeared that the war was going to end before it could be issued. Nevertheless, the House began to consider the Senate's amendments to the bill in mid-February.[33]

The House debate, which concentrated on the amendment calling for coin interest payments on the proposed bonds, further plumbed Republican attitudes toward financiers. Spaulding, Stevens, and Hooper opposed this provision, worrying that it unduly favored capitalists and would depreciate the bills by suggesting that even Congress thought them inferior to gold. Although Stevens threatened to try to scrap the bill altogether if the House accepted the amendment, many House Republicans approved the payment of interest in gold, for they believed it would lead investors to support the new notes. Gold interest payments would keep the notes close to par, they thought, for capitalists would willingly invest surplus notes in gold-bearing bonds, thus lending money to the Union at the same time that they checked depreciation of the notes caused by overexpansion of the currency. Further, the easy convertibility of the notes into bonds yielding gold would reinforce confidence in the notes themselves. The House rejected Stevens's attempt to kill the amendment by a close vote, then adopted the Senate's coin payment proposal by a wide margin. Still favoring the creation of government currency, House Republicans had retreated from their initial attempt to launch that currency without the support of financiers.

A conference committee ironed out the remaining disagreements between the two Houses over the Senate's conservative amendments, and both Houses accepted its report. The committee had agreed on the issue of $150 million worth of notes; provided for their deposit with Assistant Treasurers or in designated banks at not more than 6 percent interest; and established a fund of import duties to pay interest, and eventually principal, on notes and bonds.

Lincoln signed the Legal Tender Act, as it was called, into law on February 25, 1862, and soon the new notes, printed with green ink, filled the country. On first acquaintance, people liked the new money. The West wholeheartedly welcomed the relatively stable government bills. If not so thrilled with the "greenbacks" as Westerners, Easterners were, at least, relieved that the issue of government paper caused none of the disasters that naysayers had predicted.

It soon appeared that the monetary centralization that party members had adopted as an emergency measure might become permanent Republican policy. On June 7, 1862, Chase asked Congress for an additional issue of greenbacks to bolster the Treasury. Days later, in the House, Stevens reported a bill (H.R. 187) that authorized an additional $150 million worth of greenbacks. When the bill came up for discussion, Spaulding told the House that "the financial plan initiated six months ago as a necessary war measure" had worked so well that the Secretary recommended a continuance of it.[34]

Debate over this bill generally followed regional lines. Easterner Morrill protested this second attempt to replace state bank currencies for, he said, banks had been good to the Union. Westerners retorted that the large profits banks had made on their original investment in government bonds had amply compensated them for their early support of the Union. Popular enthusiasm for the new money further encouraged support of it. Owen Lovejoy of Illinois, who had opposed the initial issue of government paper currency, now declared himself prepared to support this one and to outlaw state bank notes, explaining that his state liked the greenbacks. His constituents, he said, "gather them up and hoard them just as much as they used to hoard gold and silver."[35]

Growing Western support for the greenbacks outweighed the East's fondness for state banking to make the issue of government currency part of regular Republican financial policy. On June 11, the House authorized the issue of $150 million worth of additional bills by a vote of 76 to 47. As on the original measure, the vote broke down largely by party, with a core of sixty-nine Republicans voting aye and a group of twenty-four Democrats and eight Old-Line Whigs voting nay. The East-West split accounted for jumping across party lines. All but one of the fifteen Republicans who voted nay were from New York or New England; six were from Massachusetts alone. The five Democrats and two Old-Line Whigs who supported the bill tended to be from Western or border states.[36]

Western and popular interests overcame banking interests in the Senate, too, although they did not gain a complete victory. As soon as Fessenden had explained the bill on July 2, Sherman went a step further and proposed a state bank note tax to give the government full control of the currency. State bank advocate Collamer condemned what he called an attempt to destroy "all the institutions sanctified by the course of years," and the two men battled ferociously. Probably anxious to avoid a long debate, the Senate overrode Western support for Sherman's amendment and killed it before passing the measure by a vote of 22 to 13. Lincoln signed the bill on July 11. It seemed that government greenbacks had become the mainstay of the Republicans' monetary policy.[37]

Despite the greenbacks' popularity, the Secretary of the Treasury did not abandon his pet scheme of creating a permanent national currency backed by private capital invested in government stocks. Republicans expected the greenbacks to disappear immediately after the war as people invested them in bonds or as the government redeemed them in specie. The retiring of the greenbacks would return control of the currency to state banks, a proposition that most Republicans increasingly disliked. On December 1, 1862, in his message to the third session of the Thirty-Seventh Congress, Lincoln indicated that he and Chase still hoped to replace the Treasury notes with national currency. Rejoicing that the greenbacks had succeeded wonderfully, the President nevertheless doubted that a sufficiently large number of them for the public's needs could be maintained without severe inflation. He called for the establishment of a national currency circulated by national banks. Secured by private property in addition to government credit, such a currency promised to be stable.[38]

Chase had probably written the sections of Lincoln's message that dealt with the Treasury, and not surprisingly, his own report on December 4 advocated his national currency plan of the previous year.

This time, he included a call for national banking institutions. Chase acknowledged that the public justly demanded a uniform currency and "at least part of the benefit of debt without interest, made into money, hitherto enjoyed exclusively by the banks." Worrying that greenbacks were susceptible to overissue at the same time that they raised "the danger of fraud in management and supervision," Chase called instead for existing and new banks to join a national scheme. An institution would invest its capital in government bonds and then deposit those bonds with the Treasury in exchange for notes of national currency. This process would combine "local and general credit" without unduly disrupting existing banks, Chase said, and base every dollar on "real capital, actually invested in national stocks." Secure, uniform national currency would supplant existing bank notes, which would be taxed out of circulation.[39]

The Secretary made it clear that to the banks that had worked "largely and boldly and patriotically on the side of the Union," he was offering an alternative to an exclusive system of government notes. Reminding bankers that many Republicans wanted the government to assume complete control over the nation's currency, he intimated that his new plan would save some of the bankers' old privileges of note issue and would "reconcile, as far as practicable, the interests of existing institutions with those of the whole people."

Despite the Secretary's pointed explanation of his plan, it found few backers in financial circles. Although Chase fondly declared that "the best thinkers and most liberal capitalists favor it," the majority of the bank lobby thoroughly disliked the scheme. Even some who had little love for the banks disapproved of so drastically changing the nation's financial system in the midst of war. The editor of *Harper's Weekly,* among others, doubted that Chase's project would meet with much favor in Congress for, he wrote, the bank interest could command enough congressional votes to defeat a measure that might destroy the banks. "Chase . . . will evidently have a close fight of it," the magazine editor concluded.[40]

In order to win his law, not only did the Secretary have to appease those who thought the plan was too hard on bankers, but also he had to attract a body of Republicans, primarily Westerners, who wanted state banks to lose altogether the privilege of issuing currency. Stevens, an aggressive spokesman of the latter group, introduced on December 8, 1862, an extreme bill that placed all authority for circulation in the government. It called for the new issue of $200 million of greenbacks, the issue of $1 billion worth of bonds, which would bear interest in legal tenders, and the severe taxation of state bank notes beyond a certain amount. In his explanation of the revolutionary bill two weeks later, Stevens made vicious swipes at bankers and brokers.[41]

The House seemed inclined to follow Stevens's lead. When, in early January 1863, Samuel Hooper proposed a national banking bill that embodied Chase's ideas, the Committee on Ways and Means immediately reported its own bill rejecting the Secretary's scheme. The committee's revenue bill (H.R. 659) proposed meeting the Treasury's financial needs by issuing an additional $300 million worth of greenbacks and by continued borrowing. Congress seemed to commit the nation to a policy of successive greenback issues when it decided on January 17, 1863, to pay the troops with $100 million worth of fresh greenbacks.[42]

At this point President Lincoln, worried about the rapidly depreciating currency, challenged the system of continued greenback issues. Although he signed the bill authorizing the new issue, he expressed to Congress his "sincere regret" that the measure was necessary. Lincoln urged that Congress, instead of repeatedly issuing greenbacks, pass a national bank bill and tax state bank notes to contract the currency.[43]

Lincoln's pressure for a national currency act and his implicit threat that he would veto more greenback legislation added to the momentum building behind Chase's scheme. Since 1861, the Secretary had urged Jay and H. D. Cooke to endorse his plan. Fearing that state banks would retaliate for any such support by ceasing to aid bond sales, the Cookes offered only private encouragement until late 1862. Then, perhaps attracted to the automatic bond market the plan offered, they resolved to help make Chase's plan law. In his *Memoirs,* Jay Cooke recalled that his agency was spending "vast sums with the newspapers for advertisements" of loans. With Chase's backing, he decided that "we had a right to claim their columns in which to set forth the merits of the new national banking system." For six weeks or more, he claimed, "nearly all the newspapers in the country were filled with our editorials condemning the state bank system, and explaining the great benefits to be derived from the national banking system now proposed." With or without Cooke's encouragement, Republican newspapers embraced Chase's idea wholeheartedly. Editorializing in its favor throughout January, they became driving forces in the bill's passage.[44]

Anxious to forestall the House's plan for more greenbacks, Chase worked hard to get Sherman to champion the currency plan in the Senate. Finally, in late January 1863, Sherman introduced a bill (S. 486) that would become the pathbreaking National Banking Act. The bill was designed to establish a national currency secured by United States securities. It provided that any five people could establish a national bank with a capital stock of not less than $50,000. Before commencing business, these people were required to pay in at least 30 percent of the bank's capital (they had to pay 10 percent installments each sixty days thereafter) and were required to invest not less than one-third of their capital stock in interest-bearing United States bonds and to deposit those bonds with the United States Treasury. In return, a new Bureau of Currency in the Treasury Department, headed by a Comptroller, would issue to the institution national currency equal to 90 percent of the current market value of the deposited bonds. The total value of the government notes was not to exceed $200 million, half of which were to be distributed according to population, the other half according to existing bank capital. National banks could circulate the national notes just as they had previously circulated their own bills, but they were required to redeem the national notes they circulated in greenbacks or specie on demand. Should one fail to do so, the government would close the bank's doors and pay the notes itself, using the proceeds of the sale of national bonds the bank had deposited with the Treasurer. In order to guarantee the success of the new system, the bill placed a tax on state bank note circulation. Once Sherman had introduced this bank bill, the Senate sent it to the Committee on Finance.[45]

In his keynote speech on the bill on February 10, Sherman stressed the growing Republican desire for monetary centralization. He reminded the Senate that Chase had requested the bill, that the administration sanctioned it, and that such a measure had gained favor with the public since Chase first suggested it in 1861. The measure offered the wartime benefits of creating a market for bonds and making additional greenback issues unnecessary, Sherman said. Of even greater importance, he continued, the plan would establish a permanent uniform national currency based on public credit and controlled, as all currency should be, by the government.

Sherman's speech revealed that wartime events had transformed early Republican ideas about a general harmony of economic interests into a call for a centralized monetary system controlled by the government. The senator impressed upon his listeners that the bill was an attempt to institutionalize a harmony of interest between the government and cooperative capitalists. Although the government initiated the bill and was its prime advocate, he explained, it had been designed so that banks would like it. Uniform currency would give their notes a wider circulation, guard against counterfeits, and stop runs on banks. Answering those who preferred that the government issue a national currency itself, Sherman said, "History teaches us that the public faith of a nation alone is not sufficient to maintain a paper currency. There must be a combination between the interests of private individuals and the Government." The bank bill would promote "a community of interest between the stockholders of banks, the people, and the Government," he claimed. The current system created "great contrariety" and "a great diversity of interests" as local bank notes clashed with government currency. The bank plan would "harmonize these interests; so that every stockholder, every mechanic, every laborer who holds one of these notes will be interested in the Government . . . whose faith and credit and security he will be more anxious to uphold." Sherman pointedly reminded senators interested in protecting the banks that the House's preference was for complete government monopoly of the nation's money supply. The House would "issue an unlimited quantity of paper without restraint or limitation."

Sherman's speech also outlined the way in which initial Republican ideas about political economy had grown during the war to a call for a powerful national government and an internationally dominant American nation. He argued vehemently in favor of the permanently increased government power embodied in the bill, claiming it would foster "a sentiment of nationality." Hamilton's concept of a strong national government spoke directly to the wartime Republicans, and Sherman tapped into that idea, arguing that states' rights theory, which elevated local above national government, was behind the Southern effort to overthrow the government. He told his colleagues that the best policy was to nationalize as much as possible. This would make men love their country before their states. "All private interests, all local interests, all banking interests, the interests of individuals, everything, should be subordinate now to the interest of the Government."

A strong government and the national sentiment it would create meant a glorious future for America, Sherman insisted. With proper national attributes "there is nothing that can be said too highly of the future of this country," he claimed. Boundless resources, a temperate climate, good location, and an enterprising population made America unique. Union triumph and a strong new nationalism would set an international example, spreading "the spirit of our republican institutions over lands that are yet living under kings and nobles and despots." By 1863, the Republicans envisioned a dominant international role for a unified American nation, and Sherman promised that the bank bill, with its implicit strengthening of the national government, would advance that goal.

Sherman's emphasis on harmony and nationalism appealed to many Republicans, and party newspapers quickly echoed the senator's sentiments. Calling on Congress to "sustain the Executive in so vital a measure," the editor of the New York *Times* argued that the bill would "consolidate" the people and the government. In the New York *Daily Tribune,* Greeley emphasized that the plan would harmonize the interests of the banks and the people. "Considered, however, as a permanent plan," concluded Greeley, "there can be no stronger argument in its favor than that it tends to strengthen the union of the States by the closely interwoven ties of common interest in the permanence and credit of the National Government."[46]

To encourage the passage of the bill, the Finance Committee offered concessions to those at both ends of the bank debate. In addition to the distribution of half the currency according to population, which the committee had designed to favor the West, Westerners won an amendment increasing the proposed amount of currency to $300 million in order to cover the issues of future Western banks. Trying to appease Western nervousness about underfunded banks, the committee also increased the amount of capital necessary to establish a national bank and made bank shareholders liable for debts not only to the amount they had invested in the bank, but also to the value of their stock. To attract bankers, the committee allowed state banks to become national institutions and deleted the tax on state bank notes, intending to provide separately for a bank note tax in a pending revenue bill.[47]

Despite these concessions, the committee insisted on the national government's exclusive control over the new banks. It tried to protect national banks from the destructive power of state taxation by providing for national taxation of the circulation of national banks and implying the banks' exemption from state taxes. The committee hoped that their deliberate vagueness about state taxation of the new banks would help the issue to slip by the spokesmen of state interests.

In spite of the committee's attempt to cater to the chief antagonists in the bank argument, party members at the far ends of the spectrum remained unsatisfied with the bill. Some Western Republicans remained convinced that notes of any private rural banks—even those organized under a national scheme—would depreciate, and they called for even more stringent safeguards on the bank plan. Jacob Howard of Michigan wanted to guarantee the security of the national notes by specifying that banks must redeem them in gold; John Henderson of Missouri tried to set the minimum capital stock of a national bank at $300,000 in order to prevent the establishment of national institutions in rural areas at all. Banks should only be established in New York, Philadelphia, Boston, and other capital centers, he said; notes issued by banks in remote areas must inevitably depreciate because the banks' inaccessibility would make the notes virtually irredeemable.

Collamer spoke for Eastern bankers, vigorously opposing the growth of government control over the currency. He charged that advocates of the bank bill and its "cognate," the pending plan for the taxation of state bank notes, intended to destroy state banks. He told Western senators who disliked banking institutions that they could not adequately understand the extent to which banks were part of New England society. "The connection of the banks enters into all the filaments of our business; it is the warp and woof of it," he said. Their destruction would cause "distress and ruin . . . through all parts of society." Collamer denied that Congress had constitutional authority to create national banks and accused Chase of attempting to construct a system of power more dangerous than the old Bank of the United States had ever been.

The wary Westerners and Collamer marked the extremes of the debate over the national banks; most Republicans were ready to try Chase's scheme. Senators were anxious over the third issue of greenbacks into a nation already full of inflated notes and were aware of the press's enthusiasm about the bank plan. Denying that the national bank proposal would create a new money monopoly, a Republican with roots in the Democratic party insisted that the new plan was "the very reverse of anything like a monopoly" because it opened control of banking to anyone who could put up the requisite capital. Eastern Republicans could find comfort in Sherman's denial that a national currency system would hurt state banks, while Western Republicans, attentive to growing popular displeasure with state banks, liked a plan that might restrain their issues. In addition, most Westerners approved of any scheme that might provide their region with secure currency, although they admitted that the West preferred greenbacks to the proposed notes. All these factors fed a growing Republican willingness to introduce government control of the nation's money and in so doing to expand permanently the national government's economic role in the nation.

On February 12, only two days after Sherman had introduced it, the Senate passed the bill, with all of the Finance Committee's amendments, by a vote of 23 to 21. The two Democrats who joined the Republican majority were both from the far Western state of Oregon, where state banks were prohibited by law, thus encouraging the senators to make a national currency available to their constituents; while the ten Republicans who opposed the bill came from states across the North.[48]

For the next week House Democrats, who recognized this bill as another assault on the privileges of state banks and thus an attack on states' rights, aggressively prevented the House from taking it up. Finally, on February 19, Spaulding gained the floor to introduce the measure. Like Sherman in the Senate, he revealed that the plan had taken on larger proportions than those of a simple question of financial policy. Conceding that the measure would not bring immediate relief to the Treasury, Spaulding maintained that it would help build a Hamiltonian system of a strong central government supported by private capital. Like Sherman, Spaulding saw the nationalization codified by the bank bill as a great step in achieving America's triumphant future. "This is our country. Let it have one national Government—one destiny," he pleaded.[49]

Democrats increasingly feared that the extraordinary war powers that the Republicans were assuming would create a permanent dictatorship, "the meanest despotism on earth," centered in Washington, and as they opposed the bill out of concern over national consolidation, their defense of state banks only succeeded in firmly associating bankers with disloyalty to the government and helped to build Republican support for the measure.[50] When the bill came up again on February 20, Hooper permitted very little debate before cutting off further discussion and any amendments to the bill. Amid a storm of protest, he demanded a vote. Many House Republicans preferred to maintain their own legal tender scheme, but they were under tremendous pressure to pass the bill. The President had made his wishes clear, and along with other Cabinet members, the Secretary of the Treasury had been present in the House since the bill came up. He was on the floor during the vote, with the Secretary of the Interior and former Secretary of the Treasury Robert J. Walker at his side. Undoubtedly, Chase's presence helped to marshal positive votes. The bill passed by a vote of 78 to 64. Most of the 23 Republicans who joined the Democrats to oppose the bill came from New England, New York, and New Jersey.[51]

Congress had passed Chase's bill after only three days of debate in the Senate and two days in the House, and Lincoln signed it on February 25, 1863. "The purpose of the measure," wrote the editor of *Harper's Weekly,* "is to institute such a connection between the public credit and the banking interest as shall, on the one hand, give the President virtual control of all the banks in the country, and, on the other, make every stockholder and banknote holder in the land an underwriter, so to speak, of the Government bonds." "It will be a peaceful but mighty revolution of the entire National currency," Greeley agreed, "at the same time effectually harmonizing the interests of both Government and people."[52]

Greeley's prediction of a monetary revolution was premature, for the new law, it seemed, was too weak to cement the government's control over the national finances. Spaulding, Hooper, the Cooke brothers, and other capitalists who supported the policies of the Treasury encouraged the establishment of national banks, but only a few patriotic citizens—mostly Westerners—took advantage of the new law. There were several legitimate reasons for financiers' reluctance to join the new system, for in its attempt to form national banks without offending state bankers, Congress had fatally weakened the new plan. It had favored state bank notes by refusing to impose the same taxes or currency limits on them that national bank notes carried, while it had also failed to guard adequately against national bank note depreciation if the bonds that secured them depreciated.[53]

Leaving the new currency weak, Congress had also failed to make the establishment of the new banks attractive. It forced converting state banks to replace their names with a number; and it did not specify what the Treasurer should do with deposited bonds, causing bankers to worry that incompetent government officers might use them as government assets. Most important, Congress had left unclear whether or not states could tax the new banks.[54]

A provision permitting states to determine the legal rate at which national banks could charge interest cemented the opposition of the New York banking community to the law. Since the legal rate in New York was 7 percent while in the West it was much higher—often 10 percent or more—New York bankers feared that Eastern capital would migrate to the West for higher returns. By late 1863, they were denouncing Chase's policy of displacing the existing state system and had decided to kill the national system by shutting its currency out of the financial markets.[55]

Aware that the national banking system would die without amending legislation, Chase pressured Congress to pass a new law. In mid-March 1864, Hooper reported from the Committee on Ways and Means an amending bill (H.R. 333) to the National Banking Act, and the battle to increase government power over the nation's peacetime monetary system recommenced.

The committee had written its bill after consultation with both the Secretary of the Treasury and the hostile bankers, although bankers disliked the result. The new bill repaired the defects of the 1863 law, strengthening the national banks and currency. It guarded against depreciation by requiring national banks to redeem their notes not only at their own counters but also at one of twelve commercial cities; made banks increase their bond deposit if the bonds depreciated; and increased the amount of necessary capital stock for the national banks. It also made the new system more attractive to state bankers by specifying that bonds deposited with the Treasury should be kept in trust for the bank depositing them, and by allowing state banks converting to the national system to keep their names.[56]

The one thing on which the new bill did not compromise was the firm assertion of national control over the new banks. The evident centralization of the bill meant that Republican sectional interest groups could use the voting strength of House Democrats, who opposed any extension of national government power, to hamstring two critically important features of the new law. A provision to establish a national 7 percent interest rate fell before Western Republicans eager to attract Eastern capital; while the prohibition of state taxation of the new banks died at the hands of Eastern banking interests anxious to reduce the competitive power of national banks. With these national elements of the bill removed, Stevens, who strongly supported national government control of banking to protect the public from unscrupulous financiers, killed the measure.[57]

But the struggle for national control of finances was not over. After Hooper, under the prodding of Treasury Secretary Chase, failed once again to get the House to accept a new bill that maintained the principle of national government control over the new banks, the Senate resumed the battle.[58] In the Senate, the Committee on Finance abandoned the fight for the national 7 percent interest rate in order to concentrate on establishing exclusive national taxation—and thus control—of the new banks. It maintained the principle of national taxation by calling for the imposition of a national tax on the new banks' circulation, deposits, and capital, allowing states to tax only an individual's personal property in a national bank. The Senate adopted the plan after further stipulating that state taxes on personal property in national banks could not exceed other state capital taxes. The Senate had finally agreed to give the national government authority over the nation's banking system.[59]

Almost as an afterthought, Republicans added to the new law one more critical provision whose significance would not emerge until after the war. Westerners, with their long-standing distrust of paper currency issued under private auspices, still doubted that the new national money would be secure. As their regional colleagues had done in the House, four Western senators advocated moving the centers of bank redemption to the East to make the currency as secure as possible. Over the protest of Sherman, who objected to "subordinat[ing] the large cities of the West . . . to the cities of the Eastern States," the Senate passed a Westerner's amendment making national bank notes redeemable in New York, Boston, or Philadelphia. Anxious to kill this plan, Sherman proposed instead that rural national banks redeem at national banks in nearby cities, and that all city banks redeem in New York. The Senate, and later the House, agreed.[60]

A conference committee brought the House around to the Senate's adjustments to the measure, and Lincoln signed the bill on June 3, 1864. It seemed that finally, thanks largely to popular discontent with the New York banks, the Republicans had established the principle of national government control over the Union's financial system. Reflecting on the Republicans' monetary changes, the editor of the New York *Times* triumphantly acknowledged that the Republicans had put into operation Hamilton's policies of linking government to capital and of having a strong central government. Reflecting that states' rights theory had strengthened the hand of Republican centralization by inciting a civil war, the editor concluded that "only great freshets can turn the wheels of progress." The legal tender act and the national currency bill, he concluded, "crystalized . . . [a] centralization of power, such as Hamilton might have eulogised as magnificent."[61]

With the establishment of the national currency going very slowly, greenbacks remained the currency of choice for most Northerners. The government notes, however, were notoriously unstable. When greenbacks depreciated, Republicans attributed the fall to a glut of state bank notes and to gold speculation, for the worth of greenbacks was measured by the price of gold. Both of these problems pointedly illustrated that the government did not yet control the currency, and Republicans undertook to remedy the situation.

Party members began to consider ways of contracting state currencies as soon as the Treasury issued greenbacks, for when the government notes appeared, state banks had issued their own notes on the basis of the government currency rather than gold. This system pumped a great deal more currency into the economy than Republicans had intended when they authorized the greenbacks, since banks issued more of their own notes than the greenbacks they held as reserves. This policy of the state banks depreciated the government currency and guaranteed that further government issues would simply fuel inflation. Many party members began to call for the taxation of state bank notes, with Chase recommending such a measure in his 1861 and 1862 reports. Newspapers had taken up the cry when the New York banks suspended specie payments and never abandoned it, and throughout the war, constituents wrote their congressmen advocating such a tax.[62]

Congressional Republicans began working for a tax on state bank note circulation during the tax debates of 1862, when an Illinois representative broached the issue. Then, in January 1863, Sherman, who was appalled by the conduct of bankers during the financial conferences of early 1862, introduced a bill to tax state bank notes. He distinguished between the functions of banking—loaning money, accepting deposits, facilitating financial transactions—and issuing money. A national currency was necessary, he said, since state currencies encouraged counterfeiting, bank failures, and inflation. Further, banks made unreasonably large profits by circulating their notes, and to maintain those profits—12.5 percent in New York, he claimed—they wanted "to issue their notes almost without limit, without interest, and without any responsibility for the principal." It was sometimes necessary to tax "in the most potent manner in order to maintain the Government," he said. His bill smothered under the national currency act, but Greeley agreed with Sherman that state bank notes should be taxed, and he continued to grumble about it in the New York *Daily Tribune*.[63]

By 1864, the Eastern bank lobby had weakened markedly, although it still wielded enough clout to block proposed taxes. Across the North, Democratic support of state banks had drawn Republican accusations of Southern sympathy, and by April 1864 state banking had become identified with disloyalty. Westerners liked the greenbacks and had begun to call for the elimination of "wildcat," "rag paper" money as early as 1862. Even some Western Democrats called for a boycott of state bank notes while Republicans called for their taxation. Taking matters into their own hands, in 1864 the businessmen of Chicago agreed to reject state bank notes. In the columns of the Chicago *Tribune*, the newspaper's editor encouraged such voluntary organizations and noted approvingly in April that national banks and other organizations in the Northwest were refusing state bank circulation. Republican newspapers and their readers across the North pressed harder and harder for the taxation of state bank notes, but in the spring of 1864, state banks were still able to resist their efforts.[64]

While the nation called for a tax on state bank notes, a more discreet monetary problem, involving only what appeared to be easily identified evil money manipulators, demanded immediate attention. By 1864, gold speculation had become the Treasury's most pressing problem. Although importers and merchants had to buy gold to pay foreign debts and customs duties, speculation overshadowed legitimate trading in gold. As soon as the Treasury issued greenbacks, people began to invest in gold, trying to anticipate its rise and fall to make a profit. As in any stock or commodities transaction, the gold market was played by "bulls" who tried to drive the market up and by "bears" who tried to force it down. Investors speculated in gold futures, buying and selling gold they did not own, to be delivered in the future. "Gold, gold, gold, gold,—hoarded, bartered, bought, and sold" became the wartime cry, one man remembered.[65]

Speculators in gold threatened the wartime Union in fundamental ways. The "feverish speculation in gold in Wall Street" had "unsettle[d] values in the whole of the country," wrote the editor of the San Francisco *Daily Alta California*. Republicans believed that as traders manipulated the price of gold the worth of currency shifted inversely. Gold had a "fixed, determinate value," explained Fessenden, but its "nominal value" fluctuated under the efforts of dealers in the money market. The belief that gold trading unsettled values profoundly disturbed Republicans, since erratic gold prices challenged the theory that labor generated all value. Value had come untied from labor and was being manipulated by speculators.[66]

Republicans believed that gold speculation undermined the proper functioning of the economy. Each man's efforts to accumulate as much as he could by his own labor would enrich the nation, but the huge profits to be made by speculating discouraged productive labor. "Speculation is taking the place of sober and persevering industry," wrote the Comptroller of the Currency, "and thousands are deluded with the notion that the wealth of the nation is being increased by the increase of its indebtedness."[67]

Speculation also had political repercussions, actively hurting the war effort by depreciating greenbacks and Union bonds, thus weakening Union credit.[68] This political aspect of gold trading tainted speculators with disloyalty to the government. It could only hurt their reputation that the Gold Room, the center of New York gold trading, received heavy "bull" orders from Washington, Baltimore, and Louisville, Kentucky, all of which were close to the South and associated with strongly secessionist operators. One veteran of the Gold Room remembered that Southerners frequented the exchange. Having watched Confederate currency plummet, they had come North to cash in when greenbacks did the same. Union victories sent gold down, Confederate victories did the opposite, and news from the battlefields could turn the Gold Room into "a den of wild beasts." Following battle news, one man wrote:

> Men leaped upon chairs, waved their hands, or clenched their fists; shrieked, shouted; the bulls whistled "Dixie," and the bears sung "John Brown"; the crowd swayed feverishly from door to door, and, as the fury mounted to white heat, and the tide of gold fluctuated up and down in rapid sequence, brokers seemed animated with the impulses of demons, hand to hand combats took place, and bystand-

ers, peering through the smoke and dust, could liken the wild turmoil only to the revels of maniacs.

Republicans believed that Southern speculators conspired to help crush the Union. For years, Greeley wrote in the New York *Daily Tribune,* Jefferson Davis had instructed his agents in New York City to drive up the price of gold. These agents believed "that they were aiding the Rebellion as truly and palpably as though they were wielding muskets in the front ranks of Lee's army."[69]

Gold speculation pointedly illustrated the control financiers exercised over the nation, and Republicans across the country begged the government to end the practice. The administration and Congress sought to oblige, believing that without the machinations of traders to drive gold up and greenbacks down, the currency would stabilize close to par, and the economic and political damage of fluctuating currency would abate. In April 1864, Chase attempted to break the market by ceasing to require gold for customs duties and by selling gold from the Treasury. Gold dropped. Quickly, though, the government found itself in need of coin from the customs to pay the interest on government bonds, and the gold market rebounded.[70]

"The price of gold must and shall come down," Chase wrote to Greeley, "or I'll quit and let somebody else try." In order to reduce gold prices, the Secretary decided to take a groundbreaking step. Chase determined to extend the economic activity of the government in an entirely new direction; he would use the national government to regulate gold transactions, thus protecting the public interest from speculators. Hoping to break the market through legislation, as other Republicans advocated, he sent to Congress a bill that Sherman introduced to the Senate on April 15, 1864. The measure (S. 106) outlawed the Gold Room and barred trading in gold futures under penalty of a fine or a prison term or both. Revealing that it promoted national control of the currency and banking systems, the bill stipulated that only greenbacks or national currency, not state bank notes, could be exchanged for gold.[71]

The object of this extraordinary bill, Sherman said as he introduced it, was not to stop legitimate exchange of gold but to "prevent gambling" in it. Speculation was vicious and notorious, "disreputable and dishonorable, and men who have regard for their characters will not be seen going and engaging in it," he insisted. Opponents of the bill, shocked at its unprecedented authorization of government interference in economic affairs, denied Congress's right to meddle with private contracts. Fessenden, however, backed Sherman and explained that the North's huge new national markets had broken down traditional checks and made many Republicans willing to take this novel step. Public opinion should have shamed speculators out of business, he said, but "in a great commercial mart like New York," the people could not exert proper pressure and the government must use its influence for the public good.[72]

Opposition to the striking new measure paled before Republican anger at speculators. "Traitors who have not the courage to face the Federal soldiers are now engaged, cowardly, assassin-like, in stabbing our country through our national currency in the hells of the city of New York," stormed one Western Republican, and enough senators agreed with him to pass the gold bill in mid-April. The count was 23 to 17: twenty-two Republicans and one California Democrat voted aye; eight Democrats, one Old-Line Whig, and eight Republicans voted nay.

House Democrats blocked the measure for almost two months. When it finally came up on June 7, defenders of state banks and opponents of this great expansion of national government authority attacked it as unconstitutional and barely failed to kill it. When the price of gold immediately soared, the House suddenly passed the bill, with no discussion, on June 14. All but one of the majority votes came from Republicans, while only seven party members joined the Democratic opposition.[73]

Lincoln signed the bill on June 17, 1864, and the law took effect on June 21. With this bill, passed hastily in outrage at gold speculation, the Republicans tried for the first time to expand the national government's role to regulate the economy for the purpose of protecting the public from specific economic harm. Their efforts failed as trading continued without the legitimacy of legality, and the price of gold jumped from 198 to at least 250. Unofficial reports put it as high as 300 as legitimate traders and bears shunned gold trading and thus ceased to counteract the gold bulls.[74]

On June 22, Maryland Democrat Reverdy Johnson introduced to the Senate a bill to repeal the gold act. He explained that businessmen had asked him to kill the ill-conceived and mischievous law. The Senate immediately passed the repeal, although thirteen Republicans still supported the measure. Despite Hooper's objections, a Democrat managed to bring the repeal into the House on July 1. It passed quickly by an overwhelming vote. The minority was solidly Republican, with key proponents of government control of the currency either voting nay or conspicuously absent.[75]

Lincoln signed the repeal on July 2, 1864, only two weeks after the gold act had passed. The Republicans' attempt to assume full control over the currency by actively using the government to protect the public interest from a specific economic threat had flopped, and the method would not be retried. In the future, the government would attempt to manipulate the market only by inducing cooperative capitalists to buy and sell gold quietly at opportune times. Despite the failure of this attempt to broaden the scope of the government's role in the economy, however, the debate over the gold bill had a lasting effect on public support for the national control of currency and banking. Newspaper articles and congressional speeches had identified defenders of state banks with tremendously unpopular gold speculators. The supporters of national control, it seemed, fought a disloyal band of wealthy men.[76]

With the failure of the gold act, Union finances in July 1864 were at their most serious crisis of the war years. News from the battlefields was grim: Grant was stalled before Richmond after leaving horrific numbers of dead from the Wilderness to Petersburg; Confederate Jubal Early threatened Washington. William Tecumseh Sherman was approaching Atlanta, but had won no major victories and was sustaining heavy losses. For the presidency, the Democrats pressed General George B. McClellan, who hoped to turn his general popularity into political victory. Despite his hard-money roots, Chase had issued $450 million worth of greenbacks, and the price of gold had become exorbitant. About to adjourn for the summer, Congress was "getting restive and discontented with the financial management" as the country tottered on the brink of financial panic. Chase's resignation at this unpropitious moment made some Republicans conclude he foresaw the Union's financial collapse.[77]

Lincoln's drafting of William Pitt Fessenden to replace Chase took into consideration the fact that Fessenden's steady, intelligent financial conservatism made him one of the few leaders in the country who could calm the money market. After he accepted the post, a string of battlefield victories joined with the efforts of helpful capitalists to break the price of gold, and the plague of speculation became less devastating. The Republicans turned back to the taxation of state bank notes to stabilize greenbacks and also to get the national banking system on its feet, hoping that when the North won the war, gold speculation would stop, paper would return to par, and the eventual return to specie payments would stabilize values permanently.[78]

In late 1864, the administration turned again to the constitutionally unremarkable idea of a bank note tax. In his December message to Congress, Lincoln strongly hinted that the Treasury needed such a measure to function. Treasury Secretary Fessenden also asked for "discriminating legislation" to force the withdrawal of state bank notes, although he did not advocate "unfriendly or severe measures likely to embarrass the business of the country." The national government must control the nation's currency, the Comptroller of the Currency wrote in his 1864 report. State banks must not "have the right to flood the country with their issues." In January 1865, Fessenden endorsed and forwarded to the Senate a currency bill drafted by the Comptroller to prevent national banks from circulating state bank notes.[79]

Congress finally imposed a tax on state bank notes as part of an 1865 revenue package. Debating a revenue bill (H.R. 744) in mid-February 1865, Hooper of Massachusetts suggested a tax of .25 percent per month on state bank notes until January 1, 1866, when the tax would increase to .5 percent. He did so, he said, to carry out the recommendations of the Secretary of the Treasury and the Comptroller of the Currency. "So long as State banks continue to issue circulation, it is intended to put a larger and disproportionate tax upon it."[80]

James F. Wilson of Iowa went a step farther and proposed prohibiting the circulation of state banks altogether after April 1, 1865. His solution was drastic but, he said, "the Government and the people need relief now, not next year." He was not trying to "make war upon any bank or any banking system," he said, but "while I am voting taxes on the people I want to make the money worth something more than it is, so as to prevent as far as practicable an unnecessary accumulation of the national debt." Hooper opposed Wilson because his proposal was "too sharp upon the banks."

New York City Democrats, who wanted both to protect their local bankers and to oppose the Republican policy of centralization, led the attack on the proposed state bank note tax. "What right have we to blot out State banks?" demanded James Brooks. Such a measure explicitly attacked state power, he said. Warning against a strong national government, he argued that Congress was usurping the traditional powers of the state legislatures. Brooks's colleague Francis Kernan tried a different approach: "if the national banks, with the great advantages which they enjoy, cannot compete successfully with the State banks," he remarked, "it simply shows that the latter subserve better the interests of the business community, and should not be destroyed." The banks have "been fairly and honestly doing great service," added New York Democrat John V. L. Pruyn, and they did not deserve to be taxed by a Republican "exercise of arbitrary power."

The House rejected Hooper's amendment, but then passed one proposed by Wilson placing a 10 percent tax on state bank circulation after January 1, 1866. The House adopted this measure by a vote of 64 to 62, with no discussion.

The Senate received the revenue bill two weeks before the close of the session on March 3, but Sherman, now the chairman of the Committee on Finance, could not introduce it until the evening of February 27. Sherman stressed the importance of the proposed tax on state bank notes, claiming that it would compel their withdrawal. "The power of taxation cannot be more wisely exercised than in harmonizing and nationalizing and placing on the secure basis of national credit all the money of the country," he declared. Whether or not they had voted for the national bank bill, other Republicans echoed Sherman's assertion that the Congress must either repeal the banking law or contract the circulation of state banks.[81]

In two debates on the measure, Democrats stressed the evils and the unconstitutionality of the Republican policy of nationalization, a theme that they emphasized increasingly stridently throughout the war years. The state bank note tax, and indeed the whole Republican financial system, were "devised in the evil spirit of ambition by one who sought by the centralization of power and force here in the Federal Government to make himself strong enough to wield this as an empire," said one. "The result of this course of legislation is utterly to destroy all the rights of the States," claimed Kentucky Democrat Lazarus Powell. "It is asserting a power which if carried out to its logical result would enable the national Congress to destroy every institution of the States and cause all power to be consolidated and concentrated here."

Despite Democratic condemnation of the Republicans' policy of centralization, on March 1, 1865, the Senate refused to strike the bank note tax by a vote of 20 to 22. One California Democrat joined twenty-one Republicans to keep the tax, while six of the twelve

Republicans who joined the opposition came from New England or New York. On March 2, opponents of the tax made a last, unsuccessful attempt to kill it. Only one senator changed his vote from the previous day. Lincoln signed the revenue bill, with the state bank note tax, on March 3. Although Lincoln's second inauguration overshadowed the passage of the bill, it was a critical final step in the Republican nationalization of the country's finances.

With their currency and banking system, the Republicans had both promoted and codified the Union government's growing strength, but in centralizing the country's financial system, Republican congressmen had gone farther than Chase originally intended. Republicans who wanted to tie banks to the government saw the greenbacks only as an emergency wartime measure and believed that, upon their disappearance, the national currency, based on private capital invested in government bonds and redeemable in gold, would come into its own. But the war had confirmed many Western Republicans' loathing of bankers, and they liked the greenbacks. They believed the government notes were the people's money, for they thought, as Fessenden originally explained, that they were based simply on Americans' ability to labor. They joined with other groups, like entrepreneurs and certain businessmen, to oppose the postwar contraction that the Republican party officially embraced. People had worried about the greenbacks initially, said an Indiana Republican congressman to his constituents in late 1864, "but I tell you today that I do not come across any man, whatever his politics may be, who does not grab at a greenback like a duck at a worm."[82]

After the war, Westerners' initial willingness to accept national banks for the secure currency they offered would crumble as the mismanagement of state bank conversions placed most of the national currency in the East. Meanwhile, as Sherman had unhappily foreseen, the pyramid system of currency redemption, adopted at the insistence of Westerners who demanded a secure currency, made New York the nation's money capital. In the postwar years, Westerners would reject the national currency notes and, adopting the class language developed during the war by the Democrats, would struggle to make the greenbacks the nation's money. The tensions between the West and the East over the two monetary systems would help create a political movement, foment social unrest, and foster financial confusion.[83]

4 | "Directing the Legislation of the Country to the Improvement of the Country": Tariff and Tax Legislation

The condition of the country is singular . . . I venture to say it is an anomaly in the history of the world. What do the people of the United States ask of this Congress? To take off taxes? No, sir, they ask you to put them on. The universal cry of this people is to be taxed.

—John P. Hale, 1864

Bond and currency legislation, as well as the war itself, required sweeping revenue measures to secure the Union's debt. Republicans formed revenue legislation not only to raise money, however, but also to promote domestic economic growth. As party members attempted to make the national finances increasingly dependent on the common man, they drew on their economic beliefs to seek ways in which they could encourage individual labor and foster production to increase wealth. The economic designs of party members created new precedents for the government. While Republican banking and currency legislation had permanently strengthened the Union government by increasing its control over the nation's financial system, Republican revenue legislation carried the economic power of the government a step further. During the war, Republicans used Congress's constitutional authority to levy taxes and set tariffs in innovative ways, which expanded the national government's role in the economy.

Republican wartime revenue legislation followed a long history of American tariff debate. Together with proceeds from the sale of public lands, tariffs, which were duties on imported goods, were the primary source of national revenue before the war. While everyone agreed that some tariffs were imperative for revenue, a battle arose during the nineteenth century over so-called protective duties. Those who believed that high tariffs on manufactured goods would encourage domestic industry and ultimately reduce the cost of manufactures fought free traders, who believed that protection only raised consumer prices for the benefit of manufacturers while offering no correspondingly higher prices for unprotected agricultural products. This debate pitted pro-tariff Whigs against free-trade Democrats, and generally set manufacturing regions in the Northeast against agricultural regions in the South and West. No corresponding political debate over taxes informed Republican revenue measures, for although Americans paid state and local taxes and land office fees, they had not paid a federal tax since the War of 1812.

In the mid-1850s, the Republicans hesitated to take a strong position on tariffs, for they needed to attract support from pro-tariff states, such as Pennsylvania, without alienating Democrats who were defecting to their standard. The Panic of 1857 and the ensuing depression permitted Republicans to develop a tariff stance, however, for many people blamed the panic on the low tariff a Democratic Congress had passed in 1857. Further, the recession had reduced imports and resulted in the Treasury's running a deficit, making an increase in revenue vital to the nation.[1] While hard-line free traders maintained that an increase in tariffs would reduce revenue by excluding imports, by early 1860, even President Buchanan, a Democrat, had decided that judicious tariffs might raise revenue with no adverse effects on imports, and had requested at least a minor tariff increase.[2]

In the spring of 1860, citing the need for revenue to bolster an indebted Treasury, Justin Smith Morrill brought before Congress a sweeping tariff bill (H.R. 338) designed to attract voters from both parties and all regions at the same time that it established a firm Republican stand on tariff legislation.[3] Morrill was particularly well suited to develop a new system of tariffs that would appeal to many different groups of Americans, for he bridged the worlds of business and agriculture: he had made his fortune in trade and commerce while he hailed from the small agricultural state of Vermont. His attitudes about tariffs were not, as a colleague recalled, "biased by a sectional feeling or the interests of his constituents." Morrill's reputation for honesty and good judgment would also help him to convince skeptical listeners of his good intentions.[4]

Morrill wrote his bill in part to woo pro-tariff Pennsylvania to the Republican ticket in the 1860 election, but he was not simply championing traditional protectionism. The Morrill Tariff bill was the first statement of a new protectionism peculiar to the Republicans. At the heart of the plan was the idea articulated by Francis Wayland and Henry Charles Carey that manufacturing, agriculture, labor, and all other economic interests interacted harmoniously and positively unless government unduly favored one or another. "The plow, the loom, and the anvil," as one man wrote in a letter to a Boston newspaper, had a "reciprocal influence." Morrill, who maintained contact with Carey throughout the debates on the bill, believed that tariff laws, if they were adjusted to encourage growth in all sectors of the economy, could be used to benefit all members of society.[5]

In order to spread the benefits of tariffs to all economic interests, Morrill reworked the traditional structure on which earlier American tariffs had been based. Traditional protectionism, as Americans understood it from their observation of England and France, required high tariffs on manufactured commodities while it dictated the free import of raw materials, including agricultural products. The theory behind this system maintained that cheap wool, coal, hemp, and so on would keep manufacturing costs low, enabling the nation to produce manufactures cheaply for the domestic market and to export excess manufactured goods at great profit, while tariffs on foreign manufactured commodities would insure that young domestic industries could develop without competition.[6]

Planning to distribute the benefits of a tariff to all sectors of the economy, and also hoping to broaden support for his party, Morrill rejected the traditional system of protection by proposing tariff duties on agricultural, mining, and fishing products, as well as on manufactures. Sugar, wool, flaxseed, hides, beef, pork, corn, grain, hemp, wool, and minerals would all be protected by the Morrill Tariff. The duty on sugar might well be expected to appease Southerners opposed to tariffs, and, notably, wool and flaxseed production were growing industries in the West. The new tariff bill also would protect coal, lead, copper, zinc, and other minerals, all of which the new northwestern states were beginning to produce. The Eastern fishing industry would receive a duty on dried, pickled, and salted fish. "In adjusting the details of a tariff," Morrill explained with a rhetorical flourish in his introduction of the bill, "I would treat agriculture, manufactures, mining, and commerce, as I would our whole people—as members of one family, all entitled to equal favor, and no one to be made the beast of burden to carry the packs of others." Attacking the traditional belief that tariffs benefited manufacturing at the expense of agriculture, Morrill and his colleagues tried to write a tariff that would, as Carey explained, spread prosperity "like the sunshine, upon every class and condition in life."

Advocates of the bill went to great lengths to explain how the new plan would benefit everyone in the nation. Relying heavily on the idea that every economic group in society shared a harmony of interest, party members argued that the strengthening of all sectors of the economy would benefit laborers, farmers, and manufacturers alike. Development would help the critical element of the economy, workers; it would support the fundamental base of society, agriculture; and it would benefit the mature stage of the economy, manufacturing.

One Republican's speech on the Morrill Tariff bill revealed the degree to which party members would argue that the bill benefited workers; it began: "I rise to advocate the rights of labor." Party members argued that a strong economy would guarantee that laborers were fully employed at fair wages that reflected the real value of labor. One representative's contention that "the steady employment of the masses should be the first care of every Christian and enlightened Government" had a great effect on his listeners, whose constituents were suffering in a recession. The collapse of domestic manufacturing in 1857 had thrown people out of work and destroyed wage scales. "The humble sons of toil" had been petitioning Congress, complaining that the previous tariff act had undermined "the value and price of [a man's] labor, which is his only capital for the comfortable maintenance of his family, and the education of his children."

The potential benefit to labor was an old argument for a protective tariff, but it gained great power in the debates over the Morrill Tariff as Republicans implied a parallel between free labor without a protective tariff and Southern slavery. Unless domestic industry recovered, the Republicans darkly threatened, American labor would be at the mercy of foreign manufacturers. The Republican image of Northern labor held in thrall by "British monopoly" dovetailed effectively with the sectional speeches against slavery that frequently interrupted the tariff debates. The alternative to the tariff was an acknowledgement of British supremacy and a sentence of hard manual labor, one speaker hinted. This threat cut to the quick a labor theory of value, for once a man's labor belonged to someone else, the whole Republican economic theory of labor, capital, and progress fell to pieces. "We are a nation of laborers," said an Ohio man, "and that

policy which shall best secure the interest of labor—our own labor—
and promote the prosperity and happiness of the whole people, should
be adopted and steadily maintained."[7]

Proponents of the Morrill Tariff also claimed that it would benefit
the previously neglected field of agriculture. The plan offered protection to farmers similar to the protection it gave to manufacturers,
party members explained, for by excluding foreign agricultural produce, it would encourage the development of the agricultural sector.
Advocates pointed proudly to the new duties on flaxseed and wool,
which would protect increasingly important products of the West, but
they acknowledged that most other agricultural products stood in
little need of protection, for America exported, rather than imported,
grain. Further undercutting the idea that the plan offered farmers
the identical protection it gave to industry, the bill placed a duty of
10 percent on all unenumerated raw materials, while unenumerated
manufactured goods bore duties of 20 percent.

Still, farmers needed a strong tariff system, Republicans insisted,
for the successful farmer depended on manufacturing tariffs as well
as agricultural ones. "Any one who has lived in the vicinity of a
manufacturing city or village," said one man, "knows the disastrous
influence of a stoppage of its industrial establishments on the interests
of the farmers of the surrounding country." In such a situation, he
maintained, demand for agricultural products dropped precipitously,
forcing farmers either to sell at ruinous prices or to send their produce
at great expense to distant markets. An Ohio Republican delivered a
speech entitled "Mutual Interest of the Farmer and Manufacturer,"
describing how the adversity of the manufacturing industry in his
district after the Panic of 1857 had crippled the farmers and broken
down every other occupation. An increased tariff would bolster
manufacturing, he declared, which would result in the hiring of more
laborers, who would eat more agricultural products. Everyone would
garner "increased wealth and prosperity." The New York *Daily Tribune* circulated a pamphlet expanding on this simple equation. It began
by pointing out that tariffs reduced competition in agriculture as men
went to work in manufactures, and ranged farther afield until it finally
argued that tariffs prevented soil depletion by keeping crop refuse in
America to replenish the soil from which the crops had grown. The
Republican party's position on the tariff, the pamphlet concluded,
demonstrated that "in it and it alone, lies the hope of American
agriculture."[8]

The emphasis on a growing American economy made it clear that an element of nationalism informed the new Republican tariff stance. Party members frankly announced that they intended the Morrill Tariff actively to develop the nation and make it independent of most foreign products. "That country is most independent, and consequently most prosperous," insisted one speaker, "which produces within her own borders all articles needful for the use of her citizens." As advocates of the bill maintained was proper for "a wholesome and beneficent system of revenue laws," Morrill had designed the new tariff system explicitly to foster American industry, in the broad sense of the word. Calling on his colleagues to support the bill, Pennsylvania's James H. Campbell cried: "Men of Missouri, men of Michigan, men from all the iron-bearing States, men of the whole land, will you not unite with us in developing the vast resources of the country?"

The development of the nation was nominally, at least, only the second object of the tariff, however; it must first raise revenue, and Morrill had designed a new system to spread the burdens of a tariff equitably throughout society. Old tariff systems set ad valorem duties—that is, fees equaling a percentage of an object's price—on a few products. But these ad valorem duties had two drawbacks. First, they were highly susceptible to fraud, for importers could claim low valuations for their products and sell them later at higher prices. Second, a system that placed high tariffs on just a few items distributed the burden of tariffs only to the handful of consumers who bought the few duted items—assuming, as Republicans did, that the laws of commerce ultimately passed any fees attached to a product on to consumers.

Objecting to a system of revenue that placed all its burdens on a few people, for this amounted to economic folly in the shape of legislation against one economic group, Morrill instituted specific charges on a wide range of commodities. His bill cut the free list, and, in addition to various enumerated duties on certain products, it established three categories of other taxable items. At 10 percent the bill duted items that Republicans deemed necessary to most people, including furs, fruit, ammonia, brass, cornmeal, and barley; at 20 percent it duted less necessary items, such as castor oil, catgut, whale oil, skins, spices and strychnine, among other things; finally, at 30 percent the bill duted luxuries, such as jewelry, perfumes, carriages, clocks, dolls, toys, silk, marble, and painted velvet. Morrill believed that this system would impose duties on virtually all consumers according to their ability to pay.[9]

The debate over the Morrill Tariff not only allowed Morrill and his supporters to expound the policy that would shape the next five years of revenue legislation, but also permitted Democratic members of the House, primarily from the South, to begin unwittingly to undermine the effectiveness of Northern Democratic opposition to later Republican wartime revenue measures. Democrats tried desperately to defeat the tariff, both because they disliked protective measures and because they recognized that the bill would attract key voters to the Republicans in the 1860 election. This stand against the bill made it easy for Republicans, who pressed the bill as an imperative revenue measure, to label their opponents as disloyal to the government. The tainting accusation of disloyalty would seriously weaken Democratic opposition to Republican measures for years to come.

The tariff bill passed the House on May 10, 1860, after some sharp parliamentary maneuvering by John Sherman and after most Republicans—a large number of them Westerners—rallied to it. The Southern-dominated Senate, however, blocked the bill. Preparing a political platform for the election of 1860, Republicans hesitated to force Westerners to accept a strong tariff plank, but, after great pressure from pro-tariff men, party leaders finally endorsed the policies of the Morrill Tariff. The Republicans' platform declared that tariffs should not only provide government revenue, but also "encourage the development of the industrial interests of the whole country," thus, as it said, securing liberal wages to working men and good prices to farmers while fostering commerce. After the Republicans won the election—capturing the pivotal high-tariff state of Pennsylvania—and the Southern senators left Washington, the bill passed and became law on March 2, 1861.[10]

The Morrill Tariff furnished the basis for Republican wartime tariff policy; as party member James G. Blaine wrote in his history of the period, it "radically changed the policy of our customs duties . . . and put the nation in the attitude of self-support in manufactures." The new law created a novel tariff system on which future Congresses could build. "The details of this act became the victim of the war," remembered one Republican, "but the general principles on which it was founded, the application of specific duties where possible, and the careful protection extended to the products of the soil and the mine, as well as of the workshop, have been maintained."[11]

Morrill's law, with its evident nationalism, also created tension between the North and England; this tension would mount over the next four years. Republicans had called aggressively for a policy designed to promote the American economy at the expense of foreign trade, and foreigners, not surprisingly, objected. The French believed that the tariff would impoverish their industry, and the English, furious at the new law, rushed goods to America before it went into effect. In New York, foreign agents agitated against the new tariff. These European reactions drew Northern anger, and newspapers quickly called for a boycott of British goods. At the end of 1861, Indianapolis newspaper carriers treated their patrons to a poem about the year's events, and after fulminations about the British, they concluded:

> So let them come on, and force us to declare, if
> They can, that we soon will abolish our tariff.
> Our tariff is Morrill, what's *moral* is right,
> And we'll stand up for that, if we *do* have to fight.[12]

Southern states had begun leaving the Union even before the Morrill Tariff passed, and the war, which started shortly thereafter, committed the Republicans to developing an extensive revenue system. Fond of quoting Hamilton's statement that "the creation of debt should always be accompanied with the means of extinguishment" in order to make public credit "immortal," Republicans were anxious not only to pay military suppliers and troops, but also to support the bond issues Treasury Secretary Chase began in March 1861.[13] Only four months after President Buchanan had signed the Morrill Tariff Act, the special session of the Thirty-Seventh Congress began the search for revenue to fund the war effort. In his report to the session, Chase stated that the government would need around $320 million for the 1861–1862 fiscal year. One-quarter of that amount could be raised by taxation, he suggested, but the rest must come from increased import duties.[14]

Ex-Democrat Chase had held tightly to his free-trade beliefs until 1860 and, not surprisingly, his suggestions for raising revenue relied on America's past experience with war tariffs rather than on Morrill's comprehensive new tariff plan. During the War of 1812, Secretary of the Treasury Albert Gallatin had supported tariffs on sugar, tea, and coffee, and Chase urged that Congress repeat these war measures. Anxious to begin the revenue process, the Committee of Ways and Means, which was reputed to have been stacked with pro-tariff men and on which Morrill sat, quickly reported a bill placing such duties. Discussion of the bill (H.R. 54) began on July 17, 1861.[15]

Democrats used the proposed tariff to attack the Republican policy embodied in the Morrill Tariff, but, paradoxically, their assaults served only to strengthen the Republicans' new tariff policy. Opposition leader Clement L. Vallandigham of Ohio at first ignored Chase's proposals and challenged the Morrill Tariff by proposing essentially to reinstate the tariff of 1857. While Republicans thought that higher tariffs would both raise money and energize the economy to break the economic recession of the last few years, Vallandigham made it clear that the Democrats wanted lower tariffs to prevent undue burdening of those the recession had left poor or unemployed. He also insisted that lower tariffs would raise more revenue by fostering imports. Then, recognizing that Chase's suggested tariffs launched a policy different from that of the Morrill Tariff, Vallandigham used to the bill at hand to complete his portrait of the Republicans as wealthy men burdening the poor while leaving their own fortunes untouched. Vallandigham said he objected to the new bill because he opposed dutying items that were "among the necessaries of life." Such tariffs would unduly burden the poor, he said, and amounted to favoritism of the rich.[16]

From his position as chairman of the Committee on Ways and Means, Morrill's close friend Thaddeus Stevens defended the Morrill Tariff, countered Vallandigham's charge that the new tariffs were intended to benefit the rich, and concluded by branding as disloyal Democrats who opposed Republican revenue policies. Insisting that the bill was solely a revenue measure, Stevens defended the tariff on necessities by explaining that, since the articles mentioned were the most widely used, they would produce the most revenue. The bill was imperative to sustain the war effort, Stevens declared, and he asked Vallandigham to declare "what objection he has . . . if he desires that the Government shall be sustained in the prosecution of this war?"

Despite Democratic opposition and a notable lack of enthusiasm for the tariff hike from Republicans representing the agricultural regions of the border states, the tariff bill passed the House on July 18, 1861, the day after debate on it had begun. The ayes were sufficient that no one asked for a roll-call vote. Public reaction to the plan mirrored the congressional debate. Only two days after the bill passed the House, a Western Republican warned a senator that the price of the duties items was already rising and that the plan "will take thousands of votes from us." The editor of an Eastern newspaper, however, reviewed the legislation and cheerfully agreed that a tariff on necessities would raise the most revenue.[17]

The House turned next to a tax bill (H.R. 71). Unlike tariffs, national taxation did not play a part in the initial Republican program to build the country, and the Republicans never intended it to continue beyond the time of absolute wartime necessity. Following Wayland and Carey, Republicans feared and hated internal taxation, for they believed that unfettered accumulation of private property enriched the nation by creating a strong incentive to labor. As a writer for the Boston *Daily Evening Transcript* declared axiomatically: "All taxes are pernicious which interfere fatally with the creation of wealth."[18]

Despite Republican reluctance, however, the war demanded national taxation. In their inexperience and haste the Committee of Ways and Means turned, as Chase had, to the laws that Gallatin had employed during the War of 1812, and this first, unsuccessful tax proposal helped to direct Republican ideas about raising revenue. The House tax bill echoed the 1813 and 1815 direct taxes that were apportioned by state according to population, and which were almost always assessed on land. Still new to the idea of a strong national government, the committee proposed a system of federal collectors to gather the tax, but permitted states to collect and deliver the tax themselves if they so desired.[19]

Even desperate need for revenue could not rally all Republicans to a direct tax and federal tax collectors. In 1861, Gallatin's system of direct taxation made less sense than it had some five decades before. Levying taxes on land would shift the burden of taxation from wealthy nonlandowning businessmen toward landowners, and Western farmers could be certain that they would pay more tax than most businessmen in Northeastern cities. Republicans from primarily agricultural states led the opposition to the imposition of a direct land tax, although they were joined by a significant number of men from other regions, notably economist Carey. A land tax was "all wrong and [would] divide the country," an Ohio man insisted. In Congress, Schuyler Colfax of Indiana, Owen Lovejoy of Illinois, and James Ashley of Ohio argued that a direct tax "must fall with very heavy, if not ruinous effect, upon the great agricultural States of the West and Southwest" and led the fight to adjust the tax burden to bear on wealthier manufacturing states. They insisted that land should not bear taxes until merchandise, personal property, and income did. "Tax all property alike," agreed a man writing to Washington from Ohio.[20]

Many other Republicans who, out of their longstanding fears of government monopoly of power, regarded expansion of the national government with suspicion, doubted the wisdom of using federal tax collectors. "It will be a horrid thing to have a crew of Federal tax gatherers quartered upon us," wrote one man. "I . . . dread and deplore the extension of the patronage and influence of the Federal Government . . . *That* government will always be corrupt and corrupting." While opponents of the national collection proposal doubted both the constitutionality of federal tax collectors and the need for creating a national system of tax collection when state systems already existed, congressmen also wanted to protect state sovereignty and their own state patronage networks.[21]

Ultimately, the need for revenue outweighed objections to the House tax bill; it passed the House in late July 1861. But Republican objections to the direct tax and party members' initial reluctance to strengthen the national government would help the Senate to shape a novel approach to the tax issue.

Not waiting for the House to finish with its tax bill, which never reached the Senate floor, the Senate took up the House tariff bill on July 25 and quickly indicated that it intended to boost Morrill's new tariff policy. The Senate adopted a substitute to the House bill, which lowered the House's proposed duty on coffee and sugar and replaced the lost revenue by increasing the existing Morrill Tariff rates on other commodities by 10 percent.[22] Although the Senate manager of the bill, James F. Simmons of Rhode Island, insisted that the tariff hike was solely a revenue device and not intended for protection at all, this bill, which would raise duties on agricultural as well as manufactured imports, revealed that war needs would promote the tariff system Morrill had launched in 1860. Indeed, the need for war revenue opened the way for higher tariff duties. Advocates of protection foresaw that the war would require "adequate" tariffs, and viewed this as "a good flowing from it far greater than all the evils the war can entail." In April, even the New York *Times,* which had not supported the Morrill Tariff, declared that all differences over tariff policy were erased by the war. "Self-preservation demands that domestic industry should be encouraged in every way," its editor declared. "Large numbers of people are suffering from want of work, and no one can question that it is our duty to employ them, in preference to the operatives in Europe."[23]

As the New York *Times* indicated, the North's growing irritation at England helped sell the Republicans' higher tariffs. The murmurs that England had caused by its opposition to the Morrill Tariff swelled into clamors when English financiers refused to invest in Union war bonds. In July 1861, when Charles Sumner, chairman of the Committee on Foreign Affairs, who had traveled widely in Europe and who maintained ties there, suggested that Congress should take care not to offend England when enacting tariffs, Finance Committee Chairman Fessenden exploded. "What right has a foreign country to make any question about what we choose to do," he demanded, echoing the angry tone of Northern newspapers. The needs of America should come first; any pressure from Europe was "an insult." When Sumner proposed to strike the 10 percent tariff, he found himself marooned in a minority of 7 against a majority of 29. All of his supporters were Democrats.[24]

Disturbed by the House's indecisive wrangling over its direct tax measure, Simmons had ventured into new waters and proposed a striking income tax amendment to the tariff bill as soon as he had introduced it. Different states had experimented with income taxes, but a federal income tax had never been seriously considered. Hoping to avoid property taxes, which had attracted such opposition in the House, Simmons recommended a 5 percent tax on annual incomes exceeding $1,000. This, he felt, represented a good living in 1861. Fessenden enthusiastically seconded Simmons's proposal, even though the proposed income tax would fall most heavily on the Atlantic states, one of which he represented. Almost echoing House Democrat Vallandigham, Fessenden conceded that the poor would feel more heavily than the rich the proposed tariffs on tea, coffee, and sugar, precisely because the tariff would fall evenly on all. An income tax would mean that "the burdens will be more equalized on all classes of the community, more especially on those who are able to bear them."[25]

Senate Republicans endorsed the expansion of the Morrill Tariff policy and accepted the attempt to equalize monetary burdens through a novel income tax, while Democrats continued to attack Republican willingness to force war funds from the poor instead of from "the politicians . . . and the property holders," who had presumably begun the war and "should pay the expenses of it." The Senate version of the tariff bill, including its income tax provisions, narrowly passed by a vote of 22 to 18 at the end of July 1861.

When the House refused to accede to the Senate amendments, the two bodies appointed a conference committee. The committee's report, which assembled different provisions from the House tariff bill, the House tax bill, and the Senate amendments to the House tariff bill, reflected the development of the Republican revenue system. From the House tariff bill, the report retained the duties on sugar, tea, and coffee that Chase had taken from Gallatin's system, although it also included new duties on liquor. From the House tax bill, the committee took a $20 million direct tax and permitted states to collect the tax themselves if they wished. This reflected Gallatin's system, but the Republicans also provided their own, new system of national tax collection. The deferment of the collection of the tax until well into 1862 showed the Republicans' continuing reluctance to levy such a tax. Revealing the innovations that the Republicans would be forced to make, the report took the income tax provisions from the Senate amendments, although it reduced the rate to 3 percent and taxable income to $800. This tax would fall due on June 30, 1862, for the year ending on December 31, 1861.[26]

The debacle of the first battle of Bull Run and constant rumors of an attack on Washington made the dangers of an empty Treasury only too apparent. The Senate approved the report of the conference committee by a vote of 34 to 8, with no Republicans in the minority. Stevens pushed the report to a quick vote in the House, and it was adopted by a vote of 89 to 39, with only two Republicans in the opposition. One Western congressman who had voted aye nervously explained to his constituents that a tax was imperative to support the war effort. Morrill expressed the same idea more confidently: "I am sure the emergency really demands from us all we are doing," he wrote, "and that the mode is as just as can be devised—taken as a whole." President Lincoln signed the bill into law on August 5, 1861.[27]

On December 9, 1861, only four months after Lincoln had signed the 1861 revenue measure, Chase told the newly convened second session of the Thirty-Seventh Congress that his previous estimates of the funds necessary to conduct the war were woefully low. Turning again to Gallatin's precedent, he encouraged still higher tariffs on sugar, tea, and coffee, but acknowledged that even these duties would be insufficient. To find the necessary money, he advocated further borrowing and taxation.[28]

Congress quickly voted Chase the tariffs for which he asked, but this stopgap measure could only begin to meet the government's revenue needs. By January 1862, with millions of dollars of bonds issued and Union credit wavering, a sweeping tax bill seemed imperative. Republicans feared that unless the government showed a willingness to raise revenue by taxation, investors would doubt that their loans could ever be repaid and would cease to buy bonds. Citizens showered their representatives with pleas for taxation to preserve the public credit, and even conservative newspapers declared that "there is not the slightest objection raised in any loyal quarter to as much taxation as may be necessary." In January, Congress passed a joint resolution committing itself to levy a tax, which, with the higher tariff duties that Morrill promised, would secure an annual revenue of $150 million.[29]

The question, then, was not whether to levy a tax, but how to do so. The income tax was untested, and Gallatin's direct land tax system was clearly unpopular. Westerners frankly told their congressmen that it was folly to talk of another direct tax, and many Easterners agreed that land was overburdened. Men flocked to Washington to offer taxation advice to Congress, and newspapers were full of suggestions about how to levy a tax. The Committee on Ways and Means received so many bills advocating different methods of taxation that Morrill complained of the expense of printing them all.[30]

At the beginning of March 1862, from the Committee on Ways and Means, Stevens introduced the tax bill (H.R. 312) that would form the foundation for Republican wartime taxation. Revealing Morrill's hand in its development, the plan led the Republicans away from tradition toward a new scheme that complemented the Republican tariff system embodied in the Morrill Tariff. When passed, the sweeping new law, which covered seventeen triple-column pages in the *Congressional Globe,* imposed a 3 percent tax on domestic manufactures and created a new Internal Revenue Bureau in the Treasury Department to collect it. It also forced the licensing of different professions, instituted a two-tiered income tax, and taxed a wide variety of commodities and services—even circuses.[31]

The Republicans based their new revenue system on what they called "indirect taxes," which were invisible sums attached to consumer goods through taxes on manufacturing, collected from manufacturers. A 3 percent tax on manufactures in the form in which each product was usually consumed and in which it had the highest value, explained a member of the Ways and Means Committee, was a simple way to tax everything, for it would sweep in all raw materials except basic foodstuffs. It would neither hurt the poor by taxing food nor cripple industry by taxing raw materials directly and thus making manufacturers unable to compete with cheaper foreign production. Republicans intended that indirect taxes would replace "direct taxes," which were enumerated individual assessments such as poll taxes, assessments, and especially land taxes, which Westerners so angrily assailed as discriminating against them. "A burden that would paralyze the agriculturists of the country will be taken on to the backs of the steam giants with alacrity and confidence," Morrill predicted.[32]

Manufacturers railed against the new system of taxation, but the Ways and Means Committee knew that indirect taxation would not ruin industrial production. The new system would require the strengthening of domestic industry to enable manufacturing to bear the brunt of national taxation. The first consideration when framing a tax bill, Horace Greeley had reminded Congress in the New York *Daily Tribune,* was that "productive industry must be encouraged and stimulated, if possible, rather than burdened and paralyzed," and indirect taxation would indeed enable the Republicans to put to a positive use the necessary evil of taxation. Fitting nicely with Republican attempts to use tariffs to develop the country, this system would require high tariffs to protect the heavily taxed domestic industries from foreign competition.[33]

By spreading taxes to consumers, indirect taxes seemed to be a domestic mirror of Morrill's tariff duties. One newspaper editor advocating "a mature system of indirect taxation" actually called these taxes "internal duties," and a Ways and Means Committee member reflected "that such a [tax], judiciously arranged, would operate like a duty on imported goods, as a tax on the consumer." Like tariffs, Republicans believed, indirect taxation would help distribute the greatest financial burden to those most able to bear it, for the more a person bought, the more he or she would pay in tax. "The weight [of taxation] must be distributed equally," Morrill said, "not upon each man an equal amount, but a tax proportionate to his ability to pay."[34]

Beginning to consider the bill in mid-March, the House turned first to a key provision, which indicated the growing Republican trend toward a centralized national government: the proposed federal system of tax collection. After reassuring his colleagues that state revenue systems would remain intact under the new plan, Morrill vigorously denied the proposition that states had a constitutional right to collect federal taxes. He attacked the practicality of state collection and challenged his colleagues to imagine a disloyal state's contribution under such a system. Vehemently asserting the growing power of the national government, Morrill insisted that the government had a right to *"demand"* 99 percent of a man's property for an urgent necessity. When the public required it, he declared, "the property of the people . . . belongs to the Government."

Morrill's position did not reflect a unanimous Northern opinion. People across the Union worried about the "army of officials" a national tax collection system would create. Democrats assailed the proposed plan, and even some Republican newspapers asserted that it would be "a very popular measure" to leave tax collection to the states. The idea of federal control over its revenue had become strong enough to overshadow state interests, however; various Republicans supported Morrill and refuted assertions that it would be cheaper to rely on state tax collection, arguing that each state would have to revamp its old systems to handle the new taxes. Without a division, the House rejected a proposed amendment to the bill maintaining state tax control. At least one newspaper saw nothing but good in the decision for nationalization of tax collection. The Chicago *Tribune* suggested that such a high price of "blood and treasure" would bring to American citizens "a sense of personal responsibility in the safety and stability of the Nation."[35]

Republican establishment of national control of the new system did not mean the end of regional animosities in the North. At the end of March, after days of technical and minor amendments to the measure, a proposed tax on whiskey made congressmen from the lower Northwest lash out at the East and the upper West. Republican William D. Kellogg from the corn-producing state of Illinois protested the whiskey tax as a heavy burden on the agricultural lower Northwest area of the nation, proposed by those from the manufacturing Northeast.

Kellogg spoke for the agricultural region in the middle of the country, which produced the North's largest corn and tobacco crops. Resenting the culturally different upper North and East, people from this area believed that Northern manufacturers and businessmen schemed to unload financial burdens on them. Democrats and some Republicans from this region went a step further than Kellogg had, attacking Easterners and challenging the entire idea of indirect taxation. They argued that manufacturing taxes would fall unduly heavily on Western consumers. Instead of these indirect taxes, they suggested taxes placed directly on raw materials such as pig iron, coal, cotton, and potato starch, with the understanding that the taxes would fall primarily on manufacturers in the regions that produced the articles: Pennsylvania and New England. Congress rejected the Northwestern plan after a New England representative on the Committee on Ways and Means insisted that manufacturing taxes automatically included a tax on raw materials. He also correctly identified the new proposals as sectional attacks which, by taxing raw materials, introduced a completely different system of taxation from the committee's manufacturing taxes.[36]

Several factors prevented these Northwestern protests against the proposed tax measure from making headway in the House, despite general Republican sympathy for agricultural regions. Most farmers from the upper Northwest liked the new bill, for commodities made from wheat, their primary crop, were untaxed to encourage competition with Canadian wheat admitted to America free of duty under the 1854 Canadian Reciprocity Treaty. In addition, the aggressive Democratic champions of the "oppressed, plundered and suffering tax payers" of the West irritated party members and made them distrust tales of the area's woes. Republicans also knew that the Union's booming agricultural production was bringing large amounts of specie to the North through exports, and they assumed that the West was prospering. Further, party members knew that critical legislation designed to benefit the agricultural sector would soon come before the House and would probably pass. Finally, most Republicans believed, as Ohio representative Valentine B. Horton insisted in a speech designed to swing members of his region behind the bill, that the measure did not levy taxes on the farmer "to any greater extent than . . . upon other classes, and perhaps, not to so great an extent."

Party satisfaction that the bill did not discriminate against any portion of the agricultural sector, however, did not relieve Northwesterners' conviction that they suffered from discrimination, and this conviction would increasingly taint the Republicans' image. Republicans Kellogg of Illinois and William Dunn of southern Indiana continued to complain in frustration that "they tax everything in the West that a farmer can raise" and then manufacturers say that "we outside barbarians" must pay the taxes. "Corn is our 'peculiar institution,'" Dunn declared, and "the corn-growing sections" must join together for their own interests.[37]

In early April, the House took up a third potentially controversial aspect of the bill, the income tax provision. This measure called for a 3 percent tax on yearly income over $600, which the Republicans claimed was a good living in 1862. Morrill apologized for maintaining the "inquisitorial" and "one of the least desirable" taxes of the previous session and claimed that the income tax was proposed only to make sure that no one could avoid a share of taxation. Morrill was also aware that indirect taxation could go only so far in allocating a fair share of taxes to the wealthy, for all families, poor or rich, needed the same basic commodities. The rich paid more than the poor only if they bought luxury goods. Attempting to raise all of the necessary wartime revenue from indirect taxes on basic goods would drive poor families into destitution. Stevens further explained that the committee had kept the income tax because its members thought "it would be manifestly unjust to allow the large money operators and wealthy merchants, whose incomes might reach hundreds of thousands of dollars, to escape from their due proportion of the burden."

Republicans from across the North had advocated an income tax for the reasons Morrill explained in Congress, and no one had much to say in opposition to the one the committee proposed. The anxiety some Republicans expressed came from a worry that the tax would fall unevenly. The Philadelphia *Daily Evening Bulletin* fretted that the proposed tax would bear too heavily on moderate incomes and suggested instead a 1 percent levy on "all incomes whatever"; *Harper's Weekly* worried that incomes in America fluctuated too much for any rational method of income taxation. These uncertain protests were unavailing, however, and Morrill's idea prevailed. After repeatedly calling for an income tax, the editor of the Chicago *Tribune* approved the one suggested, explaining, "the rich should be taxed more than the poor."[38]

In Congress, no Republican challenged the income tax. A few Democrats from agricultural regions complained that the plan would hurt farmers, ignoring the fact that in the previous session their region had advocated such a levy to balance direct taxation. "The country," Stevens retorted authoritatively, "and especially the western country, will not pay a millionth part of [the tax]." No one called for a separate vote on the income tax provision.

With the critical points settled, Stevens concluded debate on the bill by defending its principles. He emphasized that indirect taxation and the income tax would lay taxes on everyone but would distribute the bulk of the burden to the wealthy. He contrasted this system to direct or poll taxes, which would ultimately charge everyone the same heavy taxes. "We have the consolation to know that no burdens have been imposed on the industrious laborer and mechanic," concluded Stevens, and "that the food of the poor is untaxed." A colleague agreed: "It will be observed that this bill seldom reaches the poor man . . . The bill very properly, I think, adopts the indirect system of taxation."

Knowing that a vote against such a vital revenue measure would be a vote against the success of the Union, all but one Republican congressman ultimately fell into line and voted for the bill. On April 8, the measure passed the House by a vote of 125 to 14, with thirteen Democrats, eleven of whom hailed from the corn-producing region, leading the opposition.[39]

The Senate received the bill in mid-April 1862 and referred it to the Committee on Finance. Besieged by alternative plans for internal revenue, Fessenden determined to ignore all other suggestions and to deliver his friend Morrill's House bill in the best shape possible. He reported the measure in early May, but it was blocked from the floor by a group of senators who, frustrated at what they perceived to be Lincoln's weak prosecution of the war, tried to force the President to declare "some distinct line of policy"—that is, one that reflected their own heavy-handed suggestions—before they would vote a tax to continue the war effort. It was not until May 21 that Fessenden was able to bring the bill up for discussion.[40]

The two-week debate that followed the introduction of the bill revealed the same regional tensions apparent in the House between lower Northwestern agricultural interests and the upper North and Northeast, but in the Senate, as in the House, lower Northwesterners were unable to alter the Republican plan. Of the 315 amendments offered to the House bill, only those relating to the direct tax and the income tax changed Republican policy.

One of those changes dealt with the direct tax section of the 1861 tax bill, which the House had left intact. The Senate passed by a large majority an amendment to the bill limiting the direct tax levy to the $20 million tax imposed in 1861. Western Republicans Zachariah Chandler of Michigan, James Grimes of Iowa, and Timothy Howe of Wisconsin led Republicans of all regions in advocating the amendment, arguing that indirect taxation made the direct tax obsolete. Indirect taxation spread burdens equally, they maintained, by permitting commerce to distribute the burden of the manufacturing tax throughout the country. The direct tax, they argued, bore disproportionately on agricultural states and muddied the principle of indirect taxation.

In a second change, the Senate adopted an amendment graduating the income tax. Fessenden introduced the plan, which reflected an idea of Simmons's. Fessenden proposed a 3 percent tax on incomes between $600 and $10,000, a 5 percent tax on incomes over $10,000 and under $50,000, and a 7.5 percent tax on all incomes over $50,000. Although a few men had previously suggested graduated taxes to distribute taxes more evenly according to ability to pay, the Senate created this tiered system with little thought but to gain more revenue. The plan drew little debate. Congress had to find revenue to replace that from the direct tax, and to impose the high rate necessary for sufficient revenue on all incomes over $600 would have been deemed a hardship for lower-income families. A graduated tax seemed the obvious solution.[41]

The House received the amended bill in early June and promptly sent it to a conference committee, which two weeks later reported to both houses a plan reflecting the Senate's attempts to levy taxes proportionately according to wealth. Among other adjustments, the committee's report recommended suspending the direct tax for two years and establishing tiers of 3 percent for incomes over $600 and of 5 percent for incomes over $10,000. The Senate adopted the report without a division; the House adopted it by a vote of 106 to 11, with Democrats dominating the minority.

Like the revenue bill of 1861, the 1862 tax bill revealed the evolution of Republican tax policy. With this measure, the Republicans effectively shelved Gallatin's tax ideas by suspending the direct tax, which, they believed, unfairly burdened the agricultural sector of the economy. They codified their own new policy of indirect taxation in the belief that this system of taxes on manufactures would evenly distribute the tax burden. A novel, tiered income tax was to raise the war funds that the relatively low indirect taxes could not. From weeks of debate emerged "a pretty good bill," one congressman wrote, "except that the taxation descends rather too much into details." "It will answer for a beginning," he concluded. President Lincoln signed this first major tax bill of the war on July 1, 1862.[42]

On June 20, three days before the conference committee on the tax bill reported to Congress, Stevens introduced the sweeping tariff Morrill had promised earlier. Again designed by Morrill, the bill (H.R.

531) was based on the Morrill Tariff. It set the average rate on commodities affected by the tariff at around 37 percent and cut the free list in half. A three-day debate began in the last week of June.[43]

Although they were still trying to distinguish their tariff policy from traditional protectionism, Republicans did not mention agricultural tariffs when advocating this bill. The measure indeed raised the tariffs on everything encompassed in the Morrill Tariff Act—those on agricultural as well as manufacturing products—but agricultural tariffs were now irrelevant. Far from importing agricultural products, the wartime Union had aggressively developed its agricultural exports to attract foreign specie. The proposed tariff protected agriculture in case exports fell drastically, and most eastern Republicans saw no need to continue to try to attract farmers to high tariffs. They believed that the recent passage of popular homestead legislation and other agricultural measures designed to enrich the agricultural sector and thus help it to produce revenue meant that most farmers would cheerfully support other Republican revenue measures that focused on different sectors of the economy.

Instead of emphasizing the agricultural benefits of tariffs, the new manufacturing taxes made Republicans concentrate on the proposed tariff's effect on industry. They claimed that the bill was a war measure to raise revenue and to protect newly taxed domestic industries from untaxed, and therefore cheaper, foreign products. "If we bleed manufacturers we must see to it that the proper tonic is administered at the same time," said Morrill, "or we shall have destroyed the goose that lays the golden eggs." The tariff was "certainly not" intended for the purpose of protection, he insisted; but he privately reflected that it would "do much to keep our own people employed rather than those of Europe." Most pro-tariff men exulted that the measure brought closer a full-blown system of protection.[44]

An exclusive concentration on manufacturing was premature, for recent Republican efforts in favor of farmers had not dulled the agricultural regions' antipathy to tariffs, and the sectional conflicts that had surfaced in the tax debates immediately reappeared in discussions of the proposed tariff. Although in general people from the entire agricultural West disliked tariffs, those from the lower Northwest, already angry over the tax bill, were most vocal in opposition to the 1862 tariff bill. The San Francisco *Daily Alta California* declared it common knowledge that "the great valley of the West" opposed any sort of tariff, and indeed members of both parties from the corn-producing region challenged the new measure. Anticipating the new tariff bill, the Republican Cincinnati *Daily Commercial* gently suggested that New England and Pennsylvania interests stand back a bit in favor of Western interests. More vociferous, the Chicago *Times*, a Democratic "secession organ," according to a Republican rival, bitterly protested "the New England policy of the war," which, it claimed, was enriching New England through the Morrill Tariff.[45]

Congressmen of both parties from Western agricultural states made their continued opposition to protective tariffs clear. As soon as the bill came up for debate, Republican Samuel Shellabarger of Ohio warned that he would not vote for any bill that raised tariffs except to equalize tariff rates with new tax rates or to raise revenue. Democrats asserted positively that the bill was "based upon the prohibitory principle." Robert Mallory of northern Kentucky, who came from a town on the Ohio River across from Indiana, claimed that his section of the country was "oppressed to a great extent" by a tariff. "Our interests are different from the interests of that section of the country from which [Mr. Morrill] comes," he reminded the House.

The Western agricultural region's continuing dislike of tariffs commanded less and less sympathy within the Republican party, however, not only because the legislation for agricultural development the party contemplated offered significant benefits to farmers, but also because the North's growing antipathy toward Britain, France, and Canada outweighed regional feelings. The Republican press maintained a vigilant watch on England and the rest of Europe, bemoaning, among other things, Britain's blockade running and outfitting of Confederate warships. Reflecting on the apparent abundance of proofs of English hatred and jealousy, the editor of a Philadelphia paper concluded that "they are engendering a corresponding hatred in this country."[46]

Northerners believed that England's attitude reflected jealousy of the North's growing commercial and financial strength, and pro-tariff forces used this idea to promote higher duties. The New York *Daily Tribune* insisted that the Morrill Tariff had enabled the Union to survive its early financial crises without help from Europe. The Philadelphia *Inquirer* blamed British anger at Union duties on England's realization "that a new era has been reached in our tariff policy, and that the golden stream which has so long flowed to her shores from ours will now . . . be retained here to . . . give new activity to our internal trade." Having gained confidence in the Union's economic strength as the nation funded its own war without European capital,

Republicans espoused an increasingly powerful nationalistic belief that America should concentrate on making itself the wealthiest and strongest nation by enacting prohibitive tariffs, encouraging great industrial development, supporting a strong military, and increasing national pride. Newspapers charged their readers to "comprehend the brilliant destiny before us."[47]

Northerners were also becoming increasingly angry at Canada. Some maintained that Canada had violated the spirit of the Reciprocity Treaty by placing import duties on U.S.-manufactured goods while exporting the raw materials that the treaty left duty-free. They argued that the North lost millions of dollars of tax revenue because Canadian competition meant that a host of domestic commodities had to go untaxed. As Canada steadfastly maintained neutrality during the war, Republicans resented the treaty obligations even more, especially when it became clear that Canadian neutrality did not preclude giving Confederates asylum.[48]

The North's growing dislike of foreigners increased support for the 1862 tariff. Many Republicans agreed with Treasury Secretary Chase, whose report at the end of 1861 suggested that since it was the "most sacred duty" of Americans to concentrate on the reestablishment of the Union, the country should curtail trade with nations that were indifferent or unfriendly to that object. Constructing a bridge between old free-trade ideas and protectionism, Chase remarked that free trade was a "wise and noble" policy, but should only be the policy of "concordant" nations. Without friendly nations with which to trade, America should seek "a more absolute reliance, under God, upon American labor, American skill, and American soil." Trying to use national products and capital whenever possible, Northerners justified higher tariffs as a means to wean the nation from Europe. At the same time, frequent calls for abrogation of the Canadian Reciprocity Treaty made it a standard joke in House revenue debates to move that a provision be amended so it would take effect only after the treaty had ended.[49]

On July 1, the House passed the tariff bill without a division, and Fessenden reported it with minor amendments to the Senate from the Committee on Finance a week later. With the session getting old and Washington getting hot, Fessenden readily piloted the bill through the Senate. It passed with limited discussion and without a division on July 8. A conference committee took only three days to iron out the differences between the bills. Both the Senate and the House concurred in the report with almost no discussion, and the bill became law on July 14, 1862. "Congress has passed a tax law, and a tariff," wrote the editor of *Harper's Weekly*. "The two are co-ordinate parts of one integral system."[50]

The revenue measures of 1862 did not solve the Union's wartime financial problems. On December 10, 1863, Chase greeted the three-day-old Thirty-Eighth Congress with a report recommending increased taxation to cushion the Treasury against higher than projected expenditures and to help fund the staggering $1.5 billion national debt. As in 1862, Republicans throughout the North rallied to the Treasury and called for new taxes.[51]

Recognizing that a general tax revision would take time to prepare, the Committee on Ways and Means quickly proposed a new tax on whiskey and cotton. More than a revenue measure, this bill (H.R. 122) was also a Republican attempt to win advantage in the 1864 campaign. Party members believed that the large Democratic gains in the 1862 congressional elections had resulted in part from the Democratic candidates' liberal distribution of liquor in city districts. By raising the price of alcohol Republicans intended to hamper the drinking Democrats in 1864. They also hoped to label their opponents evil alcoholics who were endangering the war effort, a plan aided by the fact that a "beastly" drunk Democratic senator, Willard Saulsbury, had launched a tirade against Lincoln on the Senate floor in 1863, calling the president a weak imbecile.[52] Recognizing the Republican plan, the Democrats counterattacked ferociously, and their rhetoric helped to label the Republicans as aristocrats who plotted to ruin the poor and the agricultural West in order to enrich Eastern manufacturers.

Stevens introduced the bill in mid-January 1864, and when it came up for debate, Josiah Grinnell of Iowa, whose roots were in temperance-minded Vermont, advocated the complete cessation of whiskey production. Abolition of "that dreadful poison" would improve morals and would stop the diversion of grain from use as food. Crediting recent reports that a drunken corps commander had hampered Meade's pursuit of Lee after Gettysburg, Grinnell feared that liquor was "damaging . . . our soldiers . . . and . . . damning their souls." Many Republicans, especially those from the upper Northwest and from New England, where the temperance movement was strong, shared Grinnell's attitude. Since it was "injurious to the public health and morals," a Chicago newspaper editor wrote to a senator, liquor "should be taxed severely." One angry Democrat reacted to this argument by complaining that the Republicans were teetotaling Puritans seeking to "cure men's morals by legal penalties."[53]

On the attack, Democrats charged that the Republicans were hypocritical aristocrats whose patriotism did not extend to their pocketbooks. To pay for their war, Democrats accused, Republicans were laying an unfair tax on the poor. Whiskey, the Democratic argument assumed, was a poor man's drink. Alcohol traditionally had been considered a luxury, but the Democrats obscured that fact with their rhetoric of oppression. New York's John Chanler defended the "poor distressed creature" stalked by the "gaunt wolf of hunger and distress" who was being taxed in a spirit of tyranny akin to England's tax-hungry, labor-crushing despots. He attacked Grinnell's "aristocratic" background and "high-born air," jibing at the elegant way he dressed. Republicans retorted that "gaunt want," "poverty, ignorance, brutality, and general degradation" were born of intemperance, and that the Democrats were plotting to destroy the Union by inciting a class war.[54]

Democrats also exploited the sectional tensions already apparent over tax policy, protesting that, together with the whiskey tax, the proposed cotton tax would cripple the agricultural West. The bill called for a 2 cent per pound tax on raw cotton brought from the South, while it allowed a 2 cent per pound drawback on exported manufactured cotton goods in addition to a refund of the 3 percent manufacturing tax. Democrats identified the plan as "a heavy tax on the great agricultural interest of the country, and a bounty to the manufacturing interest." The free-for-all continued for three days, with Republicans accusing the Democrats of playing the sectional theme to gain votes, favoring foreign producers and making "pestilential assaults" on New England that echoed those of the traitors now in rebellion.

In late January, the bill passed by a vote of 86 to 68. The majority consisted of a core of Republicans, and a core of Democrats made up the minority.[55] After three committees of conference were unable to agree on the form of a final bill, the Republicans finally succeeded in passing a hodgepodge bill that Lincoln signed on March 7, but they paid a heavy price for their success. The Democratic rhetoric was the sharpest the Republicans had faced, and it had secured the party's image as a group of sectional, aristocratic tyrants.

While Congress hashed out this stopgap measure, the Committee on Ways and Means was developing a new comprehensive tax bill. The new measure took time, and it was not until mid-April 1864 that Morrill reported the internal revenue bill (H.R. 405) he had promised. The tardy introduction of the measure put Congress under a time constraint, for it hoped to get a new law in place before May 1, when income taxes would be assessed.

The 1864 bill generally built on the 1862 tax. It increased the tax on manufactures to 5 percent, reduced the free list still further, and increased the base level of the income tax to 5 percent. The committee proposed reinstating the direct tax, in part to maintain control over rebel land liberated by advancing Union armies. The law, Morrill said, should raise $250 to $300 million. One newspaper recognized the bill as "the longest . . . ever introduced into Congress." The scope of this tax bill indicated the growing power of the national tax system; the bill added so many new objects of taxation that it embraced, as one senator recalled, "nearly every source of revenue provided for by American or English laws."[56]

When the House began considering the bill, the lines of debate were much the same as on the 1862 tax bill, although the battle over the whiskey and cotton tax and the proximity of the 1864 election heightened antagonism. In their highly successful 1862 campaign Democrats had attacked Republican taxes, and they probably hoped to take advantage of this new tax bill as well. Preparing for the hustings, New York Democrats Fernando Wood and James Brooks instantly objected to the bill and held forth at length about the Republicans' mismanagement of the war.[57]

Significantly, debate on the actual bill raised no discussion of the propriety of the newly established national system of tax collection. Instead, the House reviewed the suggestions of the first director of the Internal Revenue Bureau for the Bureau's better operation. There had been surprisingly few complaints about the new system, for director George S. Boutwell and his staff had tried not to crowd taxpayers as they enforced the 1862 law.[58] Boutwell was now sitting in the Massachusetts delegation to Congress, strengthening the Bureau. By 1864, a national tax collection network had become an accepted part of the Republican tax system.

Congress broke little new ground in the first days of the tax discussion; then, in late April, Republican Augustus Frank, a railroad director from upstate New York, broached the most compelling issue of the 1864 tax debates. Frank proposed that Congress rework the income tax, graduating it in such a way that it would bear much more heavily on the wealthy. He suggested a 5 percent tax on income over $600, 7.5 percent on the excess over $10,000, and 10 percent on the excess over $25,000. As long as high taxes were necessary, Frank said, "I think it is just, right, and proper that those having a large amount of income shall pay a larger amount of tax."[59]

On its face, Frank's proposal was unremarkable. Although Congress had not discussed the principle of a tiered tax, it had in fact already graduated the 1862 tax law out of a practical need to raise revenue. The principle of a graduated tax had also been considered since Congress had first discussed an income tax. Republicans believed that "a tax properly levied, upon incomes . . . is an equitable and just tax," and many believed that to levy an income tax properly, one had to adjust it proportionately to different levels of income. A uniform, or even a slightly graduated, income tax made poorer people pay proportionately more than the wealthy. Among others, the editor of the Boston *Daily Evening Transcript* suggested "a stringent income tax, which really made people contribute to the public needs according to their income."[60]

Although the proposal to graduate the income tax seemed like a logical step to promote the proper division of tax burdens, key House Republicans attacked it. Newspaper correspondents were mumbling against the wealthy, claiming that rich businessmen were using the manufacturing tax as an excuse to raise prices far higher than necessary, then pocketing huge profits. Stevens and Morrill correctly interpreted Frank's plan as a deliberate assault on the very rich in response to these complaints. By setting his two upper tax tiers at $10,000 and $25,000 and making the rates for those income brackets significantly higher than that of the lowest bracket, Frank was clearly targeting a handful of the very richest Americans to bear disproportionate amounts of the tax. Reflecting a key Republican principle that new conditions of extreme wealth challenged, Stevens told the House that he objected strenuously to Frank's amendment because it distinguished between citizens according to their wealth, punishing a few for being very rich. Stevens firmly asserted that the use of taxation against such a narrow class of people was "vicious" and "unjust."[61]

Despite Stevens's protests, so many House members agreed to Frank's amendment that no roll-call vote was taken. Expressing the vehemence of people from the agricultural region but voicing a general Republican dislike of the extremely wealthy, Iowa's Grinnell and Ohio's Rufus P. Spalding summarized the Republican justification for Frank's graduated tax: "Go to the Astors and the Stewarts and other rich men of the country and ask them if in the midst of a war [this measure] is unreasonable." The principle, they said, was the same as a luxury tax, placing burdens on those most able to afford them.

Morrill made a last stand against Frank's tax proposal in his final speech for the bill. He objected to its "inequality" and said it was "no less than a confiscation of property, because one man happens to have a little more money than another." Echoing Wayland, Morrill worried that this sort of graduated tax would send the rich into exile. "On all other subjects we tax every man alike," Morrill reminded the House. There was a philosophy behind that system, he declared: "The very theory of our institutions is entire equality; that we make no distinction between the rich man and the poor man. The man of moderate means is just as good as the man with more means, but our theory of government does not admit that he is better." Although grounded in basic Republican ideas about political economy, Morrill's speech failed to persuade the House to drop the graduated tax, for House members reflected their constituents' increasing resentment of those who were becoming rich during wartime, often through questionable practices like speculation.

The House turned next to the direct tax. The Committee on Ways and Means revealed that the previous Congress had not laid direct taxation completely to rest; the committee proposed reinstating the tax, both to raise revenue and to enable the government to impose liens on rebel land. The House still opposed a direct tax, however, and Stevens's proposal to jettison it was popular, especially since increased income tax revenue was expected to replace direct tax receipts. Surprisingly, it was a Democrat, William Holman of Indiana, who opposed killing the tax, probably because he saw it as a more traditional, constitutional method of taxation than the Republican innovations. He moved simply to suspend the tax for another two years, and the House agreed.

The House passed the bill without a direct tax and with the sharply graduated income tax on the evening of April 28, 1864. The vote was 102 to 33, with the minority solidly Democratic.

When the Senate took up the bill in late May, its significant policy discussions concerned the same issues as the House debates had: the income tax and the direct tax. The Finance Committee recommended cutting out the top tax bracket of the income tax. Noting that the committee had discussed this point at length, Fessenden confessed that he had not made up his own mind on the subject, and he framed his ideas about it in a way that asserted the original Republican idea of equality while acknowledging the reasonableness of the popular desire to place higher tax burdens on the wealthy. Fessenden explained that the income tax itself was at best discriminatory, but in an extreme emergency was justified to raise revenue, and he recalled that he himself had advocated the two-level tax structure of 1862. Still, the impulse to place burdens on only the very wealthy should be checked unless absolutely necessary. "Men should be incited in every possible way to accumulate," Fessenden reasoned, "because as much as they accumulate by their industry they add to the national wealth." Excessive taxation of income would make people less willing to labor, they would accumulate less, and the nation would suffer. Echoing his friend Morrill, he concluded that the nation's prosperity depended on the government's even-handed treatment of individuals. Such treatment would leave the path to wealth open to everyone.[62]

Following Fessenden, the Senate indicated its willingness to tax heavily for revenue, but not to discriminate among economic classes more than was absolutely necessary for revenue. The vote to strike the top tax bracket was 22 for and 15 against. Although the yea votes were spread throughout the whole North, the minority, which included 11 Republicans, was heavily weighted toward the agricultural West and probably reflected the anger of those regions toward "the Astors and the Stewarts and other rich men" of the East.

The Senate adjusted its decision about the income tax after Grimes of Iowa successfully attacked the direct tax. The Finance Committee had recommended reinstating the direct tax, claiming that it was imperative to enable the government to tax Confederate property, but once again senators from agricultural states objected. These states did not vote cohesively on most issues, but on the direct tax they were almost unanimous. An amendment to drop the tax passed by a vote of 21 to 16. In the majority were sixteen Republicans, four Democrats, and one Old-Line Whig. With the exception of Henry Wilson of Massachusetts and John Carlile of Virginia, all of the Republicans in favor of the amendment came from Western states: Missouri,

Michigan, Wisconsin, Iowa, Indiana, Kansas, Minnesota, Illinois, and Ohio. In the negative were fourteen Republicans and two Democrats. Ten of the Republican nay votes came from New England and New York. Conspicuously absent from the vote were the two senators from Vermont, whose agricultural status would probably have led them to break the New England ranks and vote yea.[63]

The removal of the direct tax suggested a need for further income tax adjustments. Although they accepted the idea of graduation, Senate Republicans rejected the specific targeting of the very rich and redefined the tax brackets. Wilson of Massachusetts suggested a 5 percent tax on all incomes from $600 to $2,000, and a 7.5 percent tax on all incomes over $2,000. The House plan would tax all incomes under $10,000 at 5 percent; Wilson argued that his plan would produce more revenue by increasing the tax rate for moderate incomes. Wilson's proposal also promised to forestall charges of discrimination against a few rich men by placing a great many in the highest tax bracket. After raising the upper level to $5,000, the Senate adopted this plan to raise additional revenue by a vote of 18 to 11. There was little geographic or party coherence to the vote.[64]

Westerner Grimes then proposed reversing the Senate's previous decision to strike the House's tax of 10 percent on excess income over $25,000. Fessenden suggested that Grimes set the upper tax bracket at $10,000 instead, probably thinking of Wilson's suggestion about preventing charges of discrimination. A Western Democrat suggested $15,000, and Grimes agreed. His proposal passed, again probably because of the need for more revenue to replace direct tax receipts.

The bill, without a direct tax and with a graduated tax of substantially lower income brackets than the House bill had created, passed the Senate very late in the night of June 6, 1864, by a vote of 22 to 3. The minority was solidly Democratic.

Nine days later, the House took up the 636 Senate amendments, almost all of which were minor or technical. After concurring in approximately four hundred of the amendments, the House called for a committee of conference to discuss the rest. Significantly, both Morrill and Fessenden sat on the six-person conference committee.

In the last week of June, Fessenden delivered the conference committee's report to the Senate. The report reflected the desire of Morrill and Fessenden to prevent tax discrimination against the rich. It graduated the income tax to prevent overburdening lower incomes and to tax all people somewhat proportionately to their incomes, setting taxes at 5 percent for incomes from $600 to $5,000, 7.5 percent for incomes from $5,000 to $10,000, and 10 percent for incomes over $10,000. Significantly, the report omitted tax brackets for extremely high income levels, which would embrace only a few wealthy people.

Both the Senate and the House quickly concurred in the report, and Lincoln signed the bill on June 30, 1864.

Republican tax laws continued to go hand in hand with tariff propositions. In late April 1864, before a general revision of the tariff was ready to be presented, Stevens introduced a joint resolution (H.R. 67) temporarily imposing higher import duties on tobacco, liquor, iron, and wool, which were to last from the passage of the bill until July 1, 1864.[65]

This resolution, introduced less than two months after the bitter fight over the liquor and cotton tax, resulted in a sectional brawl. Border Democrats initially blocked the resolution, and amid cries of "Order!" Morrill snarled that it was a necessary war measure. Ohio Democrat S. S. Cox exploded. "New England manufacturers are getting richer every day," he said, "richer and richer and richer . . . They are . . . becoming the owners of this country . . . They are getting all the protection of the Government . . . I claim for the farmers of the West, in absolute self-defense, some little regard." Unprotected and exploited farmers, he concluded, supported parasitical New Englanders.

A substitute to the original bill, introduced by Stevens, created an across-the-board tariff increase of 50 percent for sixty days. It passed without a division.

In the Senate, too, Democratic members from agricultural states decried the bill as a "crushing" blow delivered by New Englanders. The Senate listened politely, then passed the resolution by a vote of 30 to 8. Fessenden, who believed the tariff would reduce revenue by squeezing out imports, joined seven Democrats in the minority. Lincoln signed the bill on April 29. At the end of June, the temporary tariff was extended by joint resolution to July 1, 1865.[66]

It was not until late May 1864 that Morrill reported the long-awaited tariff bill (H.R. 494) from the Committee of Ways and Means, which he now chaired. The proposed tariff raised rates to an average of around 47 percent. Like the 1862 tariff, the proposed tariff generally increased duties on the categories of items enumerated in Morrill's 1861 tariff. Morrill once again advanced this as a war necessity, claiming that it would bring increased customs revenue.[67]

For the first time Morrill admitted that the proposed tariff protected industry, although he stressed that the proposed duties were not "extravagant or prohibitory." The measure increased tariffs on agricultural products, but despite Morrill's pointed attention to its protection of wool, the initial Republican emphasis on agricultural protection had weakened markedly with the lack of agricultural imports and the increasing dependence on the manufacturing tax. The new tariff act would counterbalance the new tax, Morrill said, protecting newly taxed domestic manufactures from cheaper imports. Further, it would "shelter and nurse" domestic industry to bear the heavy taxes, eventually enabling industry alone to bear the weight of the government's support. It was necessary, Morrill said, "that the country may not languish, and that we may largely and properly stimulate the productive energies of the nation to create that wealth of which we daily use and destroy so much." Morrill also reiterated the traditional argument that protection would ultimately reduce the price of consumer goods and help to "stimulate the productive energies of the nation to create . . . wealth."

The Republican press approved the new tariff, claiming that a prohibitory tariff would be "the greatest of all blessings" because it would reduce imports and stop the flow of gold from the Union. Stopping the loss of gold would reduce its price, which in July 1864—the month Congress passed the gold bill—was above 200. Lower gold prices would reduce inflation, keeping consumer costs down. As a war necessity, the bill gained support even from those who otherwise might have balked at this "unusual and extraordinary" measure.[68]

Despite vicious Democratic attacks on the pro-tariff "vampires of the East," the House passed the bill in early June by a vote of 82 to 26. A solidly Democratic minority consisted of twenty-two votes from Ohio, Indiana, Illinois, and Wisconsin. Nineteen members from those states did not vote, and only eleven favorable votes came from there. The agricultural states still did not like tariffs.

In the Senate, the Committee on Finance reported the bill, with technical amendments, in mid-June. Making the most important point of the rambling debate on the measure, Fessenden drew applause and support for the bill by insisting that the committee had made no concessions to England when preparing the tariff. In both the House and the Senate, increasing antagonism toward Europe again fired enthusiasm for a high tariff. Although Congress and the press condemned Napoleon III's support of the puppet dictator Maximillian in

Mexico, England bore the brunt of American hatred. By the summer of 1864, it seemed clear that Britain was trying to undermine the Union. Newspapers reviewed the depredations of the British-made Confederate warship *Alabama* from October 1863 onward as a prelude to demands for reparations. In January 1864, Minnesota's governor accused Britain of giving sanctuary in Canada to the most atrocious Native American criminals, thus preventing complete Native American pacification. The Chicago *Tribune* further reported that the British had supplied Native Americans with supplies, transportation, and 300 pounds of powder with enough shot to use it. Republicans also believed that England was supporting the Democrats in the 1864 election, and newspapers equated English aristocracy and Southern "chivalry" when describing the barbarism of Confederate soldiers who murdered Union wounded. Senator Zachariah Chandler of Michigan was only one of many who wished for a "wall of fire" between America and England.[69]

Angry at England and determined to raise revenue for the desperate Treasury, which was about to hit its wartime low, Republican senators from all over the North rallied to the tariff bill. They passed the measure by a party vote of 22 to 5. Western senators Harlan and Grimes from Iowa, Lane from Indiana, Trumbull from Illinois, Brown from Missouri, Doolittle from Wisconsin, and Ramsey from Minnesota all voted aye. Although both senators from Ohio were absent, they were such staunch Republicans they undoubtedly would have backed the bill.

After a conference committee adjusted the disagreements between the House and Senate versions of the bill, both houses quickly concurred in the committee's report. Lincoln signed the bill on June 30, the same day that he signed the tax bill. Taxes and tariffs were the domestic and foreign sides of the same policy, and by signing both bills together, Lincoln put the entire 1864 system into place at once.

The Republicans subsequently completed their construction of trade barriers by abrogating the Canadian Reciprocity Treaty. Not widely popular anyway, the treaty fell before Northern anger at Canada's role in the war. Already hostile toward England, Americans became infuriated by blockade-running bases at Halifax and St. John and by Canadian asylum for Confederates, who kept the border agitated with threats of attacks on Lake Erie settlements. On April 1, 1864, the House Committee on Commerce recommended that the treaty be terminated as soon as legally possible.[70]

Republican determination to dump the treaty hardened in the next six months. In September 1864, an incursion of Confederates from Canada into the Great Lakes region led Secretary of War Stanton and Secretary of the Navy Welles to ready men to move there. A month later, a Canadian judge released a group that had raided the banks of St. Albans, Vermont, and Americans demanded an end to the Reciprocity Treaty as a reprisal. Citing the need to protect "the Canadian and provincial frontier from murder, arson, and burglary, under the pretense of rebel invasion," Congress voted to abrogate the treaty in January 1865.[71]

By 1865, the Republicans had developed a series of high tariffs and taxes that reflected the economic theories of Carey and Wayland and were designed to strengthen and benefit all parts of the American economy, raising the standard of living for everyone. As one Republican concluded during the war: "Congress must shape its legislation as to incidentally aid all branches of productive industry, render the people prosperous, and enable them to pay taxes imposed for the ordinary expenses of the Government and interest on the extraordinary war debt incurred from day to day in support of the Army and Navy."[72]

Although the Republicans had designed the income and manufacturing taxes in response to the demands of farmers and over the protests of manufacturers, the Republican revenue system fundamentally reshaped and bolstered Northern industry. In 1861, the nation's lowest tariff ever encouraged increasing dependence on imports while domestic industry suffered after the Panic of 1857. The government itself had an interest in encouraging imports because tariff duties were the Treasury's major source of revenue. The Republicans changed this system drastically. Their development of manufacturing taxes, adopted to raise revenue without crushing farmers under direct taxes, necessitated protection and encouragement of industry in order to bear the tax burden. By 1865, a national tax system of manufacturing taxes had committed the nation to a trade wall of high tariffs and the government to fostering industry.

The Republicans' ultimate, if rather backhanded, strengthening of industry gave later generations a new perspective on the bitter wartime revenue debates and obscured the fact that the revenue system was intended to avoid overburdening farmers. After the war, those horrified by the domineering corporations of the late nineteenth century paid close attention to the angry Democratic characterization of Northern Republicans as rich manufacturers legislating against poor laborers and farmers. This image, developed in sectional and political debates, took on an exaggerated importance in the postwar years.

After the war, party members followed their wartime revenue decisions to their expected ends. With the reduced need for money, Congress removed manufacturing taxes almost completely by 1868. The income tax was slated to expire in 1870; lobbying extended a weak version of it until 1872. At the same time, Congress returned to a reliance on tariffs to produce revenue generally and specifically to bring specie into the country to fund the debt with its gold interest payments. Congress increased tariffs in 1867, and then, after a reduction in 1872, increased them again in 1875 in the wake of the Panic of 1873. The death of the income tax by statutory limitation in 1872, during a very favorable period in the government's financial situation, fulfilled Republicans' initial intent for the law, but drew accusations that the wealthy had deliberately sabotaged a popular measure. Similarly, the enactment of higher tariffs after the war, inspired initially by a desire for specie, then by the protectionist impulse of manufacturers across the entire North, sparked theories of wartime schemes to develop industry at the expense of agriculture.[73]

Far from catering to a specific economic interest when they developed their revenue legislation, the Republicans tried to bolster a new national system, and most congressional Republicans were pleased with their wartime tax and tariff legislation. As economist Carey claimed, they believed that wartime protection was responsible for "a prosperity, such as, until recently, had never before been known." Tariffs had emancipated the North from the tyranny of "wealthy British capitalists" by developing the nation's resources and industry. Everyone, Carey maintained, had profited from this: laborers, who had higher wages and full employment; farmers, who were freed from uncertain European markets; investors, whose stock doubled in value as internal commerce grew; and manufacturers, whose inventories vanished as consumer demand increased. Protection, wrote Carey, had magnificently increased the wealth of the country.[74]

As they bolstered the national economy and established a system of taxes and tariffs, the Republicans turned the government's obligation to raise revenue into an opportunity to use the government to develop the economy. At the same time, the imposition of national taxes could not avoid tying individuals directly to the Union government as well as to their states. An unhappy Democratic senator noted that the government used to be a means for the people to achieve liberty and prosperity, but now, he reflected, "the Government is everything; it has become the end; and the people, and all their property, labor, efforts, and gains, at least in the West and in the Northwest, are merely the means by which the Government is to continue . . . and its powers progressively augmented."[75]

Northerners became increasingly aware of their financial power during the war, and Republican tariff and tax legislation focused the North's attention on itself as a nation as it drew away from Europe. Anger at foreign governments translated into higher tariffs and a strong American nationalism. After the war, Carey exclaimed that the country needed to continue to be *"Americanized."* When that happened, the nation could contend successfully "for the control of the commerce of [all countries]." It would thus, he said, be able to overshadow England and claim the top position in the world.[76]

"A Large Crop Is More Than a Great Victory": Agricultural Legislation

> Agriculture feeds us; to a great extent it clothes us; without it we could not have manufactures, and should not have commerce. These all stand together, like pillars in a cluster, the largest in the centre, and that largest is Agriculture.
>
> —Indianapolis *Daily Journal*, 1864

If the solvency of the government, and thus the success of the Union, increasingly depended on individual Americans, Republicans believed that they must use all the means at their disposal to increase the prosperity of those individuals. Wealth would not only enable people to buy bonds and pay taxes, but also would cement their loyalty to the Union even as their own productive efforts made it the world's greatest nation. With their agricultural legislation, the Republicans fostered what they believed to be the key sector in economic expansion and in society and, in so doing, involved the national government actively and innovatively in the economy. Although party members justified the Homestead Act, the law creating a Department of Agriculture, the Land Grant College Act, and the 1864 Immigration Act as measures designed to help the Union war effort by increasing national production and thus expanding the tax base, there was no doubt that with their agricultural legislation Republicans were consciously expanding the national government's economic role.

The Republicans' attention to agriculture grew from a long national heritage of farming. Harking back to Thomas Jefferson's praise of the yeoman farmer, antebellum Americans attached symbolic and sentimental meaning to agriculture. Believing that farming was man's primary calling, members of all parties eulogized it as the occupation most likely to bring out the best in an individual. Cultivating the land developed man, wrote one farmer, for it kept him in constant contact with his Maker.[1] Seeing nature as the root of all knowledge and beauty, a young Republican from Ohio reflected that the farmer learned "much of the elemental laws of being" and that he was "very near to the secrets of God." Farming allowed "investigations of the great truths which underlie and surround it," reflected Republican Justin Smith Morrill. Americans should promote agriculture, he concluded, in order to "improve man himself."[2]

Agriculture also seemed to be the root of American political security, for only a person who was self-supporting could remain politically independent and thus help preserve a pure republican government. In 1859, Republican Owen Lovejoy delivered to his county's agricultural society an epic poem in which he asserted that the farmer's vote was most valuable because he "knows no dependence, save upon his God / Bows to no sceptre—cowers at no one's nod."[3] "That man only is independent who feels able to support himself and family by the plow whenever other avocations are closed," Morrill agreed. For Republicans, the battle to keep the South's peculiar institution out of the territories had proven the political power of the small farmer. Senator Samuel C. Pomeroy emotionally recalled his time spent in Bleeding Kansas and told his colleagues with conviction that what had ultimately defeated slavery there, and what would defeat it everywhere, was the independent Northern small farmer.[4]

The Republicans who shaped wartime agricultural policy inherited not only these general attitudes about agriculture, but also a long national history of agitation for homestead legislation. Land policies set by the ordinances of 1785 and 1787 meant that the government usually sold public land in large parcels to speculators; individual settlers had to buy land from them at much higher prices. In the 1820s, many Americans began to resent the men who bought large tracts of land at rock-bottom prices, held them until the spread of settlement brought buyers into the area, and then sold them for huge profits. Western interests began to agitate for the free distribution of lands directly to settlers. They protested the possession of large wilderness areas by "land sharks" who made no effort to improve the land.

By the 1840s, Eastern land reformers, writing for the New York Daily Tribune and other papers, made their main theme the unemployment, poverty, and misery they saw in the burgeoning cities. The rich were enslaving the poor, they claimed, and only a policy of free land could pull the destitute out of their hovels and into the domain of free citizens. The preemption legislation of 1841, allowing those who had settled their land before the government offered it for sale to purchase it at a minimum price, failed to satisfy reformers, and by 1848 the sentiment for homestead legislation was strong enough to find its way into the platform of the new Free Soil party. In the 1850s, almost every Congress debated homestead legislation. Proponents of such measures maintained that it was "the duty of Congress to help the cities to disgorge their cellars and their garrets of a starving, haggard, and useless population."[5]

Democratic opponents of homestead legislation marshaled three strong arguments. First, they maintained that Congress had no constitutional power to give away public lands. It could sell them, or grant them in return for some consideration, but to give them away simply squandered the nation's birthright. Second, Democrats argued that Congress had no constitutional authority to meddle in the economy, and homestead plans were clearly intended to promote a specific kind of economic growth. The third argument against giving public lands to settlers was financial. Sales of public land raised revenue, and Democrats opposed alienating a source of funds. In the period between 1839 and 1860, land sales made up the 8 percent of the national income that customs duties did not cover.[6]

Over the years, strict constructionists of the Constitution, generally Southern Democrats who hoped to slow the spread of free labor, thwarted homestead legislation. Three times before 1859 the House passed homestead bills, only to have them rejected by the Senate, which was dominated by Southern Democrats. In 1859, another Homestead Act passed both the House and Senate, but President Buchanan, a Democrat, vetoed it.

During the 1850s, those who would become Republicans began to develop a new rationale for the distribution of public lands, downplaying the argument that it constituted charity for the destitute. Coming of age after the completion of the Erie Canal in 1825 made travel to the West practical, many Republicans had themselves moved West. Galusha A. Grow, the prime advocate of homestead legislation since the 1840s, was typical. He came from a farming family that had moved from Connecticut to Pennsylvania after his father's death threatened the family's financial security. Republicans like Grow were reluctant to brand emigrants as beggars. In their 1860 platform, the Republicans protested "any view of the free homestead policy which regards the settlers as paupers or suppliants for public bounty."[7]

Republicans instead attacked land monopoly, which, they said, was created by land sales to speculators, and which threatened to destroy the existence of a society built on individual labor. Over half of Minnesota's lands and around twenty million acres in Illinois and Iowa were held by speculators. Republicans believed that speculators blocked settlement, as well as squeezed capital from settlers. One newspaper editor estimated in 1860 that speculators had already cost settlers between $500 million and $600 million in higher prices, interest, losses from foreclosures, and sheriffs' fees. Republicans warned against permitting the nation's lands and property to come under the control of a relatively small number of people.[8]

Looking to Europe, Republicans believed that land monopoly created oppression and would destroy the North's free labor economy. The history of land monopoly in Europe "has been written in tears and sighs," Pomeroy explained. Land monopoly wrung the products of labor out of the poor who lived on the land, and reduced them in wealth and spirit. "It has entered like an iron into the soul of the laborer," the Kansas senator continued, "deadened his hopes and extinguished his aspirations to rise in the scale of society." Western newspapers made it clear that political parties would ignore at their peril the tremendous popularity of a homestead bill in the Northwest, and the 1860 Republican platform protested the sale of public lands to any but actual settlers.[9]

By 1861, Republicans had matured a rationale for homestead legislation based on the belief that the economic structure of society rested on agriculture. Wayland and Carey both considered the farmer the first and most vital factor in civilization. Until men produced surplus food, they taught, there was no time or material for alternative production or trade. Once a farmer's labor produced more food than he and his family could use, however, the extra food could support those in other sectors of the economy. These workers, in their turn, would produce more value than they needed to live, and their surplus labor, taking the form of capital, would employ more laborers. Thus, the more developed the nation's agricultural sector became, the more the economy would grow. As the amount of land under cultivation expanded, the nation would became wealthier and the condition of all people would improve. Man's mission on earth, Carey wrote, was to increase agricultural production.[10]

Republicans, many of whom drew on their own farming heritage, embraced this idea. Agricultural interests were "the true sources of our national prosperity," commented a reporter for the Philadelphia *Inquirer.* "Our commercial and manufacturing wealth springs from the Western prairies and the fertile acres of our Eastern States." A Westerner agreed: "The reflecting mind will at once admit that the primary interest of this country is founded on its agricultural developments," read a letter to the editor of the Indianapolis *Daily Journal,* "and that interest is not only primary, but absolutely essential to the prosperity and progress of all the other interests of the country." In Congress, Vermont's Morrill, a student of Carey, explained that "manufactures take no step until agriculture produces a surplus beyond what is required for its own consumption, and from this surplus arises raw material and cheap bread, which make the arts and manufactures flourish. From these results commerce. Trade derives all its support from the basis furnished by agriculture and manufactures." According to the Republican-dominated House Committee on Agriculture, "It is conceded on all hands that the farming interest is the basis of all other interests, and the primary source of national prosperity."[11]

Believing that agriculture supported the American economy, Republicans argued that the distribution of public lands would prove profitable for the nation. A homestead act would harness individual labor into the agricultural sector of the economy, thus increasing the North's economic base. Each level of the economy would then grow, helping the whole nation to prosper. Republicans countered constitutional objections to government involvement in the economy by arguing that Congress's role included economic development if it was demanded by the people. "What is beneficial to the people cannot be detrimental to the Government; for in this country the interests of both are identical," insisted Owen Lovejoy. "With us the Government is simply an agency through which the people act for their own benefit," he concluded.[12]

The war gave the Republicans solid justification for homestead and other agricultural legislation. In April 1861, a Philadelphia newspaper columnist noted that the North's agricultural surpluses meant that the war could not have come at a more opportune time. "It comes at a moment of extraordinary strength," he wrote, "when an unusual deficiency of grain abroad, and a great superfluity of it here, enables us to make large exports of Northern produce" in exchange for specie. Throughout the war, agricultural exports attracted European gold to fund the Union war effort. "Immense individual, corporate and national interests . . . are dependent upon [our] crops," commented the Philadelphia *Inquirer,* and a young man unable to enlist in the army reflected: "If I cannot help our cause as a soldier I certainly can as a farmer." Republicans believed that both the present and future prosperity of the Union depended on agriculture.[13]

At the same time that agricultural exports filled the Treasury with gold from Europe, public lands ceased to contribute to government finances. Once the war broke out, land sales slowed drastically. At the same time, in their desperate search for revenue, Republicans gradually developed a comprehensive system of tariffs and internal taxation, which, along with the sale of bonds, increasingly assumed the weight of government fund-raising. Party members began to feel that permitting the development of public lands to support taxpayers would be much better for the Treasury than hoarding currently unsalable public lands for later profits, and the momentum built behind homestead legislation.

On December 4, 1861, two days after the second session of the Thirty-Seventh Congress began, Owen Lovejoy of Illinois introduced a homestead bill. The "Farmer Congressman," as his constituents called him, knew well the benefits of Western land. Born and reared in Maine, Lovejoy had moved to Illinois in the mid-1830s. His 1843 marriage to a farmer's widow turned his hand from the pulpit and the newspaper press for which he was trained, and by 1858 he had a large, prosperous farm. Once in Congress, he agitated incessantly for abolition and periodically complained that the government neglected agriculture. He had supported unsuccessful homestead legislation in the past. Now, though, a homestead bill stood a good chance of passing, for Southern Democrats were absent from Congress and Grow, also a Western emigrant whose family had recovered from poverty on new land, was Speaker of the House.[14]

Lovejoy introduced his bill quickly and improperly, claiming inaccurately that he had been asked to do so by the Committee on Agriculture, which he chaired. He probably acted at Grow's urging, to forestall the bill that the Committee on Public Lands had been developing. Lovejoy and Grow feared that that committee would attach to a homestead bill a cash bounty for servicemen in lieu of bounty land grants. Such a provision would reassure constituents at home and on the battlefields that the Republicans had not forgotten the boys in blue, but it was bound to cause trouble for the financially strapped wartime government and would endanger the bill's passage.

Lovejoy's attempt to avoid a bounty provision failed; indignant members of the Committee on Public Lands managed to get his bill referred to them.[15]

A week after Lovejoy had introduced his measure, another Eastern emigrant to the West, John Fox Potter of Wisconsin, reported from the Committee on Public Lands the homestead bill it had prepared. The bill (H.R. 125) was similar to those that had passed the House previously; it offered citizens (or immigrants who had announced their intention of becoming citizens) 160 acres of unappropriated land worth $1.25 an acre or less, or 80 acres worth $2.50 an acre. After living on the land for five years and paying a $10 fee, the occupant would receive title from the federal government. Land so acquired could not be attached for any debts incurred before the issuing of the patent for the land. As Lovejoy feared, the bill also included a bounty provision for soldiers.[16]

Although homestead measures had been debated for years and had been popularly demanded, the bill's introduction to Congress attracted virtually no public comment. Newspapers concentrated instead on the imminent threat of war with England over the *Trent* affair, and one editor later noted sheepishly that nothing but war could have diverted attention so completely from such an important measure. In Congress there was almost no Republican opposition to the bill, but many party members deemed it less important than other vital legislation. A week after Potter introduced the measure, the House voted 88 to 50 to postpone its consideration in favor of more pressing business.[17]

A combination of Eastern and border state representatives passed the postponement over the votes of those from Western states, whose citizens had always vigorously supported homestead legislation. Votes against postponement came from Minnesota, Ohio, Illinois, Indiana, Wisconsin, Iowa, Kansas, and western Pennsylvania. Seven votes came from the region of New York that bordered Lake Ontario. Reflecting the regional economic differences revealed in the postponement vote, these states had boasted 663 agricultural societies when the war began in comparison to the mere 66 in all of New England, Maryland, New Jersey, and Missouri. Suddenly vocal after the paper's preoccupation with other matters, a correspondent for the Chicago *Tribune* bitterly predicted that postponement would kill the bill.[18]

At the New York *Daily Tribune,* Horace Greeley was not so ready to consider the bill dead. In the columns of his newspaper, he pressured Congress to pass the measure. A very powerful, if difficult, man, the gnomish Greeley had been reared on a farm and had worked hard for a homestead measure since at least 1848. Legend attributed to him the famous line "Go West, young man," which he reputedly delivered to a Vermont boy, Josiah Bushnell Grinnell, who later represented Iowa in the Thirty-Eighth Congress.[19] "The beneficence and sound policy of letting everyone who will take a patch of wild, vacant public land, and convert it into a homestead and productive farm, have been argued, demonstrated, established, until they have now no open opponent in the Free States," Greeley confidently declared.

Greeley's editorials reiterated the Republican theory that homestead legislation would be a catalyst for national wealth and tied to this theory the government's need to expand the tax base. The wartime necessity to raise money wherever possible should not allow pressure for land revenues to undermine the homestead policy, he wrote, for the expansion of settlement would itself create wealth through the labor it harnessed. Newly flush settlers would buy dutied imports and taxed goods, thus generating more revenue for the government. "Every smoke rising from a new opening in the wilderness marks the foundation of a new feeder to Commerce and the Revenue," he wrote. Further, such a "true policy . . . would prevent the absorption of capital in the always injurious and generally unprofitable monopoly of wild lands."[20]

Postponement did not, in fact, kill the bill. In mid-February 1862, advocates of a homestead bill successfully defeated a Senate amendment to the Legal Tender Act pledging the proceeds of land sales for the repayment of bonds. Republicans William Windom of Minnesota (a transplant from Ohio) and Lovejoy of Illinois led the opposition, reasoning that if the public lands secured bonds and thus the currency, the homestead bill would be defeated. Morrill backed them, saying that it would be a nuisance for the Treasury to keep track of the picayune sums land sales were producing. Indicating support for a homestead measure, the House rejected the Senate amendment pledging the proceeds of land sales to relieve the public debt. In an important shift, Congress thus declared it no longer considered public lands primary sources of public revenue.[21]

The House resumed its discussion of the homestead bill in mid-February 1862, when Grow took the unusual step of calling a colleague to the Speaker's chair and descending to the floor of Congress to speak in favor of the measure. He cut to the heart of opposition to the measure by attacking the constitutional argument against the bill. A large majority of the loyal public clamored for a homestead act, he said, and since "the unmistakable approval of the popular will [was] the indispensable requisite for all legislation in a free elective government," he could see no reason that the bill should not pass.

Grow echoed Greeley, explaining that taxes and tariffs, not public lands, now secured the public credit. Far from hurting the Treasury by alienating a source of revenue, he said, the measure would increase the wealth of the country and enable people to pay the taxes that Congress was imposing. If they had land on which to apply their labor, men would not only feed themselves but also produce agricultural surpluses. The extra cash they received for their produce would enable them to consume more products. Manufactures would increase and revenue from manufacturing taxes would rise. Grow told his colleagues that a homestead law would enable free men to "contribute to the greatness and glory of the Republic" as their labor built American prosperity. They would "develop the elements of a higher and better civilization."

The Speaker's dramatic descent from his chair and impassioned speech in favor of the measure gave the bill momentum. When it came up for final discussion a week later, its friends dominated the debate. Windom of Minnesota categorized opponents of the bill as foes of free labor and of the Union, *"perjured souls"* whose *"parricidal hands"* were at the throat of the government. He added to the argument that homestead legislation would increase the national wealth, marshaling statistics and examples to show how land grants would create capital and bolster the Treasury through tax revenues. The great West would "pour the wealth of empires at our feet," he told his colleagues, if only Congress would allow the labor of willing Americans and new immigrants to rouse the "giant energy of productiveness" asleep there.

Like his colleagues before him, Potter, concluding the House debate on the measure, maintained that until labor was applied to it, land could not add to the nation's general wealth. Settlement, however, promised to increase the nation's wealth dramatically and constantly. The tax base of the nation would grow through higher land values and increased consumption of taxed and dutied goods. Potter provided a critical link between the Republicans' current emphasis on increased revenue and basic Republican abhorrence of large land monopolies by reminding the House that the best use of the public lands was "the purpose for which their Creator designed them—the assignment of a limited quantity to each head of a family, for the purpose of cultivation and subsistence." Potter also foresaw the logical result of homestead legislation. He called for the government to invite immigrants and emigrants into the West, where they would invest their capital and direct their labor to developing the nation's resources.

The bill passed by a vote of 107 to 16, with only three Republicans in the minority. At least one Democrat opposed the bill because he believed the Treasury needed the proceeds of land sales, and, as Greeley gleefully pointed out, two negative Democratic votes were from railroad men who feared that the measure would devalue their company's large Western land holdings. Nineteen Democrats, however, primarily from agricultural states, voted for the bill because they were unwilling to oppose a measure popular with the powerful voting bloc of Westerner farmers, who hoped to see the fresh lands nearby opened cheaply to settlement. The Democratic support for a measure that many Democrats had previously deemed unconstitutional helped to legitimate the Republicans' new approaches to government activity and thus clear the way for further Republican expansion of the government's role in economic development.[22]

The bill went to the Senate in early March, but debate on the measure did not begin until May. Anxious to see the bill pass, the National Land Reform Association gently reminded the powerful Ohio senator John Sherman to give the measure his "especial attention." The Senate first amended the bill by limiting the benefits of the act to those who had maintained strict loyalty to the Union. Then, realizing that the Union could not afford the cash bounty to servicemen no matter how popular it might be, the Senate struck it out.[23]

On May 5, Pomeroy, an emigrant to Kansas from Massachusetts, made a long speech for the bill in which he tied homestead legislation to basic ideas about political economy more fully than the House Republicans had. Like his colleagues in the House, Pomeroy insisted first that homestead legislation was vital to the Union's financial security, for public land sales were no longer raising money. In any case, he added, turning back to basic Republican ideas, land sales caused "unprincipled land monopolies," which would destroy the Union's free society. Drawing on the idea that national prosperity would promote social development, the Kansas senator argued that as men developed unsettled lands and created wealth, they would also elevate the nation spiritually by fostering culture, patriotism, and religion. Like Potter in the House, Pomeroy called for Congress to open land to the landless of all nations and claimed that, by extending settlement into the empty prairies between the Midwest and California, a homestead law would bring freedom and civilization to the whole continent. This elevation of the nation, he noted in his advocacy of the measure, would expand the policy of nationalism the Union had established by the Morrill Tariff duties and by the tax and tariff proposals before Congress.

The following day, May 6, the bill passed by a vote of 33 to 7. Senate Democrats held more strongly to old constitutional opposition to the measure than House Democrats had, but a solidly Democratic minority failed to defeat a majority of thirty Republicans, two Democrats, and one Old-Line Whig.

Greeley joyfully announced to his readers that the homestead bill had passed the Senate. He correctly brushed aside the appointment of a conference committee, claiming that the bill only awaited Lincoln's signature. Indeed, both houses quickly accepted a conference committee report adopting the Senate's amendments, and Lincoln signed the bill on May 20, 1862. Greeley instructed readers how to take advantage of the law, thundering: "Young men! Poor men! Widows! resolve to have a home of your own!"[24]

With the passage of the Homestead Act, the Republicans demonstrated their commitment to a policy of government-sponsored economic development to increase the nation's prosperity and to expand the wartime tax base. "We have now abandoned the public lands as capital," reflected Morrill, "with the design of deriving a larger revenue from those who may settle upon them and make them fruitful." Republican senator William Pitt Fessenden confessed to a friend that he would have willingly postponed the Homestead Act until the war was less pressing, but, he said, "I can not say that the wiser course was not to make the most of our time, for no one knows how soon this country may again fall into a democratic slough." It was imperative, Fessenden realized, for his party to seize this virtually unopposed opportunity to advance its economic vision.[25]

Five days before the homestead bill became law, Lincoln signed a bill creating a Department of Agriculture. The Republicans had not advocated this project during the campaign as they had homestead legislation, but interest in this measure, too, had been growing for decades. It had begun in 1836, when the government established a Patent Office with Connecticut farmer Henry L. Ellsworth as commissioner. On his own time and at his own initiative, Ellsworth distributed seeds and plants all over the nation under the postal franks of congressmen, and every year he published agricultural statistics and information. The next Congress appropriated $1,000 for the Patent Office to continue distributing seeds and accumulating agricultural statistics. By the 1850s, the growing population of Western farmers was agitating for more government recognition; and in 1854, Congress began to make separate appropriations for agriculture. By 1860, distributing seeds and the Patent Office reports on agriculture was a very effective way for a congressman to keep in touch with his constituents.[26]

When the Secretary of the Interior, Caleb Blood Smith, reported to Congress on November 30, 1861, he devoted much of his address to the need for a "Bureau of Agriculture and Statistics." Good statistical information would help America to grow wealthier, he emphasized. Foreign governments distributed such statistics, and America suffered for the want of them. Three days later, in his annual message to Congress, Lincoln worried that "agriculture, confessedly the largest interest of the nation, has, not a department, nor a bureau." He suggested the "great practical value" of "an agricultural and statistical bureau" to provide annual reports on "the condition of our agriculture, commerce, and manufactures."[27]

Republicans responded enthusiastically to Lincoln's suggestion, for it seemed to offer both immediate and long-term benefits to the nation. Since the beginning of the war, people across the North had speculated about the amount of specie the Union's agricultural exports would bring from Europe. The more wisely farmers planted, the better their harvests would be and the more exports the North could send to Europe for gold. The United States Agricultural Society welcomed the idea of an agricultural bureau and elected Lincoln an honorary member, and a Massachusetts agricultural newspaper approvingly abstracted Smith's report. The editor of an Ohio agricultural newspaper asked Ohio senator John Sherman not to let the press of business make him overlook the endorsement of Smith and Lincoln for an agricultural department.[28]

To many Republicans, Lincoln's call for an agricultural and statistical bureau also seemed to be a positive step toward constructing an economy that used labor efficiently and thus created a high standard of living. "Political economy and statesmanship are only convertible terms for Utopian speculation, unless based upon a solid groundwork of facts," reflected a writer in the Philadelphia *Inquirer*. With the establishment of an agricultural and statistical bureau, he continued, "social theories could . . . be reduced to a certainty." This would permit enlightened guiding of economic growth. "A nation . . . with such analytic self-inspection at periodic intervals," the writer continued, "might mould its growth, and forecast its future with a knowledge of all the resources and all the forces operating to shape its destiny."[29]

Republicans believed that the dissemination of agricultural information would help to create a rich nation. In 1861, the famous orator Edward Everett gave a long speech advocating improved agricultural methods and production, which Greeley reprinted in the New York *Daily Tribune*. Everett told farmers that they must make the best use of God's land. The *Boston Cultivator* confirmed that a farmer should work in the "great field of Progress and Improvement, where reward is sure" and encouraged farmers to read and experiment in order to "reap the highest rewards for the labor and money invested." More concretely, when San Francisco was recovering from a devastating flood that had wiped out crops, the local Republican newspaper encouraged farmers to work scientifically to channel flood waters and use them to advantage rather than permitting them to erode valuable topsoil. New methods would obviously make farming more profitable. Every penny the government spent distributing agricultural information produced three pennies, Carey later maintained.[30]

Lovejoy, the "Farmer Congressman," felt strongly that the progress of agriculture depended on good seeds and proper farming techniques. In early January 1862, he introduced a bill (H.R. 269) to establish an agricultural bureau. Auguring well for the measure, the House promptly sent the bill to the Committee on Agriculture, which Lovejoy chaired. Fittingly, the Patent Office's agricultural report had just been released, and congressmen were flooded with requests for it from January on.[31]

In mid-February, Lovejoy brought the bill before the House. It called for the establishment of a Department of Agriculture, the function of which would be to acquire and distribute agricultural information, seeds, and plants. A Commissioner of Agriculture was to collect both statistics and data from experiments. With money in gravely short supply, the bill appropriated only $7,000.

Farming was "the primary source of national prosperity," said the

Republican-dominated committee in its report favoring the bill, and it was time for the government to foster agriculture as it did other trades. Scientific experiment was imperative for the advancement of agriculture, the report continued, because once a farmer understood the laws of nature, he would be able to plant and sow knowledgeably, with maximum results. Further, access to the agricultural statistics of the country would enable a farmer to calculate the approximate value of his crops and adjust his efforts to meet demand. England had provided its farmers with information and had helped them to produce more efficiently, the committee reported. America must do the same, said the committee, for the country was running out of virgin land. In a curious blend of religion and Republican economics, the committee concluded that when American farmers achieved maximum production through increased scientific knowledge and ability, man could "hope to find the whole earth transformed into the beautiful garden that he left in the olden time."

After the House amended the bill to appropriate only $5,000, Lovejoy immediately brought the measure to a favorable vote of 122 to 7. Costing little, the bill would please agricultural districts, and therefore, like the Homestead Act, it attracted Democratic votes. Twenty-three Democrats and ten Old-Line Whigs joined eighty-nine Republicans in the majority.[32]

The next day, February 18, the Senate took up the bill and, since the Senate would not have a Committee on Agriculture until the next session of Congress, referred it to the Committee on Patents and the Patent Office. While the committee was considering the bill, Republican newspapers pressured the Senate to pass it. The San Francisco *Daily Alta California* made it clear that accurate agricultural statistics were vital to California, although it did not explicitly endorse the idea of a department of agriculture. A reporter from the Patent Office for the Indianapolis *Daily Journal* went further and hinted at the need for official attention to agriculture when he rejoiced that "at least one Department of the Government is devoted to the furtherance of agriculture—that sole source of prosperity in peace, as well as the entire reliance of contending armies in the field." A writer for the Philadelphia *Inquirer* was even more explicit. An agricultural department, he wrote, "has long been demanded by the vast interests which are the true sources of our national prosperity." Agriculture supported commercial and manufacturing wealth, he continued, "and Congress exhibits an appreciation of this fact by its intention to encourage a thorough knowledge in the various branches of the noble pursuit of agriculture among the masses of the people."[33]

In mid-April, James F. Simmons, the Rhode Island cotton trader who chaired the Patent Committee, called up the bill that had already passed the House. Downplaying the fact that it created a new department and new offices, he told the Senate that the measure merely detached the agricultural bureau from the Patent office to "compliment . . . the great leading interest of industry." Agriculture, he said, constitutes "the pillar of the national strength," and the bill would remedy the fact that it had previously received little government attention. The Senate quickly passed all of the committee's rather technical amendments to the House bill before beginning debate on the measure itself.[34]

Joseph A. Wright, from the farming state of Indiana, offered a much stronger measure than the House bill for an agricultural department. Calling for the establishment of a separate statistical bureau, Wright's bill (S. 249) created an agricultural department with four separate bureaus. These bureaus were to investigate agricultural science; natural history; chemistry; and mechanics, manufactures, commerce, and agricultural statistics. There had never been a time when America depended so completely on agriculture, Wright maintained. Not only did Union finances need agricultural exports to attract specie from Europe, but also the North must work to replace vital Southern products, such as cotton and sugar, which the war had made unobtainable. Congress also needed to help Union farmers regulate their crops to fit the European and domestic market. Admitting that his plan would cost a great deal—though less than $60,000 a year, he claimed—Wright reminded his colleagues that the economic well-being of the nation rested on agriculture. "Manufactures and commerce are but the handmaids of agriculture," he told them.[35]

The Senate rejected Wright's comprehensive plan by a vote of 23 to 12. The vote did not really reflect sectional or political affiliations: yea votes came from New Hampshire, Virginia, Indiana, Missouri, California and Oregon, while nay votes came from Illinois, Ohio, Minnesota, and Iowa, as well as the New England states. More significant than geography or politics was Simmons's telling objection that Wright's bill would cost much more money than the House bill. Frugality was vital in the spring of 1862.

Although the Senate declined to make a major financial commitment to an agricultural department during wartime, it also refused to ignore the farming interest. It rejected a proposal of Connecticut's Lafayette S. Foster simply to split the department of agriculture and statistics from the Patent Office and leave it within the Department of the Interior. Simmons accurately pointed out that Foster's proposal, which could currently be accomplished at the discretion of the Interior Department, eliminated the need for any legislation at all. The Senate rejected Foster's plan by a tie of 18 to 18, leaving the House bill intact. Again, the votes were spread across sections and parties.

Because the bill establishing an agricultural department competed for time with many more spectacular wartime bills, its discussion was sporadic and carried over into May. On May 8, the House bill came up for a vote. One congressman challenged the constitutionality of the measure, objecting to appropriations of government revenues for schemes of economic development. Fessenden revealed that Republicans were willing to chart new activities for the government. He suggested that he might have agreed with that objection if years of appropriations had not established a legislative precedent. In any case, he said, the country had been reimbursed for such appropriations—"richly paid over and over again in absolute increase of wealth. There is no doubt of that." Fessenden's response indicated the prevalence of the belief that agricultural knowledge paid in increased wealth, for he spoke out despite his unhappiness at increasing expenses during wartime.

The House bill passed the Senate by a vote of 25 to 13. The negative votes came from Westerners such as Wright, who felt the bill did not do enough for farmers, and from Easterners such as Fessenden, who objected to any additional expenses during wartime. Unwilling to abandon farmers, only one Democrat voted against the measure. Four Democrats and two border state Old-Line Whigs voted for it. The yea votes were spread throughout the North.

After the House agreed to the Senate's technical amendments to the bill, Lincoln signed it on May 15, 1862. On that day, the *Bureau County Republican,* the newspaper from Lovejoy's home district, applauded "the first important movement by Congress looking directly to the interests of the man who cultivates the soil."[36]

On December 9, 1861, shortly after homestead legislation had been introduced in the House, Morrill of Vermont announced that he would introduce a bill donating public lands to the states for the purpose of establishing colleges for agriculture and the mechanical arts. Like homestead legislation and interest in a department of agriculture, the idea of federal aid to agricultural education was not new. George Washington's second annual message had suggested a national college for agricultural instruction, and in the decades since then, a government agent had studied European agricultural teaching methods and his research was reprinted twice at the direction of Congress. Movements for agricultural colleges had gained strength throughout the North, especially in New England.[37]

A college bill captivated Morrill's heart. The son of a blacksmith, the tall, earnest Vermont man had been unable to attend college and felt the loss keenly. Worrying that education would come to be available only to the wealthy, Morrill hoped for the creation of tuition-free colleges that would teach subjects of interest to farmers and mechanics. Hesitant to call for the government's creation of a national system of education, however, Morrill argued that states would build such colleges if only Congress granted them public lands to sell. The money the states would receive from land sales would establish funds to support agricultural colleges. Morrill introduced his first college bill in 1856, but Congress crushed it.[38]

When Morrill reintroduced his college measure in 1858, he tried to lend strength to his proposal by attacking the prevalent opposition argument that the Constitution did not authorize Congress to donate lands for projects outside Congress's express powers. Morrill cited previous government land grants to provide revenue for state projects and institutions. He also pointed out that the government favored commerce through improving harbors and keeping lighthouses; state railroads through land grants; authors through copyright laws; and mechanics through patent rights. Agriculture, he complained, was left out. Virtually all of Morrill's examples of government aid to economic groups fell under specific constitutional grants of power, but he nonetheless convinced the House that the national government could donate lands to foster agriculture. The House passed the bill, and the Senate followed suit in 1859. President Buchanan, however, promptly vetoed the measure, reiterating doubts about the constitutionality of giving away lands to the states without compensation.[39]

Morrill doggedly reintroduced his college land bill (H.R. 138) in mid-December 1861. The measure offered states 30,000 acres of unappropriated public land for each of a state's senators and representatives. The states would sell these lands and invest the proceeds in a permanent fund to support agricultural colleges. The House referred the bill to the Committee on Public Lands, which was chaired by Potter, who opposed the bill because it would enable Eastern states to grab large chunks of remaining public lands in Western states like his own state of Wisconsin. Because tax and tariff bills were in the offing, absorbing all of Morrill's attention, it appeared that the college bill might not see the light of day. It languished in committee until the end of May, when Potter reported it with a recommendation that it should not pass.[40]

Morrill was willing to fight for a college bill, however, because by the spring of 1862, he believed that the Union needed such a measure more than ever. In a speech shortly after Potter's committee reported, he outlined the many reasons for a college plan. As Republicans had done in debates about the homestead bill, Morrill concentrated on establishing that a college bill would increase agricultural production and thus contribute to national prosperity.

Turning first to the Homestead Act, Morrill insisted that to give land to men who did not know how to use it was "at best a bauble, and often a curse." Educating settlers would enable them to use their new land effectively. Agricultural colleges would help to improve not only the new lands but also the old, "thereby extending," as Morrill made sure to point out, "the basis of taxation and revenue." He believed that the availability of cheap public lands encouraged wasteful and destructive farming techniques. Vermont agriculture, and indeed that of all New England, had declined as new Western lands opened and Easterners had rushed to the rich prairies. Depleted soil and high emigration rates were destroying Eastern agricultural production. If indeed agriculture supported all other industries, as Republicans believed, such a decline would destroy the Union's prosperity. Tax revenues, vital to supporting the war, would drop.[41]

Particularly attractive to Morrill's Republican listeners was his argument that agricultural colleges could slow the growing emigration from rural to urban areas. Republicans disliked cities, fearing that they undermined America's free republican government by reducing independent yeomen to dependent vassals of employers or politicians. A member of Lincoln's cabinet mused that city dwellers might be incompetent to exercise self-government, for only "in an agricultural district, or a sparse population the old rule holds." An editor of the New York *Times* later went so far as to try to create in the city "a class corresponding to the yeomanry of agricultural communities."

He called for workers to join in cooperatives and "carry on their own business, manage their own affairs, sell their own goods." Morrill's solution was simpler. He maintained that the "tendency to desert the rural districts and to shun manual labor" could "only be checked by making the country more attractive and more remunerative." New information and scientific methods would increase production and make farming a more attractive profession.[42]

Morrill tried to persuade his Western colleagues, who opposed the college bill because they objected to the alienation of the public lands within their borders, that Eastern colleges would advance Western interests. Settlers from the East were pouring into their states, he argued, and emigration without education lowered the quality of men in both new and old states. Uneducated emigrants would not labor effectively in the new states, as they could only experiment ineffectually with the soil. Skilled labor in the old states would lose its edge as the dispersal of dense population reduced demand for agricultural products and permitted farming techniques to decline. The aggregate wealth of the entire country would decrease. Educating young Eastern emigrants meant that when they went West, they would be ready to begin contributing immediately to the wealth of their new states. Educating those who remained in the East would help to maintain the nation's agricultural production.

The college bill also had to overcome prejudice against "what is too often derisively called 'book-farming.'" Farmers had no use for colleges, critics charged; they needed experience. Morrill argued that the prejudice against educated farmers came from the fact that they had no real agricultural education and were unfit for farming. True agricultural education had an important role to play in a Northern society of small land owners, said Morrill, for "every man owns or expects to own land at some period in his life, and it could certainly do him no harm to be taught how to manage landed property."[43]

The bill, Morrill said, was "demanded by the wisest economy," for nothing could increase production, and therefore national wealth and power, like the education of farmers. Education trained a man to work more efficiently, concentrating his whole physical and mental ability on the task at hand. "Science, working unobtrusively, produces larger annual returns and constantly increases fixed capital, while ignorant routine produces exactly the reverse," he said. As agriculture became more productive, manufacturing and trade would become more profitable, wealth would increase, and the American people would lead better lives. Capitalizing on growing Republican hostility to England, Morrill warned his listeners that if the Union did not make the effort that Europe did to educate its farmers, America would be "dwarfed in national importance" and eventually become so poor it would be forced to import even grain. As advocates of the homestead bill had argued in debates over that measure, Morrill assured his colleagues that increased national wealth would benefit the Union tangibly as wealthier farmers paid taxes and tariffs.

Finally, to make his scheme more palatable at a time when the nation's energies had to be focused on the war, Morrill advocated military training at the agricultural colleges. "These colleges, founded in every State, will elevate the character of farmers and mechanics, increase the prosperity of agriculture, manufactures, and commerce, and may to some extent guard against . . . sheer ignorance of all military art."

Morrill did not confine his fight for the bill to the floor of the House. Anticipating Potter's attempt to kill the measure, he and the bill's friends asked Ohio senator Benjamin Franklin Wade to sponsor a similar bill in the Senate while Potter's committee was still considering the measure. Like Morrill, Wade had supported such legislation before, and he willingly introduced his own bill (S. 298) to the Senate on May 2. Wade's bill, which was virtually identical to Morrill's, proposed granting to each state 30,000 acres of unappropriated public land, worth $1.25 an acre, for each of its senators and representatives. If a state chose to accept its portion of the grant, it could select lands that would be surveyed and then sold for cash. The proceeds from the sale of the lands were to be invested in a permanent fund to support agricultural and mechanical arts colleges. No state in rebellion could take advantage of the act.[44]

When the Senate began to consider this bill in mid-May, Republican James H. Lane of Kansas led the opposition. The new Western states, with their rich untouched land and sparse population, felt much less need for agricultural education than the Eastern states, whose soil was depleted and well settled. Further, as Lane insisted to the Senate just as Potter had made clear to the House, the newer, Western states feared that, under the college bill, all their remaining public lands would be taken up by the older states that had no public land left within their own borders. Massachusetts, for instance, or—much worse in the eyes of Westerners—New York would be entitled to hundreds of thousands of Western acres under the provisions of this bill. Such a distribution would reduce the amount of land available for funding state projects. It would also give Eastern states, which could sell their land grants to whomever they chose, control over the settlement of Western states. Angry Westerners felt the bill was "a nefarious outrage on the West."[45]

Lane was aware, however, that a bill that would so benefit the older states stood a good chance of succeeding. New England was exceptionally prominent in the Senate, claiming eleven committee chairs, according to a jealous Western newspaper correspondent. In addition, whatever opposition Western states could present to such a measure had been softened by the passage of the Homestead Act, which was immensely popular in the West and much less welcome in the East, and which therefore disposed senators and representatives from Western states to vote for the college bill out of a sense of fairness.[46]

Lane wisely decided to reform the land provisions of the bill rather than try to kill it. His most powerful argument against the measure was that it would violate the principle of the Homestead Act. The college bill contained no restrictions on land sales, and the logistics of disposing of huge tracts of lands would favor speculators, who could buy in large parcels, over settlers, who would want to buy small farms for their own use. Lane claimed that the plan would simply repeat the pattern of land monopoly that the Republicans had designed the Homestead Act to prevent.

Western opponents of the bill rallied around Lane's argument. Lane first tried unsuccessfully to introduce an amendment limiting the land taken under the bill to that of unorganized lands, rather than from states or organized territories. When he proposed an amendment limiting the land taken in any state to one million acres, however, Wade was forced to concede that the provision seemed harmless, and it passed. The Senate refused to go further and limit each purchaser to 640 acres because such a restriction would make sales unwieldy. Such a provision might have stood a better chance of passing had it not been proposed by an unpopular operator, Senator Pomeroy of Kansas, who inconsistently claimed that he wanted to prevent land monopoly, even though a major railroad bill of his own contained no such provisions.

In his opposition to the bill, Lane also gave fodder to Democrats opposed to the measure and revealed his aptitude for political expediency. Despite the fact that Lane had led raiding expeditions into Missouri to capture slaves and bring them into Kansas as laborers, he now complained that under the terms of the bill, a state with a slave population could sell the Western lands it received to its own freedmen, encouraging them to leave. These emigrants, unwelcome in old states, would settle the new Western states. A Democratic Ohio newspaper picked up on this theme and cried to its readers: "Wade Proposes to Flood the New States with Free Negroes."[47]

Western opposition could not prevent the college bill from passing the Senate in mid-June by a vote of 32 to 7. In the negative were six Western Republicans and one Democrat.[48] That many Westerners ultimately approved the bill probably reflected their gratitude to the Eastern states for the Homestead Act.

A week after the Senate passed Wade's land grant college bill, Morrill moved that the House take it up. Potter tried to get it referred to the Committee on Public Lands, which he chaired, but failed by a vote of 31 to 83. He then tried to postpone consideration of the bill until January 1863, but was ruled out of order. He unsuccessfully moved to adjourn, to lay the bill on the table, and to postpone for amendments. Once Potter was neutralized, the bill passed by a vote of 90 to 25. The negative votes were primarily from members of the Western states—Indiana, Minnesota, Michigan, Ohio, Illinois, Wisconsin, Iowa—that feared they would lose lands. Lincoln signed the bill on July 1, 1862.[49]

The press had virtually ignored this bill, but once it passed, Greeley announced his unqualified approbation of the measure. It was a triumph auguring "wide and lasting good," he said, to have colleges to promote knowledge "of the sciences which underlie and control the chief processes of Productive Labor." Greeley disparaged the argument that the act would lead to monopoly and speculation. The amount of acreage appropriated, he said, was negligible. The fear that the bill would take all the nation's free land, he said, was "much like a shuddering fear that some thirsty ox may drink up the Mississippi at spring flood and leave all its vessels aground evermore."[50]

The Republican party had at least some of its roots in the nativism of the 1850s, but during the war the party's search for additional labor to increase farm production made it gradually come to champion immigration. Old ethnic and religious prejudices began to break down as soon as the war began. Since loyalty to the Union was paramount, Republicans preferred loyal immigrants to disloyal Southerners and, in the first months of the war, Republican newspapers noted that some previously unpopular groups were loyal and patriotic. Chase awarded a few clerkships in the Treasury Department to Catholics "in view of the promptitude with wh[ich] the Catholic Population came forward to the support of the Gov[ernmen]t in this crisis." In the New York *Daily Tribune,* Greeley ran two long patriotic letters from Catholics denying that the Catholic Church was proslavery and insisting on its strong antislavery, pro-Union stance. Acceptance of ethnic and religious groups hinged on perceived loyalty to the Union. The month after his defense of his appointments of Catholics, Chase worried openly about "Jew traders" who were allegedly shipping goods to the South.[51]

Throughout the war, the North's growing anger at England also mitigated Republican prejudice against foreigners. The Union's Irish community in particular won approbation as an enemy of England. The Irish would fight England, if necessary, the editor of the Chicago *Tribune* claimed in 1861, and would certainly fight the Southern aristocracy in the name of Northern freedom. Greeley agreed in the columns of the New York *Daily Tribune,* and the editor of the Indianapolis *Daily Journal* reprinted a column from a Dublin newspaper telling Irish men to stand by the Union. Even the editor of a paper in Boston, a city that bore no love for immigrants, applauded Irish disapproval of England's guarded stance toward the North. The formation of Irish-American regiments confirmed Republican faith in the community's loyalty to the Union. When draft riots in New York City during the summer of 1863 left African-Americans dead at the hands of rioters, Greeley defended the Irish community, maintaining that the mobs were not representative of New York's immigrant population.[52]

Early in the war, Republicans turned to foreigners and immigrants to fill the ranks of the army. Believing the Union cause was part of an international struggle against despotism and aristocracy, they called for men like Italy's Giuseppe Garibaldi to come fight for the Union.[53] Even foreigners without republican principles would fight, some Republicans believed. Carey wrote to Chase that men would come by the hundreds of thousands to take advantage of bounty money and army salaries. While some men did come, many native-born Americans perceived them as highly unsatisfactory soldiers. More important, many more immigrants stayed away, recognizing that high bounties were useless unless one lived to enjoy them. Immigration to America slowed during 1861 and 1862 as potential immigrants wondered if they would find themselves on battlefields if they moved. Only after 1863, when the North recognized its desperate need for labor and began to reassure immigrants that they were not going to be drafted did immigration begin to pick up. By 1865, it had returned to prewar levels.[54]

Finding men to fill regiments was never the driving force behind the Republicans' promotion of immigration. Just as they supported the Homestead Act, Republicans advocated immigration because they wanted to harness labor into the service of the country. While some skilled immigrants might be useful in urban workshops, Republicans planned for most of them to contribute to Union wealth by filling the empty Western farmlands or working on established, but labor-starved, Western farms. Greeley gloated that the free public lands provided by the homestead measure would attract "a flood-tide" of "the very best kind of immigrants . . . honest, industrious, thrifty farmers and mechanics" who would increase the country's prosperity. There was "no such thing as surplus Labor," he wrote. Attracting more laborers would make the nation vastly richer, a consideration especially pressing with the Treasury in financial straits. "Every man imported is a machine that represents a capital of at least $1000," wrote economist Carey emphatically to Chase. "Half a million men are worth more than $500,000,000—*more than the total cost of a year of war.*"[55]

From the beginning of the war, the Republicans believed that a growing agricultural sector not only would energize the whole Union economy, but also would bring gold to the Treasury through agricultural exports. Beginning in April 1861, Republican newspapers carried frequent articles about grain exports to Europe and the consequent favorable balance of trade between the Union and Europe. "The concurrence of a dearth in Europe with abundant crops in the Northern states," maintained a writer for the New York *Times,* "undoubtedly proved our salvation."[56] The drain of men to the battlefields, however, caused labor shortages in the fields. By harvesttime of 1862, newspapers reported that the labor shortage was "a serious embarrassment" and that the West could use 100,000 additional laborers. An apparent drop in agricultural production in 1863 only confirmed that the farmlands needed more labor to maintain the production levels that brought European gold to the Union.[57]

Republicans also believed that settling the West would spread the North's economic system, thereby preventing the South's peculiar institution from expanding to the territories. A passionate letter to

Senator Sherman in 1861 from a poorly educated farmer demanded that the government "protect Emegration and that will protect the Territories to Freedom." White immigration, the man told Sherman, had "hanged Slavery." Similarly, Carey confided to Lincoln his opinion that greater numbers of white settlers in the hill country of the South would have prevented secession.[58]

By concentrating their efforts on attracting immigrants to the West, Republicans minimized confrontations with city workers opposed to the arrival of cheap foreign laborers. When New York City's Chamber of Commerce ignored the possibility of angry workers and flirted with importing immigrants, it found itself in deep trouble. When "the mechanics of the city" heard a rumor that the chamber had discussed encouraging immigration, they organized a protest meeting at the Democratic stronghold, Tammany Hall. The Chamber of Commerce immediately denied that it had any plans to import labor. It accused demagogues and troublemakers of trying to stir up working men against what those demagogues called the "wealthy classes" in order to divide the North and strengthen secession.[59]

Publicly confining their aims to increasing the agricultural population, by 1862 Republicans had begun to search for ways to increase immigration. In the summer of 1862, Carey asked one of his closest friends, E. Peshine Smith, to go to Europe seeking immigrants. Smith did not relish the task, but would undertake it as "a war-service, such as a man is not at liberty to decline, if it should be thought I owe it to the country," he replied. Carey's friend had strongly supported Secretary of State William Henry Seward in New York politics; and, perhaps at Smith's urging, Seward at this time suggested to United States officials in Europe that they work to encourage immigration. By late 1862, Western newspapers were actively calling for an increase in immigration.[60]

In the late summer of 1863, Republicans began to use the national government to attract immigrants. They sent a special government agent to Europe to familiarize potential immigrants with the land and resources of the country west of the Mississippi. Although this effort was modest, a correspondent for the Indianapolis *Daily Journal* reported that "it is believed the mission will prove to be of great benefit to the development of the great west." The Indianapolis *Daily Journal's* optimism was ill-founded for, as hundreds of potential immigrants swamping American consulates abroad attested, lack of funds, not lack of interest, kept potential immigrants at home.[61]

Government promotion of immigration began in earnest in late 1863. In his message of December 8, 1863, Lincoln asked Congress to consider "the expediency of establishing a system for the encouragement of immigration." Immigrants were a "source of national wealth and strength" and were greatly needed as laborers in the agricultural and mining regions, he said. Greeley took Lincoln's cue and wrote that immigration was one of the elements of national progress. He looked forward to hosts of new settlers.[62]

A week after Lincoln's message, the House appointed a Select Committee on Immigration to consider the President's suggestion. Secretary of State Seward also acted on Lincoln's recommendation, but he directed his efforts toward encouraging private aid for the transportation of new settlers. Seward sent a circular to the Boards of Trade in Eastern cities asking them to consider ways in which they could foster immigration.

Over the next year, private immigration societies formed in Eastern cities. In Boston, a Society of Foreign Emigration, led by one of Carey's disciples, was organized in January 1864. The Boston group planned for employers and Western landowners to pool capital for importing immigrants. Once arrived, the immigrants would repay the money advanced. In the same year, a group of Philadelphia iron merchants associated with Carey merged with the American Emigrant Company, a group of New England speculators in Western lands, to form a new American Emigrant Company, organized to promote European immigration. Although it had no formal government connection, this group clearly had convinced many Republicans that it could solve the immigration problem. Its supporters included several prominent Republican politicians: Secretary of the Treasury Chase, Secretary of the Navy Gideon Welles, Secretary of the Interior James Harlan, Senator Charles Sumner, and Senator Henry Wilson, among others, endorsed the plan.[63]

Despite such prominent support, neither the American Emigrant Company nor the Society of Foreign Emigration attracted much interest from businessmen. Strikes over low wages and a dwindling labor supply were not enough to convince employers to pay to import workers. Not only could they ill afford to alienate their existing laborers, since they had few available replacements for any who decided to strike, but also employers understood that contracts made outside the country could not legally be enforced within American borders. They stood to lose investments made in transportation when immigrants discovered that they had no legal obligation to repay the debt.[64]

By the planting season of 1864, with the apparent weakness of private attempts to import laborers, Republicans clamored for government aid to immigration. "Nothing could be more wise," said an editorial in the New York *Times,* "than the encouragement of immigration. The introduction of laborers is an import of the richest source of wealth." A reporter in the Cincinnati *Daily Gazette* speculated that the government would pay for the transportation of poor immigrants to America, and Congress received countless petitions to establish a bureau of immigration. Significantly, most of these petitions were directed to the Committees on Agriculture of the respective houses of Congress.[65]

In mid-February 1864, Senator Sherman, chairman of the new Senate Committee on Agriculture, reported a bill (S. 125) to encourage immigration, and two weeks later, the Senate took it up. Reflecting the older, discredited belief that a dearth of information kept Europeans away, the Senate bill made no effort to free capital for funding transportation. The measure provided for the appointment of a Commissioner of Immigration in the Department of State who would gather information about American agricultural conditions, wage rates, and labor needs. He would disseminate the information in popular form in Europe in order to "encourage, facilitate, and protect foreign immigration to and within the United States." The commissioner would also direct a new U.S. Emigrant Office in New York City that would protect immigrants from "imposition and fraud" and help them reach their final destinations or, if the immigrant had not chosen a destination, to send him to the place "where his labor will be most profitable." No one involved with land sales or with transporting immigrants could hold office under this act. Indicating the Republicans' belief in the importance of the project, the bill included a substantial $50,000 a year appropriation.[66]

Sherman told the Senate that the Committee on Agriculture deemed this a very important project. "In the western States labor is absolutely demanded," he explained. He enthusiastically foretold that this bill could bring immigration up to 100,000 able-bodied persons within a year, and soon after that might bring it even higher. The Senate passed the bill in early March with almost no discussion.

While the Senate had been working on its immigration bill, the House Select Committee on Immigration had written one of its own, with considerable advice from Seward. In mid-April the committee reported its bill (H.R. 411), which tried to encourage immigration with funds as well as information. Reluctant to assert that the national government could assume sole responsibility for immigration, the committee had devised a system combining the efforts of government and private interests to attract new settlers. It called for a government-funded Emigrant Office in New York City to disseminate information and to protect newly arrived settlers from swindlers. The committee attempted to lower transportation costs by reducing tonnage duties on immigrant ships; and, if immigrants still could not afford to travel to America, the new bill permitted them to borrow against their future homesteads. To encourage private sponsorship of immigration, the committee declared enforceable all government-supervised contracts for labor for passage made in foreign countries; but, hoping that even city immigrants would move West quickly, it stipulated that such contracts could not exceed twelve months or be drafted to impose slavery or servitude.[67]

The House Select Committee on Immigration introduced short-term contract labor not to maintain a cheap urban labor force, as some have charged, but to prevent the need for government financial aid for the importation of immigrants to work on Western farmlands. The American Emigrant Company had written to Seward in April 1864 requesting that the government fund the costs incurred when importing immigrants: transportation, food, clothing, and so on. Despite Seward's involvement in its creation, however, the House bill stopped short of suggesting such a plan because the committee hoped to avoid a confrontation about Congress's authority to fund a project clearly outside Congress's express constitutional powers and because Republicans feared that free passage for immigrants would lead foreign governments to dump their undesirables on America. Paupers and prisoners, as Greeley said, would replace honest laborers in the immigrant ships.[68]

Despite its weak endorsement of the failing private agencies, the committee hoped to guarantee that, instead of remaining contract laborers, immigrants would enter the free labor force. Republican economic theory indicated that those who worked for themselves produced more than those who worked for others. The more immigrant laborers produced, the more their labor would help to fuel a national spiral of prosperity. While short-term contract labor might be necessary to keep the government from being forced into importing immigrants, long-term contract labor would reduce an immigrant's contribution to the economy. Indeed, most contemporary observers interpreted the bill as an encouragement to Western, not urban, immigration. Even city workers sensitive to competition gave little attention, let alone opposition, to the bill.[69]

The House passed the bill with no discussion and no division.

While the House bill sat in the Senate Committee on Agriculture, to which it had been referred, newspapers continued to press the issue. In addition to reiterating the need for labor, they continued their campaign to break down the xenophobia that might discourage immigration. The editor of the Chicago *Tribune*, who had been distinguished before the war for his nativism, now called repeatedly for immigrants, and wanted not only Germans and Scandinavians, but also Irish, Italians, Hungarians, and Poles. The editor of the New York *Times* identified the contradiction between the nationalism for which America was striving and the call for immigration. Revealing that pressure for labor did not necessarily mean welcome of heterogeneity, he resolved that tension by assuring his readers that since "yellow and brown races" such as the "Chinese, Hindoos or Turks" did not come to America, the nation could maintain its nationality as all blended into a basic Anglo-Saxon mold. He said that even Catholics, primary targets of antebellum nativism, were different in America than in Europe. Many became Protestants, and even those who retained their religion accepted American culture, he claimed.[70]

In late June 1864, when Sherman called up the House bill, the Senate instead repassed without a division or discussion the measure it had previously matured. A conference committee easily reconciled the two bills, producing a final measure based on the House bill's plan for freeing transportation capital. The measure appropriated $25,000, permitted businessmen to import workers, and assured that no immigrant who arrived after the act was passed could be drafted during the current war until he had announced his intention of becoming a U.S. citizen and renounced old allegiances. While noncitizens could not vote or share certain other citizenship rights, there was no government pressure to ask for citizenship quickly; one did not have to become a citizen to remain in the Union, and there were no time limits on citizenship eligibility. In early July, both Houses agreed to this version of the bill.[71]

Lincoln signed "an Act to encourage Immigration" on July 4, 1864. While the new law initially did little to aid private efforts at immigration, its clear bid for new settlers and its efforts to make transportation cheaper and safer helped immigration increase dramatically. By 1864, the Republican party had publicly rejected its nativist roots and devoted itself to increasing the country's labor supply. The Republican platform of 1864 called for a continued liberal policy of immigration, which "has added so much to the wealth, development of resources and increase of power to this nation."[72]

As the 1864 Republican platform indicated, party members designed their agricultural legislation to maximize farm production and, in so doing, nurture the fundamental element of the economy from which all others would grow. Republicans were so united in this goal that, except for stress between the East and West over the terms of the Land Grant College Act, their agricultural legislation neither revealed nor caused schisms within the party.

Republican agricultural legislation did much to settle the West and provide homes for farming families, but it did not ultimately create the thriving expanses of small farms Republicans had envisioned. Although the high initial costs of breaking sod and surviving until a crop matured broke many hopeful farmers, as many as 60 percent of those who took up land in the public land states in the North and West persevered and eventually built themselves Western farms, albeit with much more effort and money than the Republicans had foreseen.[73]

While the Northwest did, in fact, enjoy a huge postwar boom in agriculture, those farmers who prospered were not the self-sufficient small farmers of the antebellum world, but those who switched most successfully to a new, large enterprise system of industrial farming. The war, with its railroad boom and need to move crops in large amounts, had tied farmers directly to a national economy and promoted commercial farming at the expense of the old system of subsistence farming supplemented by surplus cash crops. By 1890, the day of the small farmer was over.[74]

As it promoted American farming to stimulate the economy's export-producing sector and to increase the tax base, agricultural legislation broke down the belief that government intervention in the economy was unconstitutional. The wartime need for money opened the way for Republicans to use the government to foster economic development, although they refused to have the government assume

sole responsibility for such unprecedented actions as establishing national schools or funding foreign immigration. Significantly, the same
agricultural legislation that established the national government's
power to develop the economy helped make such intervention necessary. Homestead legislation permanently removed public lands as a
source of revenue and thus irrevocably committed the nation to a
reliance on taxes and tariffs for national funds. From this time on, in
order to maintain Treasury revenues, the national government had a
vital interest in fostering the American economy.

6 | "It Was Statesmanship to Give
Treeless Prairies Value":
The Transcontinental Railroad

Legislation adapted to our necessities, to our growth and progress,
is the only course left for us to pursue if we would hold our place
among the nations of the earth.

—James H. Campbell, 1862

During the war, military requirements provided a convenient constitutional justification for a transcontinental railroad, but to Republicans, providing for the construction of a Pacific railroad also seemed
an economic and political necessity. Such a railroad would, they
believed, help to develop the nation and increase national productivity
by settling the Western plains and providing access to Western gold
mines. Wishing to promote American growth and greatness, Republicans also recognized that wartime railroad legislation would send a
message to the rest of the world that they had great confidence in the
eventual triumph of the Union and that Congress could "calmly and
efficiently provide for the improvement of the nation" while crushing
rebellion.[1]

As it developed the nation, Republican transcontinental railroad
legislation brought government participation in economic growth to
a new level. The increased wartime responsibilities of the government
had enabled the Republicans to explore and gain confidence in the
national economy, then to strengthen the national government's economic role in the country through banking, currency, tax, and tariff
legislation. With their homestead and land grant college acts, the
Republicans had developed an active role for the government in the
economy by using government land grants to develop agriculture.
Republican transcontinental railroad legislation went further. It used
government funds to finance national development, and it asserted
Congress's power to establish nationally chartered corporations.
Through years of wartime debate on transcontinental railroads, Re-

publicans established what they believed to be a beneficial working relationship between the government and private enterprise.

Agitation for a transcontinental railroad began in the 1840s. The tortuous overland journey from the settled Eastern states to the Pacific daunted many who wished to make the trip. A traveller to the West had to negotiate two towering mountain ranges, ford rivers, face hostile Native Americans, and brave inclement weather. A Democrat who would strongly support transcontinental railroad legislation during the Civil War, Senator James A. McDougall, found the overland trip almost unbearable. On his way to California from Illinois in the days before a railroad, he got lost, wandered at length in the mountains, barely escaped starvation, and, as a colleague later recalled, "finally reached San Francisco in rags, clothed partly in skins, without money, and not having seen a barber or razor for months."[2] Not surprisingly, the movement for a transcontinental railroad gradually gained momentum. In 1853, Stephen A. Douglas introduced to the Senate a plan for the construction of such a road. Although Douglas's plan crumbled, support for the project continued to grow. By 1860, the idea of a coast-to-coast road was tremendously popular, especially in the West.[3]

Before the war, discussions of a Pacific railroad necessarily opened debate about the role of the federal government in developing the nation.[4] State governments had always promoted local economic development; but, after a brief phase in the early nineteenth century when the national government sponsored certain economic improvements, Democrats had labeled such activity on the part of the federal government unconstitutional. Congress ceased to intervene in economic development beyond granting public lands to states to sell for funding canals, railroads, and so on. Unlike smaller state projects, however, the construction of a transcontinental railroad could not be accomplished by any one state. The route of a Pacific railroad must cross the territories, over which Congress held sole authority. Such a project also required the financial support of the national government. "It is obvious to any one," declared one Republican congressman, "that no private enterprise will take hold of a work of such magnitude, without some demonstration on the part of the Government to lend aid and assistance to the enterprise."[5] Finally, the plan was primarily advanced not by state-oriented capitalists hoping to construct the railroad for their own profit, but by the government and national politicians seeking to get it built for the public good.[6] Recognizing that a transcontinental railroad could not be built solely under state auspices, citizens resurrected the question of the national government's role in developing the country.

Many people had considerable doubts about Congress's constitutional authority to contribute materially to national development. By the mid-1850s, Democrats adhered firmly to a narrow reading of the Constitution, forbidding government involvement in internal improvements. The Democratic platform of 1856 called for military and post roads to the West, but suggested only that the national government should use "its constitutional power to the attainment of that object." In the face of increasing popular pressure for a railroad, Democratic President Buchanan's messages to Congress in 1858 and 1859 suggested that the need for military protection in the West might lend constitutional authority to the project, but many Democrats remained unconvinced of the plan's legality. In 1860, when the Democratic party broke apart over the issue of slavery, both the Charleston and Baltimore Democratic platforms advocated a transcontinental railroad, but hedged on the constitutionality of government aid to such a project.[7]

While Democrats held that government aid to a transcontinental railroad was unconstitutional, many Republicans before the war argued more and more stridently that such a project was legal, proper, and imperative, not only because the road would provide military protection, but also because it would promote commerce. Party members found authority for the national government to promote a railroad in the government's early-nineteenth-century sponsorship of the Cumberland, or National, Road and in the clauses of the Constitution giving Congress power to establish post roads, to maintain the armed forces, to provide for the common defense, and to regulate commerce among the states. The 1856 and 1860 Republican platforms called for the railroad not on military or postal grounds, but because a railroad to the Pacific was "imperatively demanded by the interests of the whole country." The national government, they said, "ought to render immediate and efficient aid in its construction." It further stated that not only land grants, but "appropriations" for national improvements, which were "required for the accommodation and security of . . . commerce, are authorized by the constitution, and justified by the obligation of the Government to protect the lives and property of its citizens."[8]

In late 1860, the House Committee on the Pacific Railroad introduced a new bill for the construction of a transcontinental railroad. Called the Curtis bill after its sponsor, Republican Samuel R. Curtis of Iowa, the bill (H.R. 646) indicated the Republicans' willingness to expand the national government's role in the economy.

Relying heavily on the Republican belief in a harmony of interest between government and business, the Curtis bill called for government investment to entice private entrepreneurs into building a Pacific railroad. The Curtis proposal named several prominent and wealthy individuals to organize a company that would construct a railroad running west from two eastern points: one from the western boundary of Iowa and the other from Missouri's western edge. The authors of the plan intended that these men would pool their own funds to begin construction. Once the railroad was under way, the government would offer to its builders not only the land grants usually given to western railroads, but also $60 million worth of 5 percent, thirty-year government bonds. The railroad company could sell the land and bonds to raise the funds necessary to continue the work. Sensitive to Democratic scruples, the Republicans justified the bill almost entirely with Buchanan's argument that Congress could help the project because it was both a military necessity and vital to postal affairs. They downplayed their own belief that the government could sponsor the project simply because of the road's commercial benefits.[9]

The Curtis bill was halfway between private and public enterprise. It stopped short of claiming congressional power to create a corporation; instead, it simply named individuals as trustees and gave them permission to organize a company. Similarly, the bill's authors offered to donate government bonds to the company not to make the government the sole sponsor of the project, but in order to encourage private investment in the scheme. The committee's design, Curtis told the House, was to "adopt a plan by which the Government will do just as much as necessary, and no more, to secure the employment of capitalists to construct this great national line of improvement."

The bond proposal was an unprecedented expansion of the government's role in economic development, and Curtis quickly grounded it in the old justification for land grants. The "prudent proprietor" theory maintained that it was proper for the government to give away land in order to enhance the value of the government lands surrounding the gift. Curtis tied the bond offer to this theory by carefully explaining that the railroad would more than repay the bonds and interest expended on its construction by slashing government transportation costs for mail, troops, and supplies, and for Indian defenses. Although the company would not expressly reimburse the government for the bonds and interest, the government would be making a prudent investment by offering the bonds. Further, Curtis said, the bonds would give the government an important first mortgage on the road, which would include the private capital that must be invested in the project before the bonds would be issued.[10]

In their attempt to create a private company with a public will, Republicans revealed their basic belief that individuals could profitably operate a company that also would benefit the public. The framers of the bill planned for wealthy individuals to pool their capital and begin to build the road, then to continue construction with government subsidies. "To act as trustees" in constructing the company, the committee "select[ed] men who they believed would, in good faith, as patriots and men of honor, carry out the will of Congress," explained Curtis. These men did not ask for this distinction, he said, and many of them did not even know they were named in the bill. The men chosen were mostly wealthy men, for "we have got to have the road built by millionaires, if ever we build it." They would permit as associates "only honest men" and, supporters of the measure argued, would sell stock only to legitimate and honest capitalists. Because they personally knew and trusted the men they named to this position, committee members expected that the trustees would act in the public interest.[11]

Although one Republican congressman advocated government control of the project, most Republicans as well as Democrats distrusted national government enterprise. As Buchanan had reminded Congress, a government railroad company would dangerously increase executive patronage and trigger an avalanche of jobbing and corruption. Only the active and careful supervision of a company by individuals financially interested in it could prevent such corruption. Democrats like Buchanan could make such assertions, but Republicans, looking back at the last several years of Southern-dominated government, were even more convinced of their validity. In their 1860 platform, Republicans expressed horror at "the systematic plunder of the public treasury by favored partisans," which had led to "frauds and corruptions at the Federal metropolis." The federal government, Republicans believed, would always invite corruption, while those involved in private enterprise watched their own interests carefully, thus promoting efficiency and honesty.[12]

Democrats opposed the Curtis plan, worrying not only about constitutional powers, but also that the honest disposition of such a vast amount of money and land was "to rest upon the mere volition and honor of men." Although Curtis protested that the trustees would get nothing until they began to construct the railroad and would also be bound by the law to build it, the House was plainly nervous that the Curtis plan gave so much money and land to a few individuals. It passed a Democrat's amendment making the trustees responsible for organizing the company and opening subscription books for stock, but not assigning the land and bonds directly to them.

The halfway status of the Curtis plan raised other obvious problems as well. Without a government charter, the trustees would have to incorporate in each state in which they operated. More worrisome, however, was what would happen should they choose not to incorporate. If they remained partners, on the death of any one of the partners the enterprise would dissolve and the ownership of the railroad would become hopelessly tangled.

The plan's many defects, a ferocious sectional battle over the location of the railroad, desires for more than one line, and Democratic convictions of the unconstitutionality of the plan itself all overrode popular enthusiasm for the bill. Recommitted, it did not reappear.

The advent of the Civil War breathed new life into the transcontinental railroad project. At the same time that the war provided concrete evidence that such a road was necessary for Northern military security, it removed most Democrats from the Union government, thus opening the field for Republican legislation. In March 1861, rumors of a plot to link California to the Confederacy had alarmed Unionists on both coasts. Although California remained loyal, Westerners grew increasingly worried about Native American uprisings as men went to war and left the country unprotected. Isolated and vulnerable, California was especially desperate for a rail link to the East. In the special session of the Thirty-Seventh Congress, which was limited to military matters, California senator McDougall declared that a Pacific railroad was "demanded" as a military necessity. Similarly, in the House, Curtis introduced a bill for the speedier transport of military supplies from the Atlantic states to the Pacific by rail. Both houses created select committees on the Pacific railroad.[13]

Although the Republicans were firmly committed to a transcontinental railroad, they remained uncertain about how best to accomplish its construction. As the second session of the Thirty-Seventh Congress got under way in late 1862, both railroad committees went right to work on a new Pacific railroad plan to replace the weak and vague Curtis bill of the previous year. Railroad men from across the country descended on the capital to offer advice. Although not so numerous that they monopolized the Washington scene, these men played an important dual role as Congress explored the active cooperation of government and business. Lobbyists explained local wishes and provided helpful information that the often inexperienced, overworked, and understaffed congressmen could not gather themselves. At the same time, as representatives of business, railroad lobbyists raised popular and congressional suspicions of corruption and special privilege.[14]

Three key railroad lobbies gathered in Washington in 1862. One, from the upper Northern states, wanted the road to follow a far northern route. Two other lobbies, one from Kansas and St. Louis, the other from Iowa and Chicago, battled over the exact location of a central route. Of the three groups, the Kansas lobby most strongly affected wartime railroad legislation.

The Kansas and St. Louis interest backed a small Kansas railroad company named the Leavenworth, Pawnee and Western Railroad Company, or LP&W. Important politicians, including popular former New York congressman Henry Bennett, backed the LP&W, and the overlap of business and political circles within the company appeared to embody the Republican belief in a harmony of interest between government and business. Contradicting this positive image, however, sporadic rumors charged that the company had purchased earlier Senate approval for a generous grant of Native American lands. Critics, who suspected the company's directors of impropriety and disliked seeing them around Congress during the preparation of a transcontinental railroad bill, constantly needled the LP&W's congressional supporters during the transcontinental railroad debates.[15]

Under the badgering of lobbyists and possibly with Bennett's help, the House railroad committee drafted a railroad bill, which committee chairman James H. Campbell reported in early April 1862. The committee patterned the bill (H.R. 364) on the Curtis bill of the previous year, offering land and government bonds for the construction of a Pacific railroad. Like the Curtis bill, the committee's 1862 Pacific Railroad bill named several incorporators—fifty-seven, in this case—

to organize as the Union Pacific Railroad Company. These individuals, as before, were handpicked by the committee from personal knowledge of their reputations, and the committee expected them to create a private company that would act in the best interests of the public. The new bill, however, repaired the Curtis bill's serious technical defects.[16]

The Union Pacific Railroad plan promoted the Republicans' willingness to involve the national government actively in the economy. In the bill, the committee boldly declared that Congress could charter a national corporation, for it authorized certain individuals to organize a corporation upon their acceptance of the terms of the proposed railroad charter. The committee did not go so far as to assert that Congress's new corporation could operate within states; it was only to build across the territories from the western boundary of Kansas to the border of Nevada Territory. State-chartered roads specified in the bill would meet the corporation's road at state boundaries. The committee's measure authorized the LP&W to build a branch line in Kansas, and Missouri state roads to build four branches from Iowa. A western line, built by the fledgling Central Pacific of California and a Nevada company, would join the Union Pacific in the West. The committee included state companies in the bill to avoid permitting the new national corporation to operate within a state, but the inclusion of those state companies itself expanded the government's economic role, for it required that the federal government give national bonds directly to state-chartered companies.[17]

At the same time that it announced a novel plan for government economic action, the committee knew that its own willingness to charter a national corporation did not guarantee public acceptance of the new scheme. Nervous that investors might shun the project, the committee provided for a return to traditional methods of railroad construction by allowing state companies to build the road if the Union Pacific failed to organize.

Aware of the need for wartime economy and sensitive to the impression giving huge sums to a few businessmen would make, the committee proposed granting to the Union Pacific itself, not to its incorporators, more land and fewer bonds than the Curtis bill had offered, and it called for cash repayment of the bonds and their interest. The new bill offered the company a 400-foot right of way across the country and ten sections of land per mile, although it attempted to prevent conferring any windfall on the Union Pacific by reserving mineral rights in the lands granted. Successive installments of 6 percent, thirty-year bonds would be issued to the company each time that government commissioners certified that railroad sections of forty consecutive miles, or twenty in more difficult places, were ready for service. The bill offered $16,000 worth of bonds per mile over the plains, $48,000 over the Rocky and Sierra Nevada mountains, and $32,000 per mile between the two mountain ranges. Although Campbell claimed that this plan offered fewer bonds to the railroad than the Curtis plan did, that was only technically accurate. Because the branch roads named in the bill received similar privileges, the total amount of bonds offered to the whole project was greater than that of the Curtis bill.

House debate on the bill began with the representatives examining the justification for the project. Its advocates touched first on the military need for a railroad. The war highlighted the necessity of binding the East and West together to prevent the Union's dismemberment, and the danger of losing California to an enemy seemed greater by 1862 than it had at the start of the war. Confederate incursions as far as New Mexico in the West and the threat of war with England over the *Trent* affair revealed the West's vulnerability. California's gold was a rich prize, tempting both the South and England. Indeed, a California congressman reminded his colleagues that England kept warships in the Pacific, and he claimed to have proof that Britain intended to seize California's mines immediately in the event of an international war. The prospect of such a disaster had tremendous impact on the nationalistic Republicans. Territorial loss would "be the first step downward in the fate of the Republic," reflected one congressman. "Whenever a nation commences to lose its territory, its history draws to an end . . . and it falls never to rise again."[18]

Republicans knew that even without external pressure California might separate from the East, and advocates of the road believed that linking the coasts would help promote a vital and growing national sentiment in the West. An early threat of some Californians to establish their own republic if the South successfully seceded emphasized that the Northeast and West coasts were developing separate cultures. The West was rapidly acquiring a sense of independence. Indeed, San Francisco newspaper editors concerned themselves as little with Eastern affairs as Eastern newspapers took notice of the West. A railroad, which would improve transportation and communication between the

Atlantic and Pacific shores, offered immeasurable political benefits. In the midst of a war to divide the nation, advocates of the road insisted, Congress must guard against any future divisions. "Unless the relations between the East and the West shall be the most perfect and the most intimate which can be established," they warned, the American "empire" would be at risk of "breaking on the crest of the Rocky mountains."[19]

The reduction of Democratic opposition in Congress freed congressional Republicans to articulate their economic justification for the railroad. "We were slandering our constituents when we said that we were paralyzed or restricted by their will from adopting the great and beneficent measures for improving the physical and moral condition of our country," asserted California's Timothy G. Phelps in his speech favoring the road. National growth, argued supporters, depended on a Pacific railroad. By spreading free Northern laborers over the country, it would increase national production and create wealth. Settlers would tap the untouched plains, bringing more than 500 million acres of a "great grazing and agricultural country" under cultivation "to add to our wealth and power," thundered railroad advocates. A road would also give ready access to the new gold and silver mines in the West. One congressman assured his colleagues that "if every acre [of the great plains] will not produce a hundred bushels of corn, it will produce a hundred dollars worth of gold, or silver, or iron, or some other useful metal."

In their belief that a railroad would help create national wealth, Republican railroad advocates were following both current political thought and their own experience of the last three decades. People who wanted to involve the government in national development made one exception to their disapproval of government enterprise, and that exception was the construction of transportation routes. One of the nation's most popular economics texts encouraged governments to "give a powerful stimulus to individual productive energy, by well-planned, well-conducted, and well-supported . . . roads," which would create value and promote prosperity by moving articles from areas of surplus to places of need.[20]

The dramatic impact of the Erie Canal on the wealth of the North seemed to Republicans to demonstrate the validity of this observation. Since the canal opened in 1825, the North had expanded rapidly. As settlers streamed West, the North had acquired new, promising states with unprecedented speed, and the population of laborers had boomed. Republicans noted that the great wealth of New York contrasted sharply with Virginia's slow decline, and they believed that Virginia had neglected its transportation routes. It boded well for railroad legislation that in the Thirty-Seventh Congress sat many men whose fortunes had taken them West through the canal; moreover, the huge Northeastern migration to the West had benefited virtually every Republican in Congress.

A railroad would not only develop America's domestic production, but would also secure control of trade from China, Japan, and India, making America the dominant sea power in the Pacific. Different nations had explored this trade, and in 1861, Russia had begun to settle the Amur River Valley on the Russian border with China. The New York *Journal of Commerce* followed this development and concluded that "the 'course of empire,' and of trade, points to the coast of Eastern Asia, China and Japan as a field for future commercial enterprise." The resources of the Amur region would eventually "find an outlet to the sea, and contribute to the wealth of our Pacific coast." A railroad would connect the markets of the East with the Pacific, placing America "in a just and merited position among the leading nations of the earth, by compelling them to pay a tribute to it for the enjoyment of a commerce, which is the chief source of their wealth," a writer for the *Journal of Commerce* concluded.[21]

Republicans in favor of the railroad offered a powerful vision that it would make America "the great central figure in the civilization of the world." Choking the westward expansion of Southerners and their peculiar economic system by filling the plains with free Northern labor, a railroad would make the American economy thrive. While production boomed, northern laborers would propagate a "high type" of culture. "The cultivated valley, the peaceful village, the church, the school-house, and thronging cities"—all traditional hallmarks of Northern culture—would spread West, an advocate predicted. America would become "the greatest nation of the earth." But if the Union failed to build the road, America would fall far behind nations that supported railroads. "Nations are never stationary," Campbell told the House. "They advance or recede. We cannot remain inactive in the midst of national activity, without the loss of trade, of commerce, and power."

The conviction that a transcontinental railroad would develop the nation made almost all Republicans support the project. Opposition to the measure came only in the shape of a move by three Easterners to postpone the bill for financial reasons until the following Congress. This attempt drew the fury of Missouri's Francis P. Blair, who accused Easterners of killing all bills that would benefit the West. People of the lower Northwest were suffering because the blockade of the Mississippi River closed their main route for transporting produce, and people from this region also resented perceived inequalities in the tax and tariff laws. Westerners "have been discriminated against since this war commenced," Blair snarled. "I say we of the West have been treated like step-children by the Government, and we shall always be treated in that way, and postponed." The clear determination of Westerners to see the bill pass, and the desire of Easterners to ease Western anger at the tax and tariff laws, stifled any further moves for postponement.

During the general debate in mid-April, Republican congressmen exposed defects in the committee's bill. Although many of the critics were motivated by regional interests, their arguments nonetheless raised key questions about the government's role in economic development. Owen Lovejoy of Illinois began the examination of the details of the measure by complaining that the many companies named in the bill made it "a conglomerate mass of confused legislation." He called for the chartering of a single company to construct the transcontinental railroad and intimated that he would prefer to let private enterprise build the road alone. "I dislike the idea of converting Congress into a railroad company," he said. "We are not here as a railroad corporation." Ironically, however, what Lovejoy proposed instead would greatly extend congressional power over economic development by permitting it to charter a company to build through states. As Campbell noted, Lovejoy's was hardly a disinterested opinion. Lovejoy and those who supported his plan wanted to give the whole project to the Maine-chartered People's Pacific Railroad Company, which would build on a far Northern route.

Following Lovejoy, two Westerners pointed out that the current bill invited the very sort of monopoly Republicans abhorred. James F. Wilson, who had replaced the battlefield-bound Curtis in the Iowa delegation, challenged the very heart of the committee's plan when he objected to making the Union Pacific a closely held corporation, for he worried that a few rich men would monopolize the company. He called instead for the public sale of stock, with a limit on what any one person could buy. Fearing the "immense . . . commercial . . . [and] political power" the corporation would wield, Wilson also wanted Congress to reserve the right to repeal the act creating the Union Pacific. "It is our duty," he said, "to guard the people against any such concentration of power as a corporation of this magnitude would possess uncontrolled by any check of the law-making power upon them." Also worried about the power of the contemplated corporation, Albert S. White of Indiana wanted the government to be represented on the company's board of directors.

In late April, Campbell told the House that the railroad committee had prepared an amendment that took into account Lovejoy's and Wilson's objections. The new plan provided for the creation of a single publicly held corporation to construct the entire road itself. Instead of organizing the company themselves, the commissioners named in the bill were now to elect a provisional board of officers and to open books for receiving subscriptions to stock. The amendment called for the company to issue a total of 100,000 shares of stock priced at $1,000 each. To prevent a monopoly while still allowing for the major investors necessary to complete the project, the committee provided that no one could buy more than 200 shares. As soon as 2,000 shares were subscribed, the stockholders would meet and elect from their midst a board of directors, which would then elect from their number a president, a vice-president, a secretary, and a treasurer.

Praising the idea of a publicly held corporation, Thaddeus Stevens nonetheless objected to the government charter of one company to build the entire railroad, including the portions of it that fell inside state boundaries. "I do not know that I share in the doubt as to the constitutionality of the United States incorporating companies to make railroads through the States," the nationalistic Stevens said, "but I know that it is entertained by a large number of people." Still unwilling to assert national power within the states, the House agreed that this proposition might hurt the bill's popularity and adopted Stevens's amendment, which restricted the Union Pacific to operation within the territories, by a vote of 59 to 39. The House also voted to make the project a popular one; it accepted the provision making the Union Pacific a publicly held corporation.

With the structure of the corporation settled, the House moved on to define the relationship of the government to the company. The active government funding of a private company added a twist to the previously abstract idea of a passive harmony of interest between government and business. Some Republicans felt that the government was doing a favor to businessmen by giving them such enticements to build the railroad, and they wanted safeguards in order to guarantee that government benefits would not be misused if unprincipled speculators, interested in short-term profits rather than in the actual completion of the railroad, came to control the project. Others objected to any provision that implied distrust of the businessmen involved in the scheme, for they believed that the railroad men were doing the government a favor by undertaking such a large and probably unprofitable project. "Gentlemen are under the impression that it is a very great benefit to these stockholders to aid them to the extent of about half the capital required," noted Campbell, and he asked his colleagues to recall that the road was the government's idea. "If the capitalists of the country are willing to come forward and advance half the amount necessary for this great enterprise," he concluded, "the Government is doing but little in aiding the company to the extent of the other half by way of a loan."[22]

Unwilling to rely on the shared interests of government and business to protect the national government's financial investment in the railroad project, many House Republicans decided to try the generally unpopular method of government oversight to guarantee that railroad men could not make the scheme serve their own purposes to the detriment of the public good. Over an objection that it would "place the interests of . . . stockholders [who had invested private capital] in the hands of irresponsible agents, whom the Government may appoint," the House provided for five government incorporators and two government directors appointed by the President. The government directors could not own stock in the company. Congressmen added another safeguard against speculator manipulation of the Union Pacific by allowing only bona fide owners of five shares of stock to be directors.

House Republicans also tried to guarantee that state railroad companies would not take the land grants and bonds to build their own branches and then quit, leaving the main road untouched, or build the profitable sections of the transcontinental railroad and then stop. They made the state companies responsible for constructing the entire railroad by passing an amendment forfeiting to the government the entire system, including all branches, if the main road was not completed by 1876.

While anxious to safeguard the government's interests in the event that unscrupulous operators came to control the railroad companies, the House did not automatically assume that the railroad men would be dishonest. It refused to make the entire line forfeit if any of the companies defaulted on any of its bonds. Trusting that the inspection of private investors would be more effective in policing the Union Pacific's affairs than government supervision would be, the House declined to make the company place its capital in the U.S. Treasury. The House also rejected an amendment striking the state companies out of the bill to prevent them from taking the government bonds and land grants while the main line went unbuilt.

Struggles between Kansas and Iowa interests over the railroad's terminus prompted the House to strengthen the government's power in the project. The committee's bill called for the Union Pacific to commence at the end of the LP&W road, thus effectively permitting the LP&W's Kansas charter to determine the starting point of the Union Pacific. Both in and out of Congress, people from Iowa and Illinois charged that "Kansas and St. Louis schemers" meant to cheat the East and Northwest out of the benefits of the railroad. It would be in the interest of the Kansas railroad, Congressman Wilson of Iowa claimed, to position the starting point in such a way that it would force the Union Pacific to build along a Southern route, and thus prevent the construction of the Iowa branch roads. If the Union Pacific started on the Kansas border, the editor of the Chicago *Tribune* agreed, the road must run up the Arkansas River, which would be two hundred miles too far south to meet existing northern lines. Northern interests wanted the road to begin at Fort Kearney in Nebraska Territory and to run up the Platte, which "God and nature," they proclaimed, had dictated as the world's "great central artery." Congressmen who distrusted the LP&W joined Iowans in calling for limits to the power of the Kansas company and for a corresponding increase of the government's authority in the railroad project.[23]

While the newspapers battled primarily over the geographical benefits of each route, congressmen from Iowa and Illinois launched an attack on the Kansas-chartered LP&W's right to locate the Union Pacific's terminus. A state should not dictate the terms of a national project, Iowa's Wilson argued. Iowa interests failed to win an amendment permitting the President and the Union Pacific to determine together the road's terminus, but they succeeded in requiring that the Union Pacific build the Iowa main branch of the road, thus guaranteeing that Kansas could not cut off the Iowa connection. They also won an amendment making the Union Pacific commence at the 102nd meridian rather than at the LP&W terminus. While the 102nd meridian was still the Western border of Kansas, the change removed the Union Pacific from Kansas control by permitting the Union Pacific, rather than the LP&W, to choose the terminus of the transcontinental railroad.

That larger issues than geographical prejudices were at stake in the debate over the railroad's terminus became clear when an attempt made solely for regional reasons to make the road begin at Fort Kearney failed. The debates over the amendments proposed by Iowa and Illinois interests confirmed that House Republicans were not yet willing to let a national work intrude on state prerogatives, for they refused to let the Union Pacific force the LP&W to terminate at a point unauthorized by its state charter. The House was anxious, however, to prevent the subordination of a national project to a state legislature, and it refused to permit the LP&W to dictate the location of the Union Pacific's terminus. In a final effort to strengthen the Union Pacific, the House lopped off several branch roads named in the bill, including the Nevada branch, thus giving the Union Pacific the task of building from Iowa to California, where it would meet with the Central Pacific. It seemed that the LP&W had been reduced to the status of a branch road.

The House passed the Pacific Railroad bill in early May 1862 by a vote of 79 to 49. Nineteen opposition members joined sixty Republicans in favor of the measure, while twenty-three Republicans joined the minority to oppose it. The voting reflected the regional tensions apparent during debate over the bill. Republicans who voted nay tended to come from the East or from states favoring the Platte route. Democrats in favor of the bill tended to be either from New York, from which would presumably come many of the company's stockholders, or from states that had been awarded branches. Once the bill had passed, most people quickly submerged their regional biases about the measure under their joy at its passage. In the New York *Daily Tribune*, Horace Greeley announced that "the clouds that have long darkened our National prospects are breaking away, and the sunshine of Peace, Prosperity, and Progress will ere long irradiate the land."[24]

The Senate railroad committee had twice reported its own measures, but the Senate waited for the House bill to begin debate. After over a month of delay, it took up the House measure in mid-June. Turning immediately to the battle over the railroad's route, senators prompted by regional interests and hatred of the LP&W reopened the question of whether a national road could operate within a state. Acceding to demands from Iowa, the Senate railroad committee proposed moving the transcontinental railroad's terminus 2 degrees east, from the 102nd to the 100th meridian, which would move the terminal from the western border of Kansas eastward about 135 miles. This would both reduce the cost of the project by shortening the Eastern branches and would force the LP&W to pick a terminus closer to Iowa than the House had required, especially if, as the committee assumed, the LP&W must build its own road to the Kansas border. The new terminus requirement would mean that the Kansas railroad must end on the western side of the northern boundary of Kansas, rather than the western border of the state. The new provision did not stipulate that the LP&W must build to a border, however, so it left open the possibility that the road could begin within Kansas. Senators voiced strenuous objections to chartering a national project to operate within a state before they rejected the plan.[25]

Senators refused to let a nationally chartered railroad intrude on state lands, but they ultimately strengthened the government's role in the project by taking control of the transcontinental railroad's terminus away from the LP&W altogether. They specified that the railroad should start between the Republican and Platte River valleys in the Territory of Nebraska, and, led by Iowa's James Harlan, who loathed the LP&W, they gave the President authority to decide on the location of the end of the transcontinental railroad. A subsequent amendment required the President also to determine the end of the Iowa branch of the railroad, which, since it too would be built by the Union Pacific, was also an important terminus of the transcontinental railroad.

The location of the terminus was not the only issue that determined the scope of government authority in the project. Despite the protests of some senators that "driving a hard bargain" with investors would make them avoid the project, the Senate tightened the terms of the railroad bill and increased the authority of the government in the scheme to protect the interests of the government in case the railroad men, like certain bankers had done, declined to act in accordance with the public good. Jacob Collamer reflected a wartime revision of the idea of a national harmony of economic interests when he explained: "We in making the grant may be governed by high national considerations, and the men who put their money and their own personal labor and services in it may be willing to contribute their labor with that of the rest of the community for a national object; but when it comes to the actual making of the road, it is to be done entirely by men who think they can make money by it."

Determined to retain power over the project, the Senate required the companies to report annually to the Secretary of the Treasury and refused to strike out a clause in the bill permitting Congress to repeal the measure. If a company defaulted on its government bonds, the Senate gave the government the right to assume the control of the road as a sort of public trustee. In order to guarantee that the entire road would be built and that investors angling for short-term profits could not take government funds without finishing the project, senators agreed to reserve in the Treasury 25 percent of the government bonds for the railroad over the plains and 15 percent of the bonds for the railroad over the mountains. They also passed an amendment forfeiting to the government the entire road and branches, rolling stock, fixtures, and all other property of the companies if the entire road and all its branches were not completed by 1876.

The railroad bill, essentially in the shape of the House plan but now with a new terminus and additional government safeguards, passed the Senate in mid-June by a vote of 35 to 5. The great popular pressure in favor of the railroad made even Collamer vote for it, despite his worry that it did not adequately guard against dishonest railroad men. Only four Republicans voted nay. Wisconsin's Howe and Minnesota's Wilkinson presumably favored a more Northern route. Wright, and maybe the others, bucked public opinion because he could not bring himself to hamper government credit during wartime. After the House accepted the Senate amendments, Lincoln signed the bill on July 1, 1862. The editor of the *American Railroad Journal* heralded the bill's passage as marking "a new era in the history of our public works."[26]

The organization of the Union Pacific began auspiciously but quickly faltered. Fulfilling the terms of the law, the Union Pacific commissioners met in Chicago on September 2, 1862. As the authors of the Republican plan hoped they would be, those joining the commissioners to express support for the project were respectable and substantial businessmen, around one thousand of "the leading railroad capitalists, shareholders and corporators, express and telegraph owners, bank presidents, and men identified with the heavy financial interests of the country." There were also government officials present: four congressmen, including Owen Lovejoy, and one governor attended.[27]

Made suspicious of the railroad project by the bad reputation of the LP&W, the North watched the meeting closely. The commissioners sent a clear message to the country that they were men to be trusted. They passed a series of resolutions declaring their patriotic determination to build the entire railroad, and, more important, they elected well-respected men, including one of the government's commissioners, to be provisional officers of the company. The editor of the Chicago *Tribune* crowed that "the Pawnee and all other tribes of speculators" could now never control "this great national work."

The Chicago meeting established the Union Pacific as a popular project. Recognizing the common distrust of anything that smacked of monopoly, the commissioners rejected a proposal to sell the first $2 million worth of stock, the amount required to fulfill the terms of the charter, to New York and Boston capitalists, declaring that "it would damn the whole enterprise if ten New York capitalists should take the whole of the stock." With their popular convictions bolstered by their suspicion that financiers were uninterested in the risky project, the commissioners played to the idea that middle-class investors would subscribe out of patriotism. "We must throw ourselves on the great national heart and then we are safe," one man concluded. The commissioners resolved to ask Congress to price shares of the required capital investment at $100 rather than $1,000 dollars so that more people could afford them. The editor of the Chicago *Tribune* caught the populist spirit of the project and demanded that every man do his patriotic duty by buying a share to promote this great national enterprise.

While boosting the project, the Union Pacific commissioners also warned that the 1862 legislation was inadequate to accomplish the construction of the railroad. Among other things, they pointed out, the law did not provide for the condemnation of lands along the road's route; its reservation of bonds would cripple construction by reducing available funds; and, critically, it did not project enough of a profit to attract investment. The commissioners resolved to petition Congress for a change in the law. Shortly after the Chicago meeting, several of the commissioners met with a group of railroad men in New York City to discuss necessary adjustments.[28]

As the commissioners had feared, investment in the Union Pacific was sluggish. Westerners were indeed investing, although slowly, but Easterners held off, "evidently wait[ing] for some amendments to the charter," one journalist observed. Worried by January 1863, the congressional railroad committees met to consider how to speed the organization of the company. In the third session of the Thirty-Seventh Congress, Senator McDougall, who had been at the Chicago meeting, introduced an amending bill to the Pacific Railroad Act. After referral to a select committee, the bill (S. 439) reemerged in late February 1863. As the *American Railroad Journal* recorded, the proposed changes to the law were those that the Union Pacific commissioners had requested: the provision of shares for $100 each, the means to procure rights of way, and the surrender of withheld bonds. "It is understood," wrote the *Journal's* editor, "that these will be met with no opposition."[29]

The editor of the *American Railroad Journal* was wrong. The provision for issuing withheld bonds to the company before the entire line was finished necessitated a reexamination of the relationship between the government and the railroad. Revealing his distrust of the Union Pacific's patriotic and vocal determination to build the entire railroad, Collamer tried to strike this provision. He argued that the existing plan had been discussed at length in 1862 and had been adopted as insurance that the whole road, not just the profitable sections of it, would be completed. But McDougall pointed out that builders needed the reserved capital to build the road and argued that the provision was an unfair burden on the patriotic and selfless individuals who were "volunteer[ing] their individual aid and energy" to help the government accomplish a great task.

The Senate took a middle stance, more in line with the apparent popular desire "that the amount retained by the Government shall not interfere practically with the construction of the road." The Senate decided to withhold bonds only for the less difficult portions of the road, paying them out for the road over the mountains. The Senate's effort was for naught; although it passed the bill without a roll call vote on February 25, the House adjourned on March 3 without considering it. The Union Pacific had gained no additional government support.[30]

With the Union Pacific languishing, the future looked good for the LP&W, for the 1862 law could be construed as permitting the company to build west without government directors or supervision should the Union Pacific fail to organize and build. In January 1863, an internationally known New York financier, Samuel Hallett, began to take over the LP&W. He rented a mansion on Fifth Avenue and entertained prospective investors, letting it be known that he planned to hire Republican politician and army general John C. Frémont as president of the concern, and mentioning Horace Greeley as "Consulting Agent." In June 1863, Hallett and Frémont acquired the LP&W with an eye to cutting out the unorganized Union Pacific.[31]

Hallett and Frémont commanded great respect in financial and political circles, but their dealings would not always withstand scrutiny.[32] Indeed, their first move as principal stockholders in the LP&W indicated that they were not the sort of statesmanlike railroad men that Congress had envisioned at the head of the transcontinental railroad company. Planning to issue a new contract for the construction of the LP&W that would win them short-term profits, they declared invalid the construction contract that had been in operation since 1862 and ordered work to halt. When the contractors, who had made large investments in materials, refused, Hallett, an old friend recalled, "by some means, unknown to any one but himself, secured control of a company of United States dragoons and rode down the contumacious contractors, agents and men." Hallett exulted that he had driven the enemy into the river and now had "all their ties, houses and works and shall hold them."[33]

Despite Hallett's and Frémont's questionable methods, circumstances seemed to favor the Kansas company's assumption of the transcontinental project. Hallett's suggestion of Greeley as "Consulting Agent" paid off as Greeley waxed enthusiastic about the Kansas line. In July 1863, he declared that the Kansas company would have to build the whole road, for the Union Pacific was "still-born—dead without having lived." Denying that Hallett and Frémont had any "sinister purposes" for the road, he encouraged his readers to shift their loyalties to the Kansas company, since "the actual working company seems to have distanced the ideal." In July, Hallett and Frémont publicly acknowledged that they planned to build the entire transcontinental railroad themselves, changing the name of the LP&W to the "Union Pacific Railway Company, Eastern Division."[34]

The threat from the Kansas company spurred the Union Pacific commissioners into action. When Hallett and Frémont bought the LP&W, the Union Pacific commissioners abruptly accepted the terms of the 1862 charter. They did this, and were permitted to do it, despite the fact that they had not yet sold the requisite 2,000 shares of stock. Clearly, neither the Union Pacific commissioners nor the government wanted the Kansas company to build the railroad.[35]

Although the Union Pacific commissioners sprang into action as soon as they perceived the Kansas threat, they could not corral invest-ment in the Union Pacific. For three more months, stock sales dragged. Then, suddenly, in late September of 1863, slightly over 2,000 shares sold and the subscription books closed abruptly. The sale astonished even the *American Railroad Journal,* which optimistically concluded that capitalists were finally showing their patriotism. In fact, railroad man Thomas C. Durant, who hoped to gain control of the Union Pacific and to profit from self-dealing construction contracts, spon-sored most of the sales through straw men. In this ambitious opera-tion, Durant both saved the transcontinental railroad from the Kansas gang and broke the spirit and the letter of the 1862 law. He saved the Union Pacific by making himself its hidden dictator.[36]

While later events revealed that Durant was not the sort of man Congress had planned to have at the head of the Union Pacific, in 1863 this was not at all apparent. A well-known, well-connected, and experienced railroad promoter, Durant could boast important and reputable politicians as references. A contemporary described Durant as "a fast man . . . a man who when he undertook to help build a railroad didn't stop at trifles in accomplishing his end." That sort of initiative and perseverance seemed exactly what was needed to save the Union Pacific. Indeed, within a month of his Union Pacific stock purchases, Durant had personally financed railroad survey teams on their way to the Rocky Mountains.[37]

The Union Pacific stockholders met in late October 1863 and elected directors of the company. Many stockholders were probably unaware that Durant had financed the stock purchases of several of the men from among whom they elected the board. An impressive set of railroad men and government officials, the directors chosen seemed to fulfill the intention of Congress that the commissioners set up an honest company. The directors then elected officers, and these, too, seemed to augur well for the railroad. Elected president was General John A. Dix, president of the Mississippi and Missouri Railroad and, more impressive in 1863, an officer on the Union battlefields. Having acted briefly as Secretary of the Treasury before Chase, Dix com-manded the respect of the administration. Durant became vice-presi-dent. John J. Cisco, the reliable longtime Assistant Treasurer in New York, was elected treasurer. As secretary of the Union Pacific, the directors chose a government commissioner, the popular and reputa-ble editor of the *American Railroad Journal,* Henry Varnum Poor.[38]

When Cisco asked Treasury Secretary Chase whether or not he

could accept the railroad position while retaining his government post, Chase confirmed that the Republicans intended the Union Pacific to be a private corporation with a public will. "An obvious distinction exists," wrote Chase, "between . . . [corporations] . . . in no wise connected with national interests . . . [and] corporations for public objects." In the former, he wrote, government officials were barred from participating. In the latter, however, government officials could, and indeed should, offer their services.[39]

Chase and the other Republicans who had adopted the Curtis plan's concept of a group of public "trustees" in charge of a private corporation operated as if they still lived in the prewar world of small communities and intimate state-oriented business circles. They assumed that those in charge of a public project would be honest and civic-minded, and that less suitable candidates would be obviously unacceptable, or thwarted by the safeguards Congress had devised. The election of the Union Pacific's officers illustrated how mistaken that belief could be in the wartime world of national enterprise. When Durant's straw stockholders became Union Pacific directors, Durant controlled enough votes to elect the corporate officers he wished. Dix's presidency was a strategic move to gain public confidence; Durant had bought stock for Dix with this plan in mind. With Dix on the battlefields, vice-president Durant actually directed the company.[40]

When they became aware of Durant's perversion of Congress's intent, some of the legitimate businessmen on the board quietly cut their ties to the company. They felt that "the Board of Directors should only be considered as the trustees of the Government," and secretly protested that "parties . . . pledged to a policy calculated to promote their own particular interests and views" controlled a majority of the Union Pacific's stock. One disgruntled director privately hinted that evil railroad men were undermining the harmony of interest between business and government. The road would certainly be good for the country and profitable for businessmen "if . . . economically constructed," resigning director J. Edgar Thompson wrote, but he worried that the present managers planned to take their profits before the road was finished and could offer benefits to the public.[41]

Whatever his hidden plans, Durant had saved the Union Pacific, and its festive groundbreaking ceremonies at Omaha, Nebraska, on December 2, 1863, drew a long, congratulatory letter from Treasury Secretary Chase. Still, the Union Pacific directors had not forgotten their need for new legislation. Desperate for money after initial surveys and purchases of materials had exhausted their cash and despairing of constructing the road under the existing law, the Union Pacific directors no longer asked for just the changes the commissioners had wanted before. They now hoped for additional funds to build the road. Two directors, Durant and Cornelius S. Bushnell, went to Washington to work for changes to the 1862 law. They arrived in late 1863 and, teaming up with the head of the California line, remained in the city for most of the congressional session. Although Bushnell later boasted that their efforts brought about the legislation of 1864, Washington newspaper correspondents took no particular notice of the men.[42]

The railroad men were not the only group interested in a new railroad law. By 1864, congressmen realized that the 1862 law could not secure the construction of a transcontinental railroad, no matter how patriotic the railroad promoters might appear. The funds that seemed ample in 1862, before Chase's second and third issues of greenbacks had entered circulation, seemed ridiculously low in the face of rampant wartime inflation.

Congress was anxious to address the Union Pacific's problems because the government had a much more pressing need for a transcontinental railroad in 1864 than it had in 1862. The 1862 arguments for the road hinged on a broad desire for an economically strong, unified nation, and also on the political expediency of pleasing the West. By 1864, the government's desperate need for specie added panicked haste to the Republican ambition to develop the nation. At the price of specie escalated, the opening of Western gold fields drew the Treasury's eye at the same time that it fired the public's imagination. In 1864, Congress was laboring under intense pressure to provide for the construction of a railroad to the gold fields.

Gold had entered the railroad debate in the summer of 1862, after the specie-carrying *Golden Gate* caught fire and sank, carrying with it not only two hundred souls but also $1.5 million worth of gold. Across the North, newspapers mourned the ship's loss. At the same time, new Colorado mines were yielding "considerable quantities" of gold and gave "encouraging indications" of being rich in ore. Government surveys of the Rocky and Sierra Nevada Mountains in late 1862 and early 1863 revealed that they were "literally stocked with minerals," capable of producing at least $300 million to $400 million worth of gold annually. Popular newspapers trumpeted the "bewildering" extent of Western riches; one recorded that Western

Indians used gold bullets in their guns. The reputable *American Railroad Journal* placed the amount of "surface gold" at hundreds of billions of dollars. Throughout 1863, talk of the West's golden riches grew more and more extravagant as the Union's financial situation deteriorated.[43]

Speculation about Western gold was not lost on the revenue-starved administration. In May 1863, shortly after the Union defeat at Chancellorsville, it began proceedings to assume control of Western mines. Panicked Western officials telegraphed Washington predicting uprisings and even secession if the plan was enforced, and the government quickly backed down. Despite this false start, no one forgot Western gold. In October 1863, the new governor of Colorado sent the Territory's first telegram to Lincoln. He assured the President that behind Colorado's "cordial support" stood "deposited in her stone vaults . . . untold millions [of dollars] of gold to the credit of the Government."[44]

Prospectors streamed to the gold fields, and they, too, demanded a transcontinental railroad. In a single month in the spring of 1863, two hundred gold, silver, and copper mining companies were organized in San Francisco. The following month, the city reported, "The mining fever is unabated. Six to eight new companies are incorporated here daily." By January 1864, miners and settlers had taken 10,041 acres of land in one Colorado district alone.[45]

Republican newspaper editors, public officials, and others across the country, anxious to promote the wealth of the nation and its individuals, called on Congress to pass new railroad legislation. The editor of the Chicago *Tribune* hoped that a railroad could be built in a year, "as fast as money and men can do it," to open up the route to the gold fields. The editor of the New York *Daily Tribune* claimed that the nation's annual gold and silver production would increase to at least $200 million as soon as just half the railroad was done. A letter to the paper's editor insisted that the completion of the road would make America "the richest and most powerful [nation] on earth." In April 1864, an Idaho judge tried to encourage congressional action by circulating an $800 gold nugget around the floor of the House.[46]

All the attention on the West made threats to California and to the nation's unity seem even more dangerous. Frequent rumors of Pacific pirates and secessionist plots kept alive the issue of California's vulnerability. Worse, England was financing a railroad across Nicaragua and another across Canada, while France was building one across

Mexico. Soon England and France would have closer contact with California than the Union's East coast did. California congressmen pressed their case for a Pacific railroad. A newspaperman in Washington recorded that Californians had long "been making urgent representations of their need of changes and reinforcements"; in early 1864 a major-general with infantry and artillery was assigned to the coast.[47]

The administration, too, was more anxious than ever for a railroad to the West. Lincoln had encouraged the project since gaining office, although his occupation with military matters prevented him from pushing it aggressively. It was perhaps even more important for new legislation that the Secretary of the Treasury, who might easily have refused any more strains on the public credit, vigorously supported the railroad. Chase backed the project in 1864 because the Treasury needed specie, because he worried that Pacific pirates would pillage seaborne gold shipments, and because California had just demonstrated its isolation from the rest of the Union by rejecting greenbacks in favor of gold circulation. Clearly, closer contact between the East and West was imperative.[48]

Promotion of the railroad would also help Chase politically, for it would gratify not only Californians, who supported his nomination for President in place of Lincoln, but also Kansas senator Pomeroy, one of Chase's chief supporters and the author of the famous "Pomeroy Circular" calling for Chase's nomination. All things considered, Chase concluded that "the earliest practicable completion of the Pacific Railroad" was of great importance to the whole country.[49]

Almost everyone—railroad men, congressmen, the public, and the administration—agreed that a transcontinental railroad was imperative and that the 1862 legislation could not achieve it. Altogether, "there was a great feeling in favor of the road [in 1864]," recalled Durant. "California was making considerable noise just then, and the Government was very anxious to get the road through to California; and we were therefore satisfied that we could get an amendment which would enable us to build the road."[50]

Each group interested in railroad legislation presented to Congress plans for a new bill, and each plan reflected a different vision of the proper relationship between the government and the railroad. Realizing that the Treasury's dire financial situation would prevent Congress from authorizing additional bond grants to the railroad companies, the Union Pacific directors advanced a proposal retaining the level of government support offered in the 1862 measure while also permitting the Union Pacific and other companies named in that bill to sell their own bonds in amounts up to one-half the amount of the government bonds issued. The company bonds would hold a lien on the railroad prior to the government's lien.[51]

The Senate Finance Committee also considered the subject, asking Chase for his ideas about a new railroad law. The Treasury Secretary replied that the importance of the project certainly "justifie[d] liberal aid by the National Government to the enterprise," but he opposed the 1862 scheme of issuing national bonds for the road's construction because he worried that these extra bonds would impair the government's credit by swelling its debt. Instead, the Secretary preferred that the government guarantee the interest on the railroad's own bonds. This plan would make the railroad's bonds more attractive to investors without harming the Treasury.[52]

Having scrutinized the two plans, the Senate railroad committee came up with its own scheme. After meeting with Chase and the Union Pacific's representatives in early April 1864, in early May the committee reported a new version of the railroad bill (S. 132) "with important amendments, understood to coincide with suggestions from the Secretary of the Treasury," as one newspaper correspondent wrote.[53]

The theory behind the new bill, its sponsors explained, was to scale down government support of the project. Indeed, although the new bill offered much that the railroad companies' directors wanted, it suggested mistrust of those involved in the project and a desire to keep the government clear of any fraudulent activity. Under the new plan, the government would no longer have a huge direct stake in the scheme; it would essentially be the guarantor of the companies named in the bill, primarily the Union Pacific, the Kansas company, and the California company. Private investment would finance the first stretch of road. The companies could then sell their own bonds, on which the government would guarantee the interest, but stockholders must continue to pay assessments on their stock until the project was complete. Committee chairman J. M. Howard explained that the committee wanted to remind stockholders "that there is a duty due from them to the company and to the Government, that they are to contribute of their own money, that this work is to be carried on by them earnestly, devotedly, at their own expense, and that 'Uncle Sam' is not the ultimate party to foot all the bills." Despite the reduction of government involvement in the project, the committee added to the 1862 bill's safeguards of the public interest by making the Union Pacific's government directors ex officio members of all the company's standing committees.[54]

The new bill offered several concessions to the Union Pacific. It included all of the amendments the commissioners had requested at their first meeting, providing for the condemnation of lands along the route, calling for the issue of one million shares of $100 each, and nullifying the old provision for withholding bonds from the company. It also gave the railroad until 1877 to finish construction, and it allowed the company to use coal and iron ore from government lands within ten miles of the road. Should the company not be able to find ten good, usable sections of land per mile under the terms of the 1862 act, it was permitted to take twenty sections of land from a wider radius. Probably to encourage private investment in the Union Pacific, the committee abandoned all liens and forfeitures listed in the 1862 bill.

Although the committee's bill offered much that the Union Pacific directors wanted, its critical removal of the government subsidy for the project would cripple the cash-starved Union Pacific. Instead of offering government bonds for the construction of the railroad, the committee's bill permitted each company named in the bill to distribute its own first mortgage bonds, on which the government offered to pay the first year's interest. The government further guaranteed the interest on the company's bonds for twenty years. The Union Pacific could issue up to $24,000 of thirty-year bonds for each mile of track east of the Rockies, $96,000 of bonds for each mile over the mountains, and $48,000 of bonds between the Rockies and Sierra Nevadas. The bonds could bear interest of up to 7 percent. Companies were forbidden to pay dividends on stock until they repaid the government for any money it had had to advance. The committee's retraction of the offer of government bonds diminished the chances that the Union Pacific would ever build, for the foundering company was out of cash and would be hard pressed to find investors. Probably aware of this, the committee permitted any companies named in the bill to consolidate and build the transcontinental railroad.

The committee may have taken this direction for any of a number of reasons. It injured the Union Pacific because it feared that speculators, interested in short-term profits, had gained control of the company; because it was biased against the company; because it decided that the public credit could not stand the issue of bonds to the railroad; or because it was simply trying to minimize the government's risk of losing money through the machinations of dishonest railroad men.

As the Senate debated the bill for four days in May, it tried to increase the Union Pacific's viability at the same time that it guarded against railroad speculators and monopolists. Worried that the 2,000-share stock limit was hampering stock sales to honest capitalists who would actually build the railroad, Lyman Trumbull advocated removing the limit altogether. Howard objected that this would enable the stock to pass "into the hands of a very few persons who will abuse their powers and privileges very much to the public prejudice and to the prejudice of individuals." The Senate tried to balance these two attitudes: it raised the stock limit to 5,000 shares.

In their efforts to protect the transcontinental railroad from the manipulations of unscrupulous railroad men, Republicans also tried to circumscribe the power of the Kansas company. It refused to allow Hallett and his colleagues to replace old contracts with ones more profitable to themselves, and it angrily rejected a reading of the 1862 law that would allow a Kansas terminus for the whole road.

Pressured by public demand for a new railroad law, Senate Republicans passed this bill by a vote of 23 to 5. New Jersey's Ten Eyck, often a critic of his party, gave the only negative Republican vote. The bill's final shape reduced the Union Pacific's viability and indicated the Senate's desire to throw construction of the road to private enterprise, although the Senate still offered significant financial benefits to the railroad companies. Senate Republicans clearly preferred that men more upstanding than Hallett should build the railroad, but fearing that further restrictions would alienate those railroad men who appeared determined to complete the road, they declined either to police the project with increased government supervision or to add more safeguards to the bill. Instead, Senate Republicans tried to protect the public interest by distancing the government from the scheme.

While the Senate had been working on its bill, the House railroad committee, under the chairmanship of Thaddeus Stevens, was developing its own. Stevens owned an iron manufacturing company in Pennsylvania and as late as February 1864 had owned full-paid stock in the Kansas railroad company. He was, not surprisingly, a staunch railroad man. Stevens also strongly favored government control of national economic affairs and utterly disapproved of Chase's financial policies. All of these predispositions helped to shape Stevens's 1864 railroad plans.[55]

In mid-February 1864, while the House committee was considering a Union Pacific bill, Stevens expressed his desire for a popular and honest railroad project by bringing up a new bill that granted lands to Maine's state-chartered People's Pacific Railroad Company, or PPRC, for a far northern railroad. This bill (H.R. 5) reintroduced the old idea of a railroad's construction by private company funded by popular subscriptions. The government's sole contribution would be a large land grant.[56]

Northern congressmen had periodically reintroduced this plan without success since Owen Lovejoy first advocated it in 1862, but Stevens had new reasons for reintroducing it now. English interests in Canada threatened to link the Northwest and Canada with their own transcontinental railroad. It was also expedient in this election year to cater to the disaffected Northwest, which had repeatedly threatened to secede from the Union. Finally, the timing of Stevens's introduction of this bill was clearly a warning to the unsavory Hallett and Durant that the whole 1862 transcontinental railroad plan could be scrapped and begun again on a new basis.[57]

The PPRC seemed to embody the old Republican ideal of harmony between business and the government. Its honorable directors, some of whom were the same influential men who had fled the Union Pacific after it fell under Durant's control, contrasted sharply with Durant and Hallett. They wanted no money from the government, asking only for traditional land grants. Basing this request on the old "prudent proprietorship" idea, the company claimed that its railroad would benefit the government by increasing one hundredfold the value of the rest of the government's northern lands. The company also offered to transport troops and government supplies free of charge so long as other companies were also required to do so. A truly popular project, the PPRC planned to build with private capital from small investors. So confident were its promoters that citizens would rally to them that the company's president privately authorized Stevens to reduce the two-year time limit for the company to sell $2 million worth of stock. He also suggested that the government could withhold up to one-half the lands requested until the road was completed as security that the company would build the entire road.[58]

With this bill under consideration, in late April, Stevens further threatened the Kansas company when he unveiled a railroad bill that promoted the government-controlled Union Pacific over the uncontrolled Kansas company. The bill fulfilled the Union Pacific commissioners' old requests, reducing the face value of stock shares, releasing bonds held by the government, providing for the condemnation of land, and allowing the Union Pacific a later completion deadline. Ignoring Chase's suggestions for a new law, Stevens used the plan the Union Pacific directors suggested. His bill authorized the railroad companies to issue their own first mortgage bonds for half the amount of the government's bond issues to each company. Because this plan would provide less revenue than the Senate package, Stevens's bill doubled the land grant offered to the companies. In order to guard against manipulation of the Union Pacific by railroad speculators, Stevens called for ten, rather than two, government directors for the Union Pacific. His bill also prevented the Kansas company from building without government supervision. Finally, Stevens's plan required the Kansas company to settle its internal strife before it received any government aid at all.[59]

Stevens bolstered the Union Pacific and attacked the Kansas company not only because of his support for an increasingly strong national government but also because, despite the Kansas company's attempt to monopolize the transcontinental railroad project, the company could never actually complete the road unless it straightened out its internal affairs. The company was embroiled in lawsuits between Hallett and Frémont, who were each struggling to wrest control of the company from the other, and the railroad's original owners. Worse, holders of old, partly paid stock certificates, most of which had been illegally distributed to help the road receive Senate approval for dubious Indian land treaties, were suing the company for its refusal to honor their shares. Stevens, who very probably still held full-paid stock in the company, was determined to force the company to make itself viable and thus profitable. Further, as a legislator, he was determined to make sure that the Kansas company did not take government subsidies and monopolize the railroad only to tumble in a morass of lawsuits.[60]

When Stevens attacked the Kansas company, Durant panicked. The railroad promoter had invested in the line, planned to make a large profit on its construction, and was considering abandoning the Union Pacific to build the unsupervised Kansas railroad west. Accompanied by his lawyers, Durant called on Stevens to discuss his assault. They found Stevens adamant that the objectionable provisions would remain unless the Kansas company settled its affairs. Stevens pointed out that the outstanding claims against the Kansas company were already more than the proposed government bond issue. This left the government's contemplated investment completely unprotected. Stevens suggested that the several contending parties and their lawyers, who were all in Washington pushing the claims of the Kansas company, should settle matters among themselves.[61]

Addressing Stevens's ultimatum, Durant revealed that he was not the sort of director Congress had envisioned at the head of the transcontinental railroad project. Durant apparently believed that Stevens would prevent the passage of any new Pacific Railroad bill, thus killing the Union Pacific as well as the Kansas road, as long as the Kansas company was in such disarray. To prevent the Kansas trouble from destroying the imperative new legislation, Durant commissioned his lawyer to buy off the battling Kansas investors; many years later, the attorney admitted that in his negotiations he parted with over $250,000 worth of Union Pacific and Kansas railroad bonds. Probably not all of this went to sort out the Kansas trouble; some undoubtedly bought off troublesome competitors.[62]

In mid-May, while Durant scrambled, Stevens brought the PPRC bill to a vote. House reaction to this measure showed how completely the Republicans were now willing to assert Congress's economic role in the country. In 1860, party members had been unwilling to allow Congress to charter a corporation or to authorize any state or national company to build through states. Made more confident of government authority by Congress's increased wartime activities, by 1862 party members announced that Congress could charter national corporations. They did not, however, assert the authority of a national corporation to operate within a state, and actually tried to prevent the Union Pacific from intruding on the rights given to the LP&W under a state charter. During the debates over the 1862 bill, sectional jealousies prompted an examination of the government's proper role in national development, and this exploration strengthened Republicans' belief in the authority of the national government over the country's economic growth. By 1864, a majority of congressmen refused to permit a state-chartered road to build a transcontinental railroad, believing that only a national company could build a national railroad. They rejected Stevens's bill.

Stevens revived the scheme a week later. His new Northern Pacific Railroad bill (H.R. 483) created the nationally chartered Northern Pacific Railroad Company. The House passed the bill on May 31 by a vote of 74 to 50 with almost no debate. Stunningly, this assertion of national power meant that the Congress had chartered a corporation with the power to build through states, although it did require that the company obtain consent from the legislatures of any states through which the road would pass. In 1862, regional interests had helped to increase the government's authority in a railroad project, and the same was true in 1864. Northwesterners, who wanted a Northern railroad, wholeheartedly supported the bill. All the votes from the upper Northern states—Wisconsin, Minnesota, and Michigan—were affirmative, while most representatives from Indiana and Ohio voted nay. The Senate passed the bill with amendments in late June without a roll call vote, and a conference committee easily reconciled the two versions. Lincoln signed the bill on July 2, 1864.[63]

In early June, after he had sent the Northern Pacific bill to the Senate, and after the Kansas railroad had announced that its affairs were settled, Stevens reported a revised Union Pacific bill (H.R. 438) to the House. Although this bill did not directly attack the Kansas railroad, it still favored the government-controlled Union Pacific. The House committee, unlike the Senate, hoped to keep the transcontinental railroad scheme from abuse by increasing the government's involvement in it.[64]

Benefiting the Union Pacific, the bill called for $100 shares, provided for the condemnation of lands, repealed the government reservation of bonds, and doubled the 1862 land grant. In a welcome offer to the impoverished corporation, it permitted companies to issue their own first mortgage bonds in an amount equal to the full amount of the government bonds. It strengthened Union Pacific credit by repealing the provision of the 1862 bill that made the entire road liable to forfeit if any branch forfeited on bonds or failed to build. To increase government supervision of the railroad's construction, the bill provided for five of the twenty Union Pacific directors to be named by the President and placed at least one government director on each of the Union Pacific's standing or special committees. In contrast to the Senate bill, this measure would enable the Union Pacific, with its government directors and central route, to mount an effective challenge to the Kansas railroad's monopoly of the transcontinental project.

The bill also made some allowances for the Kansas company as long as its directors were actually building across the country, rather than speculating for short-term gains. Removing the previous bill's restrictions on the company, the new measure permitted it to meet the Union Pacific as far west as the Kansas company deemed "practicable or desirable" and allowed it to build the whole road if the Union Pacific was not proceeding in good faith.

After four days of inconsequential debate, in mid-June two representatives attacked the House committee's bill and revealed their distrust of Durant. New York Democrat John V. L. Pruyn was the first man in the history of wartime transcontinental railroad legislation to argue seriously for government ownership of the railroad. An investor in the Union Pacific and the man who recommended to the Union Pacific commissioners in 1862 that they seek a new law, Pruyn had come to loathe Durant. Pruyn apparently recognized that Durant meant to profit by rigged construction contracts for the road, although he did not disclose his suspicions to Congress. Since the government was funding the project, Pruyn argued, the government "ought to control or own it." If the House refused to take charge of the road, he said, he would insist on having even greater control of the company than the committee's bill offered. Pruyn wanted the President to determine the road's whole route, not just its eastern end, and he wanted the Secretary of the Treasury and the Attorney General to approve the company's construction contracts before any government bonds were delivered. Pruyn presented one amendment giving control of the road to seven government commissioners and, later, one proposing government review of contracts.

Government ownership of the road was not a popular idea with Republicans for, despite their misgivings about Durant and Hallett, they felt that private individuals interested in a company made better businessmen than public servants. They also feared government corruption and the potential for government monopoly of power and, further, they doubted Congress's authority to direct a corporation. A Republican congressman had indeed suggested government ownership of the transcontinental railroad in 1860, when a Democratic administration would certainly have vetoed any such bill and long before the war drained the Treasury. Since that time, whatever confidence the Republicans might originally have had in the purity of their own administration had been sorely tried by scandal after scandal in the War Department and in the wartime public service. Lincoln himself privately dismissed government ownership of the road as impossible, citing above all the severe demands on the wartime Treasury. One congressman concluded:

> It has always been the theory, at all events of gentlemen upon this side of the House, that the Government ought not to appoint their own Federal agents for any great work of internal improvement . . . I am for intrusting this great work to men who are willing to give their time, energies, and capital to it, and am therefore opposed to breaking up the present organization and giving it to the disinterested gentlemen, acting as agents of the Government.

Pruyn's amendments failed by overwhelming margins.[65]

While Pruyn hoped to protect the government from unscrupulous operators by increasing the government's involvement in the transcontinental railroad project, Illinois Republican Elihu B. Washburne hoped to protect the government by decreasing its involvement. Washburne, too, had noted that those running the project in 1864 were not the public-spirited trustees that Congress had envisioned in 1860 and 1862, but were "bad . . . and unprincipled men . . . callous to all the obligations of patriotism or honor" who planned to plunder the government through speculation.

Washburne ruined his efforts to amend the bill by complaining that the new bill undermined government authority in the project and that it appropriated new government funds. His colleagues noted that the new bill actually increased the number of government directors in the company, while its main purpose was to prevent the Kansas railroad, which under the old bill had no government control at all, from commandeering the entire project. Further, the bill did not in fact appropriate any new funds.

Stevens, always at his best when attacking a weak position, joined Iowa's Hiram Price in ridiculing Washburne's accusations. Pointing out that the new bill gave no new government funds to the railroads, they explained that since the government was unable to give the roads enough money to build in the current inflationary climate, the committee had unanimously decided to ease the terms of the old law. The railroad could not be built without new legislation, Stevens argued, and the House bill offered less than the railroad men wanted. It also would guard the government more fully than the Senate bill, which "pledged the Government to guaranty the interest in coin upon bonds to twice the amount to which the company is entitled under existing law." Both Stevens and Price pointed to Dix's presidency of the Union Pacific as proof that the company was honorable and intended to build the whole road.

The House rejected Washburne's attempt to prevent the companies from issuing first mortgage bonds, a confused provision that would have protected the government's mortgage but would have killed government control of the railroad construction by eliminating the cash-poor Union Pacific and throwing the project to the Kansas company.[66]

Despite the fact that Republicans rejected the plans of Pruyn and Washburne, few retained the outdated view that financiers would be willing to build the transcontinental railroad solely out of public spirit, trusting to the future to determine whether or not the railroad would turn a profit. Still believing that private enterprise would prove more efficient than the government at building the road, and unconvinced that the government could either practically or legally undertake an internal improvement project alone, congressmen sought to achieve the public goal of a transcontinental railroad without suffering frauds on the public treasury. Senate Republicans scaled back government interest in the road in case railroad men proved more interested in short-term profits than in completing the project. Determined to have a railroad, House Republicans tried to guarantee that the railroad men would complete construction. Unwilling to go so far as to bar even disreputable men from the undertaking if they showed the ability to accomplish it, the House increased government involvement in the road and hedged the new bill with safeguards to protect the public purse from abuse by men like Hallett.

In late June 1864, the House passed the bill by a vote of 70 to 38. Fifty-six Republicans made up the body of the majority; twenty-seven Democrats spearheaded the minority. Of the fourteen Democrats who voted aye all but one came from the West, iron-producing Pennsylvania, or New York. Other than Washburne, the eleven Republicans who voted nay were mainly those who often switched sides in voting, including three representatives from Kentucky and one from Maryland. Pruyn declined to vote because of his position as a stockholder in the company.

When the Senate refused to replace its own bill with the House version, Congress set up a conference committee. It reported on July 1, the day before the House was to adjourn. The committee's compromise reflected House Republicans' inclination to increase the government's role in the project. It retained the House bond provision, which required the issue of government bonds and permitted the companies to issue bonds. The compromise retained the doubled land grant, but cut bond grants to the Kansas road for one of its branches. The committee also added its own provision to the plan in order to guarantee that the Kansas company could not build the entire road without government supervision. The committee allowed any two companies mentioned in the bill to consolidate and to construct any portion of the railroad left undone by the other companies, but any such consolidated organization was subject to the same "terms, conditions, restrictions, and requirements" as the Union Pacific. Both houses accepted the report, and Lincoln signed the bill on July 2, 1864.[67]

Congress had tried to adjust the terms of its wartime railroad legislation to limit the power of unscrupulous railroad men, and it expanded the government's oversight of the work; but ironically, the Republicans' desire to keep the transcontinental railroad from Hallett's grasp opened the way for later railroad corruption. In 1864, the Republicans increased the Union Pacific's privileges in an effort to keep the transcontinental railroad project from the monopoly of the unpopular Kansas company. Congress permitted the Union Pacific to issue its own bonds, up to a certain amount, for each mile of railroad construction. But Congress imposed no requirements about estimates, open bidding, or acceptance of the lowest bid for the work to be done. The men running the Union Pacific organized a construction company, the Crédit Mobilier, which was the only bidder for construction contracts. Without competition, the company could bid just slightly under the upper limit of the cost Congress had permitted. Since the actual work cost much less, the construction company pocketed huge profits. The system did not apparently violate the letter of the law, since it took no funds from the government and stayed within the legal limits of the railroad's bond issues. Further, the Crédit Mobilier scheme may well have been imperative to encourage investment in the Union Pacific. There was no doubt, however, that this twist was one that most congressmen had not foreseen when they drafted the 1864 bill.

The loophole revealed that the rapidly expanding national economy antiquated the Republican belief in a harmony of interest between government and business. With the Curtis bill, the Republicans proposed using private enterprise to achieve public ends and, throughout the war, Republican congressmen continued to legislate as if private railroad companies shared the public's interest in the speedy, efficient construction of a transcontinental railroad. With each succeeding railroad bill congressmen tried to guard against speculators, but they adhered to the expectation that members of the private companies actually intending to build the railroad would act as public trustees. Personally knowing and trusting those they initially named as incorporators, Republican congressmen legislated as if, once in power, such men would always operate the transcontinental railroad project in the public's interest.

The new American business world was no longer a small community of well-known individuals. The original, reputable trustees in charge of the Union Pacific gave way not to speculators who bilked the Treasury without laying a rail, but to businessmen who gave the public a railroad and who, having assumed great financial risk to build the road, worked hard to make the highest possible profits from their investment. One Republican wrote in disgust that these men seemed unaware of "the great purposes of Congress. They seemed to treat it as a purely private transaction, out of which they might get all the money they could, without any obligation to carry out the act according to its spirit." This was especially offensive because Oakes Ames, a key figure in the Crédit Mobilier affair, was a Republican congressman who had possibly entered the company at Lincoln's request to get construction under way. But the machinations of the Union Pacific men were, at least in part, rational responses to the difficulties of financing national projects; under its idealized 1864 investment plan, by contrast, the Northern Pacific could not build.[68]

The Crédit Mobilier gang apparently had not abused the government funds as Republicans had feared speculators would do; it had instead profited at the expense of bondholders, who could not monitor the company closely enough to detect inflated contracts. The size and scope of the Union Pacific belied the Republican idea that individual investors would force a private company into efficiency and honesty. With unknown individuals controlling private enterprise and without a guarantee that the private sector could police its companies, the government could no longer depend on businessmen, who often searched for short-term profits rather than prudent investments, to share public interests. At the same time, government-appointed directors and commissioners were often political appointees who knew nothing of railroads and had such poorly defined roles that they had little impact on the plans of the railroad men.[69]

Over the years since the Crédit Mobilier scandal, historians have repeatedly accused Republican legislators of accepting bribes for their positive votes on the transcontinental railroad bills. As in any government with close ties to business, some Republicans doubtless found their advocacy of railroads lucrative. Kansas senators Lane and Pomeroy were almost certainly involved in shady LP&W deals when railroad bills were before Congress. The votes of these two and other financially compromised representatives like them, however, could not pass these major bills alone. In 1862, a desire to develop the country and popular pressure for the railroad drove Republicans to vote for the best Union Pacific Railroad Act they could devise. In 1864, Republicans operated not only under the same desires, but also with the additional pressure of the government's need for specie and the public's frenzy to reach the gold fields.[70]

Regardless of the ways in which they may have abused Congress's intentions, railroad men did indeed build a transcontinental railroad, joining the Union Pacific and the Central Pacific at Promontory Point, Utah, in May 1869. By constructing the road, they achieved a great Republican goal.

In many ways, the impulse behind the creation of a transcontinental railroad epitomized Republican thought. A railroad to the Pacific, Republicans argued, would help to develop the country's agricultural base and thus create a great commercial nation, which would advance far beyond the countries of Europe. Wartime necessity bolstered the general Republican desire for a transcontinental railroad. The need to protect the West coast encouraged Republican support for the 1862 act from almost the beginning of the war, and in 1864 the nation's desperate need for gold and the swelling immigration West added to the Republican belief in nurturing the nation's progress. Republicans believed that a railroad to the Pacific was militarily and economically vital to the nation. As a railroad advocate had insisted in 1862, Republicans believed that a transcontinental railroad would make America "the greatest nation of the earth."[71]

"See That All Their Blessings Are the Result of Their Own Labor": Republicans and Slavery

I saw a train of some 6 or 7 thousand negroes, men, women and children, start for Wilmington and freedom today. Bundles on their heads, children in arms, some on mules, some in old wagons, all poorly clad and many with little to eat. They will do anything, suffer anything for freedom. They go they know not where. I can only think and say to myself God will care for them.

—General Oliver Otis Howard, 1865

While the war led the Republicans gradually to reform the country's monetary and revenue systems and permitted them to further agricultural progress and railroad construction, it also forced them to consider the crucial issue of what role black people would assume in the national life. First the question of slavery and later the need to facilitate the transition of black Americans from slaves to free laborers consumed much of the wartime Republicans' energies. Military exigencies dictated freedom for slaves in rebel areas, but left to Congress the tasks of both establishing freedom for slaves in nonrebel lands and helping the new freedmen fit into the Republicans' vision of political economy. While the solutions party members found to these issues drew almost hysterical Democratic accusations that the Republicans were creating a national despotism, those same solutions limited in critical ways the scope of the national government's economic activities.

The battle over slavery had been heated for decades before the war and, if it was not the sole cause of the sectional confrontation, it did much to inflame the conflict between North and South. Since racist thought influenced most Northerners before the war, only a handful of abolitionists actively opposed black slavery, and their emphasis was moral and religious rather than economic.[1] By 1860, however, Republicans generally agreed that slave labor had no part in a healthy political economy. Slavery, they argued, misused or wasted labor, and they pointed to the apparent poverty of the Southern states, especially those suffering from soil exhaustion, as proof. Republicans also argued that slave labor degraded white labor and undercut wages, and party members feared that competition from slave labor in the territories would undermine the North's economic system.[2]

Before the war, few if any Republicans made the logical step from disliking the institution of slavery to calling for emancipation. Rather than wishing to free bound workers, Republicans hated the land and money monopoly evident in the South and hoped to keep those white oligarchical tendencies from corrupting the North or the territories. Party members feared that wealthy slaveowners, characterized as the Slave Power, were plotting to destroy Northern free institutions and to spread slavery, with its classes and monopolies, to the North. In this framework, Republicans perceived slaves not as fettered free laborers but as the tools of rich Southerners who would destroy free white workers with competition from cheap slave labor.[3]

Thus, prior to the war, the Republican party called only for slavery to be contained in the states where it already existed; most Republicans insisted that they did not wish to interfere with state institutions. The Republicans' 1860 Chicago platform affirmed that "the right of each state to . . . control its own domestic institutions according to its own judgement exclusively, is essential to the balance of power on which the perfection and endurance of our political fabric depends."[4]

Revealing their lack of sympathy for the South's bound workers, Republicans devoted much of the 1860 campaign to reassuring potential Northern voters that their policies would guarantee that black slave labor would never compete with white labor in the North or the territories. With Democrats charging that the "Black Republicans" would inaugurate a new era of amalgamation and competition, Republicans anxiously sought to assuage white fears, especially in the West, where racism was strongest. Party members, including at least one long-standing abolitionist, forcefully declared that slaves were not equal to white workers and declared that black people would never move North because they were suited only to a hot climate. With the territories free for white labor, Republicans planned to leave slavery intact and black workers out of sight in the South.[5]

The outbreak of war in April 1861 might have made no difference in the status of slaves had it not been for the economic role that black people played in the conflict. Northern dislike of slavery indeed reached fever pitch after the fighting began, but calls for the abolition of slavery under the war powers were countered by pleas for the government to concentrate on restoring the Union. While many Northern citizens peppered Congress with petitions to end slavery, others asked Congress "to drop the negro question, attend to the business of the country, sustain the President and General McClellan . . . and maintain the Constitution." The war did ultimately cause much of the black slave population to run away from masters, but even this might not have altered the pattern of slavery. Without Northern willingness to abrogate the Fugitive Slave Law, the return of fugitives might well have undercut the mass movement of slaves to freedom.[6]

The black population's contribution to the Southern war effort launched a revolution in Northern attitudes about black labor shortly after the firing on Fort Sumter. Republicans had tended to disparage slave workers, but by the beginning of May 1861, Republicans had already noted that Southerners were using their slaves as laborers to support the Confederacy, and party members began to perceive black workers as important to the Confederate military.[7] As the month progressed, Republican newspapers announced that "negroes . . . have . . . been employed to do nearly all the labor of the war thus far." The New York *Times* revealed that Republicans were beginning to recognize black workers as a valuable labor force when it attributed the fall of Fort Sumter to the work of slaves. "Without the black engineers and laborers that South Carolina impressed into her service, Major Anderson might have remained in Sumter till doomsday," it insisted. Quickly, party members concluded that black labor was critical to the Southern military. "Rebels Employing Negroes," a front-page headline of the Chicago *Tribune* announced, and the editor told the South to beware: "The temper of the loyal masses will not tolerate such warfare."[8]

The "loyal masses" moved much more slowly to oppose the Southern use of slaves in the army camps than the military did. In the first month of the war, in order to appease border state sentiment, the Northern army had scrupulously returned runaway slaves to their masters. As it became clear that slaves were important army workers, however, this policy seemed suicidal. In late May 1861, General Benjamin F. Butler, commanding Union troops on the Virginia coast at Fortress Monroe, refused to continue to supply his enemy with labor. He sent a dispatch to the War Department declaring that he would not return to their masters black slaves who had been used in a military capacity. If fugitive slaves crossed his lines, Butler wrote, he would employ them as laborers and charge their care against their wages. The War Department's reply accepted the new impression of Southern slave workers and authorized Butler to "employ such persons in the service to which they may be best adapted." "The question of their final disposition," the Secretary of War cautiously concluded, "will be reserved for further determination."[9]

Republican newspapers, even those that opposed emancipation, recognized the value of slaves to the Confederacy and praised Butler's handling of "contrabands," as he termed fugitive slaves in recognition of their military value. Many newspapers had been calling for the army to cease returning runaways, both to hurt their masters economically and to weaken the Confederate war effort, and were pleased to see their advice heeded. "Bully for [Butler]!" wrote a correspondent of the Indianapolis *Daily Journal*. "Slaves can be used by the traitors in constructing fortifications, in transportation, in actual military service, and being property they are just like any other property used in such service, 'contraband of war.'"[10]

Republicans hoped that fugitive slaves taken from the Confederate war effort would aid the Union forces as they had helped the South. Party members believed that, once they knew they would not be returned to hostile masters, slaves would desert the Confederacy and help the North. "Whenever now the Federal Army moves in the rebel States," an article in the Chicago *Tribune* read,

> the black population will fall into its rear and become valuable and trusty colaborers for its success. Under the hot sun of a Virginia and Tennessee summer, they will prove their worth in the discharge of the galling and laborious duties of the camp. In fortifying positions, in providing forage, in cooking, washing, tending the sick and wounded, they will each man do a soldier's work, relieving the troops of much that is laborious and unpleasant in performance, and, in a Southern climate, injurious to the health.

Days after Butler's proclamation, the Philadelphia *Ledger and Transcript* reported that over one hundred fugitive slaves were already hard at work in Fortress Monroe. The Philadelphia editor suggested to the Southern newspapers that "have been boasting of their slaves as an element of strength in war" that the slaves might hurt, as well as help, the Southern cause.[11]

The growing belief in the importance of black labor for both armies inspired little action by congressional Republicans until the late summer of 1861. Until mid-July, much of the North perceived the Civil War as a rebellion of the hotheaded slaveholding aristocracy and believed its martial ardor would fizzle when the North crushed its army with one blow. The First Battle of Bull Run, however, which took place on July 21, left the Union army battered and bleeding, and shattered the North's complacency. Stunned, Republicans in Congress quickly moved to strike deeply at the Confederacy's war effort.

Shortly after the special session of the Thirty-Seventh Congress began, the Senate had asked the Judiciary Committee to consider a bill (S. 25) to confiscate the property of Confederates. Clearly illegal during peacetime, this plan was justified as a military necessity. The day after the Battle of Bull Run, committee chairman Lyman Trumbull of Illinois reported the bill with an amendment that revealed the Republican conviction that slave labor fortified the Confederacy.[12]

Trumbull's amendment, as he told the Senate, would forfeit the right of a master to any slave he willingly consented to use "in aid of this rebellion, in digging ditches or intrenchments, or in any other way." Henry Wilson of Massachusetts applauded the proposal, arguing that the Union should no longer return fugitive slaves, whom Southerners were "using to erect batteries to murder brave men who are fighting under the flag of their country." The Senate overwhelmingly supported Trumbull and Wilson, passing the amendment by a vote of 33 to 6 before agreeing to the confiscation bill itself. A Democrat from California and one from Oregon joined the Republican majority, while border state Democrats and Old-Line Whigs made up the minority.

House opposition members had gathered their forces to oppose the measure as the Bull Run panic cooled, for they noticed what they saw as a dangerous shift in Republican attitudes and reasoned from their observations that the confiscation plan could easily become one of outright emancipation. Republicans insisted that the bill was limited and touched only those slaves used actively for the rebellion, but Democrats recognized that Republicans were already beginning to perceive all slaves, not just military workers, as vital to the Confederacy and thus important to confiscate. Pressing their accusation that Republicans were embarked on a path of total emancipation, opponents of the bill forced its sponsor to admit that slaves producing "corn and wheat and hay" for the rebels were contributing to the Confederate military effort.[13]

Faced with Democratic charges that the Republicans were trying to subvert the Constitution and emancipate all Southern slaves, Republicans rooted their actions with regard to the slaves firmly in the authority given Congress by the war powers to do whatever was necessary to gain military advantage. On the basis of the war powers, Republicans overrode Congress's February 1861 resolution "that . . . the Congress of the United States . . . [has no] constitutional right to legislate upon or interfere with slavery in any slaveholding state." As Thaddeus Stevens announced: "I thought the time had come when the laws of war were to govern our action; when constitutions, if they stood in the way of the laws of war in dealing with the enemy, had no right to intervene." While removing Republican embarrassment over their earlier pledge not to attack slavery, this theory set early party efforts on behalf of African-Americans under extraordinary wartime powers.

After the Republicans had agreed to limit the scope of the measure to the present rebellion and to the slaves used in military labor, it passed by a vote of 60 to 48. Eleven Republicans from across the North joined the opposition; Republicans alone comprised the majority. Democrats in the Senate forced a vote on the House's minor amendments, but although they managed to marshal more Democrats for this vote than for the original vote on the bill, they could not shake the steady Republican majority.[14]

Lincoln signed the Confiscation Act on August 6, 1861, the day before the special session of the Thirty-Seventh Congress adjourned. Congress had taken its first step toward freeing what Republicans were coming to view as the South's most important laboring population. It had done so under the authority of the war powers and in response to a perceived military necessity.

As the House debate foreshadowed, limiting confiscation to the few captured slaves employed in a specifically military capacity seemed to many Republicans a weak solution to the problem of slaves working for the Confederacy, especially in light of the Confederates' repeated boast that cotton, cultivated by slaves, would win the war as cotton shortages forced European intervention in the conflict. By the summer of 1861, radical Republicans were calling actively for emancipation. When General John C. Frémont, always attuned to popular movements, obliged these party members by proclaiming in late August 1861 that slaves of disloyal masters in Missouri were free, most Republican newspapers, even those that opposed general emancipation, applauded. "What does it matter whether a slave bears a gun himself in the rebel Army, or stays at home and supports his master's family, in order that his master may be free to bear arms against the Government?" read an article in the New York *Times*. "In either case it may be said the negro furnishes a recruit to the rebel Army, and is therefore employed in hostility to the Government." One Washington reporter commented that the proclamation was universally popular, because "every slave belonging to a rebel, though employed in hoeing corn and hilling tobacco, or picking cotton, is giving aid and comfort to the rebel cause." When the President rescinded Frémont's premature proclamation, the New York *Times* admitted that the administration must run the war, but remarked that the proclamation was "beyond all question . . . in harmony with public sentiment throughout the Northern States."[15]

Republicans determined to weaken the Confederacy increasingly emphasized the value of domestic black labor (that is, field and industrial workers) to the Southern war effort. From Boston pulpits, ministers told their congregations that slaves helped the enemy. The New York *Times* reminded its readers that "it has long been the boast of the South . . . that its whole white population could be made available for the war, for the reason that all its industries were carried on by the slaves." The moderate Philadelphia *Daily Evening Bulletin* reported that while white Southerners devoted themselves to fighting, "the real hard work of the rebel armies, without which they would have been long ago compelled to disband, is done by the slaves." More radical, the Chicago *Tribune* ran article after article on the critical Southern need for black labor to back the war effort. Looking at the employment of virtually the whole Southern black population, including women and children, in the fields and in the military, the *Tribune's* editor concluded: "Those four millions of slaves off-set at least *eight millions* of Northern whites." If the South were deprived of slaves, the editor insisted, the rebellion would collapse.[16]

At the same time that they emphasized the value of Southern domestic slave labor, Republicans also began to dwell on the potential importance of black labor to the Northern military. "The Government needs their labor," the New York *Times* told its readers in August 1861, and by October, a correspondent of the Philadelphia *Daily Evening Bulletin* reported from Fortress Monroe that the more than eighteen hundred contrabands in camp "are of great use to Uncle Sam." He concluded, "I don't see how we could do without their labor." In the same month, the Indianapolis *Daily Journal* reprinted a New York *Daily Tribune* article on the critical nature of black labor at Fortress Monroe. "I venture to say," wrote the article's author, "that [the General there] can better spare from his department an equal number of soldiers than the negroes." By the end of October, the New York *Times* reported that the presence of fugitive slaves on a naval expedition was "of immediate and vast importance" because of their ability to work. "No better class of laborers could be found—indeed, none so good for the purpose, in all the population of the United States," the author concluded.[17]

It seemed that African-Americans could be as important to the Union military as to the Confederacy, but few Republicans gave much thought to their domestic value to the Union. Then, in November 1861, General T. W. Sherman captured Beaufort, South Carolina, and some of the Sea Islands of Georgia and South Carolina, giving the North a chance to test whether the fugitive slaves could provide the same domestic help to the Union cause they had apparently furnished to the Confederates. Republicans were quick to embrace the idea that contrabands would produce cash crops for the Union. "The blacks around Beaufort continue to flock into our lines," reported the New York *Times*. "There needs no suggestion what to do with them. The unpicked cotton is to be gathered now by the same hands, though those hands hold quite a new relation to the cotton and to mankind . . . It will be a splendid piece of poetic justice to hear that the King [Cotton] on whom [Southerners] relied to work out their nefarious designs is not only helpless to aid them, but is chained captive to the triumphal chariot of the advancing and conquering Union."[18]

Since the ability of black people to produce revenue was being tested, it was fitting that the Secretary of the Treasury, to whom control of abandoned lands and property fell by the terms of the Confiscation Act, began to organize black workers in the captured region. Recognizing both that the Treasury needed to exploit all available sources of revenue and that Southern African-Americans must appear productive quickly if emancipation sentiment were to continue to grow in the North, antislavery Treasury Secretary Salmon P. Chase appointed an agent to collect cotton in the captured areas after it had been picked by the local black population. Shipped north and sold, the Southern cotton would provide money for the Union treasury.

The public greeted the arrangement joyfully. Republican newspapers promised their readers that ex-slaves would produce cotton for

the market in exchange for wages, and many party members concluded that black labor would be as useful in domestic production as
in the army. Observing the Sea Islands, a New York *Times* columnist
revealed the revolution in Republican attitudes about the value of
black labor when he reported that "the labor of every slave, . . . if he
be put at the proper kind of work, and properly handled, is worth
more than the labor of two white men."[19]

When President Lincoln welcomed the second session of the Thirty-
Seventh Congress with his December 3 message, he opened the question of the role of black labor in the wartime Union. Noting that the
August Confiscation Act had liberated many slaves, Lincoln tried to
appease border states by recommending colonization for the freed
slaves and other willing free black people "in a climate congenial to
them." Some Republicans, especially in the lower Northwest, applauded the President's suggestion, but many newspapers warned that
Lincoln's plan "does not come up to the wishes of the people of the
North," and even members of his cabinet questioned a policy of
exporting black workers. The role of black people in the Union war
effort and in the Northern economy would be heavily debated in
1862.[20]

As soon as the congressional session began, propositions to free the
domestic slaves of rebels poured into Congress. The editor of the
moderate Philadelphia *Daily Evening Bulletin* reflected that few opposed confiscating "the only element of the Southern population that
gives the rebellion a formidable character," and indeed, confiscation
of rebel slaves enjoyed wide Republican support. Some conservatives
did worry, however, that Congress would "overleap [the] limits" of
confiscation of workers and advance into general emancipation, thus
alienating both the border states and much of the public.[21]

The Senate began discussion of a second confiscation measure in
January 1862. It had referred to the Committee on the Judiciary all
of the many proposed confiscation plans, and in mid-January Trumbull reported the committee's own bill (S. 151). Explaining the measure, he told the Senate that it would confiscate the property of rebels,
free their slaves, and forbid the army to return fugitives. The committee thus recognized the importance of domestic slave labor to the
Confederacy but, bowing to pressure from the border states and from
Northern conservatives, it rejected the idea that the Union could also

use free black labor in any but a military capacity. The final, critical element of the committee's bill was a provision for colonizing freed slaves who were willing to leave America.[22]

In the North, as the bill made clear, the desire to deprive the South of its domestic labor force tangled inextricably with the question of the place of black labor in a free American society. Trumbull explained that the committee intended the bill's colonization provision to address the West's aversion to free black people. Accurately gauging prevailing Western opinion, he explained: "When we tell [our constituents] that slavery has been the cause of this rebellion and that the traitors who are fighting us are supported by their slaves, they admit it"; he continued, "but they say: 'What will you do with them; we do not want them set free to come in among us; we know it is wrong that the rebels should have the benefit of their services to fight us; but what do you propose to do with them?'"[23]

Senators responding to the colonization provision of this second confiscation measure expressed a range of opinion about the place of black people in America. As soon as Trumbull finished speaking, Kansas senator Samuel Pomeroy revealed that he had come to see slaves as potential productive members of a characteristic Republican free labor political economy. He expressed a wish that black laborers be accorded a role in a free economy, preferably in a reconstructed free South, but he hinted that they could perhaps also be welcome in the North. Opposing the idea of colonization of ex-slaves, Pomeroy expressed his complete willingness to colonize slaveholders instead, for they "are dangerous, and they are not producers." The country could not spare workers, this senator from a labor-starved state insisted. He dismissed as "unworthy of the Senate" the "miserable prejudice" which maintained that a laborer would not be allowed to live in America "on account of his color."

Border state conservative Waitman Willey opposed Pomeroy and presented the opposite extreme of Republican opinion about black people's potential contribution to a free labor economy. Recoiling both from the expense of colonization and from the idea of a free black population, Willey advocated leaving the slaves as they were. The Republican from Virginia's pro-Union delegation defended his opposition to the committee's measure by emphasizing "the negro['s] . . . condition[,] . . . helplessness, . . . [and] want of all the habits of self-sustenance." If Pomeroy's black people were desirable laborers,

Willey's were useless children whose inability to support themselves made them depend on slavery to guarantee their own survival.

The committee had presented the colonization scheme because "it was thought important that the policy of the Government should be declared upon this subject," but that policy was not to be so easily decided. Many Republican senators joined Democrats to protest sweeping confiscation measures, and their opposition hobbled this bill. Arguments about whether Congress had constitutional power to confiscate property obscured the emancipation issue, and finally, in May 1862, the Senate created a select committee on confiscation to craft an acceptable measure. It would be important that, while the committee's nine members embraced a range of ideas, the committee chairman, Daniel Clark of New Hampshire, was dedicated to the abolition of slavery.[24]

Although the initial Senate second confiscation measure died, the debate over it indicated the shifting trend of Republican images of freed slaves. Northern belief in the value of slaves to the Confederacy's military organization made Republicans perceive the slaves pouring into the Union military camps as good workers who needed only jobs and wages to provide critical services to the Union army. Fugitive slave Robert Smalls's dramatic seizure of the *Planter* in May 1862, complete with its cargo of guns, and his delivery of the ship to the Union blockade offered stunning proof that black help could be invaluable to the Union military.[25]

Many Republicans, who believed that domestic slave labor kept the Confederacy afloat, were also becoming convinced of the value of domestic black labor to the Union war effort. The cotton flowing into the North from occupied South Carolina seemed to provide tangible proof that black workers would help fill the Union's treasury. The New York *Commercial Advertiser* commended the willing industry of the ex-slaves when it reported the arrival of a vessel from Port Royal carrying $50,000 worth of cotton and suggested that other such cargoes would soon follow. At the same time, other newspapers estimated the worth of current cargoes of Sea Island cotton at a quarter of a million dollars. Republicans also hoped that black workers in captured areas could grow food for the Union troops.[26]

In addition to their conviction that black labor was vital to the military, some Republicans shared Pomeroy's growing sense that black people could be productive free laborers in nonmilitary occupations. Beginning to conceive of a role for black people in a free labor economy, some party members emphasized the apparently easy transition many ex-slaves made to becoming free workers. From Washington came news that contrabands worked in hospitals and that many had been hired as servants by private families. The arrival of ninety-one contrabands in Philadelphia made some white people nervous, but many others hurried to hire "house servants and farm hands." Rumors of additional arrivals in the city increased requests for workers, and one local African-American leader concluded cheerfully that "a great scarcity of laborers exists in the country," making black workers welcome.[27]

If city dwellers seemed to welcome black workers, farmers appeared desperate for them. In the West, as farm workers went to war, the need for laborers outweighed even the virulent racial prejudice of the region to induce farmers to hire black people, although not to accord them civic or social equality. The Cincinnati *Daily Gazette* encouraged the arrival of black migrants from the South, and farmers agreed. Lamenting the lack of available farm hands, a young Kansas man declared: "It would be a great blessing if more darkies would understand their rights and come to our aid." Jayhawking raids into Missouri brought slaves into Kansas to work, and the Chicago *Tribune* suggested that the West should stop "depriving ourselves of the labor we need" and encourage the settlement of black people "so far as it may be necessary." Back East, Republicans noted that black labor was welcome and useful in the West, and suggested that "what is true . . . on a small scale, ought to hold good on a large one."[28]

While Republicans were increasingly willing to think of black people as potential free laborers, few actually advocated bringing them North. Most party members combined racial prejudice and economics to argue that, whether enslaved or free, black workers should remain in the South. A correspondent writing to the New York *Times* maintained that black people "are needed where they are—they could not be spared—their places as laborers could not readily be filled, and their immediate removal would be a far heavier blow at Southern interests than their emancipation on the soil." The Chicago *Tribune* agreed, asserting, "The negroes are to day just as necessary to the South as food is to the human body." Indeed, the apparent proof that black workers could adjust so well to life in the North, where they were generally unwelcome, offered Republicans assurance that Southerners, who traditionally preferred black labor, would try to keep their ex-slaves nearby. Even the radical New York *Daily Tribune* tried to deemphasize the idea of northward migration of freedmen. It reported that "if Slavery . . . ended to-morrow, we are confident that even South Carolina would be in no hurry to expell from her soil the most industrious and productive half of her people."[29]

Although some Republicans had begun to advocate the welcome of free black labor into the party's version of political economy, opinion was by no means unanimous. Many party members approached the question of absorbing black workers into a free economy, North or South, with ambivalence. Not only border state men like Willey, but also people throughout the North faced the reality of freed slaves nervously, sometimes emphasizing their productivity, sometimes attacking their apparent helplessness. The same newspapers that extolled black people's willingness to work often observed the horrendous living conditions of the refugee camps and characterized fugitives and Sea Island black people as degraded, destitute, and desperate for protection. Disappointed that refugees did not provide the exaggerated estimates of their labor Republicans had come to expect, some party newspapers reported that fugitives were "good for nothing," "lawless and unrestrained," "requiring to be driven by stripes to the performance of every duty." In the late spring of 1862, Republicans had begun to think of black people as potential free laborers but had not yet committed themselves to a positive stance on the position black people would take in a free economy.[30]

Like the Senate, the House had been unable to agree on a confiscation bill despite the resolution of a Republican caucus in early December 1861 that one must pass; and in April 1862, the House had appointed a select committee on confiscation. Like Senator Clark, the House committee chairman, Thomas D. Eliot of Massachusetts, opposed slavery, but the House carefully balanced the four Republicans on the committee with three opposition members.[31]

The House confiscation committee developed two related bills. H.R. 471 was a measure to confiscate the property of rebels; H.R. 472 proposed the liberation of the slaves of any person who "shall willfully aid or abet" the rebellion. The long debates over the latter bill explored both Republican and Democratic attitudes toward freed slaves, and the interaction of these differing perceptions helped to determine the Republicans' position in support of free black labor.[32]

Eliot reported the bills from the select committee in mid-May 1862. In six full days of House debates on the measures, almost all congressmen made their views known. Some long-standing abolitionists reiterated old moral arguments for emancipation, and many party members who backed confiscation maintained that slavery had caused the rebellion and must be destroyed to prevent future uprisings by the aristocratic Slave Power. Most pro-confiscation Republicans in the House, however, explained their stand by emphasizing the new image of black people as the critical labor force in the South. They further maintained that ex-slaves would be good workers for the Union.

Several elements in the debate reemphasized the Republican belief in the vital military value of slaves to the Confederacy. As before, the justification for confiscation reinforced the Republican perception of the importance of black workers to the Southern war effort, for party members insisted that constitutional authority for emancipation came from military necessity. The Southern use of black people for the war effort made slavery subject not to peacetime government authority but to the war powers.[33]

Party members in favor of the bill bolstered their constitutional argument by revisiting the changing Republican image of slaves. They emphasized the power of slaves who worked not only in the military camps but also in the fields to support the Confederacy, reminding the House that slaves were "almost the entire industrial population" of the South and as such they were "the sinews of war . . . and the main pillar . . . of the rebellion." Confiscation would, Republicans maintained, destroy the Confederacy.

Having hammered home the idea that slaves were vital to the Southern war effort, Republicans went on to reiterate their argument for strengthening the Union by using the freedmen as military laborers. "The services of slaves are needed to aid in resisting the wicked schemes of their master[s]," one representative told the House. "They build fortifications for the rebels. Why not for us? They relieve rebel soldiers from nearly all the fatigue duties of war. Why should they not aid ours? They man rebel batteries. Why not ours?" Indeed, some antislavery Republicans insisted that the committee's bill did not go far enough to secure the South's labor force for the military. Committee member Charles B. Sedgwick of New York proposed his own version of the bill, which made it a military duty for Union officers to employ ex-slaves for the Union as laborers, or even as soldiers. His plan attracted thirty-eight Republican votes before it failed.[34]

While Republicans established their belief in the importance to the Confederacy of both military and domestic slaves as well as their faith that black people would provide invaluable military aid to the North, Democrats forced Republicans to address the related question on which party members had reached no consensus. What place, Democrats asked, did Republicans believe black labor could take in a free society? Or, as a border-state slaveholder demanded: "What do you intend to do with the slaves when they are freed?" Completely opposed to any sort of emancipation, Democrats drove home the idea that the Republican plan would "turn helpless children and superannuated persons out of house and home" while providing nothing for their support. Black people needed financial aid and supervision to survive, Democrats maintained, and unless the government could place the slaves in a better condition than they currently enjoyed, opponents of the bill argued, "all sound morality and Christian duty" dictated leaving them as they were.

Anxious to defend this confiscation measure from charges that it would dump on the Union treasury and Northern states slaves who could not move unaided into freedom, congressional Republicans in favor of confiscation dropped their ambivalence about free black workers and emphasized the ability of free black people to support themselves. Triumphantly pointing to successful black businessmen in Washington, party members declared that "we do not propose to do anything with them" if slaves were freed. Ex-slaves would fit easily into a free labor market, party members argued, and they should be allowed to do so if they could. Implying that black people would fit the free labor model of independent workers if left alone as native-born white workers and immigrants were, one man insisted that "there is no objection to the negro having a fair chance in America."

Still, even those Republicans who emphasized the value of black labor were not willing to challenge Northern racist attitudes and advocate the northward migration of black workers. For the most part, they denied that freed slaves would leave the South. Emotional ties and climate would keep ex-slaves in the land of their birth, they maintained, and once freedom was established, even draw free Northern black people South. Southerners would welcome free black labor, Republicans argued, for it would be "folly" to drive out their workers.[35]

Republicans who supported free black labor outweighed party members, primarily from border states, who pleaded for leaving the slaves untouched or, if it were determined that they must be confiscated for military advantage, called for colonization. Despite support from forty-nine Republicans trying to appease Northern racism and court the border states, the House rejected an amendment to the bill providing for colonization of those freed slaves willing to emigrate and establishing "certain control" over black people remaining in America. Republicans who opposed the plan recognized no right to expatriate native-born men without their consent and also maintained that "we cannot afford to send away from the country such a vast capital of labor."[36]

In late May 1862, the House voted on the related confiscation and emancipation bills. After passing the confiscation act, it turned to the emancipation bill. To the surprise of many party members, twenty-five Republicans from across the North joined the opposition to reject the measure by a vote of 74 to 78. The next day, Republican A. G. Porter of Indiana called for the reconsideration of the emancipation bill; he perceived that its sweeping nature frightened potential supporters, and he proposed to limit the bill's provisions. Porter's motion to reconsider the measure prevailed by a vote of 84 to 64, in part because the bill's failure made many Republicans fear foreign intervention in the conflict. The majority was solidly Republican, while thirteen Republicans from across the North crossed over to vote with the opposition against reconsideration.[37]

Porter's belief that a less sweeping bill would attract enough votes to pass proved true as the House accepted a revised bill by a vote of 82 to 54 in mid-June. The new bill enumerated classes of traitors whose slaves could be confiscated, rather than allowing a blanket confiscation. It provided for commissioners to list slaves to be freed and for a judicial process to free them, and it prohibited the reenslavement of the descendants of freedmen. The bill also provided for the colonization of willing black people on foreign territory to be purchased with the proceeds of the sale of confiscated lands. This new version of the bill recognized the significance of domestic workers for the Confederacy and endorsed the idea of freedom for some black people, yet it avoided antagonizing reluctant Republicans who feared wholesale emancipation. A correspondent for the Indianapolis *Daily Journal* felt able to maintain that "not a single thought of benefitting the negro by giving him liberty entered the brain" of those advocating the new bill. The measure attracted eleven Republicans who had previously voted nay, and five party members who had not voted on the old bill. Ten Republicans from across the North continued to oppose the measure.[38]

In the Senate, radical confiscation committee chairman Clark joined Democrats, who were determined to force the adoption of a radical policy the House would reject, and moderate Republicans, who hoped to hamstring stringent confiscation, to pass a stronger measure than the House bill. This bill (S. 310) reflected the vanguard of Republican ideas about slavery. It provided for the general confiscation of slaves to prevent their use for the Confederacy and allowed the Union army to use black people as workers and soldiers. When the House over-whelmingly rejected the Senate's new version of the bill, Congress set up a conference committee on the confiscation measures, led by anti-slavery men Clark and Eliot.[39]

In mid-July, Eliot reported the work of the conference committee to the House. The committee's moderate bill enumerated carefully constructed categories of rebels whose property was at risk of confis-cation, and limited emancipation to slaves escaping from rebels to the Union army or under the army's control in captured areas. At the same time, however, it looked toward more sweeping measures by permitting the President to emancipate all slaves in rebel areas with due warning and to use black people in whatever ways he saw fit, a thinly veiled reference to African-American soldiers. In a sop to the border states, the committee also authorized colonization of willing black people.

The House approved the conference committee's report by a vote of 82 to 42. Two Old-Line Whigs, one from Tennessee and one from Kentucky, joined the Republican majority, and two Republicans joined the opposition minority. In the Senate, a solid Republican majority of twenty-seven defeated twelve opponents of the bill. Five Republicans, mainly from the border states, joined the minority. Lin-coln signed the measure, together with an explanatory joint resolution he had requested limiting property forfeiture to the life of the offender, on July 16, 1862.[40]

Over the summer of 1862, as the approaching fall elections made them defend the party against virulently racist Democratic attacks, Republicans increasingly emphasized the value of black labor to a free economy. Democrats charged that Republican confiscation plans would lead free black people North to take jobs from white men, or to live shiftlessly, draining Northern tax dollars. In return, Republi-cans began a concerted effort to destroy the idea that free black labor would hurt the North. "Every laborer in the community adds to the aggregate wealth," the Cincinnati *Daily Gazette* reminded its readers with a basic Republican economic argument the radical New York *Daily Tribune* had advanced since the first year of the war. Men who wanted to drive out workers to enhance wages would "destroy the business which furnishes the wages," the *Daily Gazette* maintained. "The State needs every laborer that has come into it, or is likely to come," the newspaper continued in a striking defense of Northern black labor. Attempting to draw black people into the Republican free labor model, the editor argued that black labor harvested the crops that supported manufacturing and commerce. "Every laboring man is worth more than his weight in gold to the country," the newspaper's editor insisted. "The desperado politicians, who are raising an outcry against negroes going to work, must have unlimited confidence that the people are ignorant of the first principles of political economy," echoed the editor of the Cincinnati *Daily Commercial*. "Will the Logan *Gazette* or the Dayton *Empire* tell us when a people were poorer from an addition to the number of laborers in their midst."[41]

The Republican effort to include black people in the free labor theory got a great boost in July 1862 from the interest of the Danish government in receiving freed slaves to populate the Danish West Indies. Although the "apprenticeship" program the foreign government offered was actually a form of forced labor, Republicans took at face value the offer to give the ex-slaves training and land. "It is a striking illustration of American short-sightedness," commented a newspaper editor, "that at the instant we are talking of the deportation of the African race, comes the earnest appeal of the Danish government to own, to possess the very labor we are willing to discard."[42]

Despite their willingness to draw black people into Republican political economic theory, however, most Republicans insisted that freedmen should contribute to the economy from a free South. As the 1862 election approached, Republicans, few of whom wanted black people in their states, tried to assuage Western fears of black migration North. They emphasized that emancipation would prevent, rather than encourage, the Northward movement of black people. Only slavery prodded runaways North, Republicans maintained. "Abolish slavery and the reason he had for directing his steps toward the north star will have passed away," Governor Morton of Indiana explained in October 1862. "Being free where he is he will have no need nor desire to visit the frozen North." The South could never expel its black population, the Cincinnati Daily *Gazette* commented, for "the laboring population is bound up with the fate of the land, and must continue so, whatever their status."[43]

As Republican attitudes about free black labor slowly changed, the party's belief in the value of domestic as well as military slave labor to the Southern war effort hardened. Two months after he signed the Second Confiscation bill into law, President Lincoln irrevocably committed the Republicans to a policy based on the idea that all slave labor was vital to the Confederacy. Building on the Second Confiscation Act, September's Preliminary Emancipation Proclamation declared that all slaves held in areas still in rebellion in one hundred days would be forever free. In the January 1, 1863, Emancipation Proclamation itself, Lincoln declared wholesale emancipation "a fit and necessary war measure" justified by military necessity. The Indianapolis *Daily Journal* applauded Lincoln's argument. "It is well known that the slaves are the producing class of the South" and slavery the Confederacy's "peculiar strength," its editor declared.[44]

With the Emancipation Proclamation, the President also committed his party to employing black labor in the military as soldiers as well as workers. He declared that ex-slaves would be received into the armed services "to garrison forts, positions, stations, and other places, and to man vessels of all sorts." It would now be only a question of time before freedmen wore Union blue.[45]

Finally, President Lincoln addressed the role of the ex-slaves in a free labor society. "I hereby . . . recommend to . . . the people so declared to be free . . . that, in all cases when allowed, they labor faithfully for reasonable wages," he wrote. In the first two years of the war, the Republicans had become convinced of the value of slave labor to the South and of black labor to the Union military. While certain Northerners had begun to welcome black workers, it remained to be seen whether black people would come to be perceived as necessary and beneficial laborers in the nation's free domestic economy.

While Republican attitudes about black labor had been shifting, the great number of displaced freed slaves in the Union had become a problem. Fugitives, who hampered movements and drew vital supplies, overran the military. Refugees without roles in army camps suffered from dislocation, poverty, and unemployment, and the dreadful living conditions in refugee settlements encouraged the rampant spread of disease. Even some of the freed slaves who had found work suffered. Government contractors or private individuals often "hired" freedmen at nominal wages, then held them to their contracts by force. In the years from 1863 to 1865, debates over what sort of aid to provide for newly freed slaves helped define both the position Republicans expected black people to assume in a free labor society and the limits of the party's willingness to expand the national government.

The government had begun to consider help for contrabands other than what the military could supply since the Union capture of the Georgia and South Carolina Sea Islands. The situation there had become so dire so quickly that shortly after arriving, General Sherman had asked philanthropic Northerners to send food and clothing. After arranging for the cotton to be gathered, Treasury Secretary Chase had appointed Edward L. Pierce, an antislavery friend who had worked with the contrabands at Fortress Monroe, to go to Port Royal, South Carolina, and report on the black population's growing needs.[46]

Pierce eventually assumed control of the black workers around Port Royal and the Sea Islands under government auspices, but he developed a private system of charity to minister to the contrabands, using his connections to missionary and abolitionist groups to bring teachers and supplies to the impoverished people. Pierce apparently maintained private control of aid to black people to guarantee that abolitionists would be able to influence events at Port Royal without interference from politicians, but the precedent he set confirmed the belief of most Republicans that only private interests, not the government, had a charitable role in society. America's limited national government had no direct jurisdiction over individuals, Republicans thought, and they expected the private sector to provide aid to those that needed help. By February 1862, private freedmen's aid societies had begun to form across the North.[47]

In the first two years of the war, Republicans opposed providing anything but temporary assistance to destitute fugitive slaves, for they feared creating a dependent race by ignoring what they believed to be the basic rule of political economy. If, as party members thought, every able-bodied man had been endowed by God with the means to support and better himself as his labor created value, no man should receive economic aid. Downplaying the needs of newly freed slaves, party members concentrated on helping freedmen join the free labor economy. Political economist Francis Wayland warned a minister on his way to occupied South Carolina "that it is of the most questionable benefit ever to *give* to a person able to work." While widows and orphans merited charity, "a man with full health and plenty of work" did not, for the elevation of black people from slavery to freedom must be carried on "upon sound political principles." Freedmen had to learn that "labor bears viable fruit," Wayland advised. They must "see that all their blessings are the result of their own labor." "Nothing will do more to elevate them into self dependent men than this," he concluded.[48]

Echoing Wayland, many Republicans advocated leaving black people to their own devices so they would become self-sufficient. The New York *Daily Tribune* sympathized with the sufferings of the ex-slaves, but insisted that, given the chance, they could help themselves. "If we can in any proper way manage to keep offensive hands off of them," agreed one representative's correspondent, "I have no fear that we can leave them, where the rest of us are, in the hands of God, and subject to the great law which feeds the industrious and sometimes lets the idle starve."[49]

Political expediency gave this theory great power. In part to defend their policies of confiscation and emancipation, by the end of 1862 most Republican congressmen adhered to the idea that freedmen would be productive workers. They expected slaves to transform themselves easily into free laborers as the military employed them, as the Treasury Department hired them to work in the abandoned Southern fields, and as individual employers bid for their services. With fugitive slaves relatively scarce, Republicans were able to dismiss the poverty in contraband camps as a normal condition of some people in a free society.[50]

Strong demand for labor during the war reinforced Republicans' belief that freedmen would not need help adjusting to freedom. Radical newspapers had noted the value of black labor since early 1862; by August 1863 the Leavenworth, Kansas, *Daily Conservative* boasted that "almost every farm is supplied with labor in the shape of one or two large healthy negroes." By the end of 1863 even a newspaper from racist Indiana rejected colonization arguments because it objected to removing "4,000,000 of valuable laborers" from America; and all the Northern requests for black workers seemed to Republicans to pale when compared to Southern demand for labor. As the New York *Times* reported, "From the South . . . we hear the same cry as ever for more negroes." "Freedom is now given to thousands at a period when the mere ability to labor is riches," commented a

Republican senator. "He who will labor now seldom needs the help of charity."[51]

Despite the power of this argument, by January 1863 two extraordinary circumstances were pushing the Republicans to explore using the government to help freedmen. First, the growing number of destitute freed slaves, whose numbers swelled after the Emancipation Proclamation, claimed the sympathies of many Northerners. Second, party members noted that their vision of productive, self-supporting freedmen was threatened by employers who abused the ex-slaves. Party members realized, as one said ruefully, that without adequate safeguards, freedmen's postwar "condition as hired hands on the immense plantations of the South may be made, by a combination of the wealthy proprietors, as oppressive as slavery has ever been."[52]

In mid-January 1863, Eliot broached the subject in Congress by introducing a bill for the creation of a Bureau of Emancipation. The bill died but the subject did not drop, for the War Department authorized three well-known reformers to investigate the condition of the refugees. The Freedmen's Inquiry Commission made a preliminary report in June 1863, indicating that freedmen needed temporary protection to become productive workers; but, the report concluded in an affirmation of Republican hopes for a productive population of freedmen, if they received such help, they could be as useful "as if the same number of loyal whites had emigrated into the northern States."[53]

Shortly after the first session of the Thirty-Eighth Congress began in December 1863, the House created a Select Committee on Emancipation. Chaired by antislavery man Eliot of Massachusetts, the committee was filled with Westerners, whose regional biases could be counted on to balance the North's racism with the nation's need for labor. In mid-February 1864, the committee presented a measure (H.R. 51) for creating a Bureau of Freedmen's Affairs within the War Department. The proposed bill, which offered only temporary government aid to help freed slaves establish themselves as free laborers, reflected the growing Republican belief that black people would become productive members of a free economy.[54]

The bill provided that under the direction of the Secretary of War, a commissioner would "make all needful rules and regulations for the general superintendence, direction, and management" of freedmen, so that both black Americans and the government "shall be mutually protected, and their respective rights and interests duly determined and maintained." Emphasizing Southern black labor, the plan called for the establishment of Southern departments, supervised by assistant commissioners and local superintendents, in which freedmen would be settled on confiscated or abandoned lands. Commissioners would organize and advise black workers and adjust the wages the workers received from their employers. In testament to the committee's faith in the value of black labor, the bill stipulated that the profits the enterprises netted after the deduction of expenses and wages would be paid into the United States Treasury.

The placing of the bureau in the War Department established two important points. First, members of the committee clearly indicated that black people could support themselves, for they maintained that the needs of the black population were occasioned by the war and were temporary. Second, by placing the bureau in the War Department, the committee set the measure solidly where other legislation benefiting African-Americans had been: under the auspices of the war powers of the government. This enabled party members to avoid the question of Congress's constitutional power to provide aid to the civilian population.

Eliot's speech introducing the measure emphasized the value of domestic black labor to the Union. He noted the freedmen's "willingness and ability to work" and argued that "by judicious and timely aid," those not in military service "will return to the Government in produce and in money more than shall be expended on their account." Eliot explained that the freedmen's problems were caused by "harpies" who exploited them and kept them laboring at starvation wages. The situation must be rectified to allow free black labor to produce with maximum results for the Union. "It is for our interests, material, political, and pecuniary, to protect these men so far as they require protection, and no further," Eliot insisted.

Emancipation committee member William D. Kelley of Pennsylvania drew on the Republicans' vision of political economy to develop Eliot's argument that domestic black labor would be valuable to the nation. Reminding the House that "in the cultivation of its lands a nation finds its wealth" and that "none can suffer from the employment of idle laborers on abandoned lands," Kelley insisted that, by employing freedmen on the fallow Southern lands, the measure would produce necessary cotton and cash—indeed, he claimed the bill was virtually a revenue measure. In case the idea of increasing national production did not attract wavering representatives, Kelley reminded them that the entrance of black people to the free labor model would "create millions of consumers, liberal consumers" of Northern goods. He painted a picture of black families with "carpets upon their floors, furniture in their rooms, and Yankee clocks upon their mantels."

Democrats opposed the measure not only because of party members' deep racism but also because they objected violently to its expansion of government powers. Democrats had watched in horror the Republicans' development of the national government, and this measure seemed designed to permit a whole new scale of government power. Ohio Democrat S. S. Cox argued that the plan was "sweeping and revolutionary" because it created a new charitable role for the national government. Cox told the House that he pitied those whom antislavery New Englanders had "thrown houseless, clothesless, foodless, medicineless, and friendless on the cold world," but that the freedmen must look to benevolent individuals for help. Congress had no constitutional authority to create a welfare system for four million freed slaves, he said, and, if begun, such a system would create "a vast opportunity for greed, tyranny, corruption, and abuse," which would doom the government. The Democrats, he concluded, wanted to limit the size of the national government to prevent the Republicans from completing their goal of establishing despotism.

Democratic outrage at the new scheme foundered under the Republicans' wartime willingness to address new situations in innovative ways to promote progress. Invoking the usual Republican justification for groundbreaking measures, one representative retorted to the opposition, "We are in the midst of a revolution, and it is no answer to the demand for a bureau to say that there has never been a Freedmen's Bureau before." "Changes," he went on, "are the sole source of hope and aspiration; they are the method and sure guarantee of progress, social and political. Stagnation," he insisted, "is death."

On March 1, 1864, after days of sporadic discussion of the measure, the House narrowly decided to use the national government to provide temporary help for enabling freedmen to enter the free labor economy. Party members thus indicated their belief that black labor was valuable enough to the nation that freed slaves merited government attention, but that that attention must be temporary and was justified only by the extraordinary circumstances of war. The House passed the bill to create a Bureau of Freedmen's Affairs in the War Department by a vote of 69 to 67. The majority was Republican, while sixteen party members joined the Democratic minority. Indicating Republicans' reluctance to launch such a novel program, Republican nay votes came from across the North. Border state party members, who feared for slavery and race control in their own states, were most likely to vote nay.[55]

While the House had been debating its measure, the Senate had created a Select Committee on Slavery and Freedmen chaired by the famous abolitionist Charles Sumner of Massachusetts and, like the House emancipation committee, dominated by Westerners. The Senate committee developed its own measure to aid freedmen, which it reported to the Senate in place of the House bill. In what was probably a blend of Sumner's desire to protect the freed slaves and Westerners' desire to control them, the Senate's new bill (still named H.R. 51) called for much more supervisory care of the freedmen than the House measure. The Senate committee's bill proposed the creation of a Bureau of Freedmen in the Treasury Department. Like the House bill, the measure outlined a plan for Southern departments overseen by commissioners and superintendents. These officials would not only settle freed slaves on confiscated and abandoned lands and adjust wages; they would also act as "advisory guardians," protecting the freedmen from ill-treatment, making sure they fulfilled labor contracts, arbitrating differences between black people or between laborers and employers, and appearing "as next friends of the freedmen" in court. Like the House bill, this measure demonstrated the committee members' basic reliance on the value of black labor. It stipulated that after the Bureau became self-sufficient, profits from it would go to the Treasury.[56]

The committee's decision to move the bureau to the Treasury Department completely changed the constitutional justification for the measure. Sumner told the Senate that the committee had moved the bureau to simplify its operations, since the Treasury Department already controlled the abandoned lands in the South. Regardless of the committee's motivations, however, placing the bureau outside of the War Department challenged the Republican belief that only the war caused freedmen's destitution and that their problems would stop with the fighting. Although Sumner insisted that the committee meant not to introduce a permanent system of government aid to freedmen, but only to help slaves in the transitional period to freedom, which would extend beyond the war, the structure of the measure clearly implied that government help would be long-term domestic aid, rather than a temporary war measure.[57]

When Sumner managed to get the Senate to take up the Freedmen's Bureau bill in early June 1864, he tried to advance the plan by equating it with another piece of novel Republican legislation for domestic economic development: the Pacific Railroad. Sumner insisted that private organizations were inadequate to address the needs of the freed slaves and enable them to become productive workers. Government alone could provide the infrastructure—networks, machinery, and organization—to perform the large operation at hand, he told the Senate. "The national Government must interfere in this case precisely as in building the Pacific railroad," in which government organization made possible a popular project of economic development too large for individuals to assume.

This strongly supervisory bill, which created a new role for the national government as a peacetime protector of individuals, met heated criticism from some Republicans. Antislavery senator James W. Grimes of Iowa tapped powerful Republican beliefs when he objected to using the government in such a way. He maintained that "the only way to treat these men is to treat them as freemen." They were no different than white men in hard times, he argued. "You have got to give them alms, you have got to exercise acts of humanity and friendship to them for awhile," he told the Senate. "They will be jostled as we are all being jostled through this life," he concluded, "but in a little while they will settle down into the position that Providence has designed that they shall occupy under the new condition of affairs in this country."

Most Republican senators stood between Sumner and Grimes, agreeing that it was "precisely the right idea" to help the freedmen temporarily through the dislocations of the war and so enable them to become good workers, but rejecting the idea that the government should provide long-term aid to freedmen. Party members maintained that black people wanted only "an opportunity to labor," which the bureau would quickly help them find, thereby making itself obsolete. Republican congressmen further denied that the national government had power to aid state inhabitants, and believed that Southern states would "assume jurisdiction over their own people and over their own property" when they rejoined the Union. When Sumner asked that the bureau be continued for two years after the war because freedmen's needs would not end with the fighting, only nine senators agreed with him. Seventeen voted to end the bureau with the war.

Republicans also continued to distrust government enterprise and wanted to make sure that freedmen would be able to direct their own work. Party members feared that the government might usurp a new role and begin hiring and organizing black labor. They noted that under government supervision the freedmen were poor and their condition was deteriorating, while freedmen who farmed for themselves "are prosperous and independent and are improving." The Senate agreed that men worked better without government management, and amended the bill to prevent government-organized farming.

Although Republicans appeared to have growing confidence in black labor, only about half of Senate party members approved of its Northward migration. Border state Republican Willey, who disliked the bill, introduced an amendment requiring commissioners to communicate with state and municipal authorities in the North to help freedmen find "homes and employment with humane and suitable persons at fair and just compensation." Willey noted the Northern cries for labor as the war had drained the region of men, and he justified his amendment as the plan most likely to enable freedmen to work while it would also solve the North's labor problem.

The amendment passed by a vote of 19 to 15. Three opposition members, intending to weaken the bill's chance of passing, joined sixteen Republicans to vote in the affirmative. Six of the Republicans who voted for the proposal came from Western states desperate for labor. Five came from border states and included both those who approved the bill and those who hoped to kill it by making it offend Northern public opinion. Four positive Republican votes came from New England and one from New York.

The nay votes on the amendment were also variously motivated. Three Democrats joined twelve Republicans to oppose the measure. Withstanding the taunts of Democrats that abolitionism was "absolute hypocrisy," for abolitionists refused to act on their professed belief that black people were their equals, Sumner and Maine's Lot M. Morrill, who had originally supported the amendment, recognized that it would probably offend public opinion and voted nay. So did antislavery senators Benjamin Franklin Wade of Ohio and Henry Wilson of Massachusetts. Showing that desire for black labor did not necessarily mean support for independent black neighbors, even James H. Lane of Kansas, who had led several jayhawking expeditions to Missouri to bring contrabands to Kansas as workers, voted against the amendment.[58]

Even Republicans willing to allow black people to move North wanted such migration to be quiet. They objected to the amendment's provision that commissioners must open correspondence with Northern governors and municipal authorities, recognizing that such actions would spark a flurry of protest in states with strong Democratic factions and would give campaign fodder to the opposition in the presidential campaign. The Senate agreed to strike the troublesome requirement.

While Republicans disagreed on the best plan for helping the freedmen enter a free economy, Democrats firmly opposed the measure on the grounds that it delegated state powers to the national government. Democrats denied the Republican image of useful black workers, insisting that "this population is incapable of taking care of themselves" [sic] and charging that Republicans sought "to give [them] advantages that the white race do not receive or claim." Democrats linked Republican support for ex-slaves and what Democrats alleged was Republican usurpation of power. The proposed plan "would swallow up . . . a very important portion of the powers enjoyed by the States," and Democrats claimed that Republicans were using the cry of "the wicked rebel and the negro" to hide their nefarious "effort to overthrow liberty and establish despotism in this country."[59]

On June 28, 1864, the Senate approved its Freedmen's Bureau bill by a vote of 21 to 9. Declaring that black people would be good workers in a free economy, Republicans permitted considerable government help for the freedmen through a brief period of transition to freedom, but rejected the idea that the national government could provide long-term aid for individual laborers. The majority in favor of the bill was solidly Republican, while three party members joined the minority.[60]

With adjournment approaching, the House postponed consideration of the measure until the next session of Congress, so it was not until late December 1864 that the House, clinging to the idea of individual self-sufficiency, refused to concur in the Senate's strongly supervisory version of the bill. To find a compromise, Congress set up a conference committee, which was dominated by antislavery men.[61]

In early February 1865, Eliot reported the conference committee's plan to the House. The new bill made a much greater commitment to the freed slaves than either of the previous bills had done. Like the old bill, the measure called for a commissioner and subordinate agents to supervise and protect freedmen in Southern districts. Strikingly, however, the new measure created not a governmental bureau, but a new government department that was to take control of abandoned lands from the Treasury Department and supervise ex-slaves, to be called the Department of Freedmen and Abandoned Lands. Tying this measure to an earlier Republican effort to develop the country, Eliot told the House that the committee had patterned the new bill on the act that created the Department of Agriculture. "The precedent seemed to be a good one," Eliot remarked. The link of the new department to the Department of Agriculture, which Republicans had created because they wanted to help what they believed to be the nation's most important economic sector, clearly indicated a Republican conviction that free black labor could greatly enhance the nation's growth and prosperity.[62]

While most party members had come to believe in the value of black labor, they also retained their belief in economic self-sufficiency, the harmfulness of intervening in the evenhanded operation of economic laws, and the danger of increasing government bureaucracy. As a result, many party members feared the committee's proposed government bureau in charge of a specific population. Auguring that far-reaching long-term aid to freedmen would run a fierce Republican gauntlet, Republican Robert C. Schenck of Ohio interrupted Eliot's introduction of the bill to tell the House that the Committee on Military Affairs had prepared an alternative measure (H.R. 698) "for the relief of refugees and freedmen," which created a temporary bureau in the War Department to aid both white and black people displaced by the war. A major general in the army before his election to the Thirty-Eighth Congress, Schenck had had personal experience with war refugees, and he maintained that no congressman could "shrink from affording immediate and speedy relief" to them.[63]

When the conference committee's plan came up again a week later, Republican James F. Wilson of Iowa questioned the sweeping new measure and revealed that most Republican representatives were convinced that freedmen could and should support themselves. "My own judgement is that the less restraint we put upon these freedmen the sooner we shall make men of them," he said. "While legislating so far as may be necessary to protect these persons, [we must] let them have the responsibility upon themselves of disposing of their own services in such a way as they deem proper, receiving compensation therefor."

The desire of many Republicans to provide only temporary, imperative help to freedmen encouraged Schenck, who once again pressed the military committee's plan. Its bill, which the clerk now read to the House, answered most of the concerns that Republicans had raised about aiding the freed slaves. Supporting the idea of individual self-sufficiency, it limited operation of the proposed bureau to the present war and assigned to it only "the supervision, management, and control of all subjects relating to refugees and freedmen from rebel States," not the freedmen or refugees themselves. Avoiding a permanent increase in government bureaucracy, the bureau would have a limited staff, supervised by the President and the Secretary of War. Seeking to provide for the immediate needs of freedmen and refugees without creating a permanent charitable role for the government, the measure authorized the President to "direct such issues of provisions, clothing and fuel as he may deem needful for the immediate and temporary shelter and supply of destitute and suffering refugees and freedmen," and permitted him to let the bureau temporarily use abandoned Southern lands for the benefit of refugees and freedmen.[64]

Schenck addressed directly the Republican beliefs in self-sufficiency and reluctance to use the government to favor one or another group. Relying on the idea that free black people could support themselves, Schenck emphasized the temporary nature of the needs of freedmen and refugees. The war had caused distress, he argued, which would end with the fighting. Permanent aid to the freedmen not only was unnecessary, but also might cause dependence, he warned, echoing Wayland. That, he said, was a result "to be guarded against either as to whites or blacks." Schenck also noted that his bill made "no discrimination on account of color." The military committee's bill "would provide for . . . refugees of all colors as well as freedmen," so that all would have relief from suffering and be able to "shift for themselves" as soon as possible.

Probably hoping to combine the two bills, House Republicans refused to reject the Freedmen's Department plan, although a majority preferred Schenck's measure. After Eliot assured the House that the proposed department would be temporary (but that it might need to continue briefly after the war), the House narrowly accepted the conference committee's version of the bill by a vote of 64 to 62 in early February 1865. The majority consisted solely of Republicans. A core of Democrats made up the minority, with fifteen Republicans, mostly border state men, joining them. Nine days after accepting the conference committee's plan, the House passed Schenck's bill to create a bureau for the relief of freedmen and refugees in the War Department without debate or a roll call vote.[65]

Senate Republicans objected even more strenuously than House members had to the apparent permanent guardianship of freed slaves inherent in the plan to establish a new government department. Reflecting that antislavery agitators had based their action on the idea that, once free, black people would support themselves, they rejected what they termed the old pro-slavery argument "that the negro is not able to take care of himself, that he needs a guardian." Indeed, most reformers only wished to see freedmen protected from abuse as they entered the free labor market. Black people knew their own interests better than white people did, some senators argued, and supervision would be counterproductive. "As long as you keep them under . . . guardianship," Indiana's Henry S. Lane maintained, freedmen would be helpless, but "the very moment you make them freemen and secure their rights in the courts," they would be able to care for themselves.[66]

Some Republicans also echoed House objections that the conference committee's bill neglected white refugees and black refugees in the Northern states while rescuing Southern freedmen. Northern newspapers carried tales of starving white refugees, and white people were reluctant, as one said, to "neglect my own kith and kin to legislate for the exclusive protection and benefit of colored men."[67]

In mid-February 1865, the Senate rejected the conference committee's plan for a new department by a vote of 14 to 24. The sixteen Republicans against the plan outweighed the fourteen in favor of it. Then, applauding the temporary nature, streamlined bureaucracy, and equal treatment of black and white refugees in Schenck's measure, Senate Republicans called for a new conference committee to reexamine the issue of aid to the freedmen. So obvious was the drift of Republican thought on the matter that the House appointed Schenck to the new committee.[68]

In early March 1865, the committee reported to the Senate a new measure slightly modifying Schenck's proposal with elements of the plan to create a new department. The report called for the establishment of a bureau in the War Department for the relief of freedmen and refugees for the duration of the war plus one year. Its limited bureaucracy would supervise and manage all abandoned lands and all subjects relating to freedmen and refugees. The measure allowed the Secretary of War to distribute temporary supplies to suffering individuals, and it also allowed the bureau to rent abandoned lands to loyal refugees and freedmen for three years, giving them an option to buy. The Senate approved the new plan without a roll call vote, while the House accepted the report by a vote of 52 to 77, on a strict party vote.[69]

Lincoln signed what became known as the Freedmen's Bureau bill on March 3, 1865. The Republicans had agreed to help individuals of all races suffering from temporary dislocation, but they denied that the government could oversee a person's affairs better than that person could. Refusing to use the government to supervise individual laborers permanently out of doubt about the legality and wisdom of such a plan, and rejecting the idea that any specific group in American society should receive special government protection, the Republicans reemphasized their belief in self-sufficiency and the ability of everyone, white or black, to advance as one's own labor created value.[70]

At the same time that Republicans grappled with the problem of helping ex-slaves enter a free economy, they addressed the question of abolishing black slavery entirely in America. As party members discussed the history and future of slavery they retraced the wartime evolution of Republican beliefs regarding the country's black population. In their ultimate resolution of the slavery question during 1864 and early 1865, Republicans largely defined the Civil War for black and white people alike.

Many Republicans feared that the Emancipation Proclamation would be effective only during the war, and they began to explore the prospect of revising America's fundamental law to prohibit slavery permanently. In January 1864, Republican John B. Henderson of Missouri introduced a joint resolution (S. 16) to the Senate, proposing amendments to the Constitution to abolish slavery. Along with numerous similar proposals, Henderson's resolution went to the Committee on the Judiciary, which reported it to the Senate in mid-February 1864.[71]

When it emerged from the committee, the joint resolution called for the submission to state legislatures of a thirteenth amendment to the United States Constitution once the amendment had received a two-thirds vote of both houses of Congress. Reflecting the hand of Judiciary Committee chairman Trumbull, whose reputation as an antislavery lawyer had been made by his successful suits applying the ill-enforced Northwest Ordinance to Illinois, the terse amendment echoed the words of that revered 1787 regulation. The new measure prohibited slavery or involuntary servitude in American territory except as a punishment for crime. The amendment also gave Congress "power to enforce this article by appropriate legislation." Revealing Republican conviction of this amendment's critical nature, William Pitt Fessenden, the Senate's financial overseer, remarked with unconscious self-parody: "This [measure] is more important than any other business except the appropriation bills." In eleven days of debate, senators helped define the proposed constitutional amendment as the crowning achievement of the Republican economic program at the same time that they advanced the wartime debate over the position of black people in America.[72]

Senate Republicans argued forcefully that the achievement of America's economic destiny depended on the end of slavery. Party members advocating the Thirteenth Amendment all maintained that slavery had caused the Civil War and that the slave system, which represented monopoly and oligarchy, must die. Harking back to the Republican antebellum belief in a "Slave Power," senators claimed that aristocratic slaveowners rebelled when they found that free laborers would not accept their domination. Party members told the Senate that "the future repose of the country . . . demands" the end of slavery to destroy the dominant aristocratic slaveholding class and to make Southerners loyal to a nation that revered liberty. As long as slavery remained viable in the South, party members insisted, the motivation for secession and war, and a rebellious group of wealthy men to act upon it, would always be present. "If [Southern slaveowners] made war once, they may make it again," worried Henderson. "Therefore the restoration of slavery is a restoration of political strife." This argument touched the deepest beliefs of Republicans throughout the North. As the Philadelphia *Inquirer* recorded, "The two terms, slavery and rebellion, are now synonymous, the one will live as long as the other, and both will expire together."[73]

Reminding listeners of the great benefits of a free labor society to all members of such a society, Republicans argued that the arrival of free labor in the South would destroy the dominant planter class and elevate all Southern workers. African-Americans would gain status as slavery ceased to tear families apart and place humans on the auction block. As freedom helped the South to bloom, Henry Wilson said, white men would also profit. "The wronged victim of the slave system, the poor white men . . . impoverished, debased, dishonored by the system that makes toil a badge of disgrace . . . will . . . begin to run the race of improvement, progress, and elevation." Similarly David Clark, stating his conviction that with emancipation "a new and regenerated people shall rise up, with an undying, ever-strengthening fealty to [the] Government," attached no color to that regenerated people.

Universal free labor, Republicans reminded listeners, would rejuvenate the Southern lands that had been ruined by slavery, and the resulting productivity would help Americans achieve their great destiny. Even Virginia, which party members noted had been devastated by the war, would become prosperous. "Commerce would cover her bays . . . products would fill her marts and luxuriant grains wave in all her fields," Clark believed. Virginia "would become the land of abundance, and on every hand would grow villages and towns, with schools and churches, and all the institutions of a higher civilization." The free South would then participate in America's climb to greatness, Wilson told the Senate in an echo of popular beliefs. The nation, "regenerated and disinthralled by the genius of universal emancipation," would run the career of development, power, and glory.[74]

As Republicans argued that the antislavery amendment would achieve their economic vision for the country, they began to embrace black people in their economic theories. Party members revisited the changing wartime ideas about black people, reminding the Senate of the great value of slave labor to the Southern war effort, insisting that black people could support themselves, and even suggesting—albeit doubtfully—that the black and white races might be equal. Then James Harlan of Iowa took the logical step, which previously only a few radicals had taken, of explicitly according black people a fundamental position in the Republican theory of free labor. Reviewing the basic laws of political economy, he reminded his colleagues that an individual's right to personal property came from the investment of labor and skill made when he created that property. "To assert the reverse would be equivalent to denying the title of the Almighty to the workmanship of His hands," Harlan claimed, "for what better right can there be to property than the right of the creator to the thing which he has made?" He denied that any man should be prevented from acquiring property and maintained that slaves were held in bondage in defiance of the laws of political economy. The proposed amendment was a matter of simple economic justice.[75]

In what became an attack on the Republicans' entire wartime

domestic policy, Democrats met with bitter acrimony the proposal to submit the Thirteenth Amendment to the states. Appealing first to racism, they denied that the slaves could survive without white control and maintained that contact with white Americans had elevated black people far beyond their condition in any other land. They insisted that a black person was inferior to a white person, "and will be so whether you call him a slave or an equal." "The law of [God's] providence is inequality," one Democrat insisted, and decried Republicans for being "vain enough to imagine that . . . we can improve upon the workmanship of the Almighty."

While Democrats slipped easily into their traditional argument against black freedom, their strongest objection to the measure came from its striking invasion of states' rights, which they opposed almost hysterically. With each piece of innovative economic legislation Republicans had advanced, Democrats had charged that their opponents were expanding the power of the national government at the expense of the states. The proposed amendment took this encroachment to a new level, for it brought the national government unprecedented power by superseding state law and allowing the government to enforce the amendment in the states directly. Democrats desperately fought this proposal as the ultimate triumph of the Republicans' wartime policies.

Democrats believed that with this amendment Republicans sought illegally to subvert the very principles on which the government stood by destroying the balance between state and national jurisdictions. States must have "the entire and exclusive control of their own local and domestic institutions and affairs," they insisted, or the structure of the government would collapse "in intolerable despotism and misgovernment." Indeed, Democrats believed that if the national government could emancipate slaves held in states, it could go to any other lengths of government intrusion, including obliterating the states altogether. They insisted that the power to amend the Constitution could not be used to restructure the government.[76]

Ignoring the fact that the proposed joint resolution called only for submitting the Thirteenth Amendment to state legislatures for ratification, Democrats charged that Republicans had become despots who were destroying the country by devising "the boldest and most revolutionary measures under the guise of law and executive administration." They claimed that the Republican party planned to remain in power indefinitely, "to protract the aggrandizement of its leaders, the pecuniary advantages of its masses, and the complete consummation of its most wicked and destructive policy and measures."

Democrats barraged the Senate with amendments to the resolution, all designed to prevent its passage by tarring those in favor of it as traitors to their race. Seeking to embarrass the Republicans and to create political fodder, they sought to add to the proposed amendment popular reform measures that the Republicans would be forced to defeat. They proposed to add to the measure new articles providing that no President or Vice-President could hold office for more than four years; preventing patronage removals in most government positions; limiting each law to one topic, to be named in the act's title; and providing a new method for electing the President and Vice-President. Next, they tried to raise the fears of Northern racists by proposing that slaves would be freed only after the government removed them from Southern states, or that after emancipation freed slaves would be distributed across the country in proportion to the white population. Finally, recognizing that the joint resolution would pass in the overwhelmingly Republican Senate, Democrats tried to forestall civil rights by providing that no black person could be a United States citizen or hold any office or "place of trust or profit" under the national government.[77]

The expected Republican rejection of these measures allowed Democrats to charge their rivals with striking down white liberties in order to liberate black people. Democrats called on Republicans to "execute the Constitution as it is before they seek to amend it" and, revisiting their opposition to Lincoln's record on civil liberties, complained that "every vital provision of the Constitution as it is is violated, and you complain not; and now you propose to amend it solely for the miserable negro, after rejecting every amendment proposed that was calculated to secure the liberties of the white man." One speaker warned the Republicans that in the fall elections, "all the conservative and honest men in the country" would "drive the Goths and Vandals from the capital."[78]

The overwhelming Republican majority in favor of the Thirteenth Amendment probably encouraged the violence of Democratic opposition to it, for when the measure to send the amendment to the states came to a vote in early April 1864, it passed by a vote of 38 to 6. Only three Democrats, two of whom were from border states that were beginning the emancipation process, joined the Republican majority.[79]

The Senate joint resolution for submitting the Thirteenth Amendment to the states came before the House at the end of May 1864. After opposition forces failed to reject the measure immediately, debate began. Like the Republicans in the Senate, House party members reiterated their beliefs about a political economy based on free labor as they maintained that the amendment would bring a new nation of free laborers to wealth and power. Covering much the same ground that the senators had, House Republicans called attention to the slaves' vital contribution to the Confederate war effort. They reminded listeners of the Slave Power's "tyrannical rule, its unholy aims, and . . . its present wicked enormities" and insisted that slavery must die, or Southern slaveowners would regain power and continue to cause trouble. House Republicans also maintained that they intended to "elevate and disinthrall that most injured and dependent class" of poor Southern white men from the power of slaveowners and to allow the freedmen to make "the broad fields that war has desolated . . . again blossom as the rose and reward the labor of the husbandman."[80]

In addition to expressing the economic beliefs they shared with their fellow senators, House Republicans firmly redefined black Americans. They stood rock firm upon the manhood of black men, arguing that by creating black soldiers to defend the country, the nation "has recognized the manhood of the negro . . . and nobly does he vindicate himself." One Republican contemptuously dismissed the Democrats' vehement arguments that black people were inferior to whites. "I will not insult the presence in which I stand by entering into an argument . . . to show that the negro is not a brute but a man," he said.[81]

Not stopping at insisting on black people's humanity, some House Republicans accepted racial equality. When Democrats asked if Republicans thought black and white people were equal, one party member told his Democratic interrogator that the question of equality was "silly." He jibingly continued: "I think some white men are better than some negroes, and that some negroes are better than some white men, especially those of the copperhead persuasion." When asked what Republicans would do with the freed slaves, he chided Democrats that, unlike their rivals, Republicans were not afraid of competing with black people. They were even willing to see black congressmen, for "the country would not suffer by such a change *in some instances*." While they had not yet made the final, critical step of including freedmen fully in a free labor economy, Republicans clearly were reconsidering the basic identity of free black people.

In the House, as in the Senate, Democrats frantically fought the proposed measure. To a man they hammered home their belief that Republicans were subverting the Constitution to foster despotism. The proposed amendment fundamentally changed the "terms and . . . spirit" of the Constitution by destroying states' rights, Democrats charged. It laid open all state domestic institutions to national intervention, and "under such a doctrine," they maintained, "States may be annihilated and a monarchy built up."

Democrats repeatedly charged Republicans with favoring black people at the expense of the white population. "The pigmy demagogues who wield the destinies of our country" were prosecuting the war "solely for the enfranchisement and elevation of the negro," they maintained. Democrats charged that Republicans had, "by grossly high coloring and unfairly exaggerating the evils of slavery . . . [excited] among the people . . . blind enthusiastic sympathy for the negro" simply to use popular passion to win dangerous amounts of power. One Democrat warned that freeing the slaves "may . . . lay the foundation for enslaving the white people of this country . . . beyond redemption and for all time to come."

In a mid-June vote on the measure, Republicans mustered a majority in favor of the joint resolution, but not the requisite two-thirds majority to pass it. Facing the 1864 election, the Republicans went before the country advocating the Thirteenth Amendment as the harbinger of a powerful new society based on free labor, while Democrats opposed it as the culmination of the Republicans' quest for despotic power. When the public returned President Lincoln to the White House and placed another Republican majority in Congress, party members felt they had a popular mandate to pass the measure. Lincoln encouraged this sentiment, telling Congress that "the voice of the people" had been "heard upon the question."[82]

On December 15, two days after the second session of the Thirty-Eighth Congress convened, Republican James M. Ashley of Ohio told the House he would call up the bill at the beginning of January. President Lincoln pressed for the measure, believing that it would speed the end of the war by demoralizing the South and eroding its labor force. With the rumor in the House that the resolution still lacked three votes to pass, the debate got under way.[83]

Democrats opposed to the measure continued to insist that black people belonged in slavery but, more powerfully, they made a last stand against "[this rash] immolation of the Constitution," which would "crush out [the] sovereign right and power" of states to regulate their own domestic affairs. "I am a believer to the fullest extent in . . . the absolute, unqualified sovereignty of the States," one representative unabashedly told the House, and Democrats still insisted that Republicans were striving to create an absolute despotism. The opposition party was not necessarily trying to protect slavery, one Democratic leader maintained; it was trying to preserve "the Constitution just as it is, just as our fathers made it."

Republicans rose to the Democratic challenge. Party members tapped all the arguments for the abolition of slavery they had used previously. Strikingly, however, in this final congressional debate on the Thirteenth Amendment, Republicans also justified their wartime strengthening of the national government and officially embraced black people in their vision of political economy, although they achieved no consensus on the equality of black and white people.[84]

Republicans seized on the debate over this amendment to advance their vision of a new, strongly governed America. They rejected the Democrats' defense of states' rights by noting not only that such an argument lay at the heart of secession but also that the doctrine had been used throughout the war to thwart legislation that the Republicans viewed as critical to the war effort. The nation now took precedence over the states, Republicans insisted, and party members who had begun the war uncertain about the extent of the power of the national government now unhesitatingly asserted its strength. "The supreme power of the national Government is rigorously maintained throughout the Constitution," commented Ashley. "We must keep steadily in view the fact that the United States are not a confederation, but a nation." Another put more directly the Republican nationalism of the late war years. "If we are not a nation," he demanded, "what are we?"[85]

Having defended their creation of a strong national government, Republicans triumphantly declared that universal freedom in America would consummate the party's vision of political economy. Reminding the House of the harmony of interest among all people in society, Republicans noted that it was fatal for a nation to forget that "whatever is beneficial to a portion" of society "is beneficial to the whole community; and whatever is injurious to a portion is injurious to the whole." Calling for the permanent destruction of the South's aristocracy, party members expressed their hope of removing distinctions between former slaveowners and ex-slaves, leaving them both, as one representative said in an often-heard echo of Republican theory, "in the hands of God, . . . and giving to each equal protection under the law, bid them go forth with the scriptural injunction, 'In the sweat of thy face shalt thou eat bread.'"

Finally, Republicans reiterated the power of their economic vision to make America the greatest nation in the world. A New York *Times* editor insisted that after the war free labor would make the South enjoy "such industrial progress as has never yet been witnessed in any country in the world," and congressmen agreed. "Under the inspiration of free labor," Ashley told the House, "the productions of the country will be . . . quadrupled." Together with emancipated slaves, the immigrants who would now flock to the South would create "a free-labor force which, under the security thus given to capital and the inspiration thus given to labor, will make the land blossom like the rose." Free labor would make America "the most powerful and populous, the most enterprising and wealthy nation in the world," he concluded.[86]

Republicans thus accorded black people a role in free labor society, insisting that "nature made all men free, and entitled them to equal rights before the law; and this Government of ours must stand upon this principle"; but Republicans reached no agreement on black and white equality. Some made implicit arguments for equality, drawing striking historical parallels between black and white slavery and maintaining that all slavery was unjust. Others tried to calm fears of competition from black labor by suggesting that competition with white workers would drive the inferior black race back to Africa. Probably most typical, Thomas T. Davis of New York denied that the races were equal, but nonetheless insisted that every race must be permitted to reach "the elevation to which its own capacity and culture should entitle it."[87]

Various circumstances affected voting on the measure when it came up at the end of January 1865. Several Democrats who had previously opposed the plan now voted aye in an attempt, they said, to save the Democratic party by bowing to what appeared to be public will. Other waverers may have been convinced to vote for any proposal designed to shorten the war by seeing pictures of starving men in Confederate prison camps, which were placed on congressmen's desks during the debate.[88]

The resolution received just over a two-thirds majority, passing by a vote of 119 to 56. Fourteen Democrats voted aye and four Kentucky

Republicans voted nay. Four years of war had finally permitted the Republicans to commit a newly strong nation to a free economy and to the prosperity party members believed free labor would create. The cheering that broke out on the floor of the House and in the galleries as the Speaker announced the vote reflected the measure's popularity in the nation. After Lincoln signed the measure on February 1, 1865, sending the Thirteenth Amendment on its way toward ratification, the editor of the New York *Times* rejoiced that the proposed amendment "perfects the great work of the founders of our Republic." With its passage, he explained, "the Republic enters upon a new stage of its great career . . . aiming at the greatest good and the highest happiness of all its people."[89]

When the resolution passed, one antislavery congressman recalled, "it seemed to me I had been born into a new life, and that the world was overflowing with beauty and joy, while I was inexpressibly thankful for the privilege of recording my name on so glorious a page of the nation's history." George W. Julian noted that a few days later— less than a decade after the Dred Scott decision had denied black people citizenship—a black lawyer from Boston was admitted to argue before the Supreme Court. Shortly thereafter a black minister preached a sermon in the hall of the House of Representatives. "Evidently," Julian concluded, "the negro was coming to the front."[90]

At the end of the war, Republican legislation regarding slavery and the freedmen seemed to consummate party members' vision for the nation. Every worker in the country had become a free agent, increasing the national wealth as he worked to better himself. At the same time, the Republicans had finally laid to rest the specter of states' rights and had confirmed America's nationhood. With the Thirteenth Amendment, soon to be ratified, the Republicans had freed the country's bound laborers and had declared the government strong enough to enforce national legislation within the states, although party members refused to use the peacetime government to aid individual workers. It would only be a question of time, it seemed, before the nation, rich with the products of millions of free laborers and strong with an enduring nationalism that prompted all Americans to work for the same goals, became the wealthiest and most powerful nation on earth.

Despite their acceptance in Republican economic theory, however, black people were neither, as Julian so optimistically put it, "coming to the front" nor secure as free laborers. Living at a time when immigrant groups had overcome great odds to construct a place for themselves in American society and believing that the ability of black people to work would win them acceptance, if not equality, Republicans underestimated the drag that white prejudice would exert on freedmen as they attempted to work their way up in a free labor economy. Even if the Republicans' belief in the ultimate power of individual labor had been realistic, the lack of Southern capital in the postwar years would still have hampered black people. After the war, racial prejudice combined with capital shortages and fluctuating labor markets to prevent the Republicans' free labor model from working for most black Americans.[91]

Epilogue

Society stands or falls—is orderly or otherwise, upon its facts, and when the acceptance of a particular theory is necessary in order to preserve its balance, there is little hope of its steadiness; and this, especially, when the theory appears to run counter to the common experience of mankind.

—Cincinnati *Enquirer*, 1862

The Republicans who struggled to preserve their country during the four tortuous years of the Civil War would have been astonished by the charges that they had legislated for the benefit of big business, or that they had merely pieced together domestic legislation to meet the exigencies of the war. During the war, party members worked first of all to hold the country together. While doing so, they turned their attention to creating a new nation based on an economic ideal that promised everyone the opportunity to advance while fueling growth. Somehow, though, the American paradise they planned turned into the very world of wealthy monopolists and impoverished workers and farmers the Republicans most abhorred. The cause of the corruption of their vision was indeed, as historians have charged, their wartime economic legislation, but the Republicans' tragic weakness was not cupidity, but self-righteous optimism.

In the summer of 1861, Republican congressmen arrived in the squalid rural capital to direct a largely passive federal government of a loose union of states. Coming from across the North, they brought their regional prejudices with them as they met in the shade of the unfinished Capitol building, but most Republicans shared a belief that labor created value and that a harmony of interest existed among all economic groups in society. As the circumstances of the war years made them revise their initial beliefs, Republicans strengthened the national government in a pathbreaking effort to nurture the American economy.

Republicans began their wartime economic activities nervously, trying simply to fill an empty war chest. When state bankers flouted the Republican expectation that capitalists would cooperate with the government, the Treasury Secretary began to bypass bankers and sell bonds directly to the public. Meanwhile, Western Republicans forced Congress to take unprecedented action to weaken the state banks and financiers that Westerners believed were monopolizing the nation's money. When banks suspended specie payments, Congress rested the nation's currency on the North's economic strength rather than gold, declaring treasury notes legal tender. The passage and amendment of the National Currency Act in 1863 and 1864, which created a new national banking system, excised uncooperative bankers from the harmonious partnership that Republicans believed should exist between government and capital and, together with the elimination of state bank notes by taxation, reduced the privileges of all bankers. By the end of the war, having acted largely because of Western political clout, Republicans had developed an innovative financial system intended to place the burden of the national debt directly on the public, prevent money monopolies, and unite Americans with a single currency.

As they restructured the country's monetary system, Republicans began to exercise unprecedented influence on other national economic issues as well. After their conflicts with bankers, party members relied on individual citizens to pay for the war though loans and taxes, so it seemed imperative for the government to foster prosperity in order for individuals to meet those added burdens. A person's labor created value, Republicans believed, so any worker could gradually accumulate enough capital to rise, provided no one obtained exclusive control of resources. Consequently, Congress took steps to guard against land and money monopolies and the creation of permanent economic classes while legislating to nurture farming and manufacturing. Enlisting wartime legislation to build a nationwide version of the rural societies from which many of them came, party members hoped to create a thriving nation of independent farmers, small manufacturers, and upwardly mobile laborers.

Even before the war, Republican congressmen had devised a new tariff system, designing it to protect domestic "industry"—that is, farming, mining, and manufacturing—at the same time that it raised revenues. When the war required domestic taxation as well, Republicans tried to avoid land taxes, which fell heavily on the Western states, and instead employed manufacturing and income taxes to spread the burden on those most able to bear it. Easterners, in turn, insisted that industry needed higher tariffs so it could pay the new taxes. Enough Westerners agreed with them to pass a series of protective tariffs. While the Republicans maintained that the tariff system benefited all sectors of the economy, by the end of the war tariff legislation concentrated on manufacturing because the agricultural sector, with its booming market, needed no protection.

Intended initially simply to raise revenue, the sweeping Republican system of tariffs and taxes expanded the government's role in the economy. Recognizing that, despite their unpopularity, taxes and tariffs could spur economic growth, party members decided to raise money in such a way that it would help Northern economic development. They turned a traditional duty to new, ambitious ends. Joined with bond policy, Republican tax and tariff legislation created a need for the government to continue encouraging economic development. Republican tax policy demanded a growing tax base, while bond policy required that the public have the resources and confidence to invest in government bonds. Republican wartime revenue measures thus depended on widespread prosperity, which party members intended to promote.

With their agricultural legislation, Republicans developed what they viewed as the sector of the economy on which all others depended. Westerners, anxious to prevent monopolization of their lands by speculators, joined Easterners, who argued that the nation needed a broader tax base, to pass the Homestead Act, which gave parcels of Western land to settlers. In addition, hoping to establish a strong agricultural foundation for the economy, Republicans funded a new agricultural department and promoted immigration to populate the West. At the request of Easterners, whose depleted lands needed scientific care, Republicans also gave lands to establish agricultural colleges.

Republican agricultural legislation represented an unprecedented government effort to speed up labor's development of the nation. Democratic opposition to such use of government was muted, for Democrats had always championed agriculture and felt unable to oppose such favorable legislation. The Republicans' agricultural program not only initiated the government's active involvement in the economy, but also committed the nation to developing national industry, for it meant that the Treasury would never again rely on land sales for revenue, but must count on taxes. Thus, these agricultural measures, which enjoyed wide support from Western farmers, ultimately dictated government support for manufactures.

Republican railroad legislation launched the party and the national government into new areas of the economy in order to increase the ability of workers to develop the nation. Anxious to move farmers across the plains, desperate to reach Western gold fields, and hoping to protect California, Republicans claimed congressional power to charter a corporation for building a transcontinental railroad. They also offered government funds to their new railroad company. Their fears of government enterprise made them limit federal regulatory powers, although they gradually expanded the government's supervision of the project. With their transcontinental railroad legislation, Republicans took the striking step of offering government credit to those who would develop the country.

Finally, with their policies toward slaves and freedmen Republicans sought to introduce black people as laborers into the free society they were constructing, although party members did not necessarily expect them to be equal to white workers. While most Republicans had excluded black labor from their prewar understanding of a society built on free labor, the evident usefulness of slaves to the Confederacy made party members recognize the value of black labor and eventually to envision a role for free black people in their plan for the American economy. Republicans gathered black Americans into their economic world, but the Freedmen's Bureau revealed a critical limit to their vision of the economic role of the national government. Convinced that the ability to labor was a person's ticket to economic success, and that the troubles of freedmen were occasioned solely by the war, the Republicans provided only temporary government aid to help freedmen through the transition from slavery to freedom, then left them alone to become laborers for the national economy. The national government's role, according to Republicans, was to encourage labor to develop the nation by preventing money monopolies, freeing land, adjusting the revenue laws, and extending government credit to entrepreneurs in public enterprises, but it was not to support any troubled economic sector.

When the war ended, the Republican vision of a prosperous society of farmers, independent laborers, and small manufacturers seemed close to realization. All American laborers were now free to contribute to the economy. The Union boasted a strong agricultural sector, which exported crops to Europe in exchange for specie; the Homestead Act drew farmers West; and the transcontinental railroad, already under construction, would soon help them get there. Not just the agricultural sector, but the whole economy boomed during the war. Laborers found work easily and, although wages did not always keep up with inflation, few complained while the fighting continued. Tariff walls encouraged Northern industry, enabling it to prosper despite taxes that, before the war, manufacturers would have found crushing. Encouraging further development, new banking policies offered capital to all regions of the country, and a uniform currency system promised an end to bank failures.

Above all, in the spring of 1865, the Union enjoyed a buoyant sense of nationalism. Bond, banking, and tax legislation had tied individuals to a strong national government and made them vitally interested in its survival, while agricultural, railroad, and emancipation legislation had won people's loyalties with tangible benefits to individuals. At the same time, the debates over tax and tariff legislation, as well as bond and railroad legislation, had exacerbated Union antagonism toward Europe, and especially England, making Northerners self-conscious boosters of America. People focused on the Union rather than individual states, defining their nation against what Republicans deemed a hostile Europe, as well as the secessionist South. Having poured out blood and money in amounts hitherto inconceivable to survive a devastating civil war, and at the end of it finding themselves prosperous as well as successful, Republicans believed in America's unlimited potential. The country was becoming, it seemed, "the greatest nation of the earth."

The years after the war, however, revealed that the Republicans' attempt to create an American utopia would not succeed. The same ideas and optimism that shaped the Republicans' plans for a strong and prosperous nation caused them unwittingly to lay the groundwork for the turmoil of the late nineteenth century. Republicans' beliefs about political economy came from a rural antebellum world of farming, small enterprise, and strong religious belief in economic justice—a world that the war and, in large part, the Republicans' own economic legislation undermined. Party members' faith in individual labor made them pass sweeping laws to enable workers to prosper and develop the nation, but the same faith made Republicans oblivious to the actual conditions they were creating for those workers. They freed the slaves, invited immigrants into the country, and offered all settlers free land, but neither recognized freedmen's, homesteaders', and Southerners' need for capital nor believed that a person's ability to work might not be enough to overcome racial or ethnic prejudice.

At the same time, Republicans' belief that employers would accord labor its full share of profits to maintain a healthy economy, follow God's law, and conform to social pressures made party members ignore workers' decreasing bargaining power in cities. Republicans constructed a world designed to offer workers an open field for advancement on the sole basis of their labor at a time when workers' recipe for success needed spicing with money, opportunity, and favorable labor markets.

Republicans' belief in a harmony of economic interests and their concomitant fear of an intrusive government underwent wartime revisions but remained fundamentally intact. Together, these beliefs both benefited and injured the nation. Party members punished certain bankers and speculators, but they remained sure enough that wealthy individuals would strive in the public interest to permit them the latitude to manage the nation's new banking system and build the transcontinental railroads. At the same time that Republicans let individuals undertake large national projects, their belief in the public spirit of such private enterprise and their fear of government interference made them reject the regulation of private organizations that might have guaranteed their probity. Party members' faith that every person understood his or her own interests, that each person's good benefited all others, and that government intrusion in private affairs invited corruption and monopoly meant that Republican legislation depended on individual responsibility and integrity. On the positive side, that meant that Republicans were willing to free the slaves without imposing a new form of government bondage. On the other hand, it made party members assign to individual investors the impossible job of policing the nation's new large businesses.

While all sectors of the economy apparently had emerged from the war healthy, the strength of agriculture and labor proved illusory. The Republicans' belief that the economy depended on agriculture led them to help individual farmers, but the realities of the wartime economy paved the way for the eventual demise of the small farm. Republicans' understanding that ever-increasing agricultural production would fuel a booming economy made them pass innovative laws to help farmers expand into new lands and put old lands to the best possible use. The antebellum notion of small enterprise, however, blinded party members to the fact that new railroads, large markets, and rising production costs, all promoted by the war, would soon favor large agricultural enterprises over the family farm.

Laborers also appeared better off at the end of the war than they really were. Republican immigration policy produced a large labor force in the postwar years, but while many immigrants did finally settle in the West, as Republicans had hoped, many more remained in Eastern cities. Competition for jobs depressed wages and undermined the idea that manufacturers and workers shared a harmony of interest. At the same time it demonstrated that labor did not possess inherent value but, rather, that its worth depended on the vagaries of the labor market. A constant influx of foreigners, all speaking different languages, having different needs, and cherishing different goals, hampered laborers' efforts to organize and weakened their bargaining power for decades. The standard of living for city workers, especially immigrants, fell to appalling levels.

Freedmen, too, seemed to many Republicans to enjoy a better position in 1865 than they really did. Republicans assumed that the freed slaves would advance in a free labor economy. Despite the devastation of the South, party members recognized no need to provide ex-slaves with assistance because they believed that an individual's ability to labor was his "pecuniary resource." Republicans made no allowances for prejudice against freedmen because, they argued, no thinking employer would turn away labor. Republican policy gave ex-slaves the same legal rights as white people, then left the freedmen on their own. Tied with Southern whites into a devastating crop lien system and suffering under race prejudice, most freedmen found themselves unable to escape from poverty.

While farmers, laborers, and freedmen appeared stronger at the end of the war than they really were, banking and business appeared weaker than they would later become. Although Republicans designed their banking measures to reduce the power of dominant bankers, Western insistence on a pyramid system of bank-note redemption increased the strength of Eastern bankers after the war. Further, the attempts of a postwar Treasury Secretary to gain bankers' support of the new system made him mismanage bank conversions, placing almost all national bank capital in the East rather than the expanding West.

Similarly, Republicans had risked the destruction of manufacturing by placing the burden of wartime taxation on it, later to find business not only healthy, as party members had hoped, but also dominant over other sectors of the postwar economy. Many businesses thrived under the new high tariffs enacted to enable manufacturers to pay taxes. While taxes fell after the war, high tariffs continued, and strong businesses remained protected against foreign competition. At the same time, the postwar push for development funneled government money and land to various corporations, giving them advantages other economic groups could not claim.

The Republicans' wartime legislation itself forestalled any postwar legislative efforts to correct its flaws. Party members' economic beliefs made them guarantee that nineteenth-century America would remain as they constructed it, for their willingness to expand the economic power of the national government firmly established the government's role in the economy for decades to come. During the war, as they broke old precedents, party members set their own powerful precedent of government support for all sectors of the national economy, but they developed no corresponding role for the government as a regulator of growth or as a protector of disadvantaged economic groups. Only once did Republicans try to use the government to protect the public interest from a specific economic harm. When the Gold Bill of 1864 failed miserably they did not try such a method again, and they explicitly rejected such a role for the government during the debates over what became the Bureau for the Relief of Freedmen and Refugees. After the war, businessmen and financiers profited handsomely from the assistance of the national government while farmers and laborers, who enjoyed no protection from the dominant manufacturing, transportation, and banking interests, suffered under the same push for development. In those years, the precedent the wartime Republicans set against government regulation of corporations and against government protection of individuals undermined American society even as the nation's economy boomed.

Adding to the turmoil of the postwar world was the wartime change in popular expectations of the central government. At the same time that Republicans expanded the activities of the government solely to increase development, Republican wartime economic legislation tied all Northerners directly to the national government. Bond sales and banking laws especially convinced Northerners that the government rested on their financial strength, that it thus belonged to them, and that it should respond to their needs. During the war, party members did in fact legislate to suit their constituents, who demanded almost exclusively laws encouraging development, and the image of a people's government grew stronger. In the postwar years, however, the nation's needs no longer seemed as clear as they had been in wartime, and the American public splintered into different groups advocating different government policies to promote their interests. The personal identification of Americans with the national government added passion to debates over national policy at the same time that wartime precedents of government action guaranteed that interest groups demanding anything but aid for development would be disappointed. The apocalyptic rhetoric of postwar third-party political movements indicated that those who identified the government as their own felt personally and profoundly betrayed when it did not respond to their needs.

During the Civil War, Republicans watched Washington turn into a thriving city, and pointed proudly to "the fact that all through this terrible struggle for the life of the Republic, the work on the new Capitol has not been suspended for a day—not even when the enemy were intrenched for months almost within drum-beat."[1] Party members recognized the symbolism of the construction, and they tried to imitate it in their own domestic legislation. In the four years of the war, while fighting for the survival of the Union, the Republican party enacted a comprehensive set of economic policies designed to create a prosperous nation. Their laws provided powerful testimony of the Republicans' trust in their fellow citizens' abilities and their optimistic confidence in their country's capacity for greatness. Their legislation was a reasonable response to the conditions at hand, and much of it benefited the nation; the party's domestic legislation brought a strong America into a new era. But the new nation was not the one that Republicans had envisioned, for the push to construct national economic might overshadowed their grand social aims until the quest for universal prosperity was abandoned. Republicans, in their optimism, pride, and self-righteousness, could not see that they had built their new America on a flawed theory that their own laws helped to antiquate.

Notes

Abbreviations

HSP   Historical Society of Pennsylvania
LC   Library of Congress
NYHS   New-York Historical Society
NYPL   New York Public Library

Introduction

The epigraph, by William Pitt Fessenden, is quoted in Francis Fessenden, *Life and Public Services of William Pitt Fessenden* (Boston: Houghton, Mifflin and Co., 1907), 1: 254.

1. W. McKee Dunn, *Congressional Globe*, 37th Cong., 2nd sess., p. 1701.
2. For a discussion of the free labor argument in America, see Eric Foner, *Free Soil, Free Labor, Free Men: The Ideology of the Republican Party before the Civil War* (New York: Oxford University Press, 1970). For an exploration of the limits of the free labor ideology, see Jonathan A. Glickstein, *Concepts of Free Labor in Ante-bellum America* (New Haven: Yale University Press, 1991).
3. For discussions of Democratic beliefs during the Civil War, see Joel H. Silbey, *A Respectable Minority: The Democratic Party in the Civil War Era, 1860–1868* (New York: W. W. Norton & Co., 1977), pp. 23–29; Jean Harvey Baker, *Affairs of Party: The Political Culture of Northern Democrats in the Mid-Nineteenth Century* (Ithaca, N.Y.: Cornell University Press, 1983); Bruce Collins, "Ideology of Ante-Bellum Northern Democrats," *Journal of American Studies*, 11 (April 1977): 103–121.
4. Historians debate whether or not leading politicans reflected the values and desires of their constituencies. I have examined the responses of congressmen to issues raised in local newspapers, to the needs of their region, and to their constituent's letters, and have noted politicians' evident determination to justify their activities to their constituencies, and I have concluded that Civil War politicians did attempt to speak for those at home.
5. For classic statements of the argument that Republicans spoke for Northern

capitalists, see Algie M. Simons, *Social Forces in American History* (New York: Macmillan, 1911), pp. 263, 289; and Charles A. Beard and Mary R. Beard, *The Rise of American Civilization* (New York: Macmillan, 1927), p. 99. Challenges to this theory include David Donald, *Lincoln Reconsidered* (New York: Alfred A. Knopf, 1956), p. 111; Stanley Coben, "Northeastern Business and Radical Reconstruction: A Re-examination," *Mississippi Valley Historical Review,* 46 (June 1959): 67–68; Glenn M. Linden, "'Radicals' and Economic Policies: The House of Representatives, 1861–1873," *Civil War History,* 13 (March 1967): 65; and Allan G. Bogue, *The Earnest Men: Republicans of the Civil War Senate* (Ithaca: Cornell University Press, 1981), pp. 315–325. On postwar economic issues, see Robert P. Sharkey, *Money, Class, and Party: An Economic Study of Civil War and Reconstruction* (Baltimore: Johns Hopkins Press, 1959); and Irwin Unger, *The Greenback Era: A Social and Political History of American Finance* (Princeton, N.J.: Princeton University Press, 1964). David Montgomery, *Beyond Equality: Labor and the Radical Republicans, 1862–1872* (New York: Alfred A. Knopf, 1967) offers a picture of the changes of the war years based on the actions and beliefs of labor and its relationship to radical Republicans. Leonard P. Curry, *Blueprint for Modern America* (Nashville, Tenn.: Vanderbilt University Press, 1968).

6. Eric Foner, *Free Soil, Free Labor, Free Men: The Ideology of the Republican Party before the Civil War* (New York: Oxford University Press, 1970). Compare Michael F. Holt, *The Political Crisis of the 1850s* (New York: W. W. Norton & Co., 1978); William E. Gienapp, *The Origins of the Republican Party* (New York: Oxford University Press, 1986); William E. Gienapp, "The Republican Party and the Slave Power," in Robert H. Abzug and Stephen E Maizlish, eds., *New Perspectives on Slavery and Race in America* (Lexington: University Press of Kentucky, 1986), pp. 51–78; and Tyler Anbinder, *Nativism and Slavery: The Northern Know-Nothings and the Politics of the 1850s* (New York: Oxford University Press, 1992). Gabor S. Boritt, *Lincoln and the Economics of the American Dream* (Memphis: Memphis State University Press, 1978).

7. Compare Richard Franklin Bensel, *Yankee Leviathan: The Origins of Central State Authority in America, 1859–1877* (Cambridge, England: Cambridge University Press, 1990).

1. The Republicans in 1861

The quotation in the chapter title is in a letter written by his father to William Pitt Fessenden, July 27, 1861, William Pitt Fessenden MSS., Bowdoin College. The epigraph from the Montreal *Herald* was reprinted in the Chicago *Tribune,* June 2, 1862, p. 6, and the Indianapolis *Daily Journal,* May 29, 1862, p. 2.

1. Thomas H. Sherman, "Squalid Capital of '60's Recalled," Washington *Evening Star,* March 14, 1935. For description of the "ragged" city, see Carl Schurz, *Speeches, Correspondence and Political Papers of Carl Schurz,* ed. George Bancroft (New York: G. P. Putnam's Sons, 1913), 1: 9.

2. Hannibal Hamlin to Ellie Hamlin, July 7, 1861, Hannibal Hamlin MSS., University of Maine at Orono.

3. Alexander K. McClure, *Recollections of Half a Century* (Salem, Mass.: Salem Press Co., 1902), p. 415.

4. James G. Blaine, *Twenty Years of Congress: From Lincoln to Garfield* (Norwich, Conn.: Henry Bill Publishing Co., 1886), 1: 325–326.

5. William Belmont Parker, *The Life and Public Services of Justin Smith Morrill* (Boston: Houghton Mifflin Co., 1924), pp. 5–6, 25–33, 151, 159, 340.

6. New York *Times,* April 12, 1861, p. 1. Fritz Redlich, *The Molding of American Banking* (New York: Johnson Reprint Corp., 1965), 2: 104.

7. George W. Julian, *Political Recollections: 1840 to 1872* (Chicago: Jansen, McClurg & Co., 1884), p. 356. Blaine, *Twenty Years,* 1: 316–317.

8. Blaine, *Twenty Years,* 1: 318. David M. Ludlum, *Social Ferment in Vermont: 1791–1850* (Montpelier: Vermont Historical Society, 1948), p. 151.

9. Edward Magdol, *Owen Lovejoy: Abolitionist in Congress* (New Brunswick, N.J.: Rutgers University Press, 1967), pp. 27–38.

10. James T. DuBois and Gertrude S. Mathews, *Galusha A. Grow, Father of the Homestead Law* (Boston: Houghton Mifflin Co., 1917), pp. 2–16, 32. For a recent biography of Grow, see Robert D. Ilisevich, *Galusha A. Grow: The People's Candidate* (Pittsburgh, Pa.: University of Pittsburgh Press, 1988).

11. A. G. Riddle, *The Life of Benjamin F. Wade* (Cleveland, Ohio: Williams Publishing Co., 1888), pp. 45–99. H. L. Trefousse, *Benjamin Franklin Wade: Radical Republican from Ohio* (New York: Twayne Publishers, 1963), pp. 17–29.

12. Isaac N. Arnold, "Recollections of the Early Chicago and Illinois Bar," speech to the Chicago Bar Association, June 10, 1880 [n.p., n.d.; probably Chicago, 1880]. Pomeroy quotation is in Edgar Langsdorf, "S. C. Pomeroy and the New England Emigrant Aid Company, 1854–1858," *Kansas Historical Quarterly,* 7 (August 1938): 227. On April 10, 1862, while the transcontinental railroad was under consideration, Lane replaced Andrew Johnson, who had returned to Tennessee.

13. Horace White, *The Life of Lyman Trumbull* (Boston: Houghton Mifflin Co., 1913), pp. 20–32. Mark M. Krug, *Lyman Trumbull: Conservative Radical* (New York: A. S. Barnes and Co., 1965), pp. 59–66.

14. On Western resentment of the East, see, for example, the Indianapolis *Daily Journal,* November 1, 1861, p. 2; and the Chicago *Tribune,* October 11,

1861, p. 2. The list of New England's government prizes is in the Indian-apolis *Daily Journal,* April 5, 1861, p. 2. Allan G. Bogue, *The Congress-man's Civil War* (Cambridge, England: Cambridge University Press, 1989), p. 10. Blaine, *Twenty Years,* 1: 323. Cincinnati *Daily Gazette,* March 6, 1863, p. 3.

15. On ties of Vermont delegation, see Justin Smith Morrill MSS., Library of Congress (hereafter LC). Cincinnati *Daily Gazette,* December 11, 1862, p. 1. Samuel C. Fessenden to Governor Abner Coburn, January 14, 1863, Samuel C. Fessenden MSS., Maine State Archives.

16. Howard K. Beale, ed., *Diary of Gideon Welles* (New York: W. W. Norton & Co., 1960), 1: 523–524. Grinnell, *Congressional Globe,* 38th Cong., 1st sess., p. 2685. Chicago *Tribune,* May 22, 1864, p. 4.

17. Lois Kimball Mathews, *The Expansion of New England* (Boston: Houghton Mifflin Co., 1909), p. 225. Philadelphia *Inquirer,* January 24, 1863, p. 3.

18. Mathews, *Expansion,* p. 206. Joseph C. G. Kennedy, *Agriculture of the United States in 1860* (Washington, D.C.: Government Printing Office, 1864), pp. xlvi–xlviii, xcvi–xcviii. Isaac N. Arnold, *Reminiscences of the Illinois Bar Forty Years Ago: Lincoln and Douglas as Orators and Lawyers* (Chicago: Fergus Printing Co., 1881), p. 19. New York *Daily Tribune,* January 22, 1863, p. 3. Charles Richard Williams, ed., *Diary and Letters of Rutherford Birchard Hayes* (Columbus: Ohio State Archaeological and Historical Society, 1922), 1: 16.

19. Edward Eggleston, *The Hoosier Schoolmaster: A Story of Backwoods Life in Indiana,* rev. ed. (New York: Grosset & Dunlap, 1899), p. 29. Henry Clyde Hubbart, *The Older Middle West, 1840–1880* (New York: D. Ap-pleton-Century Co., 1936), pp. 56–58. David Donald, "Toward a Western Literature, 1820–1860," in *Lincoln Reconsidered* (New York: Alfred A. Knopf, 1956), pp. 167–186. Cincinnati *Daily Gazette,* December 31, 1862, p. 2, January 14, 1863, p. 2, February 19, 1863, p. 1.

20. Joshua Chamberlain, *Maine: Her Place in History* (Augusta, Me.: Sprague, Owen and Nash, 1877), p. 95. Elihu B. Washburne to Algernon Sidney Washburn, May 18, 1840, A. S. Washburn MSS., Minnesota Historical Society. For an argument that the "Jeffersonian dream" was a reality in antebellum America, see Jeremy Atack and Fred Bateman, *To Their Own Soil: Agriculture in the Antebellum North* (Ames: Iowa State University Press, 1987), and Jeremy Atack, "The Agricultural Ladder Revisited: A New Look at an Old Question with Some Data for 1860," *Agricultural History* 63 (Winter 1989): 1–25. Compare Donghyu Yang, "Farm Tenancy in the Antebellum North," in Claudia Goldin and Hugh Rockoff, eds., *Strategic Factors in Nineteenth Century American Economic History* (Chicago: University of Chicago Press, 1992), pp. 135–156.

21. Chicago *Tribune,* June 11, 1864, p. 2. Speech of Jackson Grimshaw at

Clinton, Illinois, July 27, 1860, in the Chicago *Tribune,* August 1, 1960, p. 2. Albert Bushnell Hart, *Salmon Portland Chase* (Boston: Houghton, Mifflin and Co., 1899), pp. 2–13.

22. James Albert Woodburn, *The Life of Thaddeus Stevens* (Indianapolis: Bobbs-Merrill Co., 1913), pp. 24–30; Ralph Korngold, *Thaddeus Stevens: A Being Darkly Wise and Rudely Great* (New York: Harcourt, Brace and Co., 1955), p. 9, 18–19. Charles A. Jellison, *Fessenden of Maine: Civil War Senator* (Syracuse, N.Y.: Syracuse University Press, 1962), pp. 4–5.

23. John Sherman, *Recollections of Forty Years in the House, Senate and Cabinet* (Chicago: Werner Co., 1895), pp. 28–35. John Sherman to his mother, October 25, 1837, John Sherman MSS., LC.

24. William Salter, *The Life of James W. Grimes* (New York: D. Appleton and Co., 1876), p. 3–13.

25. Salmon P. Chase to Simeon De Witt Bloodgood, February 2, 1863, Chase MSS. Unless otherwise noted, all Chase manuscript letters are in John Niven, ed., *The Salmon P. Chase Papers* (Frederick, Md.:University Publications of America, 1987), on microfilm. Abraham Lincoln, Message to Congress, December 3, 1861, *Congressional Globe,* 37th Cong., 2nd sess., Appendix, p. 4. On Lincoln's views of political economy, see Gabor S. Boritt, *Lincoln and the Economics of the American Dream* (Memphis: Memphis State University Press, 1978); and James A. Stevenson, "Abraham Lincoln on Labor and Capital," *Civil War History* 38 (September 1992): 197–209. Hugh McCulloch, Report of the Secretary of the Treasury, December 4, 1865, *Congressional Globe,* 39th Cong., 1st sess., Appendix, p. 35.

26. Atack and Bateman, *To Their Own Soil,* p. 3–4.

27. Francis Wayland, *The Elements of Political Economy,* (New York: Leavitt, Lord & Co., 1837), pp. vi, 107–110. Cincinnati *Daily Gazette,* November 9, 1863, p. 2. William Henry Venable, *A Buckeye Boyhood* (Cincinnati: Robert Clarke Co., 1911), p. 5.

28. Chicago *Tribune,* November 27, 1861, p. 2. Henry Carey Baird to Henry Carey, Philadelphia, November 2, 1837, James Moore Swank MSS., Historical Society of Pennsylvania (hereafter HSP).

29. Robert Dale Owen, *Labor, Its History and Prospects: An Address, Delivered before the Young Men's Mercantile Association of Cincinnati* (New York: Fowlers and Wells, 1851). For a rejection of these ideas, see the Philadelphia *Inquirer,* March 29, 1861, p. 4. Henry Charles Carey, *Principles of Political Economy* (Philadelphia: Carey, Lea & Blanchard, 1837), p. 26. Henry Charles Carey, *Essay on the Rate of Wages* (Philadelphia: Carey, Lea & Blanchard, 1835), develops the idea of rising wages as proof that Ricardo and Malthus were wrong. So does Carey, *Principles,* pp. 48–72. See also I. W. [Israel Washburn, Jr.], "Modern Civilization," *Universalist Quarterly,* 15 (1858): 30–32.

30. S. Austin Allibone to H. C. Carey, November 8, 1858, Edward Carey Gardiner MSS., HSP.
31. Chicago *Tribune,* January 8, 1862; see also Sheffield, *Congressional Globe,* 37th Cong., 2nd sess., pp. 640–642. Chicago *Tribune,* November 27, 1861, p. 2.
32. Hamilton, *Report on Manufactures,* see discussion in Virgle Glenn Wilhite, *Founders of American Economic Thought and Policy* (New York: Bookman Associates, 1958), pp. 234–235. Elihu B. Washburne, *Sketch of Edward Coles, Second Governor of Illinois, and of the Slavery Struggle of 1823–4* (Chicago: Jansen, McClurg & Company, 1882), p. 189. George Frisbie Hoar, *Autobiography of Seventy Years* (New York: Charles Scribner's Sons, 1905), 2: 244. Roscoe Conkling, *Congressional Globe,* 37th Cong., 2nd sess., p. 633.
33. Joseph Dorfman, *The Economic Mind in American Civilization, 1606–1865* (New York: Viking Press, 1946), 2: 758. Wayland, *Elements,* pp. 6–8, 32–33. See Boritt, *Lincoln and Economics,* pp. 122–123.
34. Francis Wayland to Francis Wayland, Jr., June 27, 1861; and William Henry Seward to Francis Wayland, Jr., December 30, 1865, in Francis Wayland MSS., John Hay Library, Brown University. *Congressional Globe,* 38th Cong., 1st sess., pp. 2682, 2684. William Herndon to "Friend Weik," Springfield, Illinois, January 1, 1886, in Emanuel Hertz, *The Hidden Lincoln: From the Letters and Papers of William H. Herndon* (New York: Viking Press, 1938), p. 117.
35. Carey, *Principles,* pp. 7–19 p. 294. Paul K. Conkin, *Prophets of Prosperity: America's First Political Economists* (Bloomington: Indiana University Press, 1980), p. xi. Anna M. Storm to H. C. Carey, August 29, 1862, Edward Carey Gardiner MSS., HSP. New York *Commercial,* in New York *Daily Tribune,* June 15, 1864, p. 4. H. B. Anthony to H. C. Carey, January 2, 1858, E. C. Gardiner MSS., HSP. Salmon P. Chase to H. C. Carey, August 21, 1861, September 27, 1862, and November 18, 1862, all in Edward Carey Gardiner MSS., HSP. William B. Rogers to H. C. Carey, November 13, 1863, Edward Carey Gardiner MSS., HSP.
36. Sheffield, *Congressional Globe,* 37th Cong., 2nd sess., p. 641. New York *Daily Tribune,* December 24, 1861, p. 4; March 5, 1862, p. 4. Chicago *Tribune,* December 2, 1861, p. 2.
37. Thurlow Weed to Zachariah Chandler, August 26, 1859, Zachariah Chandler MSS., LC. New York *Daily Tribune,* November 16, 1864, p. 4.
38. For a thorough discussion of Republicans and the idea of free labor, see Eric Foner, *Free Soil, Free Labor, Free Men* (New York: Oxford University Press, 1970), esp. pp. 11–39. Wayland, *Elements,* p. 7. Over his autograph, Wayland often wrote: "Every man has a right to himself" (Francis Wayland MSS., John Hay Library, Brown University). Dorfman, *Economic Mind,* 2: 767. R. W. Hanford to W. H. Seward, January 25, 1859, William Henry

Seward MSS., New-York Historical Society (hereafter NYHS). Jackson Grimshaw at Clinton, Illinois, July 27, 1860, in Chicago *Tribune*, August 1, 1860, p. 2. On fear of the spread of slavery, see William E. Gienapp, "The Republican Party and the Slave Power," in Robert H. Abzug and Stephen E. Maizlish, eds., *New Perspectives on Slavery and Race in America* (Lexington: University Press of Kentucky, 1986).

39. Atack and Bateman, *To Their Own Soil,* pp. 3–4. Abraham Lincoln, Message of the President, December 3, 1861, *Congressional Globe,* 37th Cong., 2nd sess., Appendix, p. 4.

40. Henry Charles Carey, Letter Fifth, Philadelphia, February 18, 1865, in *The Currency Question: Letters to the Hon. Schuyler Colfax, Speaker of the House of Representatives* (Chicago: John A. Norton, 1865), p. 39. Wayland, *Elements,* pp. 49–50. The Pope quotation is on the title page of Carey's *Principles.*

41. Carey, *Essay on the Rate of Wages,* p. 81. Cincinnati *Daily Gazette,* July 15, 1862, p. 2. Chicago *Tribune,* January 8, 1862, p. 2.

42. Philadelphia *Inquirer,* March 19, 1861, p. 4. New York *Times,* April 11, 1864, p. 4.

43. Carey, *Essay on the Rate of Wages,* p. 45, 81. Wayland, *Elements,* pp. 109–117. See Abraham Lincoln's version of this idea in his speech to the New York Working-Men's Association, excerpted in the Boston *Evening Transcript,* March 22, 1864, p. 1.

44. [Washburn], "Modern Civilization," pp. 20–24. See also H. C. Carey to ———, August 12, 1861, in *American Civil War: Correspondence with Mr. H. C. Carey of Philadelphia,* reprinted from the Philadelphia *North American* and the London *Daily News* (n.p.: August-September, 1861), p. 12. On Republican fears of the Slave Power, see Gienapp, "The Republican Party and the Slave Power," pp. 51–78. On European monopolies, see Grow, *Congressional Globe,* 36th Cong., 1st sess., Appendix, p. 127. Shannon, *Congressional Globe,* 38th Cong., 1st sess., p. 2948.

45. Carey, *Principles,* pp. 7–19; also Philadelphia *Inquirer,* March 29, 1861, p. 4. Chicago *Tribune,* January 14, 1864, p. 4. See also [Washburn], "Modern Civilization," p. 24, on self-regulation of wealth.

46. Carey, *Principles,* p. 143. Chicago *Tribune,* January 14, 1864, p. 4. For moral pressure to prevent accumulations of money, see, for example, Philadelphia *Public Ledger,* June 5, 1861, p. 2.

47. For Democratic class rhetoric, see, for instance, the *Daily Illinois State Register,* May 22, 1862, p. 2; and the report of Chicago trade unions meeting, in the Chicago *Tribune,* April 27, 1864, p. 4. Cincinnati *Daily Commercial,* July 24 and 25, 1862, p. 2; quotations in the *Daily Commercial* articles are from the Cincinnati *Daily Enquirer.* Cincinnati *Daily Gazette,* October 12, 1863, p. 2. See Boritt, *Lincoln and Economics,* p. 179.

48. Philadelphia *Inquirer,* March 19, 1861, p. 4. Cincinnati *Daily Gazette,*

October 12, 1863, p. 2. Chicago *Tribune*, January 14, 1864, p. 4, quoting from Mathew Carey. New York *Daily Tribune*, November 16, 1864, and November 12, 1863, p. 4. See also ibid., December 24, 1861, p. 4.

49. Boston *Post*, January 19, 1864, p. 1. Philadelphia *Inquirer*, February 7, 1863, p. 4.

50. Carey, Letter Fourth, *Currency Question*, p. 27. Terence V. Powderly, *Thirty Years of Labor, 1859 to 1899* (Columbus, Ohio: Rankin and O'Neal, 1890), p. 57. New York *Daily Tribune*, November 12, 1863, p. 4. David Montgomery, *Beyond Equality: Labor and the Radical Republicans, 1862–1872* (New York: Alfred A. Knopf, 1967), pp. 97–101.

51. Cincinnati *Daily Gazette*, July 15, 1862, p. 2. Chicago *Tribune*, January 8, 1862, p. 2.

52. Carey, Letter Fifth, *Currency Question*, p. 39. Carey, *Principles*, p. 341. See also *Essay on the Rate of Wages*, p. 20. [Washburn], "Modern Civilization," pp. 25–26.

53. Windom, *Congressional Globe*, 36th Cong., 1st sess. (1860), Appendix, p. 174. Account of rally at Mattoon, Illinois, is in Chicago *Tribune*, August 14, 1860, p. 2. Harlan, *Congressional Globe*, 36th Cong., 2nd sess. (1861), Appendix, p. 47.

54. Wayland, *Elements*, p. 109.

55. Washburn, *Congressional Globe*, 32nd Cong., 2nd sess. (1852), p. 116.

56. Charles Sumner explained that "whether under the Constitution or outside the Constitution all that is done in pursuance of the war powers is constitutional." *The American Annual Cyclopaedia and Register of Important Events of the Year 1862* (New York: D. Appleton & Co., 1869), p. 367.

57. *American Annual Cyclopaedia, 1862*, pp. 321, 323. *Congressional Globe*, 37th Cong., 2nd sess., p. 1691. See also Lovejoy, *Congressional Globe*, 36th Cong., 1st sess., Appendix, p. 174.

58. Simmons, *Congressional Globe*, 37th Cong., 1st sess., p. 314. See also Sumner: "New occasions teach new duties; new precedents are to be made when the occasion requires" (*American Annual Cyclopaedia, 1862*, p. 301); and W. P. Fessenden: "The times are those when we are compelled to make precedents" (ibid.).

2. War Bonds

The epigraph is from a letter by Salmon P. Chase to Charles A. Heckscher, March 7, 1864, in John Niven, ed., *The Salmon P. Chase Papers* (Frederick, Md.: University Publications of America, 1987), on microfilm.

1. Jay Cooke to H. D. Cooke, March 1, 1861, Jay Cooke MSS., HSP.

2. For recent biographies of Chase, see Frederick J. Blue, *Salmon P. Chase: A Life in Politics* (Kent, Ohio: Kent State University Press, 1987); and John Niven, *Salmon P. Chase: A Biography* (New York: Oxford University Press, 1995). Jacob William Schuckers, *The Life and Public Services of Salmon*

Portland Chase (New York: D. Appleton and Co., 1874), is also useful for its reprints of letters to and from the Treasury Secretary.

3. Schuckers, *Chase,* p. 212. Robert T. Patterson, "Government Finance on the Eve of the Civil War," *Journal of Economic History,* 12 (Winter 1952): 37–39. For public concern about the tariff situation see Philadelphia *Inquirer,* March 23, 1861, p. 1; New York *Times* tariff articles of March 12, 13, 20, 22, 25, 29, 30, April 4, 5, 6, 1861. The *Mercury* quotation is in the New York *Times,* March 25, 1861, p. 4.

4. The act of June 22, 1860, authorized a $20 million bond issue, of which a previous secretary had negotiated $7,022,000. That meant that $13,978,000 was available, but was limited to issue at par. The act of February 8, 1861, authorized a $25 million bond issue at 6 percent. It had no par restriction, but it was to expire on June 30, 1861. Chase's predecessor had negotiated $8 million of it; $17 million remained. The tariff act of March 3, 1861, authorized a loan of $10 million. It could be issued either in bonds or in Treasury notes, but was not available before July 1, 1861. Chase to Lincoln, March 1861, Chase MSS. For a brief review of Civil War finances, see Paul Studenski and Herman E. Krooss, *Financial History of the United States* (New York: McGraw-Hill Book Co., 1952).

5. New York *Daily Tribune,* December 26, 1861, p. 4. See also Boston *Daily Evening Transcript,* September 20, 1861, p. 2; and "Debt Banking in England," Chicago *Tribune,* January 4, 1862. Hugh McCulloch, Report of the Secretary of the Treasury, *Congressional Globe,* 39th Cong., 1st sess., Appendix, pp. 37–38. See also I. W. [Israel Washburn, Jr.], "Modern Civilization," *Universalist Quarterly,* 15 (1858): 16–19.

6. Chase to John A. Dix, March 12, 1861, Chase MSS. New York *Times,* March 26, 1861, p. 4. Chase began advertising on March 22 for an $8 million, 6 percent bond issue, to be distributed on April 2. Since the law of February 8 had no par restriction and would expire in three months, he acted under its authority. For more detailed accounts of Chase's negotiations with bankers, see Bray Hammond, *Sovereignty and an Empty Purse: Banks and Politics in the Civil War* (Princeton, N.J.: Princeton University Press, 1970), and Wesley Clair Mitchell, *A History of the Greenbacks* (Chicago: University of Chicago Press, 1903).

7. Henry Charles Carey, *Principles of Political Economy* (Philadelphia: Carey, Lea & Blanchard, 1837), pp. 142–143. Collamer, *Congressional Globe,* 37th Cong., 3rd sess., p. 874. Hugh McCulloch, *Men and Measures of Half a Century* (New York: Charles Scribner's Sons, 1900), p. 199. For Republican reference to bankers in the Revolution, see *Congressional Globe,* 37th Cong., 2nd sess., pp. 640–642. Jay Cooke to H. D. Cooke, April 8, 1861, and Jay Cooke to Chase, April 19, 1861, Jay Cooke MSS., HSP.

8. Kellogg, *Congressional Globe,* 37th Cong., 2nd sess., pp. 1510–1512. Philadelphia *Public Ledger,* June 18, 1861, p. 3, and June 20, 1861, p. 3. Philadelphia *Inquirer,* February 16, 1861, p. 4. Horace Greeley to Schuyler

Colfax, July 1, 1863, Greeley MSS., New York Public Library (hereafter NYPL). On New York's prewar Southern sympathies, see Ernest A. McKay, *The Civil War and New York City* (Syracuse, N.Y.: Syracuse University Press, 1990), pp. 1–29. On Mayor Fernando Wood's calls for the city's secession, see ibid., pp. 33–38.

9. New York *Times,* March 28, 1861, p. 2, and April 1, 1861, p. 2. See also excerpts from the New York *Post* and *Thompson's Bank-Note Reporter* in the New York *Times,* March 30, 1861, p. 2. John J. Cisco to Chase, March 28, 1861, Chase MSS.

10. Philadelphia *Inquirer,* April 3, 1861, p. 1, 4. Chase to Lincoln, April 2, 1861, Chase MSS.

11. Chase to Lincoln, April 4, 1861, Chase MSS. Philadelphia *Inquirer,* April 4, 1861, pp. 1, 4. He accepted bids of $3,099,000. Chase to John Jay, April 6, 1861, Chase MSS. New York *Times,* April 4, 1861, p. 1. Philadelphia *Inquirer,* April 4, 1861, p. 8.

12. For bankers' belief in their patriotism, see Henry Clews, *Twenty-Eight Years in Wall Street* (New York: Irving Publishing Co., 1888), pp. 39–40. The New York Bank of Commerce got $2.5 million, according to the Philadelphia *Inquirer,* April 4, 1861, p. 4. For reports of angry rumors about Chase's arrangements with favored bankers, see John Jay to Chase, April 4, 1861; and George Opdyke to Chase, April 4, 1861, Chase MSS. For talk of a lawsuit, see the Philadelphia *Inquirer,* April 5, 1861, p. 4, New York column of April 4, 1861. Jay Cooke to H. D. Cooke, April 8, 1861, Jay Cooke MSS., HSP, reported general hostility. See also Philadelphia *Inquirer,* April 4, 1861, p. 1, and New York *Herald,* in Philadelphia *Inquirer,* April 9, 1861, p. 4.

13. Chase to John Jay, April 6, 1861, Chase MSS. H. D. Cooke to Jay Cooke, April 9, 1861, Jay Cooke MSS., HSP. New York *Times,* April 12, 1861, p. 2.

14. Chase to Hiram Barney, confidential, April 16, 1861, Chase MSS. New York *Times,* April 16, 1861, p. 4. John Jay to Chase, April 4, 1861, Chase MSS. Philadelphia *Inquirer,* April 9, 1861, p. 4.

15. Ellis Paxson Oberholtzer, *Jay Cooke: Financier of the Civil War,* 2 vols. (Philadelphia: George W. Jacobs & Co., 1907) gives a laudatory and personal portrait of Cooke, and reprints some of his correspondence. Henrietta M. Larson, *Jay Cooke: Private Banker* (Cambridge: Harvard University Press, 1936) concentrates on Cooke's business activities, exploring Cooke's role in the changing American economy of the nineteenth century. Treasury operations were often handled by such private arrangements (see Jay Cooke to H. D. Cooke, March 25, 1861, Jay Cooke MSS., HSP). Eleutheros Cooke to Jay Cooke, March 3, 1861, Jay Cooke MSS., HSP.

16. Oberholtzer, *Cooke,* 1: 131. See, for example, H. D. Cooke to John Sherman, March 25, 1856, John Sherman MSS., LC. Jay Cooke to H. D. Cooke,

March 1, 1861; E. Cooke to Jay Cooke, March 25, 1861; H. D. Cooke to Jay Cooke, May 8, 1861; Jay Cooke to Chase, July 12, 1861; and Jay Cooke to H. D. Cooke, July 9, 1861, Jay Cooke MSS., HSP.

17. Oberholtzer, *Cooke,* 1: 133–134, and New York *Times,* April 12, 1861, p. 1. Shortly after the Treasury note sale, Chase offered Cooke the position of Philadelphia's Assistant Treasurer. Cooke declined the position.

18. Chase, Report of the Secretary of the Treasury, July 4, 1861, *Congressional Globe,* 37th Cong., 1st sess., Appendix, p. 6. Chase to John A. Stevens, New York Bank of Commerce, April 11, 1861, Chase MSS. On "prosperous" Treasury, see Philadelphia *Inquirer,* April 12, 1861, p. 2.

19. Indianapolis *Daily Journal,* April 12, 1861, p. 2.

20. Francis Wayland, *The Elements of Political Economy* (New York: Leavitt, Lord & Co., 1837), pp. 342–344. New York *Daily Tribune,* July 14, 1862, p. 4, and April 11, 1863, p. 4. Spaulding, *Congressional Globe,* 37th Cong., 3rd sess., p. 116. See also reference to "the wasting results of war" in the Cincinnati *Daily Gazette,* November 6, 1862, p. 1. See also the San Francisco *Daily Alta California,* April 15, 1862. Philadelphia *Inquirer,* May 9, 1861, p. 4, and May 28, 1861, p. 4.

21. These bonds were authorized by the law of June 22, 1860. Chase to Pelatiah Perit, April 25, 1861; Chase to Dix et al., April 25, 1861; Chase to S. Hooper, April 27, 1861; Chase to Jay Cooke, April 29 and May 2, 1861; Chase to Simeon Draper, May 3, 1861; Chase to Hooper, May 7, 1861; Chase MSS.

22. Chase to Hooper, May 7, 1861, Chase MSS. These were 6 percent bonds of the same loan he had used before. Philadelphia *Inquirer,* May 13, 1861, p. 4. He could issue Treasury notes under the law of June 1860. Chase to A. T. Hall et al., May 17, 1861, in Jay Cooke MSS., HSP. Bond sales were at rates varying from 85 to 93 percent. On May 25, Chase opened over $7.5 million worth of bids at an average rate of 85, and almost $700,000 worth of bids at par for Treasury notes (Philadelphia *Inquirer,* May 28, 1861, p. 4). On May 30, he opened a second set of Treasury note bids (Chase to Jay Cooke, May 27, 1861, Jay Cooke MSS., HSP). Sales figures are in Report of the Secretary of the Treasury, July 4, 1861, *Congressional Globe,* 37th Cong., 1st sess., Appendix, p. 6. Indianapolis *Daily Journal,* May 17, 1861, p. 2, and Philadelphia *Inquirer,* May 28, 1861, p. 4.

23. Philadelphia *Inquirer,* May 22, 1861, p. 8. H. D. Cooke to Jay Cooke, May 17, 1861; Chase to Jay Cooke, May 27, 1861; Jay Cooke to H. D. Cooke, May 22, and 24, 1861; A. G. Curtin to Jay Cooke and Mssrs. Drexel and Co., May 28, 1861; Jay Cooke to H. D. Cooke, June 13, 1861; H. D. Cooke to Jay Cooke, July 9, 1861, all in Jay Cooke MSS. HSP. Chase to James H. Walton, June 14, 1861, Chase MSS.

24. Barney to Chase, May 9, 1861; Morris Ketchum to Chase, May 9, 1861, Chase MSS.

25. Chase to Ezra Lincoln, June 13, 1861; Chase to Abraham Lincoln, June 24, 1861; Chase to William Pitt Fessenden, June 18, 1861; Chase to Justin Smith Morrill, June 22, 1861, Chase MSS. Chase, Report of the Secretary of the Treasury, July 4, 1861, *Congressional Globe,* 37th Cong., 1st sess., Appendix, p. 6.
26. John A. Stevens to Chase, June 29, 1861; Chase to John A. Stevens, May 22, 1861, Chase MSS.
27. New York *Times,* April 25, 1861, p. 2. H. D. Cooke to Jay Cooke, July 9, 1861, Jay Cooke MSS., HSP. Philadelphia *Inquirer,* May 28, 1861, p. 4, and August 14, 1861, p. 4.
28. Chase, Report of the Secretary of the Treasury, December 10, 1863, *Congressional Globe,* 38th Cong., 1st sess., Appendix, p. 7. New York *Times,* April 9, 1864, p. 4. Chase to John C. Hamilton, October 1, 1861, in Schuckers, *Chase,* p. 278.
29. In the fall of 1861, Chase asked his Assistant Treasurer in New York, John J. Cisco, to investigate Napoleon's methods, which Chase admired (Cisco to Chase, September 30, 1861); Chase to August Belmont, September 13, 1861; Simeon Nash to Chase, June 23, 1864; Chase MSS. The press also recognized the loan as like Napoleon's (Philadelphia *Inquirer,* September 5, 1861, p. 4). Democratic accusations are in the *Albany Argus,* reprinted in the *Daily Illinois State Register,* August 12, 1861, p. 2.
30. Chase, Report of the Secretary of the Treasury, July 4, 1861, *Congressional Globe,* 37th Cong., 1st sess., Appendix, p. 6. Ibid., pp. 60–61, 109–110, 128.
31. Chase to Cisco, August 25, 1861; Chase to August Belmont, July 1, 1861, unofficial and private; see also Chase to Belmont, August 10, 1861; Belmont to Chase, July 3, 1861, private and unofficial; Chase MSS. For British interest in debt see the Philadelphia *Inquirer,* August 8, 1861, p. 4, and August 21, 1861, p. 4; Indianapolis *Daily Journal,* September 12, 1861, p. 2; New York *Daily Tribune,* September 9, 1861, p. 4, and September 11, 1864, p. 4.
32. Indianapolis *Daily Journal,* October 23, 1861, p. 2. Boston *Daily Evening Transcript,* September 13, 1861, p. 2. W. P. Fessenden to J. S. Pike, September 8, 1861, James S. Pike MSS., LC.
33. Chase to Cisco, August 7, 1861, Chase MSS. Philadelphia *Inquirer,* August 12, 1861, p. 4. Chase, Report of the Secretary of the Treasury, December 9, 1861, *Congressional Globe,* 37th Cong., 2nd sess., Appendix, p. 23. Philadelphia *Inquirer,* August 15, 1861, p. 4. Indianapolis *Daily Journal,* August 19, 1861, p. 2, from New York *World* of August 15. Chase to John A. Stevens, August 20, 1861, Chase MSS. Philadelphia *Inquirer,* August 15, 1861, p. 4. W. P. Fessenden to J. S. Pike, September 8, 1861, James S. Pike MSS., LC.
34. Indianapolis *Daily Journal,* September 6, 1861, p. 2. The seven-thirties were generally termed Treasury notes, but were marketed as bonds.

35. H. D. Cooke to Jay Cooke, August 7, 1861, and July 9, 1861; Jay Cooke to H. D. Cooke, May 15, 1861; Chase to Jay Cooke, September 4 and 5, 1861; H. D. Cooke to Jay Cooke, September 7, 1861; Jay Cooke to Chase, September 7, 10, and 11, 1861; Jay Cooke MSS., HSP. James Gordon Bennett to Chase, September 9, 1861, Chase MSS. Schuckers, *Chase*, p. 229.

36. Jay Cooke to Chase, September 10, 1861, Jay Cooke MSS., HSP. New York *Daily Tribune,* September 3, 1861, p. 4, September 6, 1861, p. 6, September 28, 1861, p. 4. Boston *Daily Evening Transcript,* September 10, 1861, p. 2. James Sill to Chase, September 14, 1861; Flamen Ball to Chase, September 6, 1861, Chase MSS. For popularity of loan, see also the Philadelphia *Inquirer,* October 3, 1861, p. 4.

37. James R. Doolittle to Chase, September 13, 1861; Abraham Lincoln to Chase, October 5, 1861; William Gunckel to Chase, October 3, 1861; Chase MSS. W. P. Fessenden to J. W. Grimes, September 26, 1861, William Pitt Fessenden MSS., Bowdoin College.

38. Indianapolis *Daily Journal,* September 14, 1861, p. 2, and October 7, 1861, p. 2. Philadelphia *Inquirer,* October 12, 1861, p. 4. Chase to August Belmont, September 13, 1861; John A. Stevens to Chase, September 14, 1861; S. A. Mercer to Chase, September 23, 1861, Chase MSS.

39. The Treasury used two-year, 6 percent notes. Chase to Robert Buchanan, October 4, 1861; Chase to Amos B. Eaton, October 10, 1861; William Tecumseh Sherman to Chase, October 9, 1861; Chase to Cisco, October 15, 1861; Chase to John A. Stevens, October 18, 1861; August Belmont to Chase, October 31, 1861; William D. Gallagher to Chase, November 18, 1861; Chase MSS. On Chase's insistence on receiving gold payments rather than drawing on bank funds to pay creditors, see Hammond, *Sovereignty and an Empty Purse,* pp. 79–81. For changes in the Independent Treasury Act of 1846 to avoid specie transfers, see ibid., pp. 63–70, 98–105.

40. Chase to Henry F. Vail, October 24, 1861; E. W. Chester to Chase, October 29, 1861; Chase to John A. Stevens, November 20, 1861; Henry F. Vail to Chase, November 23, 1861; Chase to John A. Stevens, November 25, 1861; John A. Stevens to Chase, December 2, 1861; Cisco to Chase, December 7, 1861, strictly private and confidential; Chase MSS.

41. George S. Coe to Chase, December 3, 1861; Chase to George S. Coe, December 4, 1861; Chase to John A. Stevens, August 17, 1861; Chase to Ezra Lincoln, August 29, 1861; Chase to Franklin Haven, September 10, 1861; George S. Coe to Chase, November 14, 1861; Chase MSS.

42. Bankers thought Chase planned a large issue of Treasury notes declared to be legal tender and exchangeable for 6 percent bonds. This would cripple banks by replacing their own bank note issues while destroying the market for bonds. George S. Coe to Chase, December 12, 1861, Chase MSS. Chase had been paying creditors with drafts against individual banks for their

parts of the $50 million advances, and an informal meeting of bankers considered ceasing to honor his drafts. Cisco to Chase, December 7, 1861, strictly private and confidential; Chase to [John E. Williams], December 10, 1861; Cisco to Chase, December 9, 1861; Cisco to Chase, December 10, 1861; Chase MSS.

43. John E. Williams to Chase, December 13, 1861; Chase to Jay Cooke, December 16, 1861; Cisco to Chase, December 16, 1861; Jay Cooke to Chase, December 27, 1861; R. W. Latham to Chase, New York, December 26, 1861; Chase MSS. See also Chase diary, December 10, 1861, in David Donald, ed., *Inside Lincoln's Cabinet: The Civil War Diaries of Salmon P. Chase* (New York: Longmans, Green and Co., 1954), p. 48.

44. New York *World,* in Cincinnati *Daily Commercial,* December 23, 1861, p. 3. Henry F. Vail to Chase, December 27, 1861; Cisco to Chase, December 16, 1861; Cisco to Chase, December 17, 1861; Chase to Cisco, December 29, 1861; George Harrington to Chase, December 29, 1861; Chase MSS. Philadelphia *Inquirer,* January 1, 1862, p. 4.

45. On the country's prosperity, see the Chicago *Tribune,* January 8, 1862, p. 3, from the New York *Times.* On money supply, see the Cincinnati *Daily Commercial,* December 9, 1861, p. 4; and the San Francisco *Daily Alta California,* January 3, 1862, p. 4. Cincinnati *Daily Commercial,* December 10, 1861, p. 4, and December 24, 1861, p. 2.

46. Hugh McCulloch, president of the Bank of the State of Indiana, December 31, 1861, in Indianapolis *Daily Journal,* January 1, 1862, p. 3. See also Indianapolis *Daily Journal,* January 7, 1862, p. 3; and January 21, 1862, p. 3. New York *Times,* January 18, 1862, p. 4. The New York *Daily Tribune,* January 5, 1864, p. 4, provides a recollection of the time of suspension. Chicago *Tribune,* January 3, 1862.

47. Chase to John A. Stevens, December 31, 1861; Chase to Cisco, January 7, 1862; Henry F. Vail to Chase, January 7, 1862; Jay Cooke to Chase, January 31, 1862; Chase MSS. Boston *Post,* January 22, 1862, p. 1; New York *Daily Tribune,* January 15, 1862, in Boston *Post,* January 16, 1862; Philadelphia *Daily Evening Bulletin,* January 20, 1862, p. 4; New York *Times,* January 16, 1862, p. 4, and January 18, 1862, p. 4; Chicago *Tribune,* January 16, 1862, p. 2, and January 17, 1862, p. 4. Banks had taken a third $50 million loan on different terms than the first two, accepting 6 percent, twenty-year bonds salable in Europe as well as the United States, but refused another installment on the same terms as the first two. On Western fury at banks, see George Carlisle to Chase, February 3, 1862; Chase MSS.

48. *Congressional Globe,* 37th Cong., 2nd sess., pp. 630–636. John Sherman, *Recollections of Forty Years in the House, Senate, and Cabinet* (London: Samson Low, Marston & Co., 1895), 1: 302. Chase to William Pitt Fessenden, February 10, 1862. Finance Committee Chairman Fessenden pushed this change through the Senate over protests that it would make the bonds

much less valuable for investors (*Congressional Globe,* 37th Cong., 2nd sess., pp. 773–775).

49. *Congressional Globe,* 37th Cong., 2nd sess., pp. 881–891, 899–901.

50. Chase to Cisco, March 22, 1862; Chase to Jay Cooke, March 22, 1862; Cisco to Chase, March 26, 1862; Chase MSS. New York *Daily Tribune,* June 12, 1862, p. 6. Philadelphia *Inquirer,* June 10, 1862, p. 4, and June 11, 1862, p. 4.

51. Philadelphia *Inquirer,* August 2, 1862, p. 7. *Samuel Hallett's North American Financial Circular,* in the Cincinnati *Daily Gazette,* August 1, 1862, p. 2. Cincinnati *Daily Gazette,* June 16, 1862, p. 2.

52. Chase to Cisco, June 5, 1862; Chase to W. P. Fessenden, June 7, 1862, Chase MSS. New York *Times,* January 14, 1862, pp. 4–5. Cisco to Chase, June 27, 1862; Chase to W. P. Fessenden, June 28, 1862; Chase MSS.

53. Chase to Elbridge G. Spaulding, June 17, 1862; Chase to John Bonner, October 4, 1862; Chase to Cisco, October 7, 1862; Cisco to Chase, October 10, 1862; Chase MSS.

54. *Congressional Globe,* 37th Cong., 2nd sess., pp. 2880–2885.

55. Chase to Cisco, September 15, 1862; Chase to Benjamin F. Butler, September 23, 1862; Chase to Cisco, October 7, 1862; Cisco to Chase, October 10, 1862; Chase MSS. Chase, September 12, 1862, *Inside Lincoln's Cabinet,* pp. 135–136. *Harpers Weekly,* 4 (November 29, 1862): 754.

56. Cincinnati *Daily Gazette,* October 8, 1862, p. 1, and October 15, 1862, p. 1. Chase to Jay Cooke, November 13, 1862; Chase MSS.

57. For brief descriptions of the Treasury Department's trouble handling bonds during the war, see Donald R. Stabile and Jeffrey A. Cantor, *The Public Debt of the United States: An Historical Perspective, 1775–1990* (New York: Praeger, 1991), pp. 56–59.

58. Kate Chase to "My dear Mr. Cooke," September 1, 1861; Jay Cooke to H. D. Cooke, March 25, 1861; Jay Cooke MSS., HSP. Jay Cooke to Chase, October 30, 1861, and October 24, 1861; Chase to Jay Cooke, October 25, 1861, and March 7, 1862; Chase to Jay Cooke, November 8, 1862, unofficial and private; Chase MSS.

59. Chase to Jay Cooke, October 23, 1862, and October 24, 1862; Jay Cooke to Chase, October 25, 1862; Chase MSS.

60. Jay Cooke to Chase, October 25, 1862; Chase to Jay Cooke, November 8, 1862; Chase MSS.

61. For examples of daily reports, see the Indianapolis *Daily Journal,* March 25, March 26, and April 8, 1863. Oberholtzer, *Cooke,* 1:234–247. Indianapolis *Daily Journal,* March 24, 1865, p. 1.

62. Chase to Jay Cooke, November 13, 1862, Chase MSS. Chase sold $13.5 million of seven-thirties in November. The temporary loan was for $10 million. Philadelphia *Inquirer,* November 19, 1862, p. 1, and November 24, 1862, p. 4.

63. For attitudes toward banks, see, for example, the New York *Times,* January 14, 1863, p. 4; and the New York *Daily Tribune,* January 15 and 21, 1863, p. 4. Stevens, *Congressional Globe,* 37th Cong., 3rd sess., pp. 145–146.

64. Chase to Jay Cooke, two letters of December 9, 1862, private, Chase MSS. Sherman, *Congressional Globe,* 37th Cong., 3rd sess., pp. 841–846.

65. Cincinnati *Daily Commercial,* January 19, 1863, p. 2. The Ohio legislature endorsed the plan. Cincinnati *Daily Commercial,* February 12, 1863, p. 4. Philadelphia *Inquirer,* January 31, 1863, p. 2. Cincinnati *Daily Gazette,* January 22, 1863, p. 2. Chicago *Tribune,* March 12, 1864, p. 2.

66. Cincinnati *Daily Gazette,* December 5, 1863, p. 1. After a month of battles, Chase agreed at the end of January to separate the banking and loan sections of his package (Chase to John Sherman, January 30, 1863, Chase MSS). "An Act to provide Ways and Means for the Support of the Government," March 3, 1863, *Laws of the United States Relating to Loans and the Currency* (Washington: Government Printing Office, 1878) pp. 54–60.

67. Chicago *Tribune,* January 23, 1864, p. 2. New York *Times,* April 9, 1864, p. 4. Hooper, *Congressional Globe,* 37th Cong., 3rd sess., p. 386. Indianapolis *Daily Journal,* April 2, 1863, p. 3. Cincinnati *Daily Commercial,* November 14, 1862, p. 2, reprinted from New York *Economist.* See also the Indianapolis *Daily Journal,* March 6, 1863, p. 1. New York *Times,* January 31, 1862, p. 4; January 11, 1863, p. 4; March 9, 1863, p. 4; May 3, 1863, p. 4. "A Veteran Observer," in the New York *Times,* March 9, 1863, p. 4. Philadelphia *Inquirer,* January 2, 1863, p. 6.

68. S. E. Browne to Chase, May 28, 1862; Chase to John P. Usher, March 30, 1863, Chase MSS. For an examination of the California situation, see Samuel C. Wiel, *Lincoln's Crisis in the Far West* (San Francisco, 1949). In January 1864, Chase sent to Congress a section of a public lands bill that would provide for sale, rather than preemption, of mineral lands. Such a law, Chase wrote, would develop the mineral regions, increase production of precious metals, and provide revenue. Over the following few months, as gold prices rose and Treasury funds fell, Chase began to press harder for the sale of gold lands. Newspapers from the New York *Times* to the Cincinnati *Daily Gazette* argued that gold from the West could solve the Treasury's problems. In June, Congress added a tax on mining products to a pending tax bill. Indianapolis *Daily Journal,* July 28, 1864, p. 3, article from New York *Post.* Chase to George Julian, January 24, 1864, Chase MSS. Chicago *Tribune,* January 23, 1864, p. 2. Cincinnati *Daily Gazette,* April 19, 1864, p. 2. New York *Times,* July 4, 1864, p. 2, and June 17, 1864).

69. Two letters from Chase to William Aspinwall and John M. Forbes, March 16, 1863; two letters from Chase to Robert J. Walker, March 30, 1863; S. Hooper to Chase, April 20, 1863; Aspinwall and Forbes to Chase, May 2, 1863; Chase MSS. In February 1863 a group of European bankers offered

Chase a $100 million loan in gold at a rate of about 15 percent, to be paid over fifty years. Chase declined the offer (J. Le Ray De Chaumont to Chase, February 17, 1863; Isaac Smith Homans to Chase, March 10, 1863; Chase MSS).

70. William Pitt Fessenden to James S. Pike, April 5, 1863, James S. Pike MSS., LC. Jay Cooke to Chase, April 23, 1863; Chase to Aspinwall and Forbes, May 14, 1863; Cisco to Chase, July 7, 1863; Chase to Cisco, January 23, 1864; Chase MSS. Indianapolis *Daily Journal,* July 25, 1863, p. 2, and August 19, 1863, p. 2.

71. Pelatiah Perit et al. to Chase, April 2, 1863; Cisco and Hiram Barney to Chase, April 8, 1863; Chase to Cisco, April 16, 1863; Chase to Perit et al., April 17, 1863; Chase to John A. Stevens, April 5, 1863; Jay Cooke to Chase, October 1, 1861; Chase to Jay Cooke, July 22, 1863; Chase to Cooke & Co., June 1, 1863; Chase to Cooke & Co., June 2, 1863; Chase MSS. Oberholtzer, *Cooke,* 1: 437–438.

72. Hiram Barney to Chase, June 16, 1863, Chase MSS. Speech of Chase at Indiana State House, in Indianapolis *Daily Journal,* October 15, 1863, p. 2. Cincinnati *Daily Gazette,* October 26, 1863, p. 1. See also Chase's Report to Congress, December 10, 1863: "The general distribution of the debt into the hands of the greatest possible number of holders has been the second object of the Secretary in its creation." (*Congressional Globe,* 38th Cong., 1st sess., Appendix, p. 7).

73. Coffroth, *Congressional Globe,* 38th Cong., 1st sess., p. 99. Hendricks, ibid., pp. 1046, 1048. Clipping sent anonymously to W. P. Fessenden, January 1864, William Pitt Fessenden MSS., LC.

74. Sherman, *Congressional Globe,* 38th Cong., 1st sess., p. 1046. See also Chicago *Tribune,* March 22, 1864, p. 2.

75. Cooke received three-eighths of one percent after the first $10 million of bonds sold. Of that, one-eighth went to his agents, one-eighth to advertising, and one-eighth to himself. Commissions to buyers for resale, who bought from Assistant Treasurers, cost another $122,000. Chase to Schuyler Colfax, April 2, 1864, Chase MSS.

76. Chase to Jay Cooke, April 8, 1864; Jay Cooke to Chase, April 11, 1864; Chase MSS. New York *Times,* April 7, 1864, p. 9. Cincinnati *Daily Gazette,* April 7, 1864, p. 3.

77. On expansion of Treasury, see the New York *Daily Tribune,* May 20, 1862, p. 6; and Fenton, *Congressional Globe,* 37th Cong., 3rd sess., pp. 1117–1119. Hendricks, *Congressional Globe,* 38th Cong., 1st sess., p. 1046. Cincinnati *Daily Gazette,* January 22, 1864, p. 2.

78. Jay Cooke to Chase, April 6, 1864; Horace Greeley to Chase, April 7, 1864; Chase to Jay Cooke, March 31, 1864; Chase to Cisco et al., March 23, 1864; Chase MSS. Chase to W. P. Fessenden, in Schuckers, *Chase,* p. 416. New York *Daily Tribune,* March 29, 1864.

79. Article from the Cincinnati *Daily Gazette,* in the Chicago *Tribune,* March 25, 1864, p. 2. In Congress, Pomeroy read an article from the New York *Post* of April 29, 1864, calling for five-twenties (*Congressional Globe,* 38th Cong., 1st sess., p. 3211). C. P. Baily to Chase, May 3, 1864; Abraham Lincoln to Chase, May 18, 1864; Chase to Cisco, March 18, 1864; Chase MSS. William Pitt Fessenden, Report of the Secretary of the Treasury, December 6, 1864, *Congressional Globe,* 38th Cong., 2nd sess., Appendix, p. 25. Oberholtzer, *Cooke,* 1:425.

80. The bond legislation of the previous session would expire at the end of June. *Congressional Globe,* 38th Cong., 1st sess., p. 2787. "An Act to Provide Ways and Means for the Support of the Government . . . ," June 30, 1864, in *Laws,* pp. 63–70. The act also authorized the sale of $200 million worth of five-twenties approved in March (H.R. 265).

81. New York *Times,* June 29, 1864, p. 4; May 5, 1864, p. 4; July 4, 1864, p. 4. New York *Daily Tribune,* June 20, 1864, p. 4.

82. Donald, *Inside Lincoln's Cabinet,* June 30, 1864, pp. 223–227. Howard K. Beale, ed., *Diary of Gideon Welles* (New York: W. W. Norton & Co., 1960), 2: 63.

83. See, for example, the Chicago *Tribune,* May 4, 1864, p. 2.

84. David S. Tod of Ohio, the first nominee, was in poor health and faced a battle for Senate confirmation. Tyler Dennett, ed., *Lincoln and the Civil War in the Diaries and Letters of John Hay* (New York: Dodd, Mead & Co., 1939), pp. 198–203. W. P. Fessenden to "My Dear Sir," Judge Tenney [?], December 17, 1864, William Pitt Fessenden MSS., LC.

85. Fessenden, Report of the Secretary of the Treasury, December 6, 1864, *Congressional Globe,* 38th Cong., 2nd sess., Appendix, p. 28. J. S. Morrill to W. P. Fessenden, July 17, 1864, Justin Smith Morrill MSS., LC.

86. W. P. Fessenden to Cisco, July 6, 1864, William Pitt Fessenden MSS., LC. New York *Commercial* of July 12, 1864, in Indianapolis *Daily Journal,* July 13, 1864, p. 3. Indianapolis *Daily Journal,* August 11, 1864, p. 4, reprint from Springfield *Republican.* New York *Times,* July 14, 1864, p. 3. McCulloch, *Men and Measures,* p. 199. New York *Post,* July 19, 1864, in Indianapolis *Daily Journal,* July 20, 1864, p. 3. Indianapolis *Daily Journal,* July 19, 1864, p. 3. Report, 38th Cong., 2nd sess., p. 28. J. S. Morrill to W. P. Fessenden, July 17, 1864, Justin Smith Morrill Misc. MSS., LC.

87. Report, 38th Cong., 2nd sess. p. 28. The bonds were three-year seven-thirties. McCulloch, *Men and Measures,* p. 191. Fessenden's Appeal is in New York *Daily Tribune,* July 26, 1864, p. 4. New York *Daily Tribune,* July 27, 1864, p. 4. Indianapolis *Daily Journal,* August 30, 1864, p. 1, from *Harper's Magazine.*

88. *Chicago Tribune,* June 4, 1864, p. 2. Francis Fessenden, *Life and Public Services of William Pitt Fessenden* (Boston: Houghton, Mifflin and Co., 1907), 1: 326–327. W. P. Fessenden to Harrington, August 12, 1864, Bixby

MSS., Huntington Library, in Charles A. Jellison, *Fessenden of Maine: Civil War Senator* (Syracuse, N.Y.: Syracuse University Press, 1962), pp. 186, 184–188.

89. Fessenden, *Fessenden*, 1: 334, 351. In September, Fessenden issued the $32 million in five-twenty bonds under the act of March 3, 1863. This was the loan that Chase had advertised and withdrawn (Report, 38th Cong., 2nd sess., p. 28). In October, Fessenden issued $40 million worth of five-twenties, which had been authorized by the act of June 30, 1864. Report, 38th Cong., 2nd sess., p. 28. Indianapolis *Daily Journal,* October 17, 1864, p. 3. Fessenden, *Fessenden,* 1: 351–353. Indianapolis *Daily Journal,* November 16, 1864, p. 3. On January 7, Fessenden withdrew the ten-forty loan. Only $170 million worth of it had sold (Fessenden, *Fessenden,* 1:359).

90. New York *Daily Tribune,* August 4, 1864, p. 4. Treasury Department Circular of December 13, 1864, Treasury Department Records, National Archives, in Jellison, *Fessenden,* p. 180. McCulloch, *Men and Measures,* pp. 190–191.

91. Fessenden got permission on January 5 to issue as seven-thirties the bonds authorized on June 30, 1864 (Fessenden, *Fessenden,* 1: 359–362). Indianapolis *Daily Journal,* February 6, 1865, p. 1, discusses the sales of February 3, 1865.

92. Philadelphia *Daily Evening Bulletin,* March 29, 1865, p. 4.

93. Fessenden, *Fessenden,* 1: 361–362. "An Act to Provide Ways and Means for the Support of the Government," March 3, 1865, in *Laws,* pp. 71–73. House debates are in *Congressional Globe,* 38th Cong., 2nd sess., pp. 1198–1205. Although there was not a roll-call vote on the passage of the bill, there was one on a motion to reconsider. The division on that motion was largely by party, with Stevens, who hated the gold provision, being the notable Republican switching sides.

94. W. P. Fessenden to Abraham Lincoln, February 6, 1865, William Pitt Fessenden MSS., LC. McCulloch was actually nominated and confirmed a few days after March 3. McCulloch, *Men and Measures,* pp. 193, 246.

95. Oberholtzer, *Cooke,* 1: 528. McCulloch, Report of the Secretary of the Treasury, *Congressional Globe,* 39th Cong., 1st sess., Appendix, pp. 34–44.

96. Article from New York *Post,* in Indianapolis *Daily Journal,* July 28, 1864, p. 3.

97. Chase, December 10, 1863, Report of the Secretary of the Treasury, *Congressional Globe,* 38th Cong., 1st sess., Appendix, p. 7. Indianapolis *Daily Journal,* March 24, 1865, p. 1. See also Sherman, *Recollections,* (London ed.), 1: 302.

98. Chase to Simeon De Witt Bloodgood, February 2, 1863, Chase MSS. Speech by Godlove S. Orth at Layfayette, Indiana, September 8, 1864, in Indianapolis *Daily Journal,* September 10, 1864, pp. 1–2.

99. Jay Cooke to Philadelphia *Inquirer,* March 19, 1868, printed March 21,

1868, in Oberholtzer, *Cooke,* 2: 47. See also, for example, Philadelphia *Inquirer,* March 20, 1867, p. 4. For references to postwar bond speculation, see Larson, *Cooke,* pp. 207–236. Larson reports that on April 14, 1866, the New York *Commercial and Financial Chronicle* estimated that Europeans held at least $200 million in U.S. securities. For a brief discussion of the Western appeal of the Democrats in 1868, see Irwin Unger, *The Greenback Era: A Social and Political History of American Finance* (Princeton, N.J.: Princeton University Press, 1964), pp. 195–199. For a discussion of the roots of the paper currency redemption plan, its elements, and its failure, see Robert P. Sharkey, *Money, Class, and Party: An Economic Study of Civil War and Reconstruction* (Baltimore: Johns Hopkins Press, 1959), pp. 81–134.

100. The actual distribution of United States securities in postwar years remains unclear. Historians of the war years tend to emphasize the wide distribution of war bonds, while those of the postwar years emphasize the gulf between wealthy bondholders and the poorer classes, who resented the taxes required to fund the bonds. A study of the subscriptions to and ownership of the bonds is necessary, especially in light of Cooke's insistence that his own examination of his sales books through 1868 revealed continuing popular ownership of U.S. securities. Available statistics from the period are unrevealing. Public Treasury records list only initial sales of postwar bonds to large investors, largely for resale (see, for example, House Exec. Doc. 52, 39th Cong., 2nd sess.; House Exec. Doc. 34, 40th Cong., 2nd sess.; House Exec. Doc. 26, 40th Cong., 3rd sess.) Banks did not absorb the majority of national bonds for reserves, either, owning at their highest level (in 1880) only about 21 percent of the total bonds issued (see tables in Studenski and Krooss, *Financial History,* pp. 174, 177). My own suspicion is that the refunding of the debt into lower interest, long-term securities in 1870–1879, which coincided with recessions in agricultural areas, along with the retirement of much of the debt in the twenty years after the war, resulted in the concentration of bonds in the hands of the wealthy, but if this is the case, the immediate postwar agitation against bondholders would bear reexamination.

3. Monetary Legislation

The epigraph is taken from the *Congressional Globe,* 37th Cong., 3rd sess., p. 1117.

1. This is, of course, a greatly simplified version of American banking. A. Barton Hepburn, *History of Coinage and Currency in the United States* (New York: Macmillan, 1903), p. 177. William B. Weeden, *War Government, Federal and State* (Boston: Houghton, Mifflin and Co., 1906), p. 355.
2. Fritz Redlich, *The Molding of American Banking* (New York: Johnson Reprint Corp., 1968), 1: 202–204. Roy P. Basler, ed., *The Collected Works*

of Abraham Lincoln (New Brunswick, N.J.: Rutgers University Press, 1953), 1: 159–179, 189, 307, 312, 317.

3. On business stagnation, see, for example, Lorenzo D. Myers to John Sherman, July 8, 1861, John Sherman MSS., LC.

4. Philadelphia *Inquirer,* April 30, 1861, p. 2. On Milwaukee riots see, for example, Boston *Daily Evening Transcript,* June 25, 1861, p. 4. James R. Doolittle to Salmon P. Chase, September 13, 1861, Chase MSS. Indianapolis *Daily Journal,* January 21, 1862, p. 3.

5. Chase's first proposal came from a plan by New York banker and theorist George Opdyke, who advocated a currency backed by government credit rather than state bank capital. After taking office, the Secretary at first worked more closely with Opdyke and his partners (one of whom had preceeded Chase in the Treasury) than with almost any other bankers. In a letter to John A. Dix, R. M. Blatchford, and George Opdyke, April 23, 1861 (in John Niven, ed., *The Salmon P. Chase Papers* [Frederick, Md.: University Publications of America, 1987], on microfilm), the Secretary gave the three men extraordinary authority to act for the Treasury Department in the event communications between Washington and New York were cut. George Opdyke, *A Treatise on Political Economy* (New York: G. P. Putnam, 1851), pp. 284–296.

6. Salmon P. Chase, Report of the Secretary of the Treasury, December 9, 1861, *Congressional Globe,* 37th Cong., 2nd sess., Appendix, pp. 25–26.

7. New York's 1838 Free Banking Act secured currency with property by requiring state banks to deposit with state bank commissioners state or government bonds in amounts equal to their proposed circulation before receiving uniform bank notes, signed by a state official, which they could circulate. In the decades before the war, monetary theorists had called for the government to develop a similar national currency scheme. Redlich, *American Banking,* 1: 191–204; 2: 100–101.

8. On the plan's unpopularity, see, for example, R. H. King to Samuel B. Ruggles, Albany, New York, December 15, 1861, Samuel B. Ruggles MSS., NYPL. On the plan's popularity, see, for example, A. A. Guthrie to J. Sherman, February 11, 1862; and J. Cooper to J. Sherman, February 24, 1862, both in John Sherman MSS., LC. Chicago *Tribune,* December 30, 1861, p. 2. Cincinnati *Daily Commercial,* December 24, 1861, p. 2.

9. Wesley Clair Mitchell, *A History of the Greenbacks* (Chicago: University of Chicago Press, 1903), pp. 37–38. On rumors of paper currency issue, see article from the St. Louis *Republican,* republished in the *Daily Illinois State Register,* December 12, 1861, p. 2; and Jay Cooke & Co. to Jay Cooke & Co., January 7, 1862, Jay Cooke MSS., HSP.

10. On Chase's trip to New York, see the Cincinnati *Daily Commercial,* December 23, 1861, p. 3, from the New York *World.* New York banks suspended on December 31, 1861; most other Eastern banks followed suit. Ohio banks suspended two weeks later; the State Bank of Indiana held out

until March 1862 (Cincinnati *Daily Enquirer,* January 11, 1862, p. 2, and January 17, 1862; Indianapolis *Daily Journal,* January 1, 1862, p. 3, and March 10, 1862, p. 2). Raymond in the New York Assembly, January 28, 1862, in the New York *Times,* February 1, 1862, p. 3.

11. New York *Daily Tribune,* December 31, 1861.

12. Elbridge G. Spaulding, *History of the Legal Tender Paper Money Issued During the Great Rebellion* (Buffalo: Express Printing Co., 1869), pp. 8–14. Mitchell, *Greenbacks,* p. 45. New York *Daily Tribune,* December 31, 1861, p. 5.

13. Some economists and legislators had ineffectively battled the "popular error that the value of money depends on the material of which it is made." On paper money as replacement for specie, rather than a debt, see Kellogg, *Labor and Other Capital,* pp. 47–48; and Opdyke, *Treatise,* pp. 52–53. On paper money as a debt, see, for example, the Chicago *Tribune,* January 8, 1862.

14. New York *Daily Tribune,* January 13, 1862, p. 4. See also the Chicago *Tribune,* January 8, 1862. Republicans also feared that the depreciation of paper currency would slow the nation's growth by encouraging the export of capital. As paper money depreciates, the price of imports rises and the price of exports falls. A nation using a paper currency, Republicans felt, would buy high and sell low, making capital flow out of the country. Chicago *Tribune,* January 8, 1862; see also Sheffield, *Congressional Globe,* 37th Cong., 2nd sess., pp. 640–642.

15. Henry Charles Carey, *Essay on the Rate of Wages* (Philadelphia: Carey, Lea & Blanchard, 1835), p. 11. Francis Wayland, *The Elements of Political Economy* (New York: Leavitt, Lord & Co., 1837), pp. 341–342. "Common Sense" editorial in the Boston *Post,* January 3, 1862, pp. 1–2.

16. Opdyke, *Treatise,* p. 303. Cincinnati *Daily Commercial,* December 9, 1861, p. 4.

17. Philadelphia *Inquirer,* June 27, 1861, p. 4. New York *Daily Tribune,* May 17, 1862, p. 4. On Confederate currency and its overissue, see Douglas B. Ball, *Financial Failure and Confederate Defeat* (Urbana: University of Illinois Press, 1991), pp. 164–176.

18. There is a difference between "currency"—a common medium of exchange determined by custom or by some other means—and "legal tender"—a special form of currency established by law that must be accepted in payment for any financial obligations.

19. Philadelphia *Daily Evening Bulletin,* January 7, 1862, p. 4. New York *Daily Tribune,* January 13, 1862, p. 4. On bank deposits, see David M. Gische, "The New York City Banks and the Development of the National Banking System, 1860–1870," *American Journal of Legal History,* 23 (January 1979): 25–27, 36. "Common Sense" in the Boston *Post,* January 3, 1862, pp. 1–2. Philadelphia *Inquirer,* January 1, 1862, p. 4; January 14, 1862,

p. 4. Compare Bray Hammond, "The North's Empty Purse, 1861–1862," *American Historical Review,* 67 (October 1961): 1–18, which argued that bankers advocated the greenbacks.

20. Chicago *Tribune,* January 17, 1862, p. 4, and February 4, 1862. See also ibid., January 3, 1862; January 13, 1862, p. 1; and January 15, 1862, p. 2, for advocacy of government notes. Similar articles appear in the New York *Daily Tribune,* December 31, 1861, p. 4; and the New York *Times,* January 6, 1862, p. 2; January 13, 1862, p. 4; and January 18, 1862. Timothy C. Day to J. Sherman, February 11, 1862, John Sherman MSS., LC. Quotation is from Cincinnati *Daily Enquirer,* January 10, 1862, reprinted from the New York *Herald.* See also Bray Hammond, *Sovereignty and an Empty Purse: Banks and Politics in the Civil War* (Princeton, N.J.: Princeton University Press, 1970) for an examination the the strengthening of the national government through wartime financial policy.

21. For the text of the bill, see the New York *Times,* January 9, 1862, p. 2.

22. Chase privately let it be known he would resign if Congress adopted the subcommittee's legal tender plan (H. D. Cooke to Jay Cooke, January 7, 1862, Jay Cooke MSS., HSP). Chase to Kate Chase [Sprague], January 14, 1862; Chase to John A. Stevens, January 17, 1862, Chase MSS. New York *Times,* January 16, 1862, p. 1.

23. Bankers worried that such a plan would depreciate the seven-thirty bonds they held. Government creditors realized that the plan meant that they, not the government, would be the ones selling bonds at a loss on a soft market. Boston banks refused to accept the plan. Bankers in New York disliked the plan for they worried that Congress would quash it (John E. Williams to Chase, January 21, 1862, New York City; Spaulding, Vail, Hunt & Co. to Chase, January 25, 1862; and Chase to John A. Stevens, January 17, 1862; Chase MSS.) New York *Daily Tribune,* January 15, 1862; Boston *Post,* January 16, 1862, p. 2; New York *Times,* January 18, 1862, p. 4. Philadelphia *Daily Evening Bulletin,* January 20, 1862, p. 4.

24. For passage of H.R. 240 through the House, see the *Congressional Globe,* 37th Cong., 2nd sess., pp. 435, 522–527, 549–552, 593–594, 614–618, 629–642, 655–665, 679–695, 707, 827–828, 874, 881–891, 899–902, 909, 938–939, 948, 953, 954. For easy access to the greenback laws, see *Laws of the United States Relating to Loans and the Currency* (Washington: Government Printing Office, 1878), pp. 44–48, 50–53, 53–54.

25. New York *Times,* January 23, 1862. New York *Daily Tribune,* January 25, 1862, p. 4. Greeley hedged his opposition in later issues (New York *Daily Tribune,* February 7, 1862, p. 4). On the Democratic dislike of the bill and its defense of banks, see Cincinnati *Daily Enquirer,* January 4, 1862, p. 2; January 8, 1862, p. 2; January 15, 1862, p. 2.

26. William Belmont Parker, *The Life and Public Services of Justin Smith Morrill* (Boston: Houghton Mifflin Co., 1924), pp. 39, 47.

27. Stevens ridiculed the substitute's creation of an interest-bearing currency, the value of which would change constantly.

28. Only 6 Democrats and 1 Old-Line Whig voted aye. The nay votes included 29 Democrats, 22 Republicans, and 8 Old-Line Whigs. The Republican nay votes broke down as follows: Vermont, 3; Rhode Island, 2; New York, 5; New Jersey, 2; Massachusetts, 3; Maine, 1; New Hampshire, 1; Indiana, Kansas, Ohio, Pennsylvania, and Illinois, 1 each.

29. See John Sherman MSS., LC., including letters there to W. P. Fessenden, forwarded to Sherman. Chase to John Sherman, October 15, 1855; H. D. Cooke to John Sherman, March 25, 1856, October 8, 1856, and January 13, 1856; John Sherman MSS., LC. H. D. Cooke to Jay Cooke, March 8, 1861, and March 24, 1861; Eleutheros Cooke to Jay Cooke, March 25, 1861, Jay Cooke MSS., HSP. Ellis Paxson Oberholtzer, *Jay Cooke: Financier of the Civil War* (Philadelphia: George W. Jacobs & Co., 1907), 1: 131.

30. The financial situation was so bad that Chase was forced to request an emergency issue of $10 million in demand notes, to which Congress agreed promptly (*Congressional Globe*, 37th Cong., 2nd sess., pp. 705, 726). Thaddeus Stevens to Dear Sir, November 17, 1862, Thaddeus Stevens MSS., LC. On deposit provision, see U. L. Schaffer to Chase, January 23, 1862, Chase MSS. For passage of H.R. 240 through the Senate, see the *Congressional Globe*, 37th Cong., 2nd sess., pp. 696, 719, 762–775, 787–804, 898–899, 911, 929, 940, 946–947.

31. Chase's discussion of the legal tender clause is in Chase to John A. Bingham, February 6, 1862, and Chase to W. P. Fessenden, February 8, 1862; Chase MSS.

32. John Young to Chase, February 11, 1862, Chase MSS.

33. The nay votes came from Collamer, Cowan (Pennsylvania), and King (New York). William Pitt Fessenden, in Francis Fessenden, *Life and Public Services of William Pitt Fessenden* (Boston: Houghton, Mifflin and Co., 1907) 1: 194. New York *Times,* February 13, 1862, pp. 3–4; February 14, p. 4; and February 19, 1862, p. 4.

34. Chase to Thaddeus Stevens, Chairman of the Committee on Ways and Means, June 7, 1862, 37th Cong., 2nd sess., Misc. H. Doc. 81. For passage of H.R. 187 through the House, see *Congressional Globe*, 37th Cong., 2nd sess.,pp. 2665, 2766–2769, 2794–2798, 2880–2889, 2903–2904, 3109, 3128, 3154, 3158, 3182.

35. Greeley, too, approved of this issue because the public liked the greenbacks (New York *Daily Tribune,* June 14, 1862, p. 4, and June 16, 1862, p. 4).

36. For bankers' reactions to this second issue, see the Philadelphia *Inquirer,* June 14, 1862.

37. For passage of H.R. 187 through the Senate, see the *Congressional Globe,* 37th Cong., 2nd sess., pp. 2916, 2917, 2987, 3071–3079, 3135, 3138, 3177.

38. For the disappearance of greenbacks after the war, see Sherman, *Congressional Globe,* 37th Cong., 3rd sess., pp. 847–849, 878; and McCulloch, Report of the Secretary of the Treasury, December 4, 1865, *Congressional Globe,* 39th Cong., 1st sess., Appendix, pp. 34–35. For insistence on repayment of greenbacks in specie, see, for instance, the New York *Times,* February 7, 1862, p. 4. Abraham Lincoln, Message to Congress, December 1, 1862, *Congressional Globe,* 37th Cong., 3rd sess., Appendix, p. 2.

39. Chase, December 4, 1862, Report of the Secretary of the Treasury, *Congressional Globe,* 37th Cong., 3rd sess., Appendix, pp. 22, 25–26.

40. Philadelphia *Inquirer,* January 12, 1863, p. 6. Chase to W. P. Fessenden, January 11, 1863, Chase MSS. New York *Daily Tribune,* December 8, 1862, p. 4. Jonathan Sturgess to John Sherman, January 24, 1863, John Sherman MSS., LC. *Harper's Weekly,* 6 (December 20, 1862): 802.

41. *Congressional Globe,* 37th Cong., 3rd sess., pp. 23, 145–146.

42. Hooper's proposal of the bill is in *Congressional Globe,* 37th Cong., 3rd sess., p. 226. The proposal was probably a modification of Spaulding's original bill by Hooper and Chase. On the bill's authorship, see Redlich, *American Banking,* 2: 104–105. For the committee's revenue bill, see *Congressional Globe,* 37th Cong., 3rd sess., pp. 235–236, 283–284. For financiers' reactions to the House's plans, see the Philadelphia *Inquirer,* January 16, 17, 22, 24, and February 16, 21, 26, 27, 1863.

43. On matters relating to the new greenback bill see the *Congressional Globe,* 37th Cong., 3rd sess., pp. 167, 245, 269–270, 314, 323, 381.

44. Jay Cooke to Chase, January 18, 1862; and Chase to Jay Cooke, December 16, 1861; Jay Cooke MSS., HSP. The paper that reflected Cooke's views, the Philadelphia *Inquirer* (see, for example, January 2, 1862, p. 6), also supported Chase's plan. Oberholtzer, *Cooke,* 1: 331–332. H. D. Cooke to Chase, December 6, 1862, Chase MSS.

45. H. D. Cooke to Jay Cooke, January 23, 1863, in Oberholtzer, *Cooke,* 1: 332–333. Sherman's bill is in U.S. Congress, *Bills and Resolutions of the House of Representatives and the Senate,* 1st–55th Cong. (1789/91–1897/90). More accessible for a review of the final form of the bill is its summary in Samuel S. Cox, *Union—Disunion—Reunion: Three Decades of Federal Legislation, 1855–1885* (Providence, R.I.: J. A. & R. A. Reid, 1888), pp. 141–142. For passage of S. 486 through the Senate, see *Congressional Globe,* 37th Cong., 3rd sess., pp. 505, 666, 703, 820–826, 840–852, 869–882, 896–897.

46. New York *Times,* January 28, 1863, p. 5; and February 2, 1863, p. 4. New York *Daily Tribune,* February 3, 1863, p. 4. See also letter from Hugh McCulloch to Morris Ketchum, Esq., May 11, 1863, in the Indianapolis *Daily Journal,* May 23, 1863, p. 1.

47. On the separation of the bank note tax, see Chase to J. Sherman, January 30, 1863, Chase MSS.

48. For mention of Oregon's bank law, see New York *Times*, January 9, 1862, p. 1.
49. For passage of S. 486 through the House, see the *Congressional Globe*, 37th Cong., 3rd sess., pp. 914, 916, 947, 1113–1119, 1141–1149.
50. On fears of Republican despotism see, for example, the Cincinnati *Daily Enquirer*, May 18, 1862, p. 2; April 9, 1862, p. 2; June 19, 1862, p. 2; and article reprinted from the Albany (N.Y.) *Argus* on March 28, 1862. See also the *Daily Illinois State Register*, March 8, 1861. A Missouri Democrat introduced a four-point amendment asking the Committee on the Judiciary to see not if, but how badly, the bill violated states' rights. He also requested the committee to determine if the bill was unconstitutional.
51. On the argument between Chase and Congress over finances, see Philadelphia *Inquirer*, January 19, 1863, p. 1. On Chase's presence during the debate, see the Cincinnati *Daily Commercial*, February 21, 1863, p. 3; and the Philadelphia *Inquirer*, February 21, 1863, p. 1, which reported that "a change came over" the representatives after personal interviews with Chase in Speaker Grow's room. On prediction of opposition, see the Philadelphia *Inquirer*, February 6, 1863, p. 1. Negative Republican votes came from the following states: New York, 5; New Jersey, 2; Massachusetts, 3; Vermont, 2; Ohio, 3; New Hampshire, Connecticut, Maine, Rhode Island, Pennsylvania, Indiana, Virginia, and Iowa, 1 each.
52. *Harper's Weekly*, 7 (March 14, 1863): 162. New York *Daily Tribune*, September 23, 1863, p. 4.
53. On the establishment of early national banks, see Redlich, *American Banking*, 2: 108–109. By the end of 1863, New York had 16 national banks, Pennsylvania 20, Ohio 38, Indiana 20, Illinois 7, Iowa 6.
54. The problems in the 1863 law became clear in the debates over H.R. 333 and H.R. 395, but were most concisely revealed by Sherman, *Congressional Globe*, 38th Cong., 1st sess., p. 1865.
55. Redlich, *American Banking*, 2: 107, 140–146.
56. It also removed the double liability of national bank stockholders for debts. For passage of H.R. 333 through the House, see *Congressional Globe*, 38th Cong., 1st sess., pp. 1099, 1254–1257, 1266–1273, 1287–1292, 1338–1344, 1350–1354, 1373–1381, 1389–1394, 1396–1402, 1409–1416, 1429–1433, 1448–1453.
57. Republicans from Maine, where the interest rate was 6 percent, also opposed the 7 percent amendment because they disliked increasing the state's interest rate.
58. Chase to Horace Greeley, April 6, 1864, Chase MSS. For passage of H.R. 395 through the House, see *Congressional Globe*, 38th Cong., 1st sess., pp. 1531, 1680–1682, 1694, 1696–1697, 2428, 2435, 2447–2452, 2476, 2639. The House amendment of the bill was deceptive, for it called for the removal of the national tax on circulation, ostensibly to promote the new

banks. In reality, this provision left the way clear for inevitable state taxation.

59. For passage of H.R. 395 through the Senate, see *Congressional Globe*, 38th Cong., 1st sess., pp. 1694, 1771, 1865–1875, 1889–1900, 1952–1959, 1989–1990, 2019–2022, 2121–2132, 2142–2155, 2174–2185, 2199–2207, 2458, 2621–2622. The vote on the tax was reported as 61 yeas, 66 nays, although the amendment passed. From the curious voting pattern listed, it seems likely that this vote was in fact on a different issue and was misplaced in the text of the *Congressional Globe*.

60. In the House, the Westerners were Iowa's James F. Wilson and Hiram Price and Michigan's Francis W. Kellogg. The four Western senators were Chandler (Michigan), Pomeroy (Kansas), Henderson (Missouri), and Grimes (Iowa). On Western preference for central redemption in New York, see the Chicago *Tribune*, March 3, 1864, p. 2.

61. New York *Times*, March 9, 1863, p. 8.

62. Chase, Report of the Secretary of the Treasury, December 4, 1862, *Congressional Globe*, 37th Cong., 2nd sess., Appendix, p. 25. For calls for note taxation, see, for example, the Chicago *Tribune*, January 1, 1862, and January 9, 1862; Charles H. Carroll to W. P. Fessenden, June 30, 1862, and G. Volney Dorsey to J. Sherman, January 9, 1863, John Sherman MSS., LC.

63. Arnold, *Congressional Globe*, 37th Cong., 2nd sess., p. 1326. Sherman, *Recollections*, 1: 286–287. John Sherman to William Tecumseh Sherman, November 16, 1862, in Rachel Sherman Thorndike, ed., *The Sherman Letters* (New York: Charles Scribner's Sons, 1894), pp. 167–168. *Congressional Globe*, 37th Cong., 3rd sess., p. 185. Sherman, ibid., Appendix, pp. 47–52. New York *Daily Tribune*, March 2, 1863, p. 4.

64. On banking and Copperheads, see the New York *Daily Tribune*, April 21, 1864, quoted in the Chicago *Tribune*, April 26, 1864. *Daily Illinois State Register*, June 6, 1862, p. 2, quotation from the Chicago *Times* and the St. Louis *Republican*. Chicago *Tribune*, April 5, 1864, p. 4; April 9, 1864, p. 4; April 10, 1864, p. 2; April 26, 1864. On Northwestern dislike of bank notes, see the Chicago *Tribune*, April 17, 1864, p. 2; and April 26, 1864, p. 2. See also the San Francisco *Daily Alta California*, April 17, 1864, p. 2.

65. On legitimate need for gold purchases, see Kinahan Cornwallis, *The Gold Room and the New York Stock Exchange and Clearing House* (New York: A. S. Barnes, 1879), p. 174. William Worthington Fowler, *Inside Life in Wall Street* (Hartford, Conn.: Dustin, Gilman & Co., 1873), p. 185.

66. San Francisco *Daily Alta California*, April 1, 1864, p. 2. Fessenden, *Congressional Globe*, 38th Cong., 1st sess., pp. 1640–1642. Philadelphia Inquirer, March 17, 1864, p. 4; and April 14, 1864, p. 4.

67. Hugh McCulloch, Report of the First Comptroller of the Currency, November 25, 1864, House Executive Documents, 38th Cong., 2nd sess., vol. 7,

no. 3, p. 52. See also the Chicago *Tribune,* March 29, 1864, p. 2; April 2, 1864, p. 2; and March 25, 1864, p. 2.

68. The stockbrokers of New York City thought it unpatriotic to buy gold, and they refused to admit gold speculation to the Stock Exchange. Gold trading migrated into the "Gold Room," originally a dark, dirty basement room near the Stock Exchange nicknamed the "Coal Hole." Outgrowing these makeshift quarters, gold brokers moved in the summer of 1864 to larger and better rooms. One year later, they ended up next door to the Stock Exchange. Cornwallis, *Gold Room,* p. 173. William Worthington Fowler, *Ten Years on Wall Street* (Hartford, Conn.: Worthington, Dustin & Co., 1870), pp. 73–74. In July 1864, the price of gold was at least 250, which meant that $1 worth of gold cost $2.50 in greenbacks.

69. Cornwallis, *Gold Room,* p. 175. Fowler, *Inside Life,* p. 188. James K. Medbery, *Men and Mysteries of Wall Street* (Boston: Fields, Osgood, & Co., 1870), p. 241. New York *Daily Tribune,* June 15, 1864. See also New York *Times,* February 4, 1864, p. 2.

70. Simeon Nash to John Sherman, January 19, 1863, John Sherman MSS., LC.; and San Francisco *Daily Alta California,* March 13, 1864, p. 2. Medbery, *Men and Mysteries,* pp. 245–250.

71. Chase to Horace Greeley, June 10, 1864, Chase MSS. For passage of S. 106 through the Senate, see *Congressional Globe,* 38th Cong., 1st sess., pp. 1618, 1640–1651, 1666–1673, 2926, 2930.

72. For newspaper support for Fessenden's position, see the Philadelphia *Inquirer,* April 20, 1864, p. 4.

73. For passage of S. 106 through the House, see *Congressional Globe,* 38th Cong., 1st sess., pp. 1635, 1658, 1695, 1814, 2690, 2694, 2726, 2743, 2788–2789, 2793–2794, 2936–2937, 2995.

74. Horace White, *Money and Banking* (Boston: Ginn & Co., 1902), pp. 143–144. Cornwallis, *Gold Room,* p. 181.

75. *Congressional Globe,* 38th Cong., 1st sess., pp. 3160, 3446, 3461, 3464, 3468.

76. For future attempts to control the gold market, see J. A. Stewart to W. P. Fessenden, October 14, 19, 28, 31, and November 7, 1864; William Pitt Fessenden MSS., Bowdoin College.

77. Howard K. Beale, ed., *Diary of Gideon Welles* (New York: W. W. Norton & Co., 1960), 2: 62. Tyler Dennett, ed., *Lincoln and the Civil War in the Diaries and Letters of John Hay* (New York: Dodd, Mead & Co., 1939), pp. 199–201.

78. On Fessenden's calming influence, see, for example, E. W[aite] to Oliver Otis Howard, July 30, 1864, Howard Family MSS., Bowdoin College. Chicago *Tribune,* April 2, 1864, p. 2.

79. Abraham Lincoln, Message to Congress, December 6, 1864, *Congressional Globe,* 38th Cong., 2nd sess., Appendix, p. 2. W. P. Fessenden, December 6, 1864, Report of the Secretary of the Treasury, ibid., Appendix, p. 29.

Hugh McCulloch, Report of the First Comptroller of the Currency, November 25, 1864, House Executive Documents, 38th Cong., 2nd sess., vol. 7, no. 3, p. 54. 38th Cong., 2nd sess., S. Misc. Doc. 21.

80. For House debate over currency portions of H.R. 744, see *Congressional Globe,* 38th Cong., 2nd sess., pp. 803–804, 832–837, 879–881.

81. For Senate debate over the currency portions of H.R. 744, see ibid., pp. 1139, 1194–1198, 1238–1244, 1286–1288.

82. Godlove S. Orth at Layfayette, Indiana, on September 8, 1864, in the Indianapolis *Daily Journal,* September 10, 1864, pp. 1–2. For two discussions of postwar financial issues, see Robert P. Sharkey, *Money, Class, and Party: An Economic Study of Civil War and Reconstruction* (Baltimore: Johns Hopkins Press, 1959); and Irwin Unger, *The Greenback Era* (Princeton, N.J.: Princeton University Press, 1964).

83. For the mechanics of the mismanagement of bank conversions, see Redlich, *American Banking,* 2: 118–119. On the results of the pyramid system of redemption, see Gische, "New York City Banks," pp. 54–65.

4. Tariff and Tax Legislation

The quotation in the chapter title is from James H. Campbell, *Congressional Globe,* 36th Cong., 1st sess., p. 1848. The epigraph is found in *Congressional Globe,* 38th Cong., 1st sess., p. 1925.

1. On the effects of the panic of 1857 on Republican policy, see James L. Huston, *The Panic of 1857 and the Coming of the Civil War* (Baton Rouge: Louisiana State University Press, 1987). Reinhard H. Luthin, "Abraham Lincoln and the Tariff," *American Historical Review,* 49 (July 1944): 612.

2. James Buchanan, December 19, 1859, Message of the President, *Congressional Globe,* 36th Cong., 1st sess., Appendix, p. 6.

3. For passage of H.R. 338 through the House, see *Congressional Globe,* 36th Cong., 1st sess., pp. 1116, 1135–1136, 1231, 1415, 1563–1564, 1826–1860, 1928–1931, 1945–1958, 1972–1987, 2012–2029, 2049–2056. For a synopsis of debates, see William Belmont Parker, *The Life and Public Services of Justin Smith Morrill* (Boston: Houghton Mifflin Co., 1924), pp. 105–109.

4. John Sherman, *Recollections of Forty Years in the House, Senate, and Cabinet* (London: Samson Low, Marston & Co., 1895), 1: 183.

5. Parker, *Morrill,* pp. 103–106. Boston *Daily Evening Transcript,* December 13, 1861, p. 1. Justin Smith Morrill to Henry Charles Carey, February 6, 1861, Edward Carey Gardiner MSS., HSP.

6. Free traders argued that traditional protectionism meant that foreign competition kept the prices of agricultural products and other raw materials low, while domestic manufacturing had a monopoly on domestic trade and could charge whatever it wished.

7. George Benjamin Mangold, *The Labor Argument in the American Protec-*

290 · Notes to Pages 107–111

tive Tariff Discussion (Madison, Wisc.: University of Wisconsin, 1908) examines the labor argument up to the Whig platform of 1844. Pennsylvania governor Curtin picked up this theme in his 1861 inaugural address (Philadelphia *Inquirer,* January 16, 1861, p. 2).

8. Henry Carey Baird, *Protection of Home Labor and Home Productions Necessary to the Prosperity of the American Farmer,* (n.p., n.d.), pp. 1, 8, 9, 13, 16.

9. John Sherman, "On the Morrill Tariff Bill," in John Sherman, *Selected Speeches and Reports on Finance and Taxation, from 1859 to 1878* (New York: D. Appleton and Co., 1879), pp. 9–12.

10. On the need for a "judicious tariff" candidate for president, see James S. Pike to William Pitt Fessenden, September 6, 1859, James S. Pike MSS., LC. For a description of how the plank was inserted and then received, see H. C. Carey to Robert McCalment, June 2, 1860, and H. C. Carey to E. B. Ward, May 21, 1865, both in E. C. Gardiner MSS., HSP. John Tweedy, *A History of the Republican National Conventions from 1856 to 1908* (Danbury, Conn.: John Tweedy, 1910), p. 47. On the benefit of Southern senators leaving, see H. C. Carey to J. S. Morrill, January 18, 1861, E. C. Gardiner MSS., HSP.

11. James G. Blaine, *Twenty Years of Congress: From Lincoln to Garfield* (Norwich, Conn.: Henry Bill Publishing Co., 1886), 1: 339. John Sherman, *Recollections of Forty Years in the House, Senate, and Cabinet* (Chicago: Werner Co., 1895), 1: 188.

12. For Republican attacks on foreign trade, see, for example, Morris, *Congressional Globe,* 36th Cong., 1st sess., Appendix, p. 252. Chicago *Tribune,* January 8, 1862. Philadelphia *Inquirer,* May 16, 1861, p. 2; April 3, 1861, p. 4; May 24, 1861, p. 4. Indianapolis *Daily Journal,* January 1, 1862, p. 1.

13. See Morrill, *Congressional Globe,* 37th Cong., 1st sess., p. 175; and Roscoe Conkling, ibid., 37th Cong., 2nd sess., p. 633. *First Report on the Public Credit,* January 14, 1790, *Second Report on the Public Credit,* January 16 and 21, 1795, in Samuel McKee, Jr., ed., *Alexander Hamilton's Papers on Public Credit Commerce and Finance* (New York: Liberal Arts Press, 1957), pp. 153, 46 (emphasis deleted).

14. Salmon P. Chase, Report of the Secretary of the Treasury, July 4, 1861, *Congressional Globe,* 37th Cong., 1st sess., Appendix, pp. 4–5.

15. For Chase's tenacious grip on his free-trade ideas, see the Philadelphia *Inquirer,* July 12, 1861, p. 4, and J. S. Morrill to H. C. Carey, July 6, 1861, E. C. Gardiner MSS., HSP. Salmon P. Chase, Report of the Secretary of the Treasury, July 4, 1861, *Congressional Globe,* 37th Cong., 1st sess., Appendix, pp. 4–5. On composition of Committee on Ways and Means, see the Chicago *Tribune,* January 22, 1862, p. 2.

16. For passage of H.R. 54 through the House, see *Congressional Globe,* 37th Cong., 1st sess., pp. 152, 171–177, 202–205, 354, 365, 415–416, 428.

17. J. Cable to John Sherman, Ohio, July 20, 1861, John Sherman MSS., LC. Philadelphia *Inquirer,* July 25, 1861, p. 4.

18. Henry Charles Carey, *Essay on the Rate of Wages* (Philadelphia: Carey, Lea & Blanchard, 1835), p. 45; and Francis Wayland, *The Elements of Political Economy* (New York: Leavitt, Lord & Co., 1837), pp. 111–116. Boston *Daily Evening Transcript,* January 15, 1864, p. 2. For passage of H.R. 71 through the House, see *Congressional Globe,* 37th Cong., 1st sess., pp. 229, 246–252, 268–274, 280–287, 299–308, 323–331.

19. Charles F. Dunbar, "The Direct Tax of 1861," *The Quarterly Journal of Economics,* 3 (July 1889): 443–445. See also Sherman, *Recollections,* 1: 303.

20. H. C. Carey to J. S. Morrill, July 28, 1861, E. C. Gardiner MSS., HSP. H. C. Carey to S. P. Chase, August 26, 1861, E. C. Gardiner MSS., HSP. *Congressional Globe,* 37th Cong., 1st sess., pp. 248–249. H. B. Hurlbut to J. Sherman, July 27, 1861, J. Sherman MSS., LC.

21. E. Peshine Smith to H. C. Carey, March 6, 1862, E. C. Gardiner MSS., HSP. Significantly, Roscoe Conkling of New York, head of a strong patronage system, led the fight against national collection of the tax.

22. For passage of H.R. 54 through the Senate, see *Congressional Globe,* 37th Cong., 1st sess., pp. 208, 253–255, 278–279, 297, 313–323, 335–336, 344, 395–400.

23. E. Peshine Smith to H. C. Carey, August 17, 1861; W. D. Lewis to H. C. Carey, August 7, 1861, E. C. Gardiner MSS., HSP. New York *Times,* in Philadelphia *Inquirer,* April 24, 1861, p. 2.

24. David Donald, *Charles Sumner and the Coming of the Civil War* (New York: Alfred A. Knopf, 1960), pp. 45–69, 78–81. See, for example, the Philadelphia *Inquirer,* August 26, 1861, p. 4; and August 31, 1861, p. 4.

25. Edwin R. A. Seligman, *The Income Tax: A Study of the History, Theory, and Practice of Income Taxation at Home and Abroad* (New York: Macmillan, 1911), pp. 399–406. Joseph A. Hill, "The Civil War Income Tax," *Quarterly Journal of Economics,* 8 (July 1894): 416.

26. For the direct tax, valuations were to be made on April 1, 1862, then a complicated series of notices were required and challenges to the valuations permitted before actual collection. *Congressional Globe,* 37th Cong., 1st sess., Appendix, pp. 34–40.

27. Albert S. White, letter to constituents, in Indianapolis *Daily Journal,* August 3, 1861, p. 2. J. S. Morrill to H. C. Carey, July 31, 1861, E. C. Gardiner MSS., HSP.

28. Salmon P. Chase, Report of the Secretary of the Treasury, December 9, 1861, *Congressional Globe,* 37th Cong., 2nd sess., Appendix, pp. 24–25.

29. *Congressional Globe,* 37th Cong., 2nd sess., pp. 169–170. On popularity of taxation, see, for example, J. R. Butler to J. Sherman, January 10, 1862, J. Sherman MSS., LC; San Francisco *Daily Alta California,* April 15, 1862;

Conkling, *Congressional Globe,* 37th Cong., 2nd sess., p. 633; and Chicago *Tribune,* January 6, 1862, and May 3, 1862. Philadelphia *Daily Evening Bulletin,* March 14, 1862. *Congressional Globe,* 37th Cong., 2nd sess., Appendix, p. 419. Morrill, ibid., p. 169.

30. Timothy C. Day to J. Sherman, January 18, 1862, J. Sherman MSS., LC. Philadelphia *Inquirer,* November 30, 1861, p. 4, and January 10, 1862, p. 4. Philadelphia *Inquirer,* January 24, 1862, p. 1, reported, "The city is crowded with merchants and manufacturers from all sections . . . eager to represent . . . their views on the question." Philadelphia *Inquirer,* March 4, 1862, p. 4, and March 10, 1862, p. 4. Morrill, *Congressional Globe,* 37th Cong., 2nd sess., p. 384.

31. For passage of H.R. 312 through the House, see *Congressional Globe,* 37th Cong., 2nd sess., pp. 1040–1041, 1194–1205, 1217–1228, 1236–1245, 1252–1259, 1273–1279, 1286–1296, 1303–1314, 1322–1330, 1342–1347, 1360–1369, 1383–1390, 1403–1415, 1432–1443, 1452–1464, 1480–1489, 1508–1514, 1527–1536, 1544–1551, 1564–1566, 1576–1577, 1614, 2620, 2680–2682, 2708, 2890–2891. See George S. Boutwell, *Reminiscences of Sixty Years in Public Affairs* (New York: McClure, Phillip & Co., 1902), 1: 303, 313. Ohio Democrat S. S. Cox complained that "the Committee of Ways and Means must have forgotten all their days of sunny childhood. A man must be lost to all sensibility who will tax a circus" (*Congressional Globe,* 37th Cong., 2nd sess., p. 1361).

32. For a discussion of the difference between direct and indirect taxes, see Seligman, *Income Tax,* p. 435.

33. Manufacturers' petition against the tax is reported in *Congressional Globe,* 37th Cong., 2nd sess., p. 1331. New York *Times,* March 17, 1862, p. 1. Indianapolis *Daily Journal,* May 3, 1862, p. 2. New York *Daily Tribune,* April 9, 1862, p. 4. See also positive use of taxation advocated in John Barr to J. Sherman, December 11, 1861, J. Sherman MSS., LC.

34. Philadelphia *Inquirer,* January 10, 1862, p. 4. *Congressional Globe,* 37th Cong., 2nd sess., p. 1194.

35. J. J. Cisco to W. P. Fessenden, April 18, 1862, J. Sherman MSS., LC. See also the Cincinnati *Daily Commercial,* December 14, 1861, p. 2. Cincinnati *Daily Enquirer,* March 11, 1862, p. 2, and April 2, 1862, p. 2, with reference to the Boston *Post.* Philadelphia *Daily Evening Bulletin,* May 7, 1862. See also the San Francisco *Daily Alta California,* April 7, 1862. Chicago *Tribune,* March 25, 1862.

36. The House later placed low taxes on coal and cotton.

37. See Democratic complaints that New England was becoming rich while the West was "being crushed into poverty" in the Cincinnati *Daily Enquirer,* January 4, 1862, p. 2; the Cincinnati *Daily Enquirer,* January 18, 1862, p. 2, and January 22, 1862, p. 2, and article reprinted from the Chicago *Post,* January 22, 1862, p. 1. For responses to these charges, see the Chicago *Tribune,* July 3, 1862. See also the Chicago *Tribune,* January 6, 1862.

38. Philadelphia *Inquirer,* November 30, 1861, p. 4; December 7, 1861, p. 4. J. Medill to J. Sherman, January 29, 1862, J. Sherman MSS., LC. Philadelphia *Daily Evening Bulletin,* March 14, 1862. *Harper's Weekly,* 6 (July 26, 1862): 466. Chicago *Tribune,* January 7, 1862, p. 2, February 14, 1862, March 18, 1862. Compare Robert Stanley, *Dimensions of Law in the Service of Order: Origins of the Federal Income Tax, 1861–1913* (New York: Oxford University Press, 1993).

39. The eleven were: Allen, from Marion, Illinois, forty miles from the Ohio River; Knapp, from Jerseyville, Illinois, near the Missouri River; Richardson, from Quincy, Illinois, on the Mississippi River; Cox, from Columbus, Ohio; Pendleton, from Cincinnati, Ohio, on the Ohio River; Vallandigham, from Dayton, Ohio, forty-five miles from Cincinnati; White, from Georgetown, Ohio, on the Ohio River; Law, from Evansville, Indiana, on the Ohio River; Voorhees, from Terre Haute, Indiana, southwest of Indianapolis, on the Wabash river; Wickliffe, from Bardstown, Kentucky, on the Ohio River; and Norton, of Platte City, Missouri, on the Missouri River. The other two Demorats who voted nay were Shiel, from Oregon, an Irish immigrant who had lived in Louisiana and studied law in Ohio, where he entered the bar; and Kerrigan, from New York.

40. Francis Fessenden, *Life and Public Services of William Pitt Fessenden* (Boston: Houghton, Mifflin and Co., 1907), 1: 190–191. James W. Grimes, May 20, 1862, quoted in William Salter, *The Life of James W. Grimes* (New York: D. Appleton and Co., 1876), p. 194. For passage of H.R. 312 through the Senate, see *Congressional Globe,* 37th Cong., 2nd sess., pp. 1603, 1966, 2254–2262, 2278–2288, 2308–2321, 2329–2341, 2344–2356, 2367–2379, 2396–2408, 2419–2430, 2443–2451, 2454–2477, 2479–2494, 2508–2526, 2540–2560, 2572–2587, 2598–2611, 2671, 2675, 2873–2877.

41. D. C. Halsted to J. Sherman, January 30, 1862, J. Sherman MSS., LC. Hill, "Civil War Income Tax," pp. 422–423.

42. Frederick A. Pike to Gov. Israel Washburn, Jr., April 10, 1862, Frederick A. Pike MSS., Maine State Archives.

43. For passage of H.R. 531 through the House, see *Congressional Globe,* 37th Cong., 2nd sess., pp. 2845, 2936–2940, 2978–2986, 3050–3055, 3208, 3213, 3216, 3267, 3268–3269. Sidney Ratner, *American Taxation: Its History as a Social Force in Democracy* (New York: W. W. Norton & Co., 1942), p. 88.

44. J. S. Morrill to H. C. Carey, July 12, 1862, E. C. Gardiner MSS., HSP. Philadelphia *Daily Evening Bulletin,* June 24, 1862. Horace Greeley to J. S. Morrill, March 18, 1862, J. S. Morrill MSS., LC.

45. San Francisco *Daily Alta California,* April 29, 1862. Cincinnati *Daily Commercial,* December 4, 1861, p. 2. Chicago *Tribune,* March 19, 1862.

46. See, among others, *Harper's Weekly,* 6 (September 27, 1862): 611; and 6 (December 6, 1862): 770; the Chicago *Tribune,* January 21, 1864; and

the Philadelphia *Inquirer,* October 10, 1861, p. 4. Philadelphia *Daily Evening Bulletin,* May 14, 1862. See also *Harper's Weekly,* 6 (March 15, 1862): 162.

47. New York *Daily Tribune,* October 11, 1861, p. 4. Philadelphia *Inquirer,* October 21, 1861, p. 4. San Francisco *Daily Alta California,* May 31, 1862.

48. New York *Times,* April 1, 1862. See also the Chicago *Tribune,* March 11 and 17, 1862.

49. Chase, Report, December 9, 1861, *Congressional Globe,* 37th Cong., 2nd sess., Appendix, p. 24. New York *Times,* April 1, 1862.

50. For passage of H.R. 531 through the Senate, see *Congressional Globe,* 37th Cong., 2nd sess., pp. 3062, 3134, 3167–3177, 3197, 3254–3255. *Harper's Weekly,* 6 (July 26, 1862): 466.

51. Salmon P. Chase, Report of the Secretary of the Treasury, December 10, 1863, *Congressional Globe* 38th Cong., 1st sess., Appendix, pp. 5–6. Chicago *Tribune,* January 13, 1864. Cincinnati *Daily Gazette,* January 25, 1864, p. 2. New York *Times,* April 8, 13, 15, 19, and 23, 1864.

52. For passage of H.R. 122 through the House, see *Congressional Globe,* 38th Cong., 1st sess., pp. 168, 215–218, 234, 268–273, 282–288, 303–313, 508, 536, 573–574, 595, 660–668, 687–693, 707–708, 738, 772, 776–779, 827, 892–893, 920, 933–935, 939, 941. Hannibal Hamlin to Ellie Hamlin, January 29, 1863, and February 2, 1863, Hannibal Hamlin MSS., University of Maine at Orono.

53. The officer in question was General William H. French. Meade blamed his failure to attack Lee on French's inability to follow orders; see Richard Meade Bache, *Life of General George Gordon Meade* (Philadelphia: Henry T. Coates & Co., 1897), pp. 387–391. J. Medill to J. Sherman, January 29, 1862, J. Sherman MSS., LC. S. S. Cox, "Puritanism in Politics: A Speech before the Democratic Union Association in January 1863 in New York City" (New York, 1863), in Joel H. Silbey, *A Respectable Minority: The Democratic Party in the Civil War Era, 1860–1868* (New York: W. W. Norton & Co., 1977), p. 76.

54. Chicago *Tribune,* January 15, 1864.

55. Since the bill had been loaded with controversial amendments, most notably a provision to tax retrospectively all liquor on hand and another exacting different taxes for domestic and foreign liquor, the nineteen Republican crossover votes had no clear explanation. For passage of H.R. 122 through the Senate, see *Congressional Globe,* 38th Cong., 1st sess., pp. 319, 331, 435, 460–462, 489–494, 699, 719, 769, 786, 814, 874, 886, 900–908, 921, 937–938.

56. For passage of H.R. 405 through the House, see *Congressional Globe,* 38th Cong., 1st sess., pp. 1532, 1697, 1715–1733, 1755–1761, 1784–1791, 1814–1827, 1832–1840, 1848–1854, 1875–1884, 1901–1918, 1934–1939, 1940–1943, 2810, 2995, 2996–3001, 3018–3021, 3024–3028,

3055, 3056–3057, 3078, 3267, 3275–3278. San Francisco *Daily Alta California,* April 18, 1864. Sherman, *Recollections,* 1: 331.

57. On Democratic election rhetoric about taxes, see, for example, the Indianapolis *Daily Journal,* October 11, 1862; and John C. Ropes to John C. Gray, Jr., November 9, 1862, in John Chipman Gray, ed., *War Letters 1862–1865 of John Chipman Gray and John Codman Ropes* (Cambridge, Mass.: Riverside Press, 1927), p. 19.

58. *Harper's Weekly,* 6 (September 27, 1862): 610.

59. Ratner, *Taxation,* p. 83.

60. New York *Daily Tribune,* May 31, 1864, p. 4. Boston *Daily Evening Transcript,* January 15, 1864, p. 2. See also D. C. Halsted to J. Sherman, January 30, 1862, J. Sherman MSS., LC.; and Geo. [?] Edmundson to J. S. Morrill, May 21, 1864, J. S. Morrill MSS., LC.

61. New York *Times,* July 1 and 4, 1864.

62. For passage of H.R. 405 through the Senate, see *Congressional Globe,* 38th Cong., 1st sess., pp. 2015, 2344, 2437–2447, 2459–2470, 2486–2501, 2512–2521, 2522–2526, 2545–2551, 2554–2575, 2589–2599, 2601–2606, 2625–2636, 2654–2663, 2665–2671, 2698–2715, 2730–2741, 2754–2770, 3039, 3254–3256, 3266, 3378.

63. For the effect of the direct tax on Vermont, see J. S. Morrill to H. C. Carey, July 31, 1861, E. C. Gardiner MSS., HSP.

64. Hill, "Civil War Income Tax," pp. 424–425.

65. For passage of H.R. 67 through the House, see *Congressional Globe,* 38th Cong., 1st sess., pp. 1695, 1697, 1702–1703, 1847–1848, 1855–1859.

66. For passage of H.R. 67 through the Senate, see ibid., pp. 1864, 1865, 1919–1933.

67. For passage of H.R. 494 through the House, see ibid., pp. 2526, 2672–2693, 2717–2722, 2743–2751, 3079, 3311–3314, 3351, 3395, 3402–3404. Ratner, *Taxation,* p. 88.

68. Chicago *Tribune,* May 5, 1864. San Francisco *Daily Alta California,* May 4, 1864.

69. For passage of H.R. 494 through the Senate, see *Congressional Globe,* 38th Cong., 1st sess., pp. 2751, 2921, 3004–3014, 3030–3039, 3040–3053, 3303, 3323, 3368, 3420. New York *Times,* April 5, 1864. See, for instance, the Chicago *Tribune,* January 21, 1864, and February 1, 1864; the San Francisco *Daily Alta California,* April 6, 1864; the New York *Times,* April 4, April 19, and May 17, 1864; the Chicago *Tribune,* January 15 and 20, 1864. Cincinnati *Daily Gazette,* July 25, 1862, p. 2, July 29, 1862, p. 2, and August 2, 1862, p. 1.

70. There was limited support for the treaty. A February 1862 report from the House Committee on Commerce, chaired by a Democrat, recommended negotiations to perfect and enlarge the treaty, warning of "enormous evils" if the United States isolated itself from Canada. (Report from the Commit-

tee on Commerce, February 5, 1862, 37th Cong., 2nd sess., H. Rept. 22.) The editor of the Chicago *Tribune* said he would support the treaty if its abrogation would endanger free navigation of the St. Lawrence for the West (April 9, 1862). Donald C. Masters, *The Reciprocity Treaty of 1854* (London: Longman's, Green and Co., 1937; rpt. Toronto: McClelland and Stewart, 1963), pp. 75–87. Chicago *Tribune*, January 14, 1864. Report of the Committee on Commerce, April 1, 1864, 38th Cong., 1st sess., Rept. 39. On Canadian Confederate sympathy, see Dennis K. Wilson, *Justice under Pressure: The Saint Alban's Raid and Its Aftermath* (Lanham, Md.: University Press of America, 1992), pp. 133–135, 139–140.

71. Howard K. Beale, ed., *Diary of Gideon Welles* (New York: W. W. Norton & Co., 1960) 2: 151–153. On the St. Albans raid, see Wilson, *Justice under Pressure*. Masters, *Reciprocity Treaty*, pp. 75–87.

72. *Harper's Weekly*, 6 (July 26, 1862): 466. Spaulding, *Congressional Globe*, 37th Cong., 3rd sess., p. 288.

73. On the postwar income tax, see Seligman, *Income Tax;* and Harold Q. Langenderfer, *The Federal Income Tax, 1861–1872* (New York: Arno Press, 1980), vol. 2. My account of postwar tariffs draws on Edward Stanwood, *American Tariff Controversies in the Nineteenth Century* (Boston: Houghton Mifflin Co., 1903; rpt. New York: Garland Publishing, 1974), 2: 145–151, which, although biased, makes some good points about postwar tariffs. On the Northwest's conversion to protectionism, see Clarence Lee Miller, *The States of the Old Northwest and the Tariff, 1865–1888* (Emporia, Kans.: Emporia Gazette Press, 1929).

74. Henry C. Carey, Letter Fourth, Philadelphia, February 17, 1865, *The Currency Question: Letters to the Hon. Schuyler Colfax, Speaker of the House of Representatives* (Chicago: John A. Norton, 1865), pp. 26–28.

75. Davis, *Congressional Globe,* 38th Cong., 1st sess., p. 1927.

76. Carey, Letter Fifth, Philadelphia, February 18, 1865, *Currency Question,* p. 40.

5. Agricultural Legislation

The quotation in the chapter title is from the Chicago *Tribune*, February 20, 1862, p. 2. The epigraph is from Richard Owen, "Late State Geologist," quoting Daniel Webster in a letter to the editor, Indianapolis *Daily Journal*, August 9, 1864, p. 2.

1. John A. Foy to the *Boston Cultivator*, January 25, 1862, p. 2.

2. William Henry Venable, *A Buckeye Boyhood* (Cincinnati: Robert Clarks Co., 1911), p. 89. *Congressional Globe*, 37th Cong., 2nd sess., Appendix, pp. 259.

3. *An Agricultural Poem, by Owen Lovejoy, M.C., delivered before the Bureau County Agricultural Society, October 1859* (Princeton, Ill.: "Bureau County Republican" Book and Job Print, 1862), p. 6.

4. *Congressional Globe,* 37th Cong., 2nd sess., Appendix, pp. 256–259, 1939.

5. Wayne E. Rasmussen, ed., *Agriculture in the United States: A Documentary History* (New York: Random House, 1975), 1: 521. John B. Sanborn, "Some Political Aspects of Homestead Legislation," *American Historical Review,* 6 (October 1900): 19–22, 27–28. Fred A. Shannon, "The Homestead Act and the Labor Surplus," *American Historical Review,* 41 (July 1936): 640–642. William R. Smith of Alabama, *Congressional Globe,* 32nd Cong., 1st sess. (1852), Appendix, p. 514.

6. Harry N. Scheiber, "Economic Change in the Civil War Era: An Analysis of Recent Studies," *Civil War History,* 11 (December 1965): 407. Democrats were initially the primary supporters of homestead legislation; Whigs opposed it. The realignment took place in the 1850s. For reasons for this change, see James W. Oberly, *Sixty Million Acres: American Veterans and the Public Lands before the Civil War* (Kent, Ohio: Kent State University Press, 1990), pp. 1–3, 45–53.

7. Grow, *Congressional Globe,* 33rd Cong., 1st sess. (1854), Appendix, pp. 240–244; Grow, *Congressional Globe,* 32nd Cong., 1st sess. (1852), Appendix, pp. 424–428. James T. DuBois and Gertrude S. Mathews, *Galusha A. Grow, Father of the Homestead Law* (Boston: Houghton Mifflin Co., 1917), pp. 62–63, 8–12. John Tweedy, *A History of the Republican National Conventions from 1856 to 1908* (Danbury, Conn.: John Tweedy, 1910), p. 48.

8. Paul W. Gates, *Agriculture and the Civil War* (New York: Alfred A. Knopf, 1965), p. 276. I. W. [Israel Washburn, Jr.], "Modern Civilization," *Universalist Quarterly,* 15 (January 1858): 24. For discussion of the reality of land monopoly, see Oberly, *Sixty Million Acres,* pp. 130–133. For closer examination of land speculation in the old Northwest, see Allan G. Bogue and Margaret Beattie Bogue, "'Profits' and the Frontier Land Speculator," *Journal of Economic History,* 17 (1957): 1–24; and Robert P. Swierenga, *Pioneers and Profits: Land Speculation on the Iowa Frontier* (Ames: Iowa State University Press, 1968).

9. Pomeroy, *Congressional Globe,* 37th Cong., 2nd sess., pp. 1937–1940. See also Grow, *Congressional Globe,* 36th Cong., 1st sess., Appendix, p. 127. Henry Clyde Hubbart, *The Older Middle West, 1840–1880* (New York: D. Appleton-Century Co., 1936), pp. 133–134. Tweedy, *Republican National Conventions,* p. 48.

10. Henry Charles Carey, *Principles of Political Economy* (Philadelphia: Carey, Lea & Blanchard, 1837), pp. 142–143. Henry Charles Carey, *Principles of Social Science* (Philadelphia: J. B. Lippincott & Co., 1858), 1: xiv, 79–80.

11. Philadelphia *Inquirer,* March 22, 1862, p. 1. F. M. F. to the editor, Indianapolis *Daily Journal,* January 24, 1865, p. 2. See also ibid., March 4, 1862, p. 2. Morrill, *Congressional Globe,* 37th Cong., 2nd sess., Appendix, p. 259. Report of the House Committee on Agriculture, ibid., p. 856. See also *American Railroad Journal,* 35 (December 20, 1862): 1005.

12. *Congressional Globe,* 36th Cong., 1st sess., Appendix, p. 174.

13. Philadelphia *Inquirer,* April 23, 1861, p. 4; and August 8, 1862, p. 7. Samuel James Reader to Martha Reader, October 21, 1861, Soldier Township, Kansas, in "The Letters of Samuel James Reader, 1861–1863: A Pioneer of Soldier Township, Shawnee Country," *Kansas Historical Quarterly,* 9 (February 1940): 47.

14. Lovejoy, *Poem,* preface, p. iv. Edward Magdol, *Owen Lovejoy: Abolitionist in Congress* (New Brunswick, N. J.: Rutgers University Press, 1967), pp. 38, 227, 184.

15. *Congressional Globe,* 37th Cong., 2nd sess., p. 14. DuBois and Mathews, *Grow,* pp. 256–257.

16. For passage of H.R. 125 through the House, see *Congressional Globe,* 37th Cong., 2nd sess., pp. 39–40, 132–140, 909–910, 1030–1035, 1972, 2069, 2081, 2158.

17. Providence [R.I.] *Journal,* July 19, 1862, p. 2.

18. The Indianapolis *Daily Journal,* April 11, 1861, p. 2, lists the number of agricultural societies registered on the mailing book of the agricultural division of the Patent Office on March 29, 1861. Chicago *Tribune,* December 27, 1861, p. 2.

19. Henry Luther Stoddard, *Horace Greeley, Printer, Editor, Crusader* (New York: G. P. Putnam's Sons, 1946), pp. 290–291. Josiah B. Grinnell, *Men and Events of Forty Years* (Boston: D. Lothrop Co., 1891), pp. 86–87. Greeley apparently did not actually give this advice; it came from John B. Soule, writing in the Terre Haute, Indiana, *Express* in 1851: see Peter Temin, "Free Land and Federalism: A Synoptic View of American Economic History," *Journal of Interdisciplinary History,* 21 (Winter 1991), footnote, p. 378.

20. New York *Daily Tribune,* February 1, 1862, p. 4.

21. *Congressional Globe,* 37th Cong., 2nd sess., pp. 889–891.

22. Charles Wickliffe explained his opposition to the bill during debates over the Legal Tender Act (ibid., pp. 889–891). Erastus Corning and Chauncey Vibbard were the President and Superintendent, respectively, of the New York Central Railroad. New York *Daily Tribune,* March 21, 1862, p. 4.

23. For passage of H.R. 125 through the Senate, see *Congressional Globe,* 37th Cong., 2nd sess., pp. 1036–1037, 1347, 1871, 1915–1916, 1937–1940, 1951, 2061, 2147–2148. William Rowe, Acting Secretary of the National Land Reform Association, to John Sherman, May 5, 1862, in John Sherman MSS., LC.

24. New York *Daily Tribune,* May 7, 1862, p. 4. The report basically paraphrased the Senate version of the bill. New York *Daily Tribune,* June 6, 1862, p. 4.

25. Compare Paul W. Gates, *History of Public Land Law Development* (Washington, D.C.: Government Printing Office, 1968), p. 435. Morrill, *Congres-*

sional Globe, 37th Cong., 2nd sess., Appendix, p. 257. William Pitt Fessenden to James S. Pike, April 5, 1863, James S. Pike MSS., LC.

26. For a brief discussion of growing American interest in a Department of Agriculture from the time of President Washington, see Wayne D. Rasmussen and Gladys L. Baker, *The Department of Agriculture* (New York: Praeger Publishers, 1972). Albert H. Leake, *The Means and Methods of Agricultural Education* (Boston: Houghton Mifflin Co., 1915), p. 13. A. G. Riddle, *The Life of Benjamin Franklin Wade* (Cleveland, Ohio: Williams Publishing Co., 1888), p. 304. For Western advocacy of an agricultural department, see articles from *Prairie Farmer* and *American Agriculturist* in Rasmussen, *Agriculture,* 1:571–572 and 594–597.

27. Caleb Blood Smith, November 30, 1861, Report of the Secretary of the Interior, *Congressional Globe,* 37th Cong., 2nd sess., Appendix, p. 13. Abraham Lincoln, Message to Congress, December 3, 1861, ibid., p. 3.

28. Indianapolis *Daily Journal,* January 10, 1862, p. 1. *Boston Cultivator,* December 14, 1861, p. 2. Thomas Brown to J. Sherman, December 15, 1861, J. Sherman MSS., LC.

29. Philadelphia *Inquirer,* December 14, 1861, p. 4.

30. New York *Daily Tribune,* September 14, 1861, pp. 6–7. *Boston Cultivator,* January 4, 1862, p. 1, and April 26, 1862, p. 2. *Boston Cultivator,* January 1, 1862, p. 2. San Francisco *Daily Alta California,* January 30, 1862, p. 2. Henry Charles Carey to [probably James Moore Swank], November [?] 3, 1871, James Moore Swank MSS., HSP.

31. Lovejoy's *Poem* concentrated entirely on better techniques and good seeds. For requests for the agricultural report, see, for example, letters of late January and early February in Benjamin F. Wade MSS., LC., J. Sherman MSS., LC., and other collections. For passage of H.R. 269 though the House, see *Congressional Globe,* 37th Cong., 2nd sess., pp. 218, 751, 855–857, 2030, 2098.

32. In the negative were four Democrats, one Old-Line Whig, and two Republicans: William G. Brown of Virginia and F. A. Conkling of New York.

33. San Francisco *Daily Alta California,* March 19, 1862, p. 2. Indianapolis *Daily Journal,* March 4, 1862, p. 2. Philadelphia *Inquirer,* March 22, 1862, p. 1.

34. For passage of H.R. 269 through the Senate, see *Congressional Globe,* 37th Cong., 2nd sess., pp. 859, 861, 1296, 1331, 1598, 1690–1692, 1755–1757, 1916, 2013–2017, 2083.

35. For passage of S. 249 through the Senate, see ibid., pp. 1370, 1690–1692, 1755.

36. In Magdol, *Lovejoy,* p. 354. See also the New York *Daily Tribune,* May 30, 1862, p. 4.

37. *Congressional Globe,* 37th Cong., 2nd sess., p. 33. Whitney H. Shepardson, *Agricultural Education in the United States* (New York: Macmillan, 1929),

pp. 16–25. *Boston Cultivator,* December 28, 1861, p. 11. Gates, *Agriculture,* pp. 251–260.

38. William Belmont Parker, *The Life and Public Services of Justin Smith Morrill* (Boston: Houghton Mifflin Co., 1924), pp. 6, 10, 23–24, 262–271. Morrill, *Congressional Globe,* 37th Cong., 2nd sess., Appendix, pp. 256–259. On Morrill's role in promoting the Land Grant College Act, compare Wayne D. Rasmussen, *Taking the University to the People: Seventy-five Years of Cooperative Extension* (Ames: Iowa State University Press, 1989), pp. 22–23, and Earle D. Ross, "The 'Father' of the Land-Grant College," *Agricultural History,* 12 (April 1938): 151–186.

39. I. L. Kandel, *Federal Aid For Vocational Education: A Report to the Carnegie Foundation for the Advancement of Teaching,* Bulletin 10 (Boston: D. B. Updike, n.d.), pp. 3–16. Alfred Charles True, *A History of Agricultural Education in the United States, 1785–1925* (Washington, D.C.: U.S. Government Printing Office, 1929), pp. 97–104. *Congressional Globe,* 35th Cong., 1st sess. (1858), pp. 1692–1697. See Buchanan's veto message in Rasmussen, *Agriculture,* 1: 587–593.

40. *Congressional Globe,* 37th Cong., 2nd sess., pp. 99, 2432. For the mechanics of choosing and selling the land grants, see Richard D. Brown, "Agricultural College Land Grant in Kansas—Selection and Disposal," *Agricultural History,* 37 (April 1963): 94–102; and Thomas LeDuc, "State Disposal of the Agricultural College Land Scrip," *Agricultural History,* 28 (July 1954): 99–107.

41. Morrill's speech is in *Congressional Globe,* 37th Cong., 2nd sess., Appendix, pp. 256–259. In the period 1850–1860 Vermont's population increased by fewer than 1,000 people. New Hampshire's population grew only 2 percent and, despite its unsettled upper frontier, Maine's grew only 8 percent. Massachusetts, Rhode Island, and Connecticut maintained their population growth overall because the industrial centers of these states were drawing newcomers. With the stunning growth of Providence, Rhode Island suffered least of all. Within the states, however, rural counties grew much more slowly than urban ones, and some rural counties actually lost population (U.S. Census records).

42. Howard K. Beale, ed., *Diary of Gideon Welles* (New York: W. W. Norton & Co., 1960), 1: 523–524. New York *Times,* May 29, 1864, p. 4. On the growing unpopularity of manual labor, see also the Chicago *Tribune,* January 14, 1864, p. 4.

43. Indianapolis *Daily Journal,* November 18, 1863, p. 1. Cincinnati *Daily Gazette,* March 17, 1864, p. 2; March 18, 1864, p. 2; and March 21, 1864, p. 1.

44. Amos Brown to Benjamin Franklin Wade, February 6, 1862, B. F. Wade MSS., LC. Parker, *Morrill,* p. 269. *Congressional Globe,* 35th Cong., 2nd sess., p. 712. For passage of S. 298 through the Senate, see *Congressional*

Globe, 37th Cong., 2nd sess., pp. 1935, 2160, 2187, 2248–2250, 2275–2277, 2328–2329, 2366, 2394–2396, 2440–2443, 2625–2634.

45. New York *Daily Tribune,* May 27, 1862, p. 4. Chicago *Tribune,* May 30, 1862, p. 2.

46. Indianapolis *Daily Journal,* April 5, 1861, p. 2. James G. Blaine, *Twenty Years of Congress: From Lincoln to Garfield* (Norwich, Conn.: Henry Bill Publishing Co., 1886), 1: 323–324. New York *Daily Tribune,* June 21, 1862, p. 4.

47. Cincinnati *Enquirer,* June 7, 1862, p. 2.

48. In the negative were Republicans Doolittle, Howe, Lane of Kansas, Wright, Wilkinson, and Grimes; and Democrat Saulsbury.

49. For passage of S. 298 through the House, see *Congressional Globe,* 37th Cong., 2nd sess., pp. 2663, 2769–2770. Compare John Y. Simon, "The Politics of the Morrill Act," *Agricultural History,* 37 (April 1963): 103–111.

50. Greeley had previously applauded the measure, but made suggestions for its improvement (New York *Daily Tribune,* May 27, 1862, p. 4). New York *Daily Tribune,* June 21, 1862, p. 4.

51. Salmon P. Chase to Charles P. McIlvaine, November 7, 1861; Chase to Enoch T. Carson, December 6, 1861; in John Niven, ed., *The Salmon P. Chase Papers* (Frederick, Md.: University Publications of America, 1987), on microfilm. New York *Daily Tribune,* September 5, 1861, pp. 4, 6; October 12, 1861, pp. 4–5.

52. Chicago *Tribune,* December 30, 1861. New York *Daily Tribune,* December 28, 1861, p. 4. Indianapolis *Daily Journal,* October 27, 1863, p. 1, from *The United Irishman,* August 29, 1863. Boston *Daily Evening Traveller,* January 4, 1862, p. 1. New York *Daily Tribune,* July 20, 1863, p. 4. On the New York City draft riots, see Iver Bernstein, *The New York City Draft Riots* (New York: Oxford University Press, 1990).

53. On the Civil War as "the last battle ground between the cohorts of freedom and the emissaries of despotism," see, for example, letter to the editor, Indianapolis *Daily Journal,* August 29, 1861, p. 2.

54. Henry Charles Carey to Chase, July 9, 1862, Edward Carey Gardiner MSS., HSP. On wartime immigration, see Ella Lonn, *Foreigners in the Union Army and Navy* (New York: Greenwood Press, 1951). She gives the numbers of immigrants arriving in the North during the war as follows: 112,705 in 1861; 114,475 in 1862; 199,811 in 1863; 221,525 in 1864.

55. New York *Daily Tribune,* February 1, 1862, p. 4; and October 15, 1861, p. 4. Henry Charles Carey to Chase, July 9, 1862, E. C. Gardiner MSS., HSP.

56. New York *Times,* January 7, 1862, p. 3.

57. Indianapolis *Daily Journal,* July 12, 1862, p. 2. Cincinnati *Enquirer,* July 29, 1862, p. 2, from Cincinnati *Daily Commercial.* The Indianapolis *Daily Journal,* September 7, 1863, p. 2, reported that crops were worse than they

had been in ten years, although the Department of Agriculture's crop reports from loyal states indicated that crops were in fact better than they had been the previous year (Indianapolis *Daily Journal,* November 2, 1863, p. 1).

58. Joseph Baldwin to J. Sherman, December 7, 1861, in J. Sherman MSS., LC. H. C. Carey to Lincoln, September 12, 1861, E. C. Gardiner MSS., HSP.

59. Philadelphia *Inquirer,* February 6, 1863, p. 4; February 7, 1863, p. 4.

60. E. Peshine Smith to H. C. Carey, September 2, 1862, E. C. Gardiner MSS., HSP. Charlotte Erickson, *American Industry and the European Immigrant* (Cambridge: Harvard University Press, 1957), pp. 7–8. William H. Seward to the Diplomatic and Consular Officers of the United States in Foreign Countries, August 8, 1862, Circular No. 19, *Foreign Relations of the United States, 1863* (Washington, D.C.: Government Printing Office, 1864), p. 1365. Cincinnati *Daily Gazette,* December 31, 1862, p. 1. See also the Chicago *Tribune,* May 8, 1862, p. 3.

61. Indianapolis *Daily Journal,* August 21, 1863, p. 1. Erickson, *European Immigrant,* p. 8.

62. Abraham Lincoln, Message of the President, December 8, 1863, *Congressional Globe,* 38th Cong., 1st sess., Appendix, pp. 1–2. New York *Daily Tribune,* December 28, 1863, p. 4.

63. Boston *Post,* January 6, 1864, p. 4. Edward Atkinson et al., Boston Board of Trade Committee on Emigration, *Foreign Emigration* (Boston, 1864). Erickson, *European Immigrant,* pp. 7, 10. John Williams, *American Emigrant Company* (New York: Office of the Iron Age, [1865]), pp. 32–33, 37.

64. New York *Times,* April 30, 1864, p. 2.

65. See the New York *Times,* April 30, 1864, p. 2, and April 18, 1864, p. 4. Cincinnati *Daily Gazette,* February 6, 1864, p. 3.

66. For passage of S. 125 through the Senate, see *Congressional Globe,* 38th Cong., 1st sess., pp. 719, 865–868, 896.

67. For passage of H.R. 411 through the House, see ibid., pp. 1673, 1764, 1793, 3316, 3388, 3530. Report of the Special Committee on Foreign Emigration, 38th Cong., 1st sess., H. Rept. 56.

68. Emerson David Fite, *Social and Industrial Conditions in the North during the Civil War* (New York: Macmillan, 1910), pp. 190–192, interpreted wartime immigration as an attempt of urban capitalists to keep wages low. Charles A. and Mary Beard more strongly charged that the Republicans intended their 1864 immigration law to benefit rapacious industrialists by guaranteeing a docile and cheap labor force: Charles A. Beard and Mary Beard, *The Rise of American Civilization* (New York: Macmillan, 1937), 2: 106, 244. Philip Foner, *History of the Labor Movement in the United States* (New York: International Publishers Co., 1947), p. 327, also endorsed the Fite view. More to the point was Louis M. Hacker's reflection that Republican encouragement of immigration kept union organization difficult: Louis M. Hacker, *The Triumph of American Capitalism* (New York: Columbia University Press, 1940), p. 372. Erickson, *European Im-*

migrant, explains industrialists' lack of interest in contract labor. H. Rept. 56. New York *Daily Tribune,* April 18, 1864, p. 4; and June 17, 1864, p. 4. See also S. Rept. 15, 38th Cong., 1st sess.

69. On the purpose of the bill, see the letter from an immigrant reprinted in the Chicago *Tribune,* May 29, 1864, p. 1. One group of striking workers who took out a front-page newspaper advertisement to explain their grievances made no mention of importation of immigrants (Chicago *Tribune,* June 7, 1864, p. 1).

70. New York *Times,* May 2, 1864, p. 4. Chicago *Tribune,* February 10, 1864, p. 2. New York *Times,* May 8, 1864, p. 5, and May 30, 1864, p. 2.

71. The Senate passed its bill as an amendment to the House bill, so it retained the House appellation. For passage of H.R. 411 through the Senate, see *Congressional Globe,* 38th Cong., 1st sess., pp. 1802, 2510, 3292, 3368, 3388, 3495. For a discussion of American citizenship, see James H. Kettner, *The Development of American Citizenship, 1608–1870* (Chapel Hill: University of North Carolina Press, 1978). For an examination of how the contract labor law worked, see Daniel Creamer, "Recruiting Contract Laborers for the Amoskeag Mills," *Journal of Economic History,* 1 (May 1941): 42–56.

72. On the revival of immigration, see Lonn, *Foreigners,* p. 574. Tweedy, *Republican National Conventions,* p. 72.

73. Gates, *Public Land Law Development,* pp. 412–413, 770. Compare Paul Wallace Gates, "The Homestead Law in an Incongruous Land System," *American Historical Review,* 41 (July 1936): 652–681; Fred Shannon, *The Farmer's Last Frontier: Agriculture, 1860–1897* (New York: Rinehart & Company, 1945), pp. 51–57; and Theodore Saloutos, "Land Policy and Its Relation to Agricultural Production and Distribution, 1862–1933," *Journal of Economic History,* 22 (December 1962): 445–460.

74. See, for example, Allan G. Bogue, *From Prairie Belt to Corn Belt: Farming on the Illinois and Iowa Prairies in the Nineteenth Century* (Chicago: University of Chicago Press, 1963); and Clarence H. Danhof, *Change in Agriculture, the Northern United States, 1820–1870* (Cambridge: Harvard University Press, 1969).

6. *The Transcontinental Railroad*

The quotation in the chapter title is from Josiah Bushnell Grinnell, *Men and Events of Forty Years* (Boston: D. Lothrop Co., 1891), pp. 297–298. The epigraph is from Campbell, *Congressional Globe,* 37th Cong., 2nd sess., p. 1578.

1. *Congressional Globe,* 37th Cong., 2nd sess., p. 1598.

2. Interest in an overland route to the Pacific dated from at least the Lewis and Clark expedition. For growth of the movement for a railroad, see Robert R. Russel, *Improvement of Communication with the Pacific Coast as an Issue in American Politics, 1783–1864* (Cedar Rapids, Iowa: Torch

Press, 1948). John D. Cruise, "Early Days on the Union Pacific," *Collections of the Kansas State Historical Society,* 11 (1909–1910): 529–532. Isaac N. Arnold, *Recollections of the Early Chicago and Illinois Bar,* speech to the Chicago Bar Association, June 10, 1880 (n.p., n.d.; probably Chicago, 1880), pp. 19–20.

3. Douglas may have produced the notorious Kansas-Nebraska bill to speed the creation of a transcontinental railroad. For popularity of the project and alternative plans, see John P. Davis, *The Union Pacific Railway: A Study in Railway Politics, History, and Economics* (Chicago: S. C. Griggs and Co., 1894; rpt. New York: Arno Press, 1973), pp. 13–96. On the history of transcontinental railroad legislation, see also Thamar Emilia Dufwa, *Transcontinental Railroad Legislation, 1835–1862* (New York: Arno Press, 1981).

4. On the relationship of government to the economy before the Civil War, see Carter Goodrich, ed., *The Government and the Economy, 1783–1861* (Indianapolis: Bobbs-Merrill Co., 1967), p. xvi. For an examination of state governments and economic development, see Oscar Handlin and Mary Flug Handlin, *Commonwealth, A Study of the Role of Government in the American Economy: Massachusetts, 1774–1861* (Cambridge: Harvard University Press, 1969); Louis Hartz, *Economic Policy and Democratic Thought: Pennsylvania, 1776–1860* (Cambridge: Harvard University Press, 1948); Milton Sydney Heath, *Constructive Liberalism: The Role of the State in Economic Development in Georgia to 1860* (Cambridge: Harvard University Press, 1954); James Neal Primm, *Economic Policy in the Development of a Western State: Missouri, 1820–1860* (Cambridge: Harvard University Press, 1954). For government promotion of railroads, see Frederick A. Cleveland and Fred Wilbur Powell, *Railroad Promotion and Capitalization in the United States* (New York: Longmans, Green, and Co., 1909), esp. pp. 240–258; Carter Goodrich, *Government Promotion of American Canals and Railroads, 1800–1890* (Westport, Conn.: Greenwood Press, 1960); and Robert William Fogel, *The Union Pacific Railroad: A Case in Premature Enterprise* (Baltimore: Johns Hopkins Press, 1960), pp. 25–50. For the mechanics of land grants to railroads, see William S. Greever, "A Comparison of Railroad Land Grant Policies," *Agricultural History,* 25 (1951): 83–90.

5. *Congressional Globe,* 36th Cong., 1st sess., pp. 2332, 2408–2409.

6. On the profitability of the project, see Fogel, *Union Pacific,* pp. 18–23. See also Goodrich, *Railroads,* p. 279.

7. On Democratic dislike of railroad projects (except in the Northwest), see Russel, *Improvement,* pp. 28–29. James Buchanan, Message to Congress, December 6, 1858, *Congressional Globe,* 35th Cong., 2nd sess., Appendix, p. 8; December 19, 1859, ibid., 36th Cong., 1st sess., Appendix, p. 6. Donald Bruce Johnson and Kirk H. Porter, compilers, *National Party Platforms, 1840–1972* (Urbana: University of Illinois Press, 1973), pp. 26, 31.

8. Davis, *Congressional Globe,* 35th Cong., 1st sess. (1858), p. 352. Johnson and Porter, *Platforms,* p. 33.

9. For passage of H.R. 646 through the House, see *Congressional Globe,* 36th Cong., 1st sess., pp. 1356, 2220, 2329–2337, 2405–2407, 2408–2419, 2439–2453.

10. On prudent proprietorship, see Goodrich, *Railroads,* pp. 171–172.

11. On the cooperation of private and public interests, see Goodrich, *Railroads,* pp. 291–294. On the history of public purpose in corporations chartered by the government and the use of corporate structure to pool capital, see Pauline Maier, "The Revolutionary Origins of the American Corporation," *William and Mary Quarterly,* 50 (January 1993): 55–58; Oscar Handlin and Mary F. Handlin, "Origins of the American Business Corporation," *Journal of Economic History,* 5 (1945): 1–23; Ronald E. Seavoy, *The Origins of the American Business Corporation, 1784–1855: Broadening the Concept of Public Service during Industrialization* (Westport, Conn.: Greenwood Press, 1982).

12. On distrust of government control of improvements, see Goodrich, *Railroads,* pp. 175–176. Buchanan, Message, December 6, 1858, p. 8; December 19, 1859, p. 6. Johnson and Porter, *Platforms,* p. 32. On government corruption before the Civil War, see Mark W. Summers, *The Plundering Generation: Corruption and the Crisis of the Union, 1848–1861* (New York: Oxford University Press, 1987). Fogel, *Union Pacific,* p. 51, suggests that acts promoting the Union Pacific Railroad were advocated "by men striving to avoid the profligacy they associated with government enterprise."

13. Philadelphia *Inquirer,* March 23, 1861, p. 1. Cruise, "Early Days," p. 532. On Confederate sympathy in the West, see Alvin M. Josephy, Jr., *The Civil War in the American West* (New York: Alfred A. Knopf, 1991), pp. 233–235, 264–268, 293–294. California newspaper editors boosted the project, while San Franciscans jammed mass meetings for the railroad (*Daily Alta California,* March 20, 1862, p. 2; March 29, 1862, p. 1, letter from "Many Citizens"; and March 30, 1862, p. 2). *Congressional Globe,* 37th Cong., 1st sess., pp. 23, 83, 91–92, 134–135.

14. Stone, Senate Executive Documents, 50th Cong., 1st sess. (1887), Doc. 51, pp. 1596–1597. One observer pinpointed seven lobbies in the city without mentioning the railroaders (Cincinnati *Daily Gazette,* December 11, 1862, p. 1). On the role of nineteenth-century lobbyists, see Margaret Susan Thompson, *The "Spider Web": Congress and Lobbying in the Age of Grant* (Ithaca, N.Y.: Cornell University Press, 1985).

15. Among those interested in the LP&W were James C. Stone, a member of the 1861 Peace Convention in Washington; Col. Andrew J. Isaacs, a recent attorney general of Kansas Territory; James H. McDowell, a member of the first Kansas state senate; and Thomas Ewing, Jr., son of a former Ohio senator and brother-in-law of William Tecumseh Sherman. Bennett had

served in Congress from 1849 to 1859 and knew many of its members. In August 1860 the Senate approved a treaty granting the LP&W the right to buy cheaply 250,000 acres of the Delaware tribe's Kansas lands; see Paul Wallace Gates, *Fifty Million Acres: Conflicts over Kansas Land Policy, 1854–1890* (Ithaca, N.Y.: Cornell University Press, 1954), pp. 106–114, and William Robinson Petrowski, *The Kansas Pacific: A Study in Railroad Promotion* (New York: Arno Press, 1981), pp. 9–19. The activities of the company became clear in 1887, and although company men apparently did not bribe congressmen directly they quietly offered large blocks of land or stock to their influential friends.

16. For passage of H.R. 364 through the House, see *Congressional Globe,* 37th Cong., 2nd sess., pp. 1577–1580, 1590–1598, 1612, 1698–1711, 1726–1728, 1846, 1888–1892, 1906–1913, 1943–1950, 1971, 2879, 2904–2906.

17. Few papers took notice that the act asserted Congress's authority to charter corporations. A striking exception was the Cincinnati *Daily Gazette,* November 6, 1862, p. 1.

18. On Confederate drives to New Mexico, see John Greiner to Salmon P. Chase, August 10, 1861, in John Niven, ed., *The Salmon P. Chase Papers* (Frederick, Md.: University Publications of America, 1987), on microfilm; and Eugene Virgil Smalley, *History of the Northern Pacific Railroad* (New York: G. P. Putnam's Sons, 1883; rpt., New York: Arno Press, 1975), pp. 106–107.

19. On secession threat, see Russel, *Improvement,* p. 294. A devastating flood in California in early 1862 received little attention in the East. The San Francisco *Daily Alta California* did not receive a true copy of the Legal Tender Act (which created a national paper currency) until March 27, 1862, although Lincoln signed the bill on February 25, 1862.

20. Jean Baptiste Say, *A Treatise on Political Economy,* 3rd ed., ed. and trans. by Clement C. Biddle (Philadelphia: John Grigg, 1827), pp. 144–146. Copy in Harvard College Library has transportation chapter marked by Charles Sumner, 1830.

21. New York *Journal of Commerce,* quoted in San Francisco *Daily Alta California,* April 16, 1861, p. 1. On trade with China, see also San Francisco *Daily Alta California,* February 7, 1862, p. 4.

22. Arthur M. Johnson and Barry E. Supple, in their *Boston Capitalists and Western Railroads: A Study in the Nineteenth-Century Railroad Investment Process* (Cambridge, Massachusetts: Harvard University Press, 1967), suggest that there were, indeed, two types of investors: those interested in short-term speculative gains, and those planning for long-term returns on a competed project.

23. Chicago *Tribune,* March 10, 1862, p. 1. In addition, the requirements of the bill were impossible for the Iowa roads to fulfill.

24. New York *Daily Tribune,* May 7, 1862, p. 4.

25. For passage of H.R. 364 through the Senate, see *Congressional Globe,* 37th Cong., 2nd sess., pp. 1983, 2055, 2081–2082, 2216–2217, 2637–2638, 2653–2656, 2659, 2675–2680, 2749–2762, 2776–2789, 2804–2818, 2832–2840.

26. Wright's speech mentioning his position on the bill is in Indianapolis *Daily Journal,* August 8, 1862, p. 2. *American Railroad Journal,* 35 (June 28, 1862): 498.

27. For reports of the meeting, see *American Railroad Journal,* 35 (September 13, 1862): 719–722; Cincinnati *Daily Gazette,* August 8, 1862, p. 4; Chicago *Tribune,* September 2, 1862, p. 4; September 3, 1862, p. 1; September 4, 1862, p. 1, 4; September 6, 1862, p. 2.

28. On the financial risks of investing in the Union Pacific, see especially Fogel, *Union Pacific,* pp. 51–60. On the New York meeting, see McDougall, *Congressional Globe,* 37th Cong., 3rd sess., pp. 1245–1246.

29. On the lack of investment, see Johnson and Supple, *Boston Capitalists,* pp. 198–199. *American Railroad Journal,* 36 (January 10, 1863): 31; 36 (February 28, 1863): 189. Philadelphia *Inquirer,* January 14, 1863, p. 1. For passage of S. 439 through the Senate, see *Congressional Globe,* 37th Cong., 3rd sess., pp. 171–172, 837, 1179.

30. Indianapolis *Daily Journal,* February 7, 1863, p. 1.

31. For Hallett's involvement with the Kansas railroad, see Alan W. Farley, "Samuel Hallett and the Union Pacific Railway Company in Kansas," *Kansas Historical Quarterly* 25 (Spring 1959): 1–16. Thomas C. Durant, "Affairs of the Union Pacific Railroad Company," H. Rept. 78, 42nd Cong., 3rd sess. (1873), pp. 514–515. On the reasoning behind this interpretation of the law, see also Waldo Crippen, *The Kansas Pacific Railroad: A Cross Section of an Age of Railroad Building* (New York: Arno Press, 1981), pp. 10–11. Philadelphia *Inquirer,* January 17, 1863, p. 6. New York *Daily Tribune,* June 4, 1863, p. 4.

32. Hallett was a bonds trader and stock market analyst who published a financial paper, *Samuel Hallett's North American Financial Circular,* for foreign investors. In 1862 he was indicted by a grand jury for illegally manipulating Indiana state bonds. Frémont had been the Republican presidential candidate in 1856 and a popular general, but he, too, had been accused of financial improprieties before being dismissed from the army. For a recent biography of Frémont, see Andrew Rolle, *John Charles Frémont: Character As Destiny* (Norman: University of Oklahoma Press, 1991).

33. Cruise, "Early Days," p. 535.

34. New York *Daily Tribune,* June 4, 1863, p. 4; June 11, 1863, p. 4; July 1, 1863, p. 4; July 3, 1863, p. 4.

35. S. Exec. Doc. 25, 38th Cong., 1st sess.

36. *American Railroad Journal,* 36 (October 3, 1863): 925. Durant, "Affairs," p. 515.

37. Durant had been a railroad promoter in Iowa for twenty years. In a letter to Lincoln, Durant offered as references John A. Dix, Thurlow Weed, and John J. Cisco (Durant to A. Lincoln, October 17, 1863, A. Lincoln MSS., LC.). Sidney Dillon, "Affairs," H. Rept. 78, 42nd Cong., 3rd sess. (1873), pp. 510–511.

38. "The Union Pacific Railway Company Official Register of Directors and Officers, 1863–1889," copy in Ames Family and Union Pacific Railroad MSS., Harvard Business School. When the war began, New York Treasury officials had been directed to follow Dix's advice when out of communication with Washington. (Chase to Hiram Barney, April 24, 1861, Chase MSS.) *American Railroad Journal,* 36 (November 7, 1863): 1047.

39. Chase to J. J. Cisco, December 9, 1863, Chase MSS.

40. John A. Dix to Durant, July 6, 1863, in Charles Edgar Ames, *Pioneering the Union Pacific: A Reappraisal of the Builders of the Railroad* (New York: Merideth Corp., 1969), p. 20. Cornelius S. Bushnell, "Affairs," H. Rept. 78, 42nd Cong., 3rd sess. (1873), p. 542.

41. J. Edgar Thompson to Thaddeus Stevens, Private, January 26, 1864, Thaddeus Stevens MSS., LC.

42. Chase to John A. Dix, November 25, 1863, Chase MSS. Bushnell, "Affairs," H. Rept. 78, 42nd Cong., 3rd sess. (1873), pp. 38–39. Lobbyists for various canal projects were much more visible than railroad lobbyists.

43. For the *Golden Gate* story, see *American Railroad Journal,* 35 (August 16, 1862): 637; and the New York *Daily Tribune,* August 8, 1862, p. 4. On the Colorado mines, see the Cincinnati *Daily Commercial,* August 25, 1862, p. 1. Reports of government surveys are in Commissioner of the Land Office, Report to the Secretary of the Interior, *American Railroad Journal,* 35 (December 20, 1862): 990–991. Cincinnati *Daily Gazette,* December 13, 1862, p. 1. San Francisco *Daily Alta California,* March 28, 1864, p. 1. *American Railroad Journal,* 36 (October 3, 1863): 925.

44. Roy P. Basler, ed., *The Collected Works of Abraham Lincoln* (New Brunswick, N.J.: Rutgers University Press, 1953–1955), 4: 205–206, 393–394. Samuel C. Wiel, *Lincoln's Crisis in the Far West* (San Francisco: privately printed, 1949). Gov. John Evans to A. Lincoln, October 26, 1863, A. Lincoln MSS., LC.

45. Cincinnati *Daily Commercial,* April 2, 1863, p. 3; April 27, 1863, p. 1; February 16, 1864, p. 3.

46. Chicago *Tribune,* January 28, 1864, p. 1 and 2; January 29, 1864, p. 2. New York *Daily Tribune,* June 20, 1864, p. 4; February 19, 1864, p. 4. Cincinnati *Daily Gazette,* April 2, 1864, p. 3.

47. The Philadelphia *Inquirer,* January 30, 1863, p. 2, carried a rumor that the Confederate ship *Alabama* was on its way to California. The Cincinnati *Daily Commercial,* April 2, 1863, p. 3, told of a secessionist conspiracy to conquer California. The New York *Daily Tribune,* May 25, 1864, p. 4,

explained the political importance of a railroad in the face of European construction efforts. For California's demands, see the Cincinnati *Daily Gazette,* January 8, 1864, p. 3.

48. On Lincoln's enthusiasm, see Grenville M. Dodge, *How We Built the Union Pacific Railway* (Council Bluffs, Iowa: 1911–1914; rpt. ed., Denver, Colorado: Sage Books, 1965), pp. 11–12. Chase rather extravagantly claimed to be one of the railroad's earliest and most earnest advocates (Chase to Kate Chase, August 18, 1863, and Chase to John A. Dix, November 25, 1863, Chase MSS.). For worries of Pacific pirates, see Chase to A. Lincoln, March 29, 1864, Chase MSS. On California's monetary measures, see Chase to Thompson Campbell, February 8, 1864; Chase to John Conness, February 8, 1864; Thomas Brown to Chase, February 12, 1864; Chase to Thomas Brown, March 8, 1864; all in Chase MSS.

49. Edwin B. Crocker to Chase, June 27, 1863; Richard C. Parsons to Chase, February 6, 1864; Thomas Brown to Chase, April 6, 1864; all in Chase MSS.

50. Durant, "Affairs," H. Rept. 78, 42nd Cong., 3rd sess. (1873), p. 515.

51. Petrowski, "Kansas Pacific," p. 91. Stewart, "Affairs," H. Rept. 78, 42nd Cong., 3rd sess. (1873), p. 179. U.S. Congress, *Bills and Resolutions of the House of Representatives and the Senate,* 1st–55th Cong. (1789/91–1897/90), on microfilm.

52. Chase to John Conness, March 22, 1864, Chase MSS.

53. John Sherman to Chase, April 6, 1864, Chase MSS. Cincinnati *Daily Gazette,* April 20, 1864, p. 3.

54. For passage of S. 132 through the Senate, see *Congressional Globe,* 38th Cong., 1st sess., pp. 786, 921, 936, 960, 1022, 1703, 1802, 1900, 2171, 2327–2332, 2351–2358, 2376–2384, 2395–2404, 2417–2424.

55. Simon Stevens to Thaddeus Stevens, February 5, 1864, Thaddeus Stevens MSS., LC.

56. For passage of H.R. 5 through the House, see *Congressional Globe,* 38th Cong., 1st sess., pp. 658, 1533, 1698–1702, 2291–2297. On March 3, 1864, the Senate committee reported back a similar bill (S. 11) adversely because "the bill . . . is based upon a State charter granted by the State of Maine. The committee think it not right to act upon a State charter in so large a concern" (ibid., p. 921).

57. On linking Canada with the Northwest, see report of a business meeting in St. Paul, from Chicago *Tribune,* in *American Railroad Journal,* 36 (October 10, 1863): 956. On Northwest disaffection and Northwest Democrats' threats of secession, see the Cincinnati *Daily Gazette,* January 14, 1863, p. 2; February 13, 1863, p. 1; and the Cincinnati *Daily Commercial,* March 12, 1863, p. 2.

58. As soon as the company sought national support (it was originally exclusively a New England concern), William B. Ogden, former president of the

Union Pacific, and J. Edgar Thompson, one of the Union Pacific's directors, became directors of the new company (Smalley, *Northern Pacific*, pp. 111–124, 141–144). Josiah Perham to Thaddeus Stevens, May 1, 1864, Thaddeus Stevens MSS., LC.

59. Congress, *Bills and Resolutions*.

60. Petrowski, *Kansas Pacific*, pp. 68–79. For the very complicated outcome of these suits, which after Hallett's murder in 1864 pitted Durant against the Kansas directors, see Petrowski, *Kansas Pacific*, pp. 102–141.

61. In February 1864, Durant agreed to provide Hallett with funds to build the Kansas railroad, using the LP&W's securities to help raise the money. In exchange, Durant would receive one-third of all profits from a rigged construction contract that Hallett promised to arrange (Petrowski, *Kansas Pacific*, pp. 68–79). Durant, "Crédit Mobilier Investigation," H. Rept. 77, 42nd Cong., 3rd sess. (1873), pp. 515–516. Stewart, "Affairs," H. Rept. 78, 42nd Cong., 3rd sess. (1873), pp. 178–179. Crippen, *Kansas Pacific*, p. 16.

62. Stewart, "Affairs," H. Rept. 78, 42nd Cong., 3rd sess. (1873), pp. 175–179, 388–393. Durant, "Credit Mobilier," H. Rept. 77, 42nd Cong., 3rd sess. (1873), pp. 386, 515–517. This was the "suspense account" (so named because the assets were suspended) that caused such a furor in 1873.

63. For passage of H.R. 483 through the House, see *Congressional Globe*, 38th Cong., 1st sess., pp. 2427, 2448, 2611–2612, 3316, 3388, 3479. For passage of H.R. 483 through the Senate, see ibid., pp. 2622, 2664, 3062, 3290–3291, 3360, 3459.

64. For passage of H.R. 438 through the House, see ibid., pp. 2671, 2842, 3021–3024, 3060, 3062, 3079–3080, 3115, 3148–3156, 3180–3186, 3244, 3266–3267, 3317, 3357, 3388, 3479, 3480–3481. Bill H.R. 438 is in House Records, National Archives. House rules meant that Stevens's introduction of this bill stifled the Senate's bill. In addition to the other reasons discussed in this chapter, Stevens introduced the bill because the House railroad committee had been at work for six months and did not want to start again and because he was furious with Chase and probably welcomed the opportunity to show once again that he despised the Secretary's financial ideas. This stifling of the Senate bill later led to accusations that Durant had bribed Stevens.

65. For Horace Greeley's dismissal of government ownership of the road, see the New York *Daily Tribune*, February 19, 1864, p. 4. Dodge, *How We Built*, p. 12.

66. Some historians have followed Washburne's biased 1868 account of this debate and have thus attributed much more coherence to his proposal than it merited, concluding that the rejection of his amendment was proof of congressional corruption (see Davis, *Union Pacific*, pp. 120–126). For an account of the 1868 attacks on the railroad by Elihu B. Washburne and his

brother C. C. Washburn, see William F. Huneke, *The Heavy Hand: The Government and the Union Pacific, 1862–1898* (New York: Garland Publishing Co., 1985), pp. 26–29.

67. For passage of H.R. 438 through the Senate, see *Congressional Globe,* 38th Cong., 1st sess., pp. 3251, 3266, 3289, 3291–3292, 3298, 3458–3459.

68. On the risk assumption in building the railroad, and on the profits to Crédit Mobilier stockholders, see Johnson and Supple, *Boston Capitalists,* pp. 195–221. Fogel, *Union Pacific,* estimated profits for Crédit Mobilier investors at between $13 and $16.5 million, which he argued was commensurate with the risk they assumed. Huneke, *Heavy Hand,* estimated profits to have been at least $30 million, a larger profit than their risk merited. On the financial necessity for Crédit Mobilier, see Huneke, *Heavy Hand,* pp. 19–23. George F. Hoar, *Autobiography of Seventy Years* (New York: Charles Scribner's Sons, 1905), 1: 320. On Lincoln's request that Ames get involved in the railroad, see "Oakes Ames, A Biographical Sketch," by H. B. Blackwell [1882], in the Ames Family and the Union Pacific Railroad MSS., Harvard Business School. Winthrop Ames, *The Ames Family of Easton, Massachusetts* (privately printed, 1938), p. 145, says that in her diary, Mrs. Oakes Ames noted the meeting on January 20, 1865. Charles Edgar Ames, *Pioneering the Union Pacific: A Reappraisal of the Builders of the Railroad* (New York: Merideth Corp., 1969), p. 89, noted that the diary has been lost. Oakes Ames himself, however, later denied categorically that he had ever become involved in the railroad for patriotic rather than economic motives (Testimony of Oakes Ames, in "Affairs," H. Rept. 78, 42nd Cong., 3rd sess. (1873), p. 29). For the uncovering of the Crédit Mobilier scandal, see Huneke, *Heavy Hand,* pp. 32–48. On the Northern Pacific's monetary problems, see Smalley, *Northern Pacific.*

69. On government supervision of the railroads, see Huneke, *Heavy Hand,* pp. 48–53.

70. Republican legislation concerning national railroads has been seen more often than not as "preferential treatment . . . [for] powerful economic interests," a time when federal "bounty" was used selectively for the benefit of a few, a situation that led to graft and corruption; see Leonard P. Curry, *Blueprint for Modern America* (Nashville, Tenn.: Vanderbilt University Press, 1968), pp. 246–247, and chapter 6: "Congress and Public Improvements: Transportation Legislation." Citing the tremendous amounts of public land given to railroads—over the years an area larger than Texas, one study suggests—historians have generally "had a negative view" of railroad land grants, as one points out: see Lloyd J. Mercer, *Railroads and Land Grant Policy: A Study in Government Intervention* (New York: Academic Press, 1982), pp. 7–8, and Mercer's historiographical essay, pp. 8–15. Wallace D. Farnham, "The Pacific Railroad Act of 1862," *Nebraska History,* 43 (September 1962): 141–167, claimed that "the overriding principle of the

first law, response to private interests, continued its reign thereafter, with ever-growing results."
71. *Congressional Globe,* 37th Cong., 2nd sess., p. 1701.

7. Republicans and Slavery

The quotation in the chapter title is from Francis Wayland to Rev. L. Peck, D.D., February 19, 1862, Francis Wayland MSS., John Hay Library, Brown University. The epigraph is from Oliver Otis Howard to [Lizzy], New Fayetteville, N.C., March 16, 1865, Howard Family MSS., Bowdoin College Library, Brunswick, Maine.

1. On Northern racism before the Civil War, see V. Jacque Voegeli, *Free but Not Equal: The Midwest and the Negro during the Civil War* (Chicago: University of Chicago Press, 1967); and Leon F. Litwack, *North of Slavery: The Negro in the Free States, 1790–1860* (Chicago: University of Chicago Press, 1961). In an 1860 speech against slavery, Charles Sumner's first four arguments against slavery were moral and religious; an economic point came fifth (Chicago *Tribune,* July 6, 1860, p. 4).

2. On slave labor, see, for example, *Congressional Globe,* 37th Cong., 2nd sess., Appendix, p. 182; and Oliver Otis Howard to [Grace], November 17, 1863, Howard Family MSS., Bowdoin College. For Republican comparison of energetic Northerners and lazy Southerners, see *Congressional Globe,* 38th Cong., 1st sess., p. 1459.

3. Jackson Grimshaw at Clinton, Illinois rally of July 27, 1860, in Chicago *Tribune,* August 1, 1860, p. 2.

4. John Tweedy, *A History of the Republican National Conventions from 1856 to 1908* (Danbury, Conn.: John Tweedy, 1910), p. 46.

5. See, for example, speech of Owen Lovejoy at Chicago on October 15, 1860, in Chicago *Tribune,* October 18, 1860, p. 2; and Chicago *Tribune,* December 4, 1860, p. 2.

6. For petitions to end slavery, see long list of such petitions in *Senate Journal,* 37th Cong., 2nd sess.—for example, pp. 146, 271, 318. For petitions that Congress concentrate on the war, see *Senate Journal,* 37th Cong., 2nd sess., p. 475. For other petitions that Congress drop the slavery question, see ibid., pp. 80, 22, 146, 309.

7. For notice of black people in the Confederate army camps, see, for example, Chicago *Tribune,* May 3, 1861, p. 1; Philadelphia *Public Ledger,* May 7, 1861, p. 1; Indianapolis *Daily Journal,* May 16, 1861, p. 2. Strikingly, the New York *Daily Tribune* made no mention of the Southern use of slaves, apparently trying to paint slaves as good Unionists who would not fight for the Confederacy and who therefore should be freed.

8. Philadelphia *Daily Evening Bulletin,* May 28, 1861, p. 4; see also the

Philadelphia *Public Ledger,* May 30, 1861, p. 2. New York *Times,* May 12, 1861, p. 4; see also the Indianapolis *Daily Journal,* May 16, 1861, p. 2. Chicago *Tribune,* May 3, 1861, p. 1. On slave labor in the Southern military, see Bell Irvin Wiley, *Southern Negroes, 1861–1865* (New Haven: Yale University Press, 1938), pp. 110–172.

9. Fred A. Shannon, "The Federal Government and the Negro Soldier," *Journal of Negro History,* 11 (October 1926): 567. See also *Private and Official Correspondence of Gen. Benjamin F. Butler during the Civil War Period* (Privately issued, 1917), 1: 112–119.

10. For approbation of Butler's action, see, for example, the Philadelphia *Daily Evening Bulletin,* May 28, 1861, p. 4. The Boston *Evening Transcript* opposed emancipation, but approvingly observed Butler's course (see, for example, Boston *Evening Transcript,* June 3, 1861, p. 4; and August 12, 1861, p. 1). On the need to confiscate property to hurt Southerners economically, see the New York *Times,* May 16, 1861, p. 4. On the weakening of the war effort, see the Chicago *Tribune,* May 28, 1861, p. 2, and June 13, 1861. See also the Philadelphia *Daily Evening Bulletin,* June 5, 1861, p. 4. Indianapolis *Daily Journal,* May 31, 1861, p. 2.

11. On desertions if the Fugitive Slave Law were superseded, see the Philadelphia *Daily Evening Bulletin,* May 28, 1861, p. 4. Chicago *Tribune,* June 1, 1861, p. 1. On use of black people in hot areas, see also the New York *Times,* May 12, 1861, p. 4. Philadelphia *Ledger and Transcript,* May 30, 1861, p. 2.

12. For passage of S. 25 through the Senate, see *Congressional Globe,* 37th Cong., 1st sess., pp. 120, 218–219, 426, 427, 434. Trumbull introduced S. 25 on July 15, 1861, and the Senate sent it to the Judiciary Committee. Trumbull had personally introduced the measure the day before Bull Run, July 20, and he reported the bill from the committee on July 22.

13. For passage of S. 25 through the House, see ibid., pp. 231, 409–415, 430–431, 447. The House Judiciary Committee, to which the Senate confiscation bill was referred, reported it back with a substitute. Probably forced through by Democrats on the committee, who hoped to kill the bill by making it appear to be an abolitionist measure, the substitute dropped the confiscation of rebel property and called only for the confiscation of slaves. The House killed the measure.

14. Republican nay votes came from the following states: Pennsylvania, 3; New York, 2; Indiana, 2; Ohio, 1; Rhode Island, 1; Kentucky, 1; New Jersey, 1.

15. For examples of newspapers embracing the proclamation when they had previously opposed emancipation, see the Boston *Evening Transcript,* against emancipation August 26, 1861, p. 2; for proclamation, September 2, 1861, p. 2. See also the Indianapolis *Daily Journal,* September 16, 1861, p. 2. New York *Times,* September 1, 1861, p. 4. Even Republicans ada-

mantly opposed to emancipation liked the idea of threatening the South with it to shorten the war (see, for example, the Philadelphia *Daily Evening Bulletin*, September 2, 1861, p. 4). New York *Times*, September 16, 1861, p. 1.

16. Sermon of Dr. Ellis of Charlestown, Massachusetts, in the Boston *Evening Transcript*, September 27, 1861, p. 2. New York *Times*, September 2, 1861, p. 4. Philadelphia *Daily Evening Bulletin*, November 27, 1861, p. 4. Philadelphia *Daily Evening Bulletin*, December 3, 1861, p. 4. Chicago *Tribune*, August 22, 1861, p. 2.

17. New York *Times*, August 13, 1861, p. 4. Philadelphia *Daily Evening Bulletin*, October 19, 1861, p. 1. Indianapolis *Daily Journal*, October, 3, 1861, p. 1. New York *Times*, October 27, 1861, p. 4.

18. New York *Times*, November 29, 1861, p. 4.

19. Boston *Evening Transcript*, December 6, 1861, p. 2. New York *Times*, December 23, 1861, p. 4.

20. Lincoln, Message of the President, December 3, 1861, *Congressional Globe*, 37th Cong., 2nd sess., Appendix, p. 3. See Indiana senator Henry S. Lane's speech in Washington in favor of the policy, reprinted in Indianapolis *Daily Journal*, December 16, 1861, p. 2. Philadelphia Daily *Evening Bulletin*, December 4, 1861, p. 4. Secretary of War Simon Cameron had to be forced to modify the sections in his report calling for the employment of black laborers, even as soldiers if necessary.

21. Philadelphia Daily *Evening Bulletin*, December 3, 1861, p. 4. On popular support for confiscation, see *Congressional Globe*, 37th Cong., 2nd sess., p. 2274, and Appendix, p. 226. See also the Indianapolis *Daily Journal*, April 8, 1862, p. 2; the Chicago *Tribune*, March 1, 1862, p. 2; and April 11, 1862, p. 2. For worries about general emancipation, see, for example, the Indianapolis *Daily Journal*, November 26, 1861, p. 2; December 7, 1861, p. 2; Washington column of December 2, in Indianapolis *Daily Journal*, December 9, 1861, p. 2; December 10, 1861, p. 2; December 12, 1861, p. 2.

22. For passage of S. 151 through the Senate, see *Congressional Globe*, 37th Cong., 2nd sess., pp. 334, 849–850, 942–946, 986, 1040, 1049–1054, 1074–1077, 1136–1142, 1157–1162, 1544, 1557–1562, 1569–1575, 1604–1607, 1626–1628, 1652–1655, 1680, 1714–1720, 1757–1763, 1776–1787, 1808–1814, 1845–1846, 1856–1861, 1873–1886, 1895–1904, 1916–1924, 1953–1966, 1991. My discussion necessarily slights the complicated constitutional issues at stake in the confiscation debates. For more on this topic, see J. G. Randall, *Constitutional Problems under Lincoln* (Urbana: University of Illinois Press, 1951), pp. 275–341; and Patricia M. L. Lucie, "Confiscation: Constitutional Crossroads," *Civil War History*, 23 (December 1977): 307–321.

23. Trumbull's mail reflected both the popularity of confiscation and the wish to keep black people from the West. See, for example, a letter from Du

Quoin, Illinois, to Lyman Trumbull, April 11, 1862; F. C. White to Trumbull, Whitesboro, New York, April 11, 1862; a letter from Canton, Illinois, to Trumbull, May 2, 1862; W. Jayne, Yankton, Dakota Territory, to Trumbull, May 2, 1862; and Daniel D. Meriam to Trumbull, Quincy, Illinois, May 14, 1862, all in Lyman Trumbull MSS., LC.

24. The committee consisted of Clark (R-New Hampshire), Collamer (R-Vermont), Cowan (R-Pennsylvania), Wilson (R-Massachusetts), Harris (R-New York), Sherman (R-Ohio), Henderson (R-Missouri), Willey (R-Virginia), Harlan (R-Iowa).

25. See, for example, the Philadelphia *Daily Evening Bulletin,* January 10, 1862, p. 4. See also the Indianapolis *Daily Journal,* December 25, 1861, p. 2; and January 11, 1862, p. 2. On Smalls's actions, see the Indianapolis *Daily Journal,* May 22, 1862, p. 2; speech of Governor Wright of Indiana on August 2, 1862, in the Indianapolis *Daily Journal,* August 7, 1862, p. 2; Chicago *Tribune,* May 21, 1862, p. 1, and May 22, 1862, p. 2.

26. Article from the New York *Commercial Advertiser,* reprinted in the Boston *Evening Transcript,* December 21, 1861, p. 2. Philadelphia *Daily Evening Bulletin,* December 20, 1861, p. 1. William F. Messner, *Freedmen and the Ideology of Free Labor: Louisiana, 1862–1865* (Lafayette: Center for Louisiana Studies, University of Southwestern Louisiana, 1978), p. 35.

27. See Washington column in the Philadelphia *Daily Evening Bulletin,* April 5, 1862, p. 5. See also news from the *Washington Republican,* May 10, 1862, in the Chicago *Tribune,* May 14, 1862, p. 2. Letter of William Still, Corresponding Secretary of S.C. and Statistical Association of the Colored People of Pennsylvania, in the Philadelphia *Daily Evening Bulletin,* April 7, 1862, p. 1.

28. On black people in Kansas during the war, see Albert Castel, "Civil War Kansas and the Negro," *Journal of Negro History,* 51 (April 1966): 125–138. Cincinnati *Daily Gazette,* April 3, 1862, p. 1; and April 5, 1862, p. 2. "Letters of Samuel James Reader, 1861–1863, Pioneer of Soldier Township, Shawnee County, Kansas," *Kansas Historical Quarterly,* 9 (May 1940): 151 (letter dated July 8, 1862). See also letter of May 4, 1862, on p. 147. Chicago *Tribune,* December 18, 1861, p. 2. Philadelphia *Daily Evening Bulletin,* January 10, 1862, p. 4, including quotation from the New York *World.* See also the Chicago *Tribune,* January 21, 1862, p. 2; the New York *Times,* March 14, 1862, p. 3.

29. Z. B. to the New York *Times,* September 22, 1861, p. 5. See also J. B. Lyon to the New York *Times,* September 6, 1861, p. 2. Chicago *Tribune,* August 10, 1861, p. 2. New York *Daily Tribune,* March 11, 1862, p. 4.

30. Boston *Evening Traveller,* February 1, 1862, reported in the Philadelphia *Daily Evening Bulletin,* February 3, 1862, p. 8. New York *Times,* November 30, 1861, p. 4. Philadelphia *Daily Evening Bulletin,* January 2, 1862, p. 8.

31. On the caucus, see the Philadelphia *Daily Evening Bulletin,* December 10, 1861, p. 8. The committee members were Eliot (R-Massachusetts), Noell (D-Missouri), Hutchins (R-Ohio), Mallory (OW-Kentucky), Beaman (R-Michigan), Cobb (D-New Jersey), and Sedgwick (R-New York) (*Congressional Globe,* 37th Cong., 2nd sess., pp. 1846, 1861).

32. For passage of H.R. 471 and H.R. 472 through the House (they were debated together), see ibid., pp. 1886, 2128, 2232–2246, 2265–2274, 2292–2305, 2321, 2323–2327, 2341, 2356–2363, 2393, 2764–2766, 3106–3107, 3187–3188, 3266–3268, 3293.

33. Republicans spent much of their time defending the constitutionality of the proposed measures. The two arguments underlying these defenses were, first, that confiscation would weaken the Confederacy and, second, that confiscation would punish the rebels.

34. U.S. Congress, *Bills and Resolutions of the House of Representatives and the Senate,* 1st–55th Cong. (1789/91–1897/90), on microfilm.

35. Some antislavery representatives cautiously suggested that they would work to combat Northern racism, but others admitted their impotence to enlighten "unreasoning brute prejudice" (*Congressional Globe,* 37th Cong., 2nd sess., p. 2243).

36. Border state representatives argued that such broad confiscation would horrify their constituents and could well turn them against the Union. Many Republicans recognized that turning the war into an "abolition war" might divide the troops and hurt morale, as Democrats repeatedly charged. People who feared the liberty of "lawless, thieving, marauding and murderous negro savages" had called for government aid to and supervision of freedmen since 1861. The New York *Times* was an early proponent of this argument. See, for example, *Supplement to the New York Times,* December 4, 1861, p. 4. The body of Republicans in favor of the bill included both those who opposed Sedgwick's plan for arming the slaves and those who approved it. Any sort of emancipation was still unpopular in the border states; only six border-state representatives voted for the amendment.

37. New York *Times,* May 29, 1862, p. 4. Of the twenty-five Republicans who opposed the bill, four came from Virginia, five from Massachusetts, seven from the lower Midwest, two each from New York, Pennsylvania, and New Jersey, and one each from Michigan, Delaware, and Rhode Island. *Congressional Globe,* 37th Cong., 2nd sess., p. 2363. The Indianapolis *Daily Journal* approved confiscation of domestic slaves but thought that this bill went too far (R. M. H. in the Indianapolis *Daily Journal,* June 3, 1862, p. 2). On fears of foreign intervention, see the Chicago *Tribune,* May 31, 1862, p. 2, Washington letter of May 26, 1862.

38. The *Congressional Globe* lists only fifty-three names but gives the number of nay votes as fifty-four. U.S. Congress, *Bills and Resolutions.* R. M. H. in the Indianapolis *Daily Journal,* July 11, 1862, p. 2. *Congressional Globe,*

37th Cong., 2nd sess., p. 2793. Changed votes were Dawes (Massachusetts), Dunn (Indiana), Fisher (Delaware), Killinger (Pennsylvania), Mitchell (Indiana), Nixon (New Jersey), Porter (Indiana), A. H. Rice (Massachusetts), Stratton (New Jersey), Train (Massachusetts), Trimble (Ohio). The Republicans previously absent were Bingham (Ohio), Hale (Pennsylvania), Low (California), Shellabarger (Ohio), Sherman (New York). Of the Republicans opposing the measure, one each came from Virginia, New York, Michigan, Pennsylvania, Illinois, and Rhode Island, and two each from Massachusetts and Ohio.

39. For passage of S. 310 through the Senate, see ibid., pp. 2112, 2163–2173, 2188–2205, 2217–2229, 2842–2843. For passage of H.R. 471 through the Senate, see ibid., pp. 2364, 2878–2879, 2896–2903, 2916, 2917–2933, 2959–2975, 2989–3006, 3111, 3166, 3178, 3274–3276. Seventeen Republicans and two Democrats supported Clark's measure, while one Old-Line Whig and sixteen Republicans, including well-known antislavery men Grimes of Iowa, Hale of New Hampshire, Pomeroy of Kansas, Sumner of Massachusetts, and Wade of Ohio, opposed it. The vote was 28 to 13, the majority solidly Republican. The vote on the House rejection of the bill was 8 to 124. Fourteen Republican senators also tried unsuccessfully to get the Senate to recede from its version of the bill and approve the House bill. The conference committee consisted of Clark (New Hampshire), Harris (New York), and Wright (Indiana) from the Senate; and Eliot (Massachusetts), Wilson (Iowa), and Corning (New York) from the House.

40. House Republicans who voted nay were Granger (Michigan) and B. F. Thomas (Massachusetts). Senate Republican nay votes were Browning (Illinois), Carlile (Virginia), Cowan (Pennsylvania), Henderson (Missouri), and Willey (Virginia) (ibid., p. 3276). For discussion of Lincoln's request, see ibid., p. 3374. For reaction to the bill, see, for example, the New York *Times*, July 15, 1862, p. 4

41. Democrats had been charging that emancipation would lead free black people North to take jobs from white laborers since the confiscation debates of 1861 (Cincinnati *Enquirer*, July 11, 1861, p. 2). Their anger increased with the Second Confiscation Act. For tales of lost or threatened jobs, see the Cincinnati *Enquirer*, May 1, 1862, p. 2; see also April 18, 1862 p. 2; July 1, 1862, p. 2. Cincinnati *Enquirer*, March 29, 1862, p. 2. One congressional Democrat claimed that support for freed slaves in the South would cost a minimum of $90 million a year. In ten years, he said, the sum would add up to well over a billion dollars, on which interest alone would require a doubling of national taxes (Noell, "Emancipation of the Slaves of Rebels, the Views of the Minority," 37th Cong., 2nd sess., H. Rept. 120). For an argument that labor was not scarce enough to require black labor, see also item from the Quincy (Illinois) *Herald*, in the *Daily Illinois State Register*, October 29, 1862, p. 2. Cincinnati *Daily Gazette*, July 15, 1862,

p. 2. Quotation from the Cincinnati *Daily Commerical* in the Cincinnati *Enquirer,* July 18, 1862, p. 2. See also quotation from the Cincinnati *Daily Commerical* in the Cincinnati *Enquirer,* July 29, 1862, p. 2.

42. For a discussion of the situation on the Danish islands, see Leila Ames Pendleton, "Our New Possessions—The Danish West Indies," pp. 267–288, and documents on pp. 289–324, in *Journal of Negro History,* 2 (July 1917). Chicago *Tribune,* July 8, 1862, p. 2. For other discussions of the Danish offer, see the Philadelphia *Inquirer,* July 25, 1862, p. 1.

43. See letter of Massachusetts governor John A. Andrew to F. Blair, Sr., November 8, 1862, in Blair Family MSS., LC, on microfilm, for an abolitionist's reasons why black people should not move North. Governor Morton's speech in Washington, October 6, 1862, in the Indianapolis *Daily Journal,* October 10, 1862, p. 2. See also the Chicago *Tribune,* June 17, 1862, p. 2. Cincinnati Daily *Gazette,* September 25, 1862, p. 2.

44. Mario M. Cuomo and Harold Holtzer, eds., *Lincoln on Democracy* (New York: HarperCollins, 1991), pp. 257–260. For positive reaction to the emancipation of all domestic Southern slaves, see the Indianapolis *Daily Journal,* September 27, 1862, p. 2; and October 10, 1862, p. 2. Indianapolis *Daily Journal,* January 5, 1863, p. 2.

45. Cuomo and Holtzer, eds., *Lincoln on Democracy,* pp. 270–272. On freedmen and fugitive slaves in the Union service, see Dudley Taylor Cornish, *The Sable Arm: Black Troops in the Union Army, 1861–1865* (Lawrence: University Press of Kansas, 1987); James M. McPherson, *The Negro's Civil War* (New York: Pantheon Books, 1865), pp. 161–239; and Benjamin Quarles, *The Negro in the Civil War* (New York: Russell & Russell, 1968), pp. 183–232, 296–311. For a history of black soldiers by a black volunteer, see George W. Williams, *A History of the Negro Troops in the War of the Rebellion, 1861–1865* (New York, 1888; rpt. ed., Bergman Publishers, 1968).

46. Willie Lee Rose, *Rehearsal for Reconstruction: The Port Royal Experiment* (London: Oxford University Press, 1964), pp. 20–22.

47. Rose, *Rehearsal,* pp. 28–31. Chase himself encouraged private philanthropy to care for the educational and physical needs of the black population while the government organized the workers to produce cotton (see, for example, Chase to Rev. Hamilton W. Pierson, February 1, 1862, Chase MSS). See also the Indianapolis *Daily Journal,* September 4, 1863, p. 2; the Chicago *Tribune,* March 8, 1862, p. 2; the Chicago *Tribune,* April 2, 1862, p. 2; and the Philadelphia *Inquirer,* February 10, 1864, p. 4. G. K. Eggleston, "The Work of Relief Societies during the Civil War," *Journal of Negro History,* 14 (July 1929): 272–299.

48. Francis Wayland to Reverend Peck, D.D., Providence, Rhode Island, February 19, 1862, in Francis Wayland MSS., John Hay Library, Brown University.

49. New York *Daily Tribune,* December 24, 1861, p. 4. Charles M. Storey to Henry Wilson, April 26, 1862, Henry Wilson MSS., LC.

50. For a successful enterprise helping black people's transition from slavery to freedom, see Steven Joseph Ross, "Freed Soil, Freed Labor, Freed Men: John Eaton and the Davis Bend Experiment," *Journal of Southern History,* 44 (May 1978): 213–232. See also the Chicago *Tribune,* June 9, 1864, p. 3.

51. Albert Castel, "Civil War Kansas and the Negro," *Journal of Negro History,* 51 (April 1966): 129–130. Indianapolis *Daily Journal,* December 7, 1863, p. 2. New York *Times,* March 22, 1864, p. 4. Henderson, *Congressional Globe,* 38th Cong., 1st sess., p. 1463. On black employment in Ohio during the war, see David Allison Gerber, "Ohio and the Color Line: Racial Discrimination and Negro Responses in a Northern State, 1860–1915," (Ph.D. diss., Princeton University, 1971), pp. 276–285.

52. For abolitionists' efforts to win government aid for the freedmen, see James M. McPherson, *The Struggle for Equality: Abolitionists and the Negro in the Civil War and Reconstruction* (Princeton, N.J.: Princeton University Press, 1964), pp. 178–181. For similar efforts by freedmen's aid societies, see Message of the President of the United States, communicating a letter addressed to him from a committee of gentlemen . . . S. Exec. Doc. 1, 38th Cong., 1st sess. See also the Cincinnati *Daily Gazette,* December 9, 1863, p. 1. Philadelphia *Inquirer,* January 11, 1864, p. 4.

53. *Congressional Globe,* 37th Cong., 3rd sess., p. 381. S. Exec. Doc. 53, 38th Cong., 1st sess., "Preliminary Report Touching the Condition and Management of Emancipated Refugees, made to the Secretary of War by the American Freedmen's Inquiry Commission, June 30, 1863." For standard histories of the Freedmen's Bureau, see Paul S. Peirce, *The Freedmen's Bureau: A Chapter in the History of Reconstruction* (Iowa City: University of Iowa Press, 1904); and George R. Bentley, *A History of the Freedmen's Bureau* (University of Pennsylvania Press, 1954; rpt. New York: Octagon Books, 1970).

54. *Congressional Globe,* 38th Cong., 1st sess., p. 37. The members were Eliot (R-Massachusetts), Kelley (R-Pennsylvania), Knapp (D-Illinois), Orth (R-Indiana), Boyd (R-Missouri), Kalbfleisch (D-New York), Cobb (R-Wisconsin), Anderson (R-Kentucky), and Middleton (D-New Jersey). For passage of H.R. 51 through the House, see ibid., pp. 19, 21, 88, 190, 566–573, 708–713, 740–743, 760–763, 772–776, 799–805, 825, 888–892, 893–895, 909. U.S. Congress, *Bills and Resolutions.*

55. Republican nay votes were distributed as follows: Michigan, 1; Missouri, 1; West Virginia, 3; Kentucky, 4; New York, 1; Oregon, 1; Maine, 1; Maryland, 2; and Pennsylvania, 2.

56. *Congressional Globe,* 38th Cong., 1st sess., p. 197. The committee members were: Sumner (R-Massachusetts), Howard (R-Michigan), Carlile (R-Virginia), Pomeroy (R-Kansas), Buckalew (D-Pennsylvania), Brown (R-Mis-

souri), and Conness (R-California). Sumner introduced S. 227, to establish a Bureau of Freedmen, on April 12, 1864. The Senate committee reported the House bill with its own bill as an amendment in the form of a substitute. For passage of H.R. 51 through the Senate, see ibid., pp. 896, 908, 1559, 2457, 2786–2787, 2798–2804, 2931–2935, 2966–2977, 3292–3293, 3299–3309, 3327–3337, 3341–3350. U.S. Congress, *Bills and Resolutions.*

57. For a discussion of the committee's motives in moving the bureau, see David Donald, *Charles Sumner and the Rights of Man* (New York: Alfred A. Knopf, 1970), pp. 175–176.

58. Lane had also opposed the Land Grant College Act in part because it would allow slaveholding states to send their black populations to Western states. Sumner later tried to strike the amendment. The vote was a tie, 14 to 14. All of the votes to strike the proposal came from Republicans, including Clark of New Hampshire, who had originally supported the plan.

59. Democrats forced a vote on an amendment to the bill guaranteeing the constitutional rights of white people. This jab at both Lincoln's wartime abridgment of civil rights and Republicans' alleged concern for black people failed by a vote of 8 to 29, with Democrats comprising the minority. House Democrats had also made the argument that Republicans favored black people at the expense of white people. See, for example, Martin Kalbfleisch and Anthony L. Knapp, Bureau of Freedmen's Affairs, Report of the Minority of the Select Committee on Emancipation, January 18, 1864, 38th Cong., 1st sess., H. Rept. 2; and *Congressional Globe,* 38th Cong., 1st sess., pp. 761, 891, 3346, 2803.

60. Two of the Republican nay votes came from Virginia and West Virginia; the third came from Pennsylvania's Edgar Cowan, who often switched sides in voting.

61. The House received the bill at the end of June and sent it to the select committee on emancipation, which recommended that the House refuse to agree to the Senate's version of the bill. The House voted on July 2, 1864, to postpone consideration of the bill until December 20, 1864 (ibid., pp. 3397, 3427, 3527). The House appointed Eliot and Kelley and the Senate chose Sumner and Howard of Michigan to the conference committee. Representative Warren P. Noble of Ohio and Senator Charles R. Buckalew of Pennsylvania provided the Democratic voices on the committee, but they refused to endorse the committee's work.

62. For passage of the conference committee's H.R. 51 through the House, see *Congressional Globe,* 38th Cong., 2nd sess., pp. 79–80, 90, 562–565, 688–694, 1004, 1402.

63. *Robert C. Schenck, U.S.A., Major General of Volunteers* (Ohio: Published by order of Union Central Committee, 3rd Congressional District [1863]). Anxious to report his bill to the House, Schenck took the floor to do so immediately after the discussion on Eliot's bill, but failed to accomplish his

purpose. For passage of H.R. 698 through the House, see *Congressional Globe*, 38th Cong., 2nd sess., pp. 565–566, 908.

64. New York *Times*, February 9, 1865, p. 4.

65. The lack of a roll call vote on Schenck's proposal indicated overwhelming support, while the conference committee's bill passed by only two votes. See also *Congressional Globe*, 38th Cong., 2nd sess., p. 985, for an argument that the House prefered the more limited plan.

66. For passage of conference committee's H.R. 51 through the Senate, see *Congressional Globe*, 38th Cong., 2nd sess., pp. 77, 79, 674, 711–712, 743, 766–768, 785–786, 958–964, 983–990, 1007, 1182, 1307–1308, 1348. McPherson, *Struggle for Equality*, pp. 181–188.

67. Chicago *Tribune*, February 21, 1865, p. 2.

68. The Senate appointed Wilson, Harlan, and Willey; the House sent Schenck, Boutwell, and J. S. Rollins.

69. The House did not vote directly on the report, but on whether or not to lay it on the table, so it is possible that this vote is slightly inaccurate. Herman Belz, *A New Birth of Freedom: The Republican Party and Freedmen's Rights, 1861–1866* (Westport, Conn.: Greenwood Press, 1976), argues that the principle of nondiscrimination embodied in the bill made it promote African-American equality before the law; compare Louis S. Gerteis, *From Contraband to Freedman: Federal Policy toward Southern Blacks, 1861–1865* (Westport, Conn.: Greenwood Press, 1973).

70. For examinations of the problems of imposing free labor beliefs on the South after the war, see Paul A. Cimbala, "The 'Talisman Power': Davis Tillson, the Freedmen's Bureau, and Free Labor in Reconstruction Georgia, 1865–1866," *Civil War History*, 28 (June 1982): 153–171; Messner, *Freedmen and the Ideology of Free Labor;* and Eric Foner, "Reconstruction and the Crisis of Free Labor," in *Politics and Ideology in the Age of the Civil War* (Oxford: Oxford University Press, 1980), pp. 97–127.

71. On public agitation for complete emancipation, see, for example, the New York *Times*, January 18, 1864, p. 1; and the Philadelphia *Inquirer*, April 23, 1864, p. 1. Mark M. Krug, *Lyman Trumbull: Conservative Radical* (New York: A. S. Barnes and Co., 1965), p. 219. For passage of S. 16 through the Senate, see *Congressional Globe*, 38th Cong., 1st sess., pp. 145, 553, 694, 921, 1130, 1313, 1346, 1364–1370, 1405–1406, 1419–1425, 1437–1447, 1448, 1456–1465, 1479–1490. For histories of the Thirteenth Amendment, see Howard Devon Hamilton, *The Legislative and Judicial History of the Thirteenth Amendment* (Ph.D. diss., University of Illinois, Urbana, 1950; university microfilms, 1982); and George H. Hoemann, *What God Hath Wrought: The Embodiment of Freedom in the Thirteenth Amendment* (New York: Garland Publishing, 1987).

72. Krug, *Lyman Trumbull*, pp. 59–66, 218. Horace White, *The Life of Lyman Trumbull* (Boston: Houghton Mifflin, 1913), pp. 20–21.

73. Philadelphia *Inquirer,* April 12, 1864, p. 4. See also the New York *Times,* June 26, 1864, p. 4.

74. On Virginia's devastation, see the Philadelphia *Inquirer,* February 19, 1864, p. 4. Philadelphia *Inquirer,* April 12, 1864, p. 4.

75. See Lea S. VanderVelde, "The Labor Vision of the Thirteenth Amendment," *University of Pennsylvania Law Review,* 138 (December 1989): 437–504, for the concepts of free labor embodied in the amendment, and for postamendment definitions of "involuntary servitude."

76. In illustration of the idea that the government would be free to do as it wished with the states, the Democrats offered an amendment to the proposed measure consolidating all six New England states into two large states: East and West New England.

77. They also attempted to replace the joint resolution with a new bill that offered a Democratic program for a compromise with the South.

78. On Lincoln and civil liberties, see Mark E. Neely, Jr., *The Fate of Liberty: Abraham Lincoln and Civil Liberties* (New York: Oxford University Press, 1991).

79. The third Democrat in favor of the measure came from the far northwestern state of Oregon. Border state Democrats in favor of the measure were Wilson (Missouri) and Johnson (Maryland).

80. For passage of S. 16 through the House, see *Congressional Globe,* 38th Cong., 1st sess., pp. 2612–2621, 2722–2723, 2939–2962, 2977–2995, 3000, 3357.

81. On the role that the existence of black soldiers played in the passage of the Thirteenth Amendment, see Mary Frances Berry, "Toward Freedom and Civil Rights for the Freedmen: Military Policy Origins of the Thirteenth Amendment and the Civil Rights Act of 1866" (Washington, D.C.: Department of History, Howard University, 1975).

82. For political articles on the measure and the election, see the Philadelphia *Inquirer,* June 17, 1864, p. 4; and the New York *Times,* June 17, 1864, p. 4. John Tweedy, *A History of the Republican National Conventions from 1856 to 1908* (Danbury, Conn.: John Tweedy, 1910), p. 71. For Lincoln's endorsement of the platform see ibid., p. 79. Abraham Lincoln, Message of the President, December 6, 1864, *Congressional Globe,* 38th Cong., 2nd sess., Appendix, p. 3.

83. For passage of S. 16 through the House, see ibid., pp. 53–54, 138–156, 214–225, 478–488, 523–531. Samuel S. Cox, *Three Decades of Federal Legislation, 1855 to 1885* (Providence, R.I.: J. A. Reid, 1888), pp. 320–321. See also Earl S. Pomeroy, "Lincoln, the Thirteenth Amendment, and the Admission of Nevada," *Pacific Historical Review,* 12 (December 1943): 362–363.

84. For articles equating rebellion and slavery, see, for example, the New York *Times,* January 16, 1865, p. 4; and the Boston *Evening Transcript,* January 10, 1865, p. 2.

85. Philadelphia *Inquirer*, April 9, 1864, p. 4. For an article supporting this position, see the New York *Times*, January 14, 1865, p. 4.
86. New York *Times*, January 20, 1865, p. 4.
87. Nathaniel B. Smithers of Delaware noted the bondage of Saxons, as well as of Christians in Algiers. John M. Broomall of Pennsylvania attacked a Democratic opponent of the measure by pointing out that the man's own ancestors had been slaves, "bought and sold with the land upon which they lived."
88. Some Democrats who were tempted to cross over and vote aye suddenly changed their minds on hearing that the government was on the verge of a peace conference with Confederate commissioners. They feared that a positive House vote on the proposed constitutional amendment would doom the meeting (Cox, *Three Decades of Federal Legislation*, pp. 327–328). This was the Hampton Roads conference. It is also possible that Ashley persuaded one Democrat to vote aye with a promise of an office for the man's brother; another received hope of political support; and a third absented himself on the condition that a private bill he opposed would be postponed (White, *Lyman Trumbull*, p. 228).
89. The four Republicans were Clay, Grider, Harding, and Mallory. On the popularity of the measure, see the New York *Times*, February 3, 1865, p. 4; and the Boston *Evening Transcript*, February 2, 1865, p. 2. New York *Times*, February 1, 1865, p. 4. For a similar article, see the Philadelphia *Daily Evening Bulletin*, February 2, 1865, p. 4.
90. George W. Julian, *Political Recollections, 1840 to 1872* (Chicago: Jansen, McClurg & Co., 1884), pp. 251–252. For another joyful recording of the measure's passage, see the Chicago *Tribune*, February 1, 1865, p. 2.
91. For a striking example of the gulf between the wartime optimism of those who recognized the worth of black labor and the general public dislike of black people, see the correspondence between General Oliver Otis Howard and his wife about a freed slave, Julia, whom Howard sent to his wife in Maine to employ as a servant: Oliver Otis Howard to [Lizzie], January 8, 1864, March 14, 1864, and September 22, 1864; Lizzie Howard to Oliver Otis Howard, July 24, 1864, September 4, 1864, October 2, 1864, and October 14, 1864. All letters in the Howard Family MSS., Bowdoin College. For freed slaves' acquisition of land after the war, see Loren Schweninger, "A Vanishing Breed: Black Farm Owners in the South, 1651–1982," *Agricultural History*, 63 (Summer 1989): 41–60.

Epilogue

The epigraph is from a Democratic paper, the Cincinnati *Enquirer*, July 18, 1862, p. 2.

1. New York *Times*, March 30, 1863, p. 4.

Bibliography

Primary Sources

GOVERNMENT DOCUMENTS

The *Congressional Globe* is by far the most valuable source for information about Republican wartime economic legislation. Many other government documents are also important, however, and can be found primarily in the volumes of the *Executive Documents,* the *Miscellaneous Documents,* and the *Reports* of the House and Senate. For this book, I found two House Reports and one Senate Executive Document especially useful. "Affairs of the Union Pacific Railroad Company," H. Rept. 78, 42nd Cong., 3rd sess. (1873); and "Crédit Mobilier Investigation," H. Rept. 77, 42nd Cong., 3rd sess. (1873) reveal much of the story of the wartime machinations of the railroad builders. Senate Executive Documents, 50th Cong., 1st sess. (1887), Document 51, explains the wartime operations of the Leavenworth, Pawnee and Western Railroad Company as well as Thomas C. Durant's activities. The volumes of *Foreign Relations of the United States* were also useful for information on immigration plans during the war. Although not officially a government document, *The American Annual Cyclopaedia and Register of Important Events* (New York: D. Appleton & Co.) gives highlights of congressional debates and other important government events.

Most of the bills and laws of the wartime Republicans can be found in U.S. Congress, *Bills and Resolutions of the House of Representatives and the Senate,* 1st–55th Cong. (1789/91–1897/90), on microfilm. Gaps do occur in this collection, however. Notably, the railroad bill H.R. 438, from which the 1864 railroad law evolved, is available only from the House Records at the National Archives. The wartime currency laws are most easily accessible in *Laws of the United States Relating to Loans and the Currency* (Washington. D.C.: Government Printing Office, 1878).

For information on agriculture in America shortly before the war, Joseph C. G. Kennedy, *Agriculture of the United States in 1860* (Washington, D.C.: Government Printing Office, 1864) is invaluable, as are the U.S. Seventh and Eighth Census Records, 1850 and 1860, for information on population trends in the country.

MANUSCRIPTS

Ames Family and the Union Pacific Railroad MSS., Harvard Business School.
James G. Blaine MSS., Library of Congress, on microfilm.
Blair Family MSS., Library of Congress, on microfilm.
Zachariah Chandler MSS., Library of Congress, on microfilm.
Salmon P. Chase MSS., John Niven, ed., *The Salmon P. Chase Papers*
    (Frederick, Md.: University Publications of America, 1987), on microfilm.
Jay Cooke MSS., Historical Society of Pennsylvania.
James R. Doolittle MSS., Library of Congress, on microfilm.
Samuel C. Fessenden MSS., Maine State Archives.
William Pitt Fessenden MSS., Bowdoin College.
William Pitt Fessenden MSS., Library of Congress, on microfilm.
Edward Carey Gardiner MSS., Historical Society of Pennsylvania.
Horace Greeley MSS., New York Public Library.
Hannibal Hamlin MSS., University of Maine at Orono, on microfilm.
Howard Family MSS., Bowdoin College.
Abraham Lincoln MSS., Library of Congress, on microfilm.
Justin Smith Morrill MSS., Library of Congress, on microfilm.
Lot Morrill MSS., Maine State Archives, Augusta, Maine.
Frederick A. Pike MSS., Maine State Archives.
James S. Pike MSS., Library of Congress.
Samuel B. Ruggles MSS., New York Public Library.
William Henry Seward MSS., New-York Historical Society.
John Sherman MSS., Library of Congress.
Thaddeus Stevens MSS., Library of Congress.
James Moore Swank MSS., Historical Society of Pennsylvania.
Lyman Trumbull MSS., Library of Congress, on microfilm.
Benjamin F. Wade MSS., Library of Congress, on microfilm.
Algernon S. Washburn MSS., Minnesota Historical Society.
Francis Wayland MSS., John Hay Library, Brown University.
Henry Wilson MSS., Library of Congress.

NEWSPAPERS

American Railroad Journal
Boston Cultivator
Boston *Daily Evening Transcript*
Boston *Daily Evening Traveller*
Boston *Post*
Chicago *Tribune*
Cincinnati *Daily Commercial*
Cincinnati *Daily Gazette*

Cincinnati Enquirer
Daily Illinois State Register
Harper's Weekly
Indianapolis *Daily Journal*
New York *Daily Tribune*
New York *Times*
Philadelphia *Daily Evening Bulletin*
Philadelphia *Inquirer*
Philadelphia *Public Ledger*
Providence *Journal*
San Francisco *Daily Alta California*

REMINISCENCES

Arnold, Isaac N. "Recollections of the Early Chicago and Illinois Bar," a
    speech to the Chicago Bar Association, June 10, 1880 [n.p., n.d. Probably
    Chicago, 1880].
———. *Reminiscences of the Illinois Bar Forty Years Ago: Lincoln and
    Douglas as Orators and Lawyers.* Chicago: Fergus Printing Co., 1881.
Blaine, James G. *Twenty Years of Congress: From Lincoln to Garfield.* 2 vols.
    Norwich, Conn.: Henry Bill Publishing Co., 1886.
Boutwell, George S. *Reminiscences of Sixty Years in Public Affairs.* 2 vols.
    New York: McClure, Phillip & Co., 1902.
Clews, Henry. *Twenty-Eight Years in Wall Street.* New York: Irving Publishing
    Co., 1888.
Cornwallis, Kinahan. *The Gold Room and the New York Stock Exchange and
    Clearing House.* New York: A. S. Barnes, 1879.
Cox, Samuel S. *Union—Disunion—Reunion: Three Decades of Federal
    Legislation, 1855–1885.* Providence, R.I.: J. A. & R. A. Reid, 1888.
Cruise, John D. "Early Days on the Union Pacific." *Collections of the Kansas
    State Historical Society,* 11 (1909–1910): 529–549.
Cullom, Shelby M. *Fifty Years of Public Service.* Chicago: A. C. McClurg &
    Co., 1911.
Dodge, Grenville M. *How We Built the Union Pacific Railway.* Council Bluffs,
    Iowa: 1911–1914; rpt. ed., Denver, Colorado: Sage Books, 1965.
Fowler, William Worthington. *Inside Life in Wall Street.* Hartford, Conn.:
    Dustin, Gilman & Co., 1873.
———. *Ten Years on Wall Street.* Hartford, Conn.: Worthington, Dustin &
    Co., 1870.
Grinnell, Josiah B. *Men and Events of Forty Years.* Boston: D. Lothrop Co.,
    1891.
Hoar, George F. *Autobiography of Seventy Years.* 2 vols. New York: Charles
    Scribner's Sons, 1905.

Julian, George W. *Political Recollections: 1840 to 1872*. Chicago: Jansen, McClurg & Co., 1884.

McClure, Alexander K. *Recollections of Half a Century*. Salem, Mass.: Salem Press Co., 1902.

McCulloch, Hugh. *Men and Measures of Half a Century*. New York: Charles Scribner's Sons, 1900.

Medbery, James K. *Men and Mysteries of Wall Street*. Boston: Fields, Osgood, & Co., 1870.

Powderly, Terence V. *Thirty Years of Labor, 1859 to 1899*. Columbus, Ohio: Rankin & O'Neal, 1890.

Schurz, Carl. *The Reminiscences of Carl Schurz*. 3 vols. New York: McClure Co., 1907.

Sherman, John. *Recollections of Forty Years in the House, Senate and Cabinet*. 2 vols. Chicago: Werner Co., 1895; also London: Samson Low, Marston & Co., 1895.

Spaulding, E. G. *History of the Legal Tender Paper Money Issued During the Great Rebellion*. Buffalo: Express Printing Co., 1869.

Venable, William Henry. *A Buckeye Boyhood*. Cincinnati: Robert Clarke Co., 1911.

[Washburn, I., Jr.] *Notes of Livermore*. Portland, Me.: Bailey and Noyes, 1874.

Wilson, Henry. *History of the Rise and Fall of the Slave Power in America*. 3 vols. Boston: James R. Osgood and Co., 1874.

DIARIES, LETTERS, SPEECHES, AND CONTEMPORARY WRITINGS

An Agricultural Poem, by Owen Lovejoy, M.C., delivered before the Bureau County Agricultural Society, October 1859. Princeton, Ill.: "Bureau County Republican" Book and Job Print, 1862.

Atkinson, Edward, et al., Boston Board of Trade Committee on Emigration. *Foreign Emigration*. Boston, 1864.

Bancroft, Frederic, ed. *Speeches, Correspondence and Political Papers of Carl Schurz*. 6 vols. New York: G. P. Putnam's Sons, 1913.

Basler, Roy P., ed. *The Collected Works of Abraham Lincoln*. 9 vols. New Brunswick, N.J.: Rutgers University Press, 1953–1955.

Beale, Howard K., ed. *Diary of Gideon Welles*. 3 vols. New York: W. W. Norton & Co., 1960.

Cuomo, Mario M., and Holtzer, Harold, eds. *Lincoln on Democracy*. New York: HarperCollins Publishers, 1991.

Dennett, Tyler, ed. *Lincoln and the Civil War in the Diaries and Letters of John Hay*. New York: Dodd, Mead & Co., 1939.

Donald, David, ed. *Inside Lincoln's Cabinet: The Civil War Diaries of Salmon P. Chase*. New York: Longmans, Green and Co., 1954.

Hertz, Emanuel. *The Hidden Lincoln: From the Letters and Papers of William H. Herndon.* New York: Viking Press, 1938.

"The Letters of Samuel James Reader, 1861–1863: A Pioneer of Soldier Township, Shawnee Country." *Kansas Historical Quarterly,* 9 (February 1940): 26–57.

"The Letters of Samuel James Reader, 1861–1863, Pioneer of Soldier Township, Shawnee County, Kansas." *Kansas Historical Quarterly,* 9 (May 1940): 141–174.

Private and Official Correspondence of Gen. Benjamin F. Butler during the Civil War Period. 5 vols. Privately issued: 1917.

Report on Emigration by a Special Committee of the Chamber of Commerce of the State of New York. New York: John W. Amerman, 1865.

Russell, William Howard. *My Diary North and South.* Edited by Eugene H. Berwanger. New York: Alfred A. Knopf, 1988.

Sherman, John. *Selected Speeches and Reports on Finance and Taxation, from 1859 to 1878.* New York: D. Appleton and Co., 1879.

Thorndike, Rachel Sherman, ed. *The Sherman Letters.* New York: Charles Scribner's Sons, 1894.

War Letters 1862–1865 of John Chipman Gray and John Codman Ropes. Cambridge, Mass.: Riverside Press, 1927.

[Washburn, Israel, Jr.]. "Modern Civilization." *Universalist Quarterly,* 15 (January 1858): 5–31.

Williams, Charles Richard, ed. *Diary and Letters of Rutherford Birchard Hayes.* 5 vols. Columbus: Ohio State Archaeological and Historical Society, 1922.

Williams, John. *American Emigrant Company.* New York: Office of the Iron Age [1865].

———. *Considerations in favor of the Accompanying Proposed Amendmendments to the Act entitled an Act to encourage Immigration, approved July 4, 1864. Offered by the American Emigrant Company* [n.p., n.d.; probably 1866].

ECONOMIC TEXTS

Baird, Henry Carey. "Protection of Home Labor and Home Productions Necessary to the Prosperity of the American Farmer." n.p., n.d.

Carey, H. C. *The Currency Question: Letters to the Hon. Schuyler Colfax, Speaker of the House of Representatives.* Chicago: John A. Norton, 1865.

———. *Essay on the Rate of Wages.* Philadelphia: Carey, Lea & Blanchard, 1835.

———. *The French and American Tariffs Compared; in a Series of Letters to Mons. Michel Chevalier.* Philadelphia: Collins, 1861.

———. *Principles of Political Economy.* Philadelphia: Carey, Lea & Blanchard, 1837.

———. *Principles of Social Science.* Philadelphia: J. B. Lippincott & Co., 1858.

Kellogg, Edward. *Labor and Other Capital.* New York: published by the author, 1849.

McKee, Samuel, Jr., ed. *Alexander Hamilton's Papers on Public Credit Commerce and Finance.* New York: Liberal Arts Press, 1957.

Opdyke, George. *A Treatise on Political Economy.* New York: Published for the Proprietor by G. P. Putnam, 1851.

Owen, Robert Dale. *Labor, Its History and Prospects.* Address delivered before the Young Men's Mercantile Association of Cincinnati. New York: Fowlers and Wells, 1851.

Say, Jean Baptiste. *A Treatise on Political Economy.* Edited and translated by Clement C. Biddle. Philadelphia: John Grigg, 1827.

Wayland, Francis. *The Elements of Political Economy.* New York: Leavitt, Lord & Co., 1837.

Bibliographical Essay

On the beliefs of the antebellum Republican party, see Eric Foner, *Free Soil, Free Labor, Free Men* (New York: Oxford University Press, 1970); Gabor S. Boritt, *Lincoln and the Economics of the American Dream* (Memphis: Memphis State University Press, 1978); William E. Gienapp, "The Republican Party and the Slave Power," in Robert H. Abzug and Stephen E Maizlish, eds., *New Perspectives on Slavery and Race in America* (Lexington: University Press of Kentucky, 1986), pp. 51–78; James L. Huston, *The Panic of 1857 and the Coming of the Civil War* (Baton Rouge: Louisiana State University Press, 1987); and Jonathan A. Glickstein, *Concepts of Free Labor in Ante-bellum America* (New Haven: Yale University Press, 1991). On wartime Republicans, see Leonard P. Curry, *Blueprint for Modern America* (Nashville, Tenn.: Vanderbilt University Press, 1968). David Montgomery, *Beyond Equality: Labor and the Radical Republicans, 1862–1872* (New York: Alfred A. Knopf, 1969), follows the interaction of labor and radical Republicans in the postwar years.

On the wartime Democrats, see Leonard P. Curry, "Congressional Democrats, 1861–1863," *Civil War History,* 12 (September 1966): 213–229; Joel H. Silbey, *A Respectable Minority: The Democratic Party in the Civil War Era, 1860–1868* (New York: W. W. Norton & Co., 1977); Jean Harvey Baker, *Affairs of Party: The Political Culture of Northern Democrats in the Mid-Nineteenth Century* (Ithaca, N.Y.: Cornell University Press, 1983); and Bruce Collins, "Ideology of Ante-Bellum Northern Democrats," *Journal of American Studies,* 11 (April 1977): 103–121.

BANKING AND CURRENCY

Albert S. Bolles, *The Financial History of the United States from 1861 to 1885*, vol. 3 (1894) (rpt.: New York: Augustus M. Kelley, 1969), offers a review of Republican financial policies from the perspective of a hard money man; Paul Studenski and Herman E. Krooss's *Financial History of the United States* (New York: McGraw-Hill Book Co., 1952), is a review of Civil War financial measures. Fritz Redlich, *The Molding of American Banking: Men and Ideas* (New York: Hafner Publishing Co., 1947; rpt.: New York: Johnson Reprint Corp., 1968), 2 vols., explains wartime bank operations, introduces individual bankers, and traces the development of banking ideas. Donald R. Stabile and Jeffrey A. Cantor, *The Public Debt of the United States: An Historical Perspective, 1775–1990* (New York: Praeger, 1991), give a very brief, readable overview of wartime and postwar debt and funding. *Laws of the United States Relating to Loans and the Currency* (Washington, D.C.: Government Printing Office, 1878) pp. 54–60, collects the wartime financial legislation itself.

E. G. Spaulding, *History of the Legal Tender Paper Money Issued during the Great Rebellion* (Buffalo: Express Printing Co., 1869), gives Spaulding's version of events and contains reprints of correspondence and proposed bills. Wesley Clair Mitchell's *A History of the Greenbacks* (Chicago: University of Chicago Press, 1903), is the best monetary history of early bond negotiations and the greenbacks despite Mitchell's abhorrence of the instruments that he believed cost the Union more than they produced. Don C. Barrett, *The Greenbacks and Resumption of Specie Payments, 1862–1879* (Cambridge: Harvard University Press, 1931), reiterates Mitchell's argument that the greenbacks were unnecessary, maintains that they could have been retired in 1865–1866, and heralds resumption as a triumph. Robert P. Sharkey argued that greenbacks were in fact necessary and, challenging the idea that a cohesive group of radicals drove Republican postwar economic policy, examined the economic interests of wartime and postwar financial groups in his *Money, Class, and Party: An Economic Study of Civil War and Reconstruction* (Baltimore: Johns Hopkins Press, 1959), attributing financial attitudes to the economic needs of bankers, workers, farmers, and manufacturers. Irwin Unger took exception to Sharkey's economic determinism in *The Greenback Era: A Social and Political History of American Finance* (Princeton, N.J.: Princeton University Press, 1964), which explored cultural and social influences on postwar financial attitudes. Bray Hammond, "The North's Empty Purse, 1861–1862," *American Historical Review*, 67 (October 1961): 1–18, returned to an exclusive emphasis on the greenbacks and argued that bankers were the driving force behind greenback legislation. Hammond's *Sovereignty and an Empty Purse: Banks and Politics in the Civil War* (Princeton, N.J.: Princeton University Press, 1970), a good chronological review of the financial events of the Civil War from 1861 through the February 1863 banking act, emphasized the construction of national sovereignty through the nation's wartime financial needs. David M. Gische, "New York City Banks and the Development of the National Banking System, 1860–1870," *American Journal of Legal History,* 23 (January 1979): 21–67, offers a review of the mechanics of banking in New York City during the war years and examines the interplay of the government and bankers in the construction of the National Banking Acts.

TARIFFS AND TAXES

Three scholars concentrated on the entire history of nineteenth century tariffs in America; each wrote to take a stand on turn-of-the-century protectionism. Edward Stanwood, *American Tariff Controversies in the Nineteenth Century* (Boston: Houghton Mifflin Co., 1903; rpt. New York: Garland Publishing, 1974), 2 vols., supported protectionism and offers some insights into reasons for postwar expansion of the tariff. Ida Tarbell, *The Tariff in Our Times* (New York: Macmillan, 1915), blamed unnecessary high wartime tariffs on the manipulations of businessmen. In *The Tariff History of the United States* (New York: G. P. Putnam's Sons, 1892), F. W. Taussig argued for free trade but, while condemning postwar tariffs, blamed the Civil War tariffs on the need for revenue. Studies focusing specifically on Civil War tariffs include Richard Hofstadter, "The Tariff Issue on the Eve of the Civil War," *American Historical Review,* 64 (October 1938): 50–55, which argued that Northern business had little interest in a new tariff in 1860; Clarence Lee Miller, *The States of the Old Northwest and the Tariff, 1865–1888* (Emporia, Kans.: Emporia Gazette Press, 1929), which explored the Northwest's conversion to protectionism; and Reinhard H. Luthin, "Abraham Lincoln and the Tariff," *American Historical Review,* 49 (July 1944): 609–629, which investigated Pennsylvania's role in the tariff plank of the 1860 Republican platform.

Frederic C. Howe, *Taxation and Taxes in the United States Under the Internal Revenue System, 1791–1895* (New York: Thomas Y. Crowell & Co., 1896) generally reviewed the operation of the different Civil War taxes. Harry Edwin Smith, *The United States Federal Internal Tax History from 1861 to 1871* (Hart, Schaffner & Marx, 1914), provided what remains a good synopsis of wartime taxation. Charles F. Dunbar, "The Direct Tax of 1861," *Quarterly Journal of Economics,* 8 (July 1889): 436–461, examined the direct tax, but much of the history of wartime taxation has concentrated on the income tax. Joseph A. Hill, "The Civil War Income Tax," *Quarterly Journal of Economics,* 3 (July 1894): 416–452, 491–498, reviewed the income tax to see if it should be reimposed. Edwin R. A. Seligman, *The Income Tax: A Study of the History, Theory, and Practice of Income Taxation at Home and Abroad* (New York: Macmillan, 1911), examined the progressive logic of the income tax while supporting the Sixteenth Amendment. Similarly, Sidney Ratner, *American Taxation: Its History as a Social Force in Democracy* (New York: W. W. Norton & Co., 1942) saw the history of

American taxation as part of the progress of democracy. Robert Stanley, *Dimensions of Law in the Service of Order: Origins of the Federal Income Tax, 1861–1913* (New York: Oxford University Press, 1993) disagreed. Harold Q. Langenderfer, *The Federal Income Tax, 1861–1872* (New York: Arno Press, 1980), 2 vols., provides a close examination of the details, and the legal and practical questions, of the wartime laws.

AGRICULTURE

The history of Civil War agriculture begins with Thomas Donaldson's *The Public Domain: Its History, with Statistics* [House Exec. Doc. 47, Part 4, 46th Cong., 3rd sess.] (Washington, D.C.: Government Printing Office, 1884), which gives the congressional history of public lands, surveys, laws, and land statistics, albeit with a few errors and a prejudice against immigrants who took up land. George M. Stephenson, *The Political History of the Public Lands from 1840 to 1862* (Boston: Richard G. Badger, 1917), offers an old-fashioned political history concentrating on sectional struggles over land policy. Paul Wallace Gates, "The Homestead Law in an Incongruous Land System," *American Historical Review,* 41 (July 1939): 652–681, maintained that public land policies favored special interest groups over homesteaders. Benjamin Horace Hibbard, *A History of the Public Land Policies* (New York: Macmillan, 1924; rpt. Madison, Wisc.: University of Wisconsin Press, 1965), agreed that government policies failed to keep land in the hands of farmers, as did Roy M. Robbins, *Our Landed Heritage: The Public Domain, 1776–1936* (Princeton, N.J.: Princeton University Press, 1942; rpt. New York: Peter Smith, 1950).

Allan G. Bogue and Margaret Beattie Bogue, "'Profits' and the Frontier Land Speculator," *Journal of Economic History,* 17 (1957): 1–24, challenged the idea of speculation as a bonanza business; Robert P. Swierenga, *Pioneers and Profits: Land Speculation on the Iowa Frontier* (Ames: Iowa State University Press, 1968), argued that speculators helped the settlement of the public lands. Paul W. Gates tempered his earlier position, suggesting that agriculture thrived before the Civil War, in *The Farmer's Age: Agriculture 1815–1860* (New York: Holt, Rinehart and Winston, 1960) and *Agriculture and the Civil War* (New York: Alfred A. Knopf, 1965), but maintained that the postwar years spelled bad times for farmers. Allan G. Bogue, *From Prairie Belt to Corn Belt: Farming on the Illinois and Iowa Prairies in the Nineteenth Century* (Chicago: University of Chicago Press, 1963), argued that midwestern farming had boomed after the Civil War; Clarence H. Danhof, *Change in Agriculture: The Northern United States, 1820–1970* (Cambridge: Harvard University Press, 1969), explored the increasing productivity of postwar farms and its effect on family farm units. Gates's revision of his initial stance is in Paul W. Gates, *History of Public Land Law Development* (Washington, D.C.: Government Printing Office, 1968). The debate over public land policy in the nineteenth century is covered in Robert P. Swierenga, "Land

Speculation and Its Impact on American Economic Growth and Welfare: A Historiographical Review," *The Western Historical Quarterly,* 8 (July 1977): 283–302, and Lawrence B. Lee, "American Public Land History: A Review Essay," *Agricultural History,* 55 (July 1981): 284–299.

More recently, Jeremy Atack and Fred Bateman, *To Their Own Soil: Agriculture in the Antebellum North* (Ames: Iowa State University Press, 1987), maintained that antebellum Northern farmers could be self-sufficient, own land, and make more money than Southerners or urban dwellers. Jeremy Atack, "The Agricultural Ladder Revisited: A New Look at an Old Question with Some Data for 1860," *Agricultural History,* 63 (Winter 1989): 1–25, further argued that the agricultural ladder moving individuals upward to prosperity and land ownership worked well in the mid-nineteenth century; this argument has been challenged by Donghyu Yang, "Farm Tenancy in the Antebellum North," in Claudia Goldin and Hugh Rockoff, eds., *Strategic Factors in Nineteenth Century American Economic History* (Chicago: University of Chicago Press, 1992) pp. 135–156.

RAILROADS

Lewis H. Haney's *A Congressional History of Railways in the United States* (Madison: University of Wisconsin, 1908 and 1910; rpt. New York: Augustus M. Kelley, 1968), 2 vols., is a good synopsis of congressional promotion and regulation of railroads. Emphasizing sectional tensions in the debate over transcontinental travel, Robert R. Russel's *Improvement of Communication with the Pacific Coast as an Issue in American Politics, 1783–1864* (Cedar Rapids, Iowa: Torch Press, 1948), remains an excellent history of the forces promoting a Pacific railroad. A more sketchy, but still useful, history with a similar slant is Thamar Emelia Dufwa, *Transcontinental Railroad Legislation, 1833–1862* (New York: Arno Press, 1981).

Many histories of the Union Pacific have been written. Most useful remain John P. Davis's *The Union Pacific Railway: A Study in Railway Politics, History, and Economics* (Chicago: S. C. Griggs and Co., 1894; rpt. New York: Arno Press, 1973), which gives a negative but generally accurate history of the Union Pacific. Nelson Trottman, *History of the Union Pacific: A Financial and Economic Survey* (New York: Ronald Press Co., 1923), concentrates on the postwar history of the railroad. On the Kansas Pacific, see Waldo Crippen's *The Kansas Pacific Railroad: A Cross Section of an Age of Railroad Building* (New York: Arno Press, 1981); and William Robinson Petrowski's *The Kansas Pacific: A Study in Railroad Promotion* (New York: Arno Press, 1981), which offers a very thorough picture of the machinations of the Kansas Pacific men. On the Northern Pacific, see Eugene Virgil Smalley, *History of the Northern Pacific Railroad* (New York: G. P. Putnam's Sons, 1883; rpt. New York: Arno Press, 1975).

For investigation of investment strategies of the railroad builders and financial risks of Union Pacific construction, see Robert William Fogel, *The Union*

Pacific Railroad: A Case in Premature Enterprise (Baltimore: Johns Hopkins Press, 1960); Arthur M. Johnson and Barry E. Supple, *Boston Capitalists and Western Railroads: A Study in the Nineteenth-Century Railroad Investment Process* (Cambridge: Harvard University Press, 1967); and William F. Huneke, *The Heavy Hand: The Government and the Union Pacific, 1862–1898* (New York: Garland Publishing, 1985).

On government aid to internal improvements, see Frederick A. Cleveland and Fred Wilbur Powell, *Railroad Promotion and Capitalization in the United States* (New York: Longmans, Green, and Co., 1909), and Carter Goodrich, *Government Promotion of American Canals and Railroads, 1800–1890* (Westport, Conn.: Greenwood Press, 1960). On the mechanics of land grants to railroads, see William S. Greever, "A Comparison of Railroad Land Grant Policies," *Agricultural History,* 25 (1951): 83–90.

SLAVERY

Although dated, Paul S. Peirce's *The Freedmen's Bureau: A Chapter in the History of Reconstruction* (Iowa City: University of Iowa Press, 1904), and George R. Bentley's *A History of the Freedmen's Bureau* (Philadelphia: University of Pennsylvania Press, 1955; rpt. New York: Octagon Books, 1970), are useful general surveys of the Freedmen's Bureau. Louis S. Gerteis, *From Contraband to Freedman: Federal Policy toward Southern Blacks, 1861–1865* (Westport, Conn.: Greenwood Press, 1973), argues that federal policy toward the ex-slaves, including the Freedmen's Bureau, was designed to prevent great change. Herman Belz, *A New Birth of Freedom: The Republican Party and Freedmen's Rights, 1861–1866* (Westport, Conn.: Greenwood Press, 1976), disagrees, explaining how the very limits of Republican policy promoted racial equality.

On Northern attitudes toward Southern labor, see George Winston Smith, "Some Northern Wartime Attitudes toward the Post-Civil War South," *Journal of Southern History,* 10 (August 1944): 253–274. William F. Messner, *Freedmen and the Ideology of Free Labor: Louisiana, 1862–1865* (Lafayette: Center for Louisiana Studies, University of Southwestern Louisiana, 1978); Steven Joseph Ross, "Freed Soil, Freed Labor, Freed Men: John Eaton and the Davis Bend Experiment," *Journal of Southern History,* 44 (May 1978): 213–232; Eric Foner, "Reconstruction and the Crisis of Free Labor," in *Politics and Ideology in the Age of the Civil War* (Oxford: Oxford University Press, 1980), pp. 97–127; and Paul A. Cimbala, "The 'Talisman Power': Davis Tillson, The Freedmen's Bureau, and Free Labor in Reconstruction Georgia, 1865–1866," *Civil War History,* 28 (June 1982): 153–171, examine the implementation of the free labor ideal in the postwar South.

Works on the Thirteenth Amendment still begin with James G. Randall's *Constitutional Problems under Lincoln,* rev. ed. (Urbana: University of Illinois Press, 1951); while Harold M. Hyman, *A More Perfect Union: The Impact of the Civil*

War and Reconstruction on the Constitution (New York: Alfred A. Knopf, 1973), fits the amendment into the story of larger constitutional changes. Howard Devon Hamilton, *The Legislative and Judicial History of the Thirteenth Amendment* (Ph.D. diss., University of Illinois, Urbana, 1950; university microfilms, 1982) provides a comprehensive examination of the creation of the amendment, while George S. Hoemann, *What God Hath Wrought: The Embodiment of Freedom in the Thirteenth Amendment* (New York: Garland Publishing, 1987), concentrates on the role of war in making the amendment possible. Mary Frances Berry, "Toward Freedom and Civil Rights for the Freedmen: Military Policy Origins of the Thirteenth Amendment and the Civil Rights Act of 1866" (Washington, D.C.: Department of History, Howard University, 1975), argues that the presence of black soldiers dictated legislation. Lea S. VanderVelde, "The Labor Vision of the Thirteenth Amendment," *University of Pennsylvania Law Review,* 138 (December 1989): 437–504, examines the concepts of free labor embodied in the amendment.

Index